C. Vann Woodward

Southerner

C. Vann Woodward

Woodward

Southerner

John Herbert Roper

The University of Georgia Press

Athens and London

© 1987 by the University of Georgia Press
Athens, Georgia 30602
All rights reserved
Designed by Richard Hendel
Set in Linotron 202 Garamond Number 3
with ITC Garamond Light display

The paper in this book meets the guidelines for
permanence and durability of the Committee on
Production Guidelines for Book Longevity of the
Council on Library Resources.

Printed in the United States of America

91   90   89   88   87   5   4   3   2   1

Library of Congress Cataloging in Publication Data

Roper, John Herbert, 1948–
    C. Vann Woodward, southerner.

    Bibliography: p.
    Includes index.
    1. Woodward, C. Vann (Comer Vann), 1908–   .
2. Historians—United States—Biography.   3. Southern
States—Historiography.   I. Title.
E175.5.W66R67   1987   978'.0072024[B]   86-25020
ISBN 0-8203-0933-8 (alk. paper)

British Library Cataloging in Publication Data available.

For Rita

Contents

Acknowledgments

There is no way to express adequately the extent of my debts or the depths of my gratitude to those who have taken special pains to help me on this project. Inevitably it has involved controversy and ambiguities, and there seems to be more than the usual number of places where an author could make serious mistakes, as well as many areas where it was hard to find out information. Those parts of this book which readers find interesting and informing are likely the product of comments and suggestions made at different times and in different places by the following people: anonymous referees at *Southern Humanities Review, Phylon,* and the University of Georgia Press, Ann Abadie, Ron Bayes, Janis Bolster, Bev Bowen, Lolita Brockington, Neal Bushoven, Malcolm Call, Bill Carleton, Hunter Chase, Isaac Copeland, Georgia Craven, Manning Dauer, Ralph Gabriel, Judy Green, John Hall, Julia Hall, Evans Harrington, Joe Herzenberg, Leslie Hosfeld-Leeuw, Michael Johnson, Neal Jones, Charles Joyner, Howard Kaminsky, Edna Ann Loftus, Cathy Lowry, Bill McFeely, Tom McHaney, Don Mathews, George Melton, Molly Nolan, Mabel Parker, Betty Parnell, Michelle Peck, Allison Pickering, Darden Pyron, Mary de Rachewiltz, Sam Ragan, Glenn Rainey, Jim Roark, Ed Roper, Jr., Frank Ryan, Anita Shepperd, Bob Simpson, Barbara Slaughter, Joe Steelman, George Tindall, Peter Walker, Bell Wiley, Joel Williamson, Anna Woodson-Williamson, Jan Woodward.

Note to Readers

Throughout most of Vann Woodward's career, *Negro* was both the technically correct and the polite term, and one that he and his friends consciously used in preference to the grotesque violence of the word *nigger* and in preference to the spirit-draining condescension of the word *colored*. Until about 1963 or 1964, the term *black* essentially had negative connotations and for those reasons was seldom used by those seeking improvement of race relations; one of the crucial aspects of the black pride movement was the mission, ultimately successful, to transform the language of race relations so that black people could take pride in what they are. Because of this historical dimension in the development of language and attitudes, Negro and black are used interchangeably in this text for that long period of time between 1908 and 1964.

Introduction

This is not a biography in the traditional sense, for there is no attempt here to describe every phase in the long life and distinguished career of C. Vann Woodward. Nor is it historiographical analysis, at once extensive and rigorous, of all the many things he has written. Rather, this is an extended essay about one southerner's struggle to understand his section of the country, a process which has involved an effort to get the rest of the nation to help change a number of southern practices but a process which has induced no less effort to get the rest of the nation to accept, and even to adopt, other southern practices. There are tensions both external and internal in this man's efforts, and one is tempted to subtitle the essay "the well-wrought irony of the ironist." This, however, would express two serious inaccuracies, the first duplicity in Woodward's character, and the second a greater control of events and environment than he has actually enjoyed. No, Woodward must be seen instead as a figure of authorial activism, one who has sincerely wanted fundamental change of southern regions, and indeed of the Western world, but also one who has deeply regretted the many unintended effects borne along by the tides of reform. The ambivalence he so frequently demonstrates, then, is not only honest and conscious, what his compadre Robert Penn Warren calls an "earned" irony: it is also fundamentally healthy in the way it reminds both reactionaries and reformers that all human visions encompass very little of what actually is. [1]

In the old rural parlance, he has hoed a tough row, for American reformism has shown, in addition to its moral fervor, special impatience with tradition, and Woodward has often found his works inspiring a kind of thoroughgoing housecleaning he never intended. By the same token, his clearly defined family ties, his undisguised preference for a distinctly southern style, and his admiration for much of the southern past have moved some of his readers to a worshipful celebration of Dixie, a response which he also dislikes. While misreadings of his complex essays abound, there are good reasons for the paradoxical reactions to what he has said and done, partly because some of his ideas have evolved considerably over time, but largely because of the powerful, counterpoised dualities in his thoughts and deeds. In fact, much as he expresses disdain for dialectics, his career embodies a long-running dialogue between radicalism and conservatism; and furthermore, we are the better for it, since his interior debate, forced into the open by scholars probing his work, has raised fundamental questions about ourselves and our society, questions which we ignore at our peril.

Not only has there been this significant dialogue between Woodward and his critics, as well as his own interior dialogue, but also there has been a unique dialogue between his ideas and his own experiences—in David Minter's felicitous phrase, "deep reciprocities."[2] Woodward has seen and has written, has heard and has written, and for all his far-flung travels, the sound of the Ouachita River and the feel of the rolling Ouachita hills are always there in his works. Many of his renowned themes of analysis—certainly the southern economic "colonialism," the radical changes wrought by Civil War, the "strange career" of Jim Crow segregation, the irony of southern uniqueness—are things which he has not only seen and heard but has also lived. And his passionate attraction to dissident eccentrics of the documented past has doubtless been inspired by the equally powerful effects on him of contemporaneous dissident eccentrics in Arkadelphia, Oxford, Druid Hills, Chapel Hill, Gainesville, Claremont, Baltimore, and New Haven.

Born and reared very much on the inside of a limited regional circle of leadership, Woodward eventually came inside the national circles of leadership, and yet there has always been something strangely centrifugal in his personality which has impelled him toward the outer circles. For all the ease with which he has moved among the elite, he is ultimately no real friend of power or authority: this man is about change and motion, and the impulses of Populism have been central to his being. This man Woodward, then, is a peculiar blend of activism with detachment, of radical egalitarianism with aristocratic provenance, or profound localism with universal concerns. He is sui generis and is himself largely responsible for the actual blending of seemingly disparate and even contradictory elements in his character.

In addition to significant advantages of birth and station, Woodward also benefited from the fortunes of time and of place which graced one who came to maturity in the late 1920s after a group of southern intellectuals—in retrospect almost a shock wave—had prepared the way for others to follow. This matters because southern historians in particular, unlike their New England contemporaries, are almost always first-generation academics. For all that Woodward himself has done to point out the consciousness of time and tradition in his region, there have been few historian families in the South to record and interpret that history. There is yet no equivalent of the Adamses in Massachusetts, or the Smith/Mayo-Smithes in New York, where generation after generation of academics instructs and learns from family members as well as from professional colleagues. Few southern scholars are reared in homes where academia pervades the air, preceding one's formal donning of the profession's cloth. Thus it was that Georgia's great conservative historian Ulrich Bonnell Phillips, at the top of his form in the 1930s, still drew snickers at Yale when he referred to Edward Coke as if the jurist's name rhymed with *broke* instead of *brook*. And by like sign, Tennessee's great liberal historian Bell Irvin Wiley, though recruited arduously to study at the same institution, scared off more than one hostess at welcoming teas because he so looked the part of the hill boy that he was.[3]

Woodward's case was different, and the difference was a boon. He had enormous talent and much pluck and luck, of course. But an extensive network of friendly uncles and avuncular friends was also there to help out at crucial times. As Woodward recalled in retrospect, there was a "decisiveness of southern 'accidents,'" whether in Morrilton and Arkadelphia, Arkansas; Oxford and Atlanta, Georgia; or Chapel Hill, North Carolina. At each place, these men arose, "all improbably, . . . wildly accidental, but there they were," to help Woodward when events had otherwise conspired against him.[4]

The network was essentially a closed circuit, and the men in it were jealous of intrusion. Thus Chapel Hill's Howard Washington Odum, miffed at a newspaper account of young Vann Woodward criticizing the Georgia activist Will W. Alexander, wrote testily to Alexander to inquire, "Who is Professor Vann Woodward?" Reassured by Alexander that the account was in error, Odum happily welcomed Woodward and, in a few years, was writing enthusiastically to friends at the Rockefeller Foundation that fellow Carolina sociologist Rupert Bayless Vance "and I are talking with him to be sure he finishes his . . . study and gets himself all ready to become one of the younger leaders of the South." For Odum, as for all the members of this circuit, leading the South was defined as changing the South, increasing its gross economic production, diversifying the kinds of its economic activities, improving educational levels in all spheres, ameliorating (though not actually challenging) racism, cleaning up dirty political systems. Tall orders all, and all to be accomplished by the steady application of research and teaching by activist academics committed to reform.[5]

In their context, research meant asking questions about class structure and who makes whom do what, while teaching meant nagging young folk along à la Socrates to find their own answers to leading questions. Both research and teaching started on the campus, but neither stopped there. As Charles Wooten Pipkin, yet another in Woodward's circle of patrons, announced on taking charge of the graduate school at Louisiana State University, research must always be for the good of the region, and a graduate school should positively influence the life of a region. As for research of a pure kind, a kind not to be applied to social problems, Pipkin spoke for the whole crowd: "If Dr. Johnson were alive today, he would say it was research [of that kind] which is the last refuge of the scoundrel."[6]

In later life, Woodward would often disdain this brand of activist and committed scholarship, especially where it was carried to excess; at times, he even hinted of a need for *ars gratia artis* in scholarship, of scholarship virtually disembodied from political context. Yet such occasional expressions were sentimental as Johann von Goethe defined sentimentality: will attempting to do the work of the imagination. Most of the time Woodward's fundamental instincts guided him toward imaginative scholarship which could be, and generally was, used for political ends. Moreover, the "deep reciprocities" between his character and experiences often drew him back into activist research and publication regardless of what he was saying about detached observation or the needs of the academic. For instance, in 1974, after a period of virtual retreat from such involvements in the polity, he surfaced as organizer and editor for *Responses of the Presidents to Charges of Misconduct,* a major salvo in the assault on Richard Milhous Nixon; and in 1981, after again making noises about disenchantment with politics, he appeared before the House Committee on the Judiciary as its members took testimony on the extension of the Voting Rights Act of 1965. And on that occasion he sent a friend a note that he felt especially invigorated when so occupied, for "it was a thrill to see old friends and students rally around" the one cause, civil rights, which was his abiding and transcending passion.[7]

Reformism and withdrawal are thus one more duality in this mind which, after all, insisted correctly that American history was a story of conflict and not consensus. Nor should we discount too greatly his efforts at resolution of these inner complexities. Besides opening our eyes to significant but previously unexamined questions, he has moved us a long way down the road to answering the questions. His very best works, while never didactic, express a clear moral direction; and even his works most flawed by contradictions which cancel out any meaningful conclusions express moral impulses of depth, strength, and goodness. To speak of anyone in such language of judgment is unfashionable nowadays, but this man and these struggles, these questions and these answers, demand nothing less than a full discussion and a frank, and fair, evaluation. In spite of and even because of his flaws and imperfections, this man is the most significant historian of our age.

1

Arkansas Youth, 1908–1928

He was born in the land of cotton on a frosty morn, 13 November 1908, as celebrated for the mythical southerner in the song "Dixieland": how fitting, for he intensely disliked that genre of tubthumping southernism and yet he was much of what the song describes; fitting also because the song was performed most memorably by whites in black face in the "Jim Crow" stage routine and it would be Jim Crow racism which would most fully engage him in his career. His naming, Comer Vann Woodward, was equally significant: Woodward originally meant "warder of the wood," fully apt for one whose ancestor owned large tracts of timberland; Comer was in honor of his "sainted uncle"; and Vann, as he was called almost immediately, was for his mother's family, the people who founded and named the village of his birth.[1]

I

The Arkansas of that era was an intensely rural place where, although even the larger towns could be dismissed by a knowing cosmopolite as "out of the way," there was a rich and varied history. In fact, the state was situated at the crossroads of conflicting regional identities, and given the contrapuntal notes in the refrain of his youth, it is no wonder that the historian has written so often and so eloquently of irony. Arkansas was "new" in the salad days of the Old South, attracting its first large settlements in 1818 and joining the Union in 1836. Wealth, for a few, developed quickly because of the international demand for short-staple cotton in the 1850s, but it disappeared in a twinkling with the Civil War. Where Virginians and Carolinians viewed "The War" as a destruction, perhaps even a self-destruction, of what they had built since the seventeenth century, Arkansans had scarcely had the chance to get used to their cotton wealth. Of course, a huge majority were self-sustenant farmers who did not own slaves, who had been coerced by an elite minority into secession, who had subsequently suffered terribly in such battles as Pea Ridge and Prairie Grove, and who thus had an especially jaundiced view of the rapid rise and fall of other men's fortunes.

Moreover, the state had always been divided in half by the Arkansas River, which effectively created two regional identities, one northern, one southern; and Woodward, living in both regions, would inherit things from each. In addition, geography, time, and experience further subdivided the northern and southern regions, since this was a state where rivers formed the routes of communication and transportation and where citizens checked the daily newspapers for reports on river levels, the most pertinent information about the weather. The north had an eastern corner presided over by Memphis shipping and commerce, and here was Vanndale, "way up in the hills . . . where the gentry was not much in control," as Woodward remembered it. Cotton and slaves there were, but not on a grand scale, and politics was often dominated by small freeholders instead of large planters. Smaller-scale slavery and relatively early conquest in the Civil War made race and sectionalism less of an issue than in the south, but the northeast was still notably preoccupied with race when compared with the Ozarks region of the northwest.[2]

By contrast, the south, along its eastern edge, was dominated by the Mississippi River and, while not really Delta, was geographic and cultural first cousin to the Mississippi and Louisiana Delta. West of the Father of Waters and hard by the Arkansas River lay Morrilton, and south of it lay Arkadelphia; these were the two towns where Woodward grew up, and here, too, he sensed, "they didn't have the gentry as much in charge as did the low-country near Memphis"; class distinctions were never flaunted, for "you knew the town's taxi driver's boy" and the son of the banker: "you knew them all."[3] On the other hand, there were enough black people and the Confederacy persisted long enough so that race and sectionalism often crowded out other things from the political arena. For example, immediately before the war, men from the Cotton Belt proposed a law which would again enslave those few blacks fortunate enough to have been freed, an extreme response even for an age of fire-eating extremism.

It is a fair question whether each of these Arkansas regions developed its own aristocracy; some have even questioned the existence of an aristocracy anywhere in the South at all. Despite these disclaimers, there were certainly many who intended to become aristocrats, whose families claimed continuity of economic and political dominance in their communities, and who enjoyed a fair degree of control over the social direction of their communities. To the objection that the latter component of aristocracy was lacking in the South because of the section's youth and rudeness, Woodward's own rebuttal rang true: all aristocracies begin parvenu. Thus Woodward's family tooks its position and presumed its entitlements: his mother's family, the Vanns, had left the coastal plain of Carolina during the flush times of slavery and established the community of Vanndale, Arkansas, where Vann Woodward was born three generations later. Such beginnings have always granted power and a long tether on behavior, and the Vann family of the early twentieth century had both. It was, after all, the privilege of the aristocrat to lead while standing a little distance apart, a trait often seen in Woodward later.[4]

The historian's great-great-grandfather John Vann had migrated from Hertford, North Carolina, to Tennessee and thence to St. Francis County in northeastern Arkansas, establishing in 1850 what became the Mount Zion Methodist Church and the Arcadia Lodge of the Masonic Temple near the St. Francis River. The next generation of Vanns, Rensalear and Emily Maget Vann, who owned twenty-six slaves and some six hundred acres, established a general store and post office, and when they moved these operations to the Noble Branch of the Iron Mountain Railroad line, they created the village of Vanndale. By ordinary standards, anyone who owned as many as twenty slaves counted as a large slaveholder, and it is this measure which helps establish the maternal side of the family as parvenu aristocracy.

The little postage stamp of Faulknerian territory, with its train station, post office, two hotels, three general stores, and three hundred
people, came to serve as the county seat; and there was optimism,
what with railroad construction extending lines both north-south
and east-west and with land values rising. By April 1861, however,
Vanndale and its hopes were overwhelmed by the Civil War. Soon
after the killing began, Rensalear and Emily's eldest son, John
Maget Vann, was conscripted into the Confederate army as a teen-
ager. He survived the conflict, having not yet reached his majority
when Robert Edward Lee and Joseph Johnston handed over their
swords four Aprils later.[5]

But the Vanns' antebellum style of life did not survive the war, an
element of personal family history which may explain some of the
conviction in the mature historian's thesis that the Civil War was a
Second American Revolution (a term he borrowed with thanks from
Charles Austin Beard) which destroyed the Old South and created a
New South. John Maget Vann returned from the fighting to find
changes of considerable magnitude, since the Thirteenth Amendment meant that he would not inherit the family's twenty-six slaves as
his personal property and since the war's course had caused his plantation land to decline in value as real property. Further, as scholars of
Reconstruction social history Hortense Powdermaker, Joel Williamson, Peter Kolchin, and Carol Bleser have demonstrated effectively,
the freed blacks fully intended to be treated as wage-earning farm
laborers. Thus much of the oft-noted "wandering" and "roaming" of
Vanndale's blacks in 1865–67 was nothing less than the black version
of the traditional geographic mobility of American labor in search of
better wages or better working conditions.[6]

Despite overwhelming military defeat and daunting economic
reversals, however, the Vanns and others could still take a position
and presume certain entitlements. Before the war, powerful assumptions of racial superiority had rationalized the planters' station
and their concomitant claims to hold blacks in caste slavery. Now
equally powerful assumptions of the landholders as a class embold-
ened postbellum planters to bind the poor of both races in sharecropping contracts where no wages were involved. Yet the planters'
assumptions encountered a genuine revolution of expectations in the
ranks of the freedmen, who were by no means willing to accept
passively a continuation of their status as slaves. So well docu-

mented is this intent of the black laborers to become wage earners and so well known are the economic models which predict the felicitous consequences of self-conscious bargaining by "rational" owners of labor resources that neoclassical economists have built an elegant paradigm of the regional "negotiations" after 1865. To these authorities, such as Robert Higgs, sharecropping, far from a tragedy, was the result of rational choice and self-interested trading between former slaves and former masters. The freedmen, having available the very labor desperately needed to tend the cotton which remained the most marketable product of the area, were unwilling to function as slaves anymore—and demanded wages. The former masters, providing the only opportunity for employment in the area, were unwilling to pay wages and established Black Codes which rationalized the freedman's status as a kind of serf-of-color bound to the land. When the Black Codes were declared illegal, the landowners lost a bargaining chip, but they remained unwilling to pay wages; moreover, the landowners were so strapped for liquid capital that they in many cases could not have paid wages even if their racism had not been in the way.[7]

What then ensued, according to this model, was a time of negotiation as blacks attempted to establish their rights as mobile labor able to look for work where they pleased. The upshot of these negotiating processes, from the perspective of labor, was that blacks accepted less than wages by winning contracts in which they traded their work for payment in kind, that is, a share of the crop. On the employer side, landowners had to *hire* free men to work, and while they could hedge that freedom about with many restrictions, they held by no means the amount of power over black people which they had had in the days of thralldom. In the classical description of the marketplace trade, then, postbellum sharecropping emerged as a compromise which was less than either laboring man or landowner sought, but "better" than a complete surrender by one or the other.[8]

Persuasive as this model of bargaining behavior may be in the abstract, it was unlikely that John Maget Vann and his croppers experienced anything like it in northeastern Arkansas. Federal intervention in the region, not atomistic negotiations, ended the Black Codes. And subsequently, federal policy impelled black labor to accept the payment in kind of sharecropping agreements, with few alternatives other than unemployment or, in a number of cases, prison for vagrancy. As Eric Foner has observed of this issue, given the particularities of local conditions, the neoclassical model has an almost perverse relationship to the actual events, and to call the resultant peonage a product of bargaining is to rob discourse of all rational meaning.[9] In time, déclassé whites would also be drawn into the web of the same system as sharecroppers, so that the racist attitudes associated with slavery attained a much less direct relationship with the economics of southern farm labor. Thus whatever traditions of paternalism, moderation, and compassion were involved in the Vann family history, John Maget Vann after 1867 took full advantage of one of the most abusive work systems ever devised.

A related development in this part of Arkansas was the system of tenantry in which small-time farmers of both races borrowed money from a third party and then rented acreage from the large landowners. The distinction between tenantry and sharecropping has often been blurred, but the laborer, capitalist, and landowner of the era certainly perceived it clearly: a tenant owed a third-party creditor, while the cropper owed the man whose land he rented and worked. For the laborer, the advantage lay with tenantry, and the eventual legal recognition of the validity of such off-the-land borrowing gave the tenant a welcomed independence from the landed gentry. Unfortunately for the poor of both races, these new creditors were not banks or thrift institutions as they are known today, but were instead the infamous country stores often operated by a newly risen merchant class. Functioning as "territorial monopolies" without competitors in their localities, these merchants were able to charge their debtors interest rates as high as 50 to 60 percent per year. Much controversy exists among scholars about the identity of the new class of merchant creditors and whether they were the old landholding aristocracy transformed or a new bourgeoisie displacing the old planters; John Maget Vann was to some degree both, inheritor of land now reduced in value and worked by sharecroppers, but also owner and operator of a country store whose credit network soon gained him tenants as well. Irony as well as interest was thus compounded in this environment, as the Vanns and other landholders eventually recaptured their black labor while also gaining a new source of white labor through the intertwined systems of sharecropping and tenantry.[10]

In fact, credit and capital soon became the most vexing of problems for the postbellum southerner regardless of race or station: even some who farmed on a large scale found themselves deeply in debt to the local country store; and landholders of all kinds and the entrepreneurs managing the new factories were often in their turn deeply in debt to New York and Philadelphia and Providence firms which extended credit against future deliveries of raw cotton and of finished yarn. To this rondelet of debt was added the dilemma of transportation and communication, for the Vanns and their neighbors faced great difficulties in moving their crops to market over the state's poor roads or over the rails operated by monopolies which charged discriminatorily high rates for hauling southern and midwestern farm products; and they faced no less of a problem in making contact with their potential markets, since communication lines, too, were controlled by monopolists. Certainly these ancestral problems for the Arkansas farmer, problems which began with John Maget Vann's return home from the Civil War and persisted into Vann Woodward's student days in the New Deal, made an ineffable, irrefragable impression on the historian in his youth, and he would retain throughout his career a lingering distrust of "unrestrained capitalism."[11]

But there were also problems in this era for which neither racism nor the loss of the war, neither credit monopoly nor rail monopoly, could take the blame. During the 1860s many new sources of cotton were discovered, developed, and exploited. In time, the cotton supplied by Mexico, India, and Egypt more than made up for the supply from the United States which was effectively cut off by "Mr. Lincoln's blockade" of southern ports; with the postwar resumption of southern shipping, there developed a catastrophic drop in international demand for cotton, and prices drifted down perilously close to the Arkansans' actual cost of production, even taking account of the low wage-in-kind cost of labor. In other words, even if John Maget Vann had been able to get capital at low interest charges and even if he had enjoyed a good cheap transportation system, his cotton farming would have been less profitable after 1865 than his father's before him.[12]

For these and other reasons, Vann engaged in a different kind of work and a new way of life after his discharge from the Confederate army. He was still a cotton grower, but the status of planter no longer obtained, for the operations in that part of Arkansas were too small to merit the term. Using croppers and tenants, he shared in the regional landowners' responsibility for victimizing black and white labor; running a country store, he shared in the regional creditors' responsibility for the victimization of debtor farmers. Living as he did in the South, he was in turn victimized by out-of-state rail haulers for his shipping. No longer dominating, but hardly a peasant, Vann and his fellows formed part of a new elite, decidedly more bourgeois in tone than their fathers had been. Among other things, he and his neighbors were far more receptive to business enterprise, and business was managed best "at the North." Bitter as were memories of the defeat in battle, there was a considerable aping of the conqueror, though the mimicry was attempted at a great distance, for as Woodward put it, the North seemed especially far away, another country, really, a place where there were prosperity and power and good reasons for confidence about the present and optimism about the future. [13]

Vann tried to adjust to the times, experimenting with timber industry on three-quarters of his acreage and attempting to use the St. Francis River to transport the logs; and he encouraged his neighbors to diversify by grazing cattle in the west of the county, now named Cross County, and by growing clover, corn, and grasses in the basin of the St. Francis River. Essentially, however, he was the major cotton ginner and the creditor to cotton farmers in a land-rich, money-poor part of the world. This became even more the case when he married Ida Hare, a woman whose family members were leaders in the Methodist church which dominated much of the community; in fact, Ida Hare was largely credited with raising the money to relocate the Mount Zion Methodist Church through ticket sales to suppers given by her Ladies' Aid Society. Not only were the Hares important in Methodist circles, but they were also major stockholders in the only other banklike institution in town, the American Building Loan and Ponteen. Finally, the Hares counted in their number a preponderance of the town's newly emerged professionals, a lawyer and a doctor as well as the financial agents. [14]

One of John and Ida Hare's three children, Emily Branch (Bess) Hare, was a tall and handsome woman who in 1907 married Hugh Allison (Jack) Woodward in ceremonies conducted by Jack's brother, the Reverend Comer McDonald Woodward. Where the Vanns brought societal prominence and economic power to the family union, these Woodwards brought with them moral stewardship and cultural power, for they were leaders in the educational wing of the Methodist Episcopal Church, South. Jack and Comer Woodward were particularly influential, the former as an astute administrator, the latter as an outspoken educator and activist. Although devoted to the same cause—quality education under the aegis of the Methodist church—Jack and Comer employed very different styles in the pursuit of their tasks. Comer ran out to the end of his long tether, speaking against lynching and other abuses and damages to the Negroes of the South; while Jack was ever the conciliator, the reconciler, the irenic man who forgave the extremist racists—and who sometimes overlooked what they did. [15]

Jack and Comer, so different in the means they used to seek the same end, were also products of New South economics, being in part responsible for the training and supervision of postbellum industrial and commercial management and labor. Moreover, they were Methodists, fervently Methodist, in an era and in a place where fundamentalist religiosity peaked in intensity. Yet the Woodwards were simultaneously proof that the New South bodied forth many types, since they were reform gospelers resentful at once of the chiliastic antiintellectualism of the small town and of the Mammon-worshipping homocentricism of the industrial metropolis. Among other things, their attitudes toward education for women reflected changing times: Bess dropped out of Galloway College in Searcy, Arkansas, to marry and start her family with Jack, but it was always understood that she would finish her college degree, which she eventually did with Jack's and Comer's encouragement. [16]

I I

It was these economic, genetic, and environmental endowments from the Vanns, the Woodwards, and the Hares that Vann Woodward inherited in Vanndale, spending the first years of his life in a town peopled with Confederate veterans and ex-slaves, tenants and croppers, creditors and illiquid farmers, gentle churchmen and violent Negrophobes. There were love for northern money and hatred for the northerner who had money, need for northern credit and frustration with its price in interest, the power of regional monopoly creditors themselves beholden to New York creditors; and there were tenants and croppers united by poverty, debt, and malnutrition, but divided by racism and ignorance. As Woodward expressed it once, "The Faulknerian repertoire was all represented."[17]

Possibly to escape the dominance of Faulkner's Snopeses, who fed on southern ignorance, state senator Sam Vann, nephew of John Maget, introduced a bill into the Arkansas General Assembly which created a special school district for Vanndale, whose citizens had earlier sent their children to neighboring Wynne township. But this bill came too late for young Vann, since by the time of the measure's enactment the Woodwards had moved to Arkadelphia, arriving in time to witness Armistice Day commemorations. The very move, even more than the economic activities of the Vanns and the Hares, was one of the things which marked off the New South from the Old South. This was a new attitude toward mobility and toward cultural identity. Men and women of the Old South had found their identity in the soil they worked and in the vagaries of the seasons which dictated their actions. They moved often, but always in search of better land, for land, with slaves to work it, made one wealthy and powerful. The New South, by contradistinction, encouraged mobility in quest of capital, not land, and it was industrial expertise combined with financial backing and the entrepreneur's lucky roll of the dice that brought wealth and power to postbellum leaders. Soil and season, formerly prideful elements of identity, became less important and, where relevant, were often considered primarily to be worrisome obstacles which impeded progress. So it certainly was for the Woodwards. Uncle Comer took a doctoral degree from the then-new University of Chicago, the beneficiary of Rockefeller oil money, and then went out to Dallas to teach at the equally young Southern Methodist University before settling in Atlanta at Emory University, also new and the beneficiary of the Candler family's Coca-Cola money. In the same way Jack moved from town to town, not in search of better soil or happier season, but in quest of better wages.[18]

Thus Jack took his family to Arkadelphia on such a quest and, after several years there, to Morrilton; and then he brought them back to Arkadelphia. The boy Vann and his sister, Ida, were a little disoriented by the moving, and Vann, for his part, enjoyed summer stays with grandparents John and Ida back in Vanndale. On the other hand, there were some spectacular occurrences in Arkadelphia and in Morrilton, things which stamped an imprint deep and forever into the still-plastic sensibility of the adolescent. All in some way involved race relations, the phenomenon which would always be at the heart of his historical research and writing and at the heart of his political activism and "journalism" writing. The first incident was a lynch mob formed in Morrilton to punish some real or imagined abuse by a black man by executing him summarily without the pretense of a trial. The boy Vann "saw the mob, knew of it, knew what was to be," though he did not see the man. Living in a home suffused with Christian ethics, the youth was struck hard by the disparity between the gentle teachings of Jesus and the grisly death of a black man destroyed by a white mob. The disparity became a yawning abyss in a succeeding incident when members of the Ku Klux Klan came into the First Methodist Church in Morrilton one Sunday, "in full regalia," deposited a monetary donation with the minister, and left. The minister and the congregation there assembled appeared thankful for the gift and not displeased with its source. [19]

While still unbalanced by the specter of the klan, young Vann thrilled to the visit of former governor Charles Hillman Brough, one churchman who was doing something about lynching and racial brutalization. Brough, a deacon in the Baptist church, had dinner with the Jack Woodwards while touring the Chatauqua speaking circuit after his second term as governor ended in 1920. Brough was a native Mississippian who had earned the Ph.D. from Johns Hopkins University, studying alongside such scholars as Woodrow Wilson and Frederick Jackson Turner, and who had then returned to his home state to teach at the main Baptist institution there, Mississippi College. During the war to end all wars, he had taught economics and sociology at the University of Arkansas before resigning in 1916 to run for governor on a reform ticket. As governor, Brough built good roads, some twenty-five hundred miles of them; he built good schools, several hundred; and he instituted woman suffrage, making Arkansas the only southern state to permit it before the passage of the Nineteenth Amendment to the Constitution. More to the point for young Vann, Brough consistently and vigorously spoke against the crime of lynching and once personally answered an appeal to come to Phillips County to stop a race riot. The activist politico temporarily restored Vann's trust in churchmen and educators, and he was proud that his father was friends with such men.[20]

Brough's visit was followed by another visit with another reformist dinner guest, but this visit did not leave the boy in the same frame of mind about children, politics, school, or his family. Uncle Comer, then at Southern Methodist University, sat at the same table and "issued ringing denunciations of the klan." Essentially a minister "of the old school of good works," Comer could hold forth with the effectiveness of the local evangelists, who could keep throngs attentive during protracted meetings; and although hardly a great scholar, he could also articulate a set of intellectual perceptions in a style foreign to the Bible Belt. But as Comer waxed eloquent in his protests, much as had Brough several weeks before, his namesake "came to the realization" that Jack—freer and more open with his own brother than he had been with the distinguished former governor—"did not feel this way and was not going to react to the klan." Subsequently, as Vann reflected on this incident, the full impact of his newly gained understanding became a crushing weight; and it occasioned some rebellion by the son against the father's brand of administrative pragmatism and against the Methodist church. In later decades he could at least understand the necessity of his father's compromises with extreme racism; otherwise, "the poor man would have risked his whole life and his whole family"; and he could make his peace with Jack. On the other hand, the Methodist church, and all religions, became to Vann increasingly less relevant at best and, at worst, insultingly hypocritical.[21]

Of course, this kind of filial reconciliation with a parent was a long way off in those Arkansas days; "youth is impatient with compromise," the elder could announce of himself six decades later, and this impatience would only worsen as Jack's administrative duties grew more and more complex. Nothing dramatic is recorded or remembered of rebellious protest, though it was there in several forms. For one, whenever possible Vann eschewed churchly duties, demonstrating the selective quality of adolescent protest, since Comer and Governor Brough were both far more religiously active than his father. At any rate, as he understood his generation of southern boys, religion was no longer "fashionable," much less meaningful, regardless of the depth of the faith of their predecessors. For another, he attempted little revolts comically typical of youthful lack of focus. His father's position as public school administrator gave Vann many opportunities to embarrass Jack with minor misbehavior: childhood friend Cyrus Richard (Dick) Huie recalled Morrilton visits during which he saw Vann's pet snake, which went to many unauthorized places; and Dick also remembered following Vann on a "freight train-hopping," "trolley-hopping" expedition to Little Rock, followed by a visit to a "big city" swimming pool. Just desserts, Vann judged these tiny embarrassments of a father whose occupation as superintendent caused his son to be "victimized and singled out" by the other boys. [22]

A dispute over one issue involved a deeper, more fundamental resentment which Vann felt toward his father, and demonstrated nothing less than the incompatible inheritance of an upright Protestant and ne'er-do-well wealth. On this occasion Jack's maternal ancestors, the Lockharts of Warren County, Tennessee, emerged as a group with a past fully as interesting as the Vanns', the Hares', and the Woodwards'. In fact, there was some evidence that Jack's mother, Amelia Elizabeth Lockhart, was related to the novelist Sir Walter Scott; for Amelia Elizabeth may have been the daughter of Walter Lockhart, the descendant of Scott's daughter's husband and, given the circumstances, potential heir to a portion of a considerable fortune. Furthermore, a British lawyer was interested in pressing Jack's legal claims to the estate left by Walter Lockhart, a rounder who evidently died at the hands of criminals and was buried without ceremony in Versailles. Besides the excitement which the bookish and imaginative youth sensed about this possible kinship, however attenuated, with the famed novelist, Vann was delighted at the prospect of a comfortable existence once Jack asked for the inheritance which his now-deceased mother had never known to claim. But if the lawyer were correct, then Amelia Elizabeth was likely illegitimate and likely in Tennessee at the behest of an irresponsible father who had given her a little money and then shipped her overseas. And Jack was not about to claim filthy lucre at the expense of his mother's good name. It was also possible that the scatalogical Scottish Lockhart and the upright Tennessee Lockhart were merely namesakes "related" by a barrister's hope for a commission and a boy's hope for an exciting past. For all that, Vann was angry that his "impecunious schoolmaster" father would pass up this opportunity.[23] Again, it was the selective rebellion of adolescent: where before he thought his father too pragmatic, placing the ideals of justice secondary to the demands of office, in this case he judged his father too idealistic, putting the abstraction of a righteous family name above a material legacy.

In this dispute, and in all the other episodes, Vann created no "primal scene" of defiance, and friends noted only that he was obviously closer to his mother than to his father, a relationship that was itself part of a larger pattern of parent-child relationships in the South of that era. More than anything else, Vann simply adopted Uncle Comer as his hero, and he emulated the scholar as much as possible, though much of the imitation was inevitably based on an idealized abstraction instead of a real man. Vann cultivated the intellectual's life, for Comer was a man of ideas and a fashioner of policy, while Jack, in reality an honors graduate of Emory College, was viewed by his son as a man who got the little things done—effective, but often dull. Vann read widely, questioned all things skeptically, and was always on the lookout for bright dissidents who were able to challenge his own mind and, more important, who were willing to challenge the racial minds of southerners. Besides Comer, these included Charles Pipkin and Rupert Vance, both from Morrilton and Henderson-Brown College, men he met in his youth and whom he would come to know well in his adult life.[24]

Pipkin was the boy wonder of the town of Morrilton, already in 1925 a full professor of political science at Louisiana State University after graduating from the Methodist college in Arkadelphia. From there, he earned a Rhodes Scholarship, a master's degree at Vanderbilt University, the Ph.D. at Oxford University, and a Carnegie Fellowship for study at the University of Paris. Descended from a line of ministers, Pipkin even as a youth was fashionably secular, but knowing observers discerned the evangelistic fervor in his demands for reform. To his passion for economic development of the South, his travel in Europe in the 1920s added an equally powerful passion for world peace, and Pipkin served Vann not only as an example of activist reform but also as a material benefactor, when the Baton Rouge professor loaned the boy money for his own European tour.[25]

While Pipkin in his early career approached the Greek ideal of the complete man beautiful in body and mind, Vance was crippled at age three by poliomyelitis, which shriveled his legs and bent his frame; thus Vance became the Greek ideal of arete, the struggle against overwhelming odds. Following therapy in St. Louis, he was able to walk with braces and crutches, and he returned to Morrilton to enter school, eventually catching up with his classmates. As George Brown Tindall puts it, "What he lost in physical development he gained in mental development. While other children romped and played he read books, exhausting the resources of the town and school libraries and the family's private collection." Grandchild of a Civil War veteran and child of a dairy and beef farmer who also operated a country store, Vance shrewdly observed the transformation of Arkansas in the twentieth century, and he developed an encyclopedic knowledge of postbellum politics. Vann had heard of this scholar, and he met him on the grounds of the Morrilton high school in the 1920s when Vance was visiting his parents during a vacation from the Georgia school where he was teaching before moving on to prominence with the Regionalists at the University of North Carolina. Even more than Pipkin, Vance was a multitalented man with wide-ranging interests: trained in classics and literature at Henderson-Brown, he earned graduate degrees in economics at Vanderbilt University and in sociology at the University of North Carolina; and he made contributions in history and geography. Finally, like Pipkin, Vance was dedicated to reforming the southern economy as well as the section's race relations. The combined influence of Comer Woodward, Rupert Vance, and Charles Pipkin was near-total: as Woodward put it in his eightieth decade, "I've been an academic all my life and never knew any other life except four years in the navy."[26]

In a way, he would have enjoyed a pure rebellion, a complete rejection of his region's famous antiintellectualism. How grand to be like Rupert Vance, the Renaissance polymath who embraced all academic subjects and who made no pretense of interest in the local boys' amusements! But Vann bowed at least once to communal pressure, taking up the game of football despite his classmates' passion for it to the virtual exclusion of meaningful labor. There was not much other way to win the attention of the Morrilton girls, and when his father pushed exactly the right buttons on the teenaged keyboard at a public assembly of the high school, Vann "went out" for the team. Having grown over six feet two inches tall and broad-shouldered with a powerful frame, Vann "was entrusted with the position of center . . . low on the totem pole," but in the middle of the often confusing action. He was an effective center and remained athletic all his life, but he retained a contempt for such team sports, especially football, which would continue to grow exponentially in popularity all over Dixie.[27]

Graduating in 1924, Vann enrolled at the same Henderson-Brown College (HBC) which had trained Pipkin and Vance, thus returning to the town of Arkadelphia as well as rejoining his partner in teenaged mischief, Dick Huie. HBC, a private institution which decades later became part of the state's system, was in those days very Methodist, sitting as it did across Eighth Street from the "self-consciously Baptist" Ouachita Baptist College. That he would go to college somewhere was always assumed, for the "impecunious Woodwards" had somehow managed to obtain training and certification in higher education despite the costs. Moreover, Vann contemplated an academic career, though what discipline he would master, what profession's colors he would wear, was quite murky in his vision. Thus he went off with a plan for the future whose grandness of scale was somewhat overmatched by its vagueness of concept.[28]

His plans were set into motion on the campus with enthusiasm, and when he took a job cleaning out the chemistry building, he suddenly realized that laboratory science had to be his appointed future. Practical science in the service of the people of the Southland, vigorous mental exercise, the exacting standards of the chemist's academy—all those elements were there in his scenario. The only thing missing was execution, the actual doing of chemistry, at which he failed and from which he retreated, laying aside the great campaign in a matter of weeks, although he did continue to clean the laboratory for pay. There ensued a "miscarriage of majors," since he would do well in all his other courses without hitting on any which caught his fancy. The only thing he did with real distinction was expository writing, this the result of his response to the stern but superlative drill under the eyes of Misses Boulware Martin and Mary Sue Mooney, two feisty teachers of English who would declare to students for half a century thereafter that it was they who "taught Vann Woodward how to write properly," a claim more or less fairly made.[29]

As in so much else, it was fitting that Vann be unclear about his status and his station and that he be eloquently describing the complexities of his confusion, for his host institution was no less beset with conflicting claims on its human, material, and capital resources. Besides the HBC campus of 130 students, the state's Methodists were supporting two other colleges, Hendrix in Conway and the Galloway in Searcy, which Bess Woodward had attended. Three seemed too many and there was persisting talk in the churches and at the conference meetings in Little Rock about establishing one of the schools as *the* four-year institution while demoting the other two to junior-college status. In Arkadelphia, one of Arkansas's few eighteenth-century settlements but a community which also boasted no small amount of New South entrepreneurial wealth, hopes were high that the "HBC Reddies" would become the flagship, but equally high were countervailing fears that HBC would be designated one of the two tugboats. Vann's father, Jack, and Dick Huie's father, Robert, were both quite active in raising money for HBC and in pressing its case with their fellow Methodists at conference.[30]

Moreover, the campus also refracted oddly angled rays of light from the southern lens being ground by the changing economics of the New South. A few hundred yards obliquely away from the college main hall sat two imposing houses which all but glared at each other. One, an elegantly simple Greek Revival piece of architecture, was built before the war by heirs to the fortune of Jacob Barkman, the man who learned from the area's Caddo Indians how to mine salt from the "saline bayou," the man who then learned how to build a steam-drive sidewheeler and subsequently shipped enough salt along the Caddo and Ouachita and along the riverways to the Mississippi and thence to New Orleans so that he could buy twenty-two thousand acres and build a plantation of grandiose scale. The other house, such a complex mess of Victorian excess, with eaves like giant gumdrop balls, that it is actually attractive in its quirky way, was raised by Charles Christopher Henderson, a postbellum industrialist, railroad builder, and prominent banker who climbed his way to leadership from a starting point as a small-time farmer, bought the old Barkman land, gave it to the Methodists for the college, and then financed much of the HBC construction in the 1890s. The sharp discrepancies between the two styles of architecture and leadership were noted by the teenaged Woodward in an address to those of his classmates who donned green beanies in Saturday evening meetings of the Garland Society, which met to debate current events and contemporaneous politics.[31]

There were other contradictions in the corporate personality of HBC. On the surface it was only another sleepy academic backwater staffed by teachers barely known outside the region; furthermore, there was not even a separate library facility, and the volumes scattered over the shelves of instructional rooms, if brought into one place, would have constituted only a good-sized library for one family. And times were especially tough in the late 1920s, for even the school's existing material resources were diminished: the north wing of Goodloe Dormitory burned down during the winter of 1928, evidently because of a poorly tended heating stove, the front-loading door of which a sleepy student left open on a cold night. Yet the little, financially strapped school which the Methodists thought of abandoning could enumerate some fine scholars in its classrooms, in addition to the already prominent graduates Pipkin and Vance. Vann was not alone in becoming what the campus newspaper phrased a "Reddie worth watching"; Dick Huie would become a fine lawyer, eventually an officer in the state bar, and like his father a major benefactor of the college; Edward Brown Williams would become a successful corporate lawyer in Washington, D.C.; John Paul McConnell would become prominent in the armed forces, serving as secretary of the air force in the Joint Chiefs of Staff; and Amy Jean Green, styled "the spirit of Henderson," would become a valued member of the school's faculty. Again, the scale was often regional rather than national, but the subsequent record shows that Vann was studying with talented and active men and women who were on their way to leadership in the New South.[32]

Moreover, they were already quite active on the campus, demanding, and responding to, academic challenges beyond the ordinary offerings in an undergraduate curriculum. All of them in general and Vann in particular relied on Mooney and Martin to establish and enforce the standards of national achievement against which some of the Reddies wanted to be measured. Mooney, whose portrait hangs today in an academic building named for her, was from Tennessee, where she had become friends with Mary Noailles Murfree, a local colorist who wrote under the nom de plume Charles Egbert Craddock. The portrait reveals a large-framed, imposing, and rather stern figure of a woman. She taught anything involving English literature and grammar and had also instructed in mathematics, for she had earned a master's degree in literature from Bellevue College and one in law from Memphis Conference Female Institute and later a bachelor's degree in science from the University of Chicago and a master's degree in teaching from George Foster Peabody College. Certainly she had, as the novelist Walker Percy once observed, that passion found in the upper South for academic degrees and titles. What she also had was a real dedication to scholarship, editing the works of Murfree/Craddock and pushing her students hard, whether making them parse or differentiate. Nor was it only the pupils who admired her, for the school trustees officially denominated her "a valuable asset to the college and a strong influence as a Christian example in building character."[33]

By contrast, Martin ("Bola" even to students) in those years worked little influence on her fellow professors or on the administration; her impact was much more directly on her students than Mooney's. She read widely and always with an inquiring mind, and she inspired a similar curiosity in her pupils. Where Mooney gave the answers and sternly developed correct techniques, Bola found the questions and fondly urged her charges not only to discover their own answers but also, eventually, to discover their own questions. There was another contrast which could not be blinked: Mooney fully looked the role of the taskmaster, but Bola was a handsome lady, only a few years older than the seniors and still very much in the bloom of youthful charm. More than one young male student was attracted by attributes other than the purely cerebral; but she kept them at a properly late-Victorian distance, and she maintained successfully her role as the one who helped students find the probing questions.[34]

This kind of inquiring mentality was well served by HBC, ironically because the little school was in no hurry for its instructors to finish their graduate training. "In those days," she remembered, "you could go after graduate studies at several schools. We were not required to go at it fast and furious in the matter of getting a degree. You could go at your own pace," freely exploring studies in several fields and on different campuses. Bola took advantage of this freedom, traveling to the University of Chicago and to Columbia University in an era of intellectual ferment on both campuses and also traveling to the University of Oklahoma before taking her master's degree from Tulane University. In these peregrinations, she was emphatic about studying within the discipline of literature and not in teachers' colleges or in the programs of teacher education. As holder of HBC's first degree in oratory, Bola specialized only in elocution and rule of debate, while she made a general assault on the avant-garde fiction and poetry which she had encountered in Chicago and New York.[35]

For Bola and these freshman and sophomore students, the possibility that the Methodists might withdraw their support and the straitened circumstances of the school combined with a nagging sense of parochialism to make not so much a threat as a challenge: if Bola and Vann and Dick and Amy Jean and Ed rushed to the barricades, then perhaps the day could be saved after all. The group used the campus newspaper, the *Oracle,* for which all of them worked, Vann first as "special correspondent" and eventually as editorial writer, as a means to state their case for higher standards and political reform. They also used the Garland Society for Literature in the same way, honing their skills in discussion under Bola's coaching, while consistently taking left-wing postures in subsequent Pi Kappa Delta debating society meets: the United States should cease to protect by force capital invested overseas; war should be outlawed; jingoist acts against the Mexican revolutionary government must be stopped; the Philippines should be granted immediate independence; the direct primary must be retained; Nicaragua's Augusto Cesar Sandino deserves our sympathy; businesses should no longer benefit from inequitable tax advantages.[36] When the same clutch of students spoke in the Garland Society, debated in favor of the Left at Pi Kappa Delta, and then recorded their activities and publicized their attitudes in the *Oracle,* they achieved a powerful symbiosis between written and spoken word—and quite a circularity of tendentious reasoning.

Whatever else, Vann and his fellows labored mightily to escape the kind of snide denunciation which H. L. Mencken had recently made of the South as "the Saharra of the Bozart." In the next decade Vann would take as a special authorial hero Thomas Wolfe, and at times he foreshadowed that novelist's hero Eugene Gant, for Bola declared that the young man seemed intent on reading every book on campus. But Bola, and John Paul and Amy Jean and Dick and

Ed, were all equally like that; as Bola said deferentially of herself, "I've done an awful lot of opening and closing books . . . and I enjoyed [the students'] skills" of interpretation. Dick's mother, Mrs. Robert Huie, did her best to help the ambitious scholars: trained in library science at the University of Illinois, she finally got a separate library building after some years of begging, then borrowed and bought more books for it, catalogued them by the Dewey Decimal System, and over time thus developed an adequate library service on the campus. In the meantime, Vann and his friends created their own personal lending service, obviously highly informal, through which they could share the books that excited them.[37]

This was also a fun-loving group, known for its wit and humor as well as for its talent and reformism. The school's strict social regulations posed no problems for Vann and Dick, who simply ignored the rules which prohibited drinking or driving. Cars, especially those driven by students, were a rare sight in Arkadelphia, but Vann and Dick often were able to borrow them to take excursions, the mood of which was lifted considerably by "Virginia Dare Tonic," their collective term for the distilled spirits of the Prohibition era. And Vann's sense of humor was specifically remarked by many in the campus and community, though always with the caveat that he was both subtle and of the opinion that, as Bola put it, "If you got it, okay, if you didn't, you didn't." His friends Dick and Bola each felt that he had a real chance to be a writer of humorous fiction and of satiric essays; Dick thought nothing less than another Mark Twain.[38]

When summer 1927 arrived, Vann found that neither his intellectual wanderlust nor his sense of adventure was ably served in Arkansas, and so he hitchhiked to New York City. Eventually he found work as a seaman on a Dutch freighter, which paid his passage across the Atlantic but left him no spending money. He spent weeks roaming around France and the Netherlands and even made his first of several visits to the Union of Soviet Socialist Republics, a place and a system which fellow Arkansan James William Fulbright says in those days was less known to a southern boy than remotest Africa. Dick said of his summer's trip, "How he managed his passport business and money for his travel I do not know except for the fact that he was quite adept at hitching rides on trains without buying a ticket." What is known for certain of the trip is the way it rekindled Vann's passion to know about international affairs and the way it influenced his preexisting antiwar sentiments, his sympathies with socialism, and even his tolerance for communism.[39]

After returning to campus from his unique tour of Europe, Vann delivered an address to his friends in the Garland Society and, in the process, pulled together a number of previously disparate notions into a coherent direction; in fact, as historian Julia Hall has demonstrated, the speech "Romance and Reality," written seven years before he thought seriously about becoming a historian, forecast some of the most significant historiographical themes which he would develop in his career in the profession. It concerned the difficulty of laying aside cherished abstractions in order to face the concrete particularities of the present. Such abstractions are cherished because they comfort the soul oppressed by new and poorly understood circumstances; yet the comfort is actually a sham, and a dangerous sham at that, since nothing is as harmful in the long run as failing to recognize change wrought over time: this was the message central both to Thomas Wolfe, whom he already admired, and to William Faulkner, whom he would come to appreciate much later. The Europeans he had encountered were certainly living in utterly different circumstances after World War I—circumstances only made more difficult by "romantic" appeals for traditional responses to the environment of another day. In the same way, the South after the Civil War faced a new reality and could only hurt itself by pretending that traditions recalled from the Old South plantation system could adequately respond to the challenge of freedom, urbanism, and industrialism.[40]

Closer to the students' home there was another bit of romance and realism, what Vann had called "the reality of historical events in contrast to romantic or accepted illusions." While many were understandably anxious about what the Methodists in Arkansas would do with the school, Hendersonians actually faced an equally great threat *inside* their administrative offices: Vann felt that the school bid fair to implode from mismanagement. The college president, Clifford E. Hornaday, was an adequate scholar who had enjoyed teaching success in other schools and who might have enjoyed administrative success in another era. A strict disciplinarian, Hornaday on the one hand took with deadly seriousness the rules for gentlemanly behavior and on the other hand was unable to imagine women seriously attempting an education. Given the realities of a new social context in which only vestiges of agrarian gentlemanliness remained, and given the steep ascent of the parabola of women's rights, especially at a school of more women than men, Hornaday was expressing and acting on attitudes utterly inappropriate for the Henderson of that day.[41]

Add to those attitudes and actions a ham-handed style, a lack of commitment to the faculty's scholarship, and hints of petty corruption and nepotism, and one had the makings of institutional self-destruction. Once Hornaday angrily told all the male students to leave school, and only intervention—pleading, in fact—in the dormitory by several professors kept them on campus. This assault on the men's feelings was a one-time occurrence; but the women, especially Amy Jean Green, felt singularly offended almost all the time, hemmed in as they were by dress restrictions and codes of behavior fashionable in antebellum finishing schools where Queen Victoria was taken seriously as the arbiter of conduct. Withal, it was the finishing-school style of teaching which most angered the little set of dissidents who wrote for the *Oracle:* anxious for more of the rigor of Mooney's instruction and for more of the sprightliness of Bola's discussions, many students complained that Hornaday was more interested in hiring teachers of deportment and enforcers of discipline than he was in finding and promoting talented scholars. The *Oracle,* in editorials usually written by Vann and in features written by Amy Jean and John Paul, raised the cry of "scholarship first," belittling the Hornaday administration's plans while redundantly praising the labors of teachers such as Bola.[42]

Where Hornaday was most vulnerable, especially with the trustees and the supporters of the school, was in another area: he was most conspicuously in trouble with the penny-ante affairs of the tiny campus bookstore run by members of his family. Books needed for classes were not always readily available, and more vexing, they were consistently priced well above the manufacturers' suggested retail levels. Vann and Dick recognized Hornaday's tactical error and exploited it cleverly: they wrote to the manufacturers to obtain price lists and then printed those lists alongside the bookstore's lists. Student reaction to this information was no angrier than it was already, but publication of the discrepancies quickly caught the eyes of school trustees and the ministers who were relied on to send students to Arkadelphia—as well as those fearful that the Little

Rock Conference might be looking for excuses to demote the school to junior-college status in favor of Hendrix, where there were, presumably, happy students and no scandal. Considering that Dick's father was perhaps the single most important trustee of the college, that Vann's father was a fund raiser, that Amy Jean had the ear of Mooney, who was herself officially proclaimed an "asset" and "example" by the trustees, Hornaday had blundered by making these young people his enemies, and he was not long for the administrative world of HBC.[43]

But Vann himself was not long for Arkadelphia either. Much as he appreciated Bola and Mooney, Amy Jean and Dick, by the end of the sophomore year he came to an understanding about himself and his aspirations. Even if HBC could be saved—as it eventually was in complex maneuvers which transformed it into a state teachers' college—he still felt unduly restricted by the pleasant little community and its nice little college, both in the middle of a small state in the upper South. When the vaunted Comer became dean of students at Emory University in Atlanta and offered his nephew room and board in his Druid Hills house, it seemed time to transfer. After all, that very year Uncle Comer had also goaded Jack with these words: "It is my hope that you and Sister Bess can keep yourselves in the frame of mind that you now reflect. Occasionally in life we need to pull up, root and branch, and plant ourselves in a new and different soil. To make the transition successful, good judgment must be used. Yet the whole thing turns on the will to get up and do it. The timid and fearful cannot risk large adventure. Some of those who do, risk them and fail. But the chance and the game are worth the trying. If you will swing entirely free from your present situation and come up here and go to work . . . it is my opinion that other things will work out all right. Remember also that the achievers do not stay always close to the shore."[44]

What a glorious mixture of metaphors from the beckoning Comer! But it did not really matter whether the images involved moving a plant, turning on a pivotal point, or sailing the high seas; what mattered was to be up and doing. The nephew heard the message clearly and responded at once; the brother hesitated and responded later. Football and cotton raising, writing drill and skipping chapel, newspapers and debates in Arkadelphia were for others. Vann Woodward was to "swing entirely free from [his] present situation" and "study . . . and get himself all ready to become one of the younger leaders of the South."[45]

There was a final chance to shine for the Reddies in May before he left them. Under Bola's coaching and the titular direction of Professor Percy Winfield Turrentine, Vann had won at least ten contests involving debating teams and individual debaters from colleges in Arkansas and Mississippi. Speaking at Hendrix College in competition with orators from all of Arkansas's universities and colleges, Vann took top honors for his "The Outlawry of War" and found his name engraved on a trophy still housed at Henderson. In later years, those who have witnessed one of Woodward's oddly inflected, mumbling speeches—in the words of fellow historian Jack Pole, "He's really a throwaway lecturer"—have often wondered how he could have won this honor. Bola has explained that the grading was partially on delivery, for which Vann was graded down even in those days, but mostly on substance; and the judges, examining the text of the remarks, were overwhelmed by the boy's powerful style of argument.[46]

After 1928, this would be no less the case in Atlanta.

2

The City

Youthful Activism
and Revolt,
1928–1934

Vann Woodward's was hardly the only road which led to Atlanta in the 1920s. The region's vital center of modern industrial and commercial energies, this city self-consciously styled itself Phoenix because of its postbellum renascence after its destruction during the Civil War. Along with the economic and political activities came a rejuvenated intellectual life, especially in the colleges—the black Atlanta University System, the Georgia Institute of Technology, and the transplanted and transformed Emory of Comer Woodward. There was no question that this Atlanta was becoming so influential that it would dwarf the other urban centers of the South. Whether it was lovely and useful, as its contemporaneous enthusiasts claimed, or the pestilential force which young Vann Woodward decried is another level of question which will continue to elicit hot debate for generations. What is clear is that a powerful beast was in full flight, for good or ill, by 1928, and Vann Woodward was aboard for the ride.

This development seemed the more notable because the South had fallen well behind the pace of growth set by the rest of the nation; and Atlanta's success, perhaps because atypical, made it the very embodiment of the self-proclaimed New South Movement.

Spokesman for the movement was Henry Woodfin Grady, whose editorials and features in the *Atlanta Constitution* celebrated the coming day of industrialism and urbanism. The novelty of the new day which Grady welcomed was more than newspaper rhetoric, though there was certainly much of that. Much of the South looked, and perhaps was, as it had been before the Civil War; but Atlanta was bigger and it moved faster than it had in its antebellum identity. There was change not only in degree but also in kind: in the levels of labor specialization, in technological innovation, and in the means and uses of credit. The relevant knowledge was now scientific; the language of economic rationalism was now franker and more overt, as the city man's neatly kept double-entry ledgers replaced the country man's more haphazard notations; and the scene of power and wealth and influence moved from the drawing rooms and courthouses of Charleston and Savannah and Wilmington to the corporate boardrooms of railroads and the banking headquarters of Atlanta and Richmond and Charlotte. To be sure, a good number were with varying degrees of success resisting the New South Movement, for as economist Aleksandr Gerschenkron has noted of the processes of industrial development in an essentially agrarian society, a considerable "tension" is created by the contrast between the "promises inherent" in the "potentialities of development" and the "existing obstacles" in the "actualities" of the relatively undeveloped economy. But such resistance to the contrary, there was no doubting Atlanta's dominance in the spiritual and material leadership of the movement.[1]

Woodward's Atlanta started on the grounds of Emory University, where he found that his uncle Comer, who had first taken a post as professor of sociology in 1919 and then had advanced up the ladder of administrative responsibilities, was also a great hero to the boys on this campus. Thomas H. English, a young literature instructor in those days, remembered that there was little controversy or unhappiness on the campus in the 1920s or early 1930s, but that even taking account of the relative harmony, Comer was an extremely popular figure and, after assuming the position of dean of men in 1929, enjoyed more success than any subsequent holder of that office. In the same year, Vann's senior year, Jack became dean of the junior college at Oxford, Georgia, and Vann's sister, Ida Elizabeth, a concert cellist, began her course of instruction at both campuses,

Oxford and Emory, which would culminate in a performing career with several major symphonies. Finally, in the next decade Vann's mother, Bess, would at last complete her college education, earning a degree from Oglethorpe College across town. Thus several chapters from the story of Emory and Atlanta are germane to the cultural experiences which formed young Vann Woodward's education.[2]

I

In a city on the make, Emory was the school on the make. It was called into being by the powerful Candler family, which seized the propitious moment to expand its empire and to set a monument to itself in the Druid Hills north and east of town. The school was more than a talisman, however, for it was to become an excellent training center for the young elite who would direct the New South. Emory could do so because of its fidelity to the traditional values of the Methodist church, a fidelity shown by the elastic bonds between church and school. These bonds could expand a great deal, but not far enough for the school to gain true independence, a factor which may partly explain Emory's brushes with greatness, each brush followed by a return to the academic norm.[3]

The Candlers who built Emory were a study in their own right: a big family of big men with vision, some good sense, and the political and economic wherewithal to achieve their dreams. In this family three brothers reigned over Georgia industry, religion, and jurisprudence: respectively, they were Asa Griggs Candler, scion of the Coca-Cola Bottling Company and its subsidiary empire; Warren Akin Candler, Methodist bishop; and John S. Candler, state supreme court justice. It was the first two who stretched the elastic from the Methodist church around a family fortune to the new school. The occasion for their action was a convention meeting to resolve the dilemma posed by the Vanderbilt University Board of Trustees who successfully declared their independence from the church.

The school in Nashville, itself largely built by the donations of railroad and financial entrepreneur Commodore Cornelius Vanderbilt, had by 1910 established a program of education which was decidedly secular and decidedly free of the bishops. In that year the bishops ordered "Vandy" back into the fold, but this particular lamb so resisted the blandishments of the shepherds that the issue became a court case not resolved until 1913. By then the university had gained still more money from the industrialists, this time from steel man Andrew Carnegie's foundation; and the court's ruling, which legally severed Vanderbilt's ties of obligation to Methodism, only affirmed an economic fait accompli.[4]

In the aftermath of the Vanderbilt decision, the Methodist Conference sought to reestablish quality scholarship under the aegis— and the direction—of the church. This time there would be two centers, one east and one west of the Mississippi River. Smooth, efficient collaboration between Warren and Asa Candler won the day for Atlanta, the eastern site for the new school and the new site for the old Emory. Atlanta's Emory University would have four years of liberal arts instruction, graduate programs in the arts and in some sciences, a divinity school, a law school, and a medical university attached to a research hospital. By contrast, there was a reduction in status for Emory's parent institution at Oxford, Georgia, which had been founded in 1836 by the Methodist Episcopal Church in response to the Oxford Movement in education led by disciples of John and Charles Wesley. This original Emory College became in 1919 Oxford College, which featured a two-year program of instruction in liberal arts and a divinity school which was largely ancillary to Atlanta's, so that the Oxford that Jack Woodward joined suffered the very fate which he had labored to avert for Henderson-Brown in Arkadelphia.

For their part, the Candlers put considerably more than soul into the new site for Emory: a cash gift of one million dollars, priceless family land for the campus physical plant and for faculty housing, and other real estate which could be sold to meet expenses in the future. Even the marble facades for the buildings came from the Candler quarries in north Georgia. Not surprisingly, such generosity found an immediate reward this side of heaven's treasure trove: Warren Candler became chancellor of the university which opened in 1919; and there were busts of Warren and Asa Candler on prominent display in the main library and in the divinity school. And understandably enough, Bishop Candler sought as well to exercise a full measure of spiritual influence over the faculty and administration.[5]

The quality of that spiritual direction was high, albeit a little narrow, for the bishop was a man of intelligence and usually a man of compassion. Quite conservative temperamentally as much as politically, Warren Candler attempted to protect Emory by shielding it from attack as he had done for Methodist institutions since the turn of the century. Then the big patriarch—"I'm six feet one way and four feet the other way"—stretched a sheltering arm over school, church, and family in an incident illustrative both of his mentality and of his era's preoccupations.

In 1902 Andrew Sledd was a bright young professor of classics at Emory, Oxford. A fine scholar, Sledd also excelled in theology and in translating Latin and classic Greek; in those days he rated as a provocative instructor as well as an outgoing, spirited citizen of the community. During this era of obsession with race, Sledd jumped in to offer his own verdict on the black place in society. He drew on Cicero, who during the days of tumult in the first century B.C. which ended the Roman republic and replaced it with empire had considered the status of former slaves and had decided that they should gain full rights of citizenship. In Cicero's judgment, the former slaves should be able to vote, hold office, enter into business contracts, and even marry into families of citizens with no damage to the fabric of society. Sledd, writing in the *Atlantic Monthly,* found parallels between Roman emancipation and southern emancipation; and he announced that the American culture could survive the extension of citizenship to the freed blacks just as the Roman culture had survived. Being acutely conscious of the extreme racism stalking his land in this era, Sledd tried to avoid real provocation by excluding racial intermarriage from his catalog of citizen rights for the freedman.[6]

But provoke he did. John Temple Graves, a popular and usually rather moderate columnist for Georgia dailies, came after Sledd in print, insisting that the professor be dismissed. When Candler, who was father-in-law to the young rebel, publicly supported Sledd, Graves began a series of attacks on the "fat bishop," as did Rebecca Latimer Felton, wife of one-time Georgia congressman William Felton and a woman with tremendous intellectual and political energies, who was by no means ready to follow her older husband into retirement from debates about public policy. Both Graves and Rebecca Felton could play roughly and never so roughly as on the race question. In their speeches and articles, widely and enthusiastically followed throughout the South, the freedman was said to be "the black beast rapist," an animal on a suicide mission of destruction for self and for the white women of the region. Moreover, as Rebecca Felton and John Graves would have it, Sledd was the fool of the clever beast rapist while Candler was a knave in league with the beast; all were equally dangerous—knave, fool, and beast—and all deserved eradication.

When these people talked about eradication, they were in deadly earnest. In 1897 Rebecca Felton, speaking before Georgia's most prominent planters at a Tybee Island convention, had called for a "thousand lynchings a week." She was not rewarded with that ghastly number of murders, but she exulted in the wide dissemination of her address, a notice of which was entered in the congressional report for Georgia's General Assembly, as she exulted in the subsequent number of lynchings: 165 recorded for 1897 and 127 recorded for 1898. Graves never stirred emotions as intensely as Felton, but he enjoyed a considerable readership and, in tandem with the more volatile Felton, helped to bring great notoriety to Sledd. Angry readers sent hateful correspondence to Sledd, and some even made threats to his life; in this violent era, he took these threats seriously enough to carry a gun with him to his bedside in the evenings.[7]

The Candler family, which after all represented economic, political, and moral power, closed ranks around Sledd; but the little school in Oxford could not stomach any more confrontation, regardless of the manpower it could call to its side. Emory "accepted" Sledd's resignation in circumstances which demonstrated simultaneously Candler power and the school community's sense of collective guilt. His resignation included a sizable "fellowship"— really a salary—to finance doctoral studies at Yale University. After completing this degree, Sledd became a prime mover at the University of Florida, which was involved in a major curricular revision and a program of physical expansion. In short, Sledd endured little material suffering, but he certainly suffered the obloquy of exile.[8]

By the First World War, extreme racism had waned, being replaced by the softer glow of patronizing conservatism, and Sledd was thus permitted to rejoin the Emory faculty. When classes commenced in Atlanta, Sledd was one of the luminaries in the new sky, a restoration which showed that times had changed for Georgia. Significantly, however, Sledd had changed as well. The man who taught in Atlanta in the twenties scrupulously avoided the race question and even altered his style of instruction. Where once he had provoked vigorous discusssion, in and out of class, now he sought no influence beyond Druid Hills, and in his classroom he brooked no interruption of any kind. As a scholar, Sledd continued to excel, producing a fine English translation from the Greek of St. Mark's Gospel. As a lecturer he was crisp and occasionally brilliant, but he forbade students to offer their opinions on the subject matter. Every now and again he also cautioned students against social activism, vaguely referring to his own youthful action and the punishment it brought him. In seminary classes and in chapel services, Sledd told students that his activism had once been so controversial that he slept with a shotgun, and that he, and they, should avoid such activism.[9] In other words, by the late 1920s, when Vann arrived on campus, Emory again had room for Sledd, but the Sledd it made a place for was a markedly different man.

Sledd's case was the kind of fight which Warren Candler had experienced during a dangerous era in social relations, the time from 1896 to 1919, which Joel Randolph Williamson has designated usefully as "the crucible" of race relations. The scars remaining from such struggles, and the memory of the scarring, had fixed in the bishop a determination to prevent future wounds by preventing future fights. He permitted on his campus none of the Felton-Graves obscene celebration of lynchings, but that particular message had never been acceptable on such a conservative campus anyway. What he did permit was the brand of condescending disdain for Negro intelligence which formed the conservative defense of racial segregation. Thus students witnessed a campus ritual in which an Emory administrator kept small Negro children off the campus by chasing them with a broom. In part, this talismanic enactment was a comic sport enjoyed by the black boys and girls, who laughed at the man's discomfiture; but it was to larger degree clear evidence that town and gown were for whites only.[10]

Concomitant with segregation by color went the bishop's desire to segregate by creed, to keep Emory a Protestant enclave. In this struggle he generally failed, the failure a sign of intellectual growth and toughness in the school faculty. But Candler did not fail from laxity of effort. He once attempted to discipline LeRoy Loemker, professor of philosophy, because the recent graduate of Boston University and the University of Berlin dared to speak to a gathering of Jews about the career of Benedict Spinoza. First Candler publicly denounced the study of non-Christian philosophers such as the excommunicated Jew and pantheist Spinoza. Then he insisted on Loemker's resignation. But in this shadowy reminder of the Sledd incident, the university administration held firm around Loemker. A compromise was arranged whereby Loemker met with the bishop to defend, but not to apologize for, studying and teaching about Spinoza; and Candler, permitted to demonstrate his compassionate side, not only accepted the principle but also enthusiastically proclaimed himself Loemker's friend. Over the next years, as the Great Depression developed, the bishop, in Loemker's words, "was still fighting the battles of the twenties," but the fighting was strictly rhetorical and Candler did not again interfere with the professors.[11]

By the fall semester of 1928, Emory had thus become a very good school freed of disastrous intervention for reasons of race or of religion. The campus grounds and the faculty residential development were maturing gracefully, as lawns with flowers and shrubbery broke the monotony of red clay and pine trees. Students, predominantly from small southern communities, came to school in considerable awe of the relatively cosmopolitan faculty and generally worked hard in the classrooms, especially after the economic reversals of 1929. Members of the faculty, in turn, were generous with students, finding housing and board for the poorest and, in one case, virtually adopting an indigent Swedish migrant whom they assisted financially through the undergraduate science program and then through the medical school.[12]

On first arriving, Vann Woodward was almost as overwhelmed by the campus and its faculty as were his classmates who hailed from Dalton or Dothan or Anderson or Swainsboro. But unlike his fellows, Woodward felt deeply the influence of a family and a network of friends accustomed to the privilege of dissent. Before long, Woodward found the nice campus too nice, too staid. Other students frolicked on the grounds, playing with a huge rubber sphere in the popular game of pushball; but that game was not for Woodward. Nor did he share the students' enthusiasm for the campus basketball and boxing teams; and he did not attend the hilarious mock trials in the convocation halls in which the "district attorney"

ended up as the man on defense. Instead, he was soon riding the
trolley downtown, frankly looking for windmills to tilt at. It was in
such exercises in activism that he formed the third part of the triptych of Emory dissidents: Glenn Weddington Rainey, Ernest Hartsock, and Vann Woodward.

I I

Ernest Hartsock was the center of this triptych, more spirited,
brighter, more ambitious than his friends; but like the center of any
triptych, he also relied on Woodward and Rainey to support him,
emotionally, financially, and sometimes even physically. Hartsock,
the man of vision, was already an excellent poet; in 1929 he would
win the first prize of the American Poetry Society for this poem:

> Ages of earth are in me. I am made
> Of time's immortal matter, which is dust.
> I am old atoms in a new parade;
> I am new iron miracled from rust.
>
> This that is I had not been I forever;
> Once it was pearl or spider, flame or fly.
> Nature's destination is endeavor;
> There is no dust that beauty will let die.
>
> This that is flesh of me may once have ridden
> The saddle of the stallions of the sun
> Which leap from hidden glory unto hidden,
> Knowing their goal and origin are one.
>
> Last among sulphurous meteors I come;
> Vanished in smoky mystery I go
> Where cooling comets crackle like a drum
> To ether's weird electric tremolo.
>
> From space to space the flaming planets scatter,
> Crashing and splitting in the black abyss.
> Still onward hurls the starry march of matter:
> Each Armaggedon is a Genesis.

There is no height nor depth beyond our border
Of isolated vision in the earth;
And all there is is cataclysmic order
Moving in rhythms of ironic mirth.

There is no East nor West. Only an aching
Cyclone of chaos hurtling forever on.
There is no day or night. Only the breaking
Of eerie shadows in eternal dawn.

Out of the chaos and the dark and thunder,
Flung to new glamour in earth's diagram,
I stand upon the citadel of wonder
And shout the terrible miracle—I Am![13]

Moreover, as the dominant intellect in the threesome, Hartsock urged his fellows to improve their own writing. Woodward and Rainey both harbored the desire to become auteurs, the former as novelist, the latter as poet; and as the first phase of that plan, the two honed their prose on the sharp edges of Hartsock's critiques. All three cared passionately about style and all three labored for the *Bozart,* the offbeat literary magazine which Hartsock produced despite a number of emotional and fiscal problems that slowed his basement printing presses. They chose the title *Bozart* from the acerb observation of H. L. Mencken, who dismissed the South as the "Saharra of the arts" and insisted that the "gaping primates" of Dixie would render *beaux-arts* as *bozart.* Hartsock was a brilliant, albeit slender, reflection of a literary and artistic star burst at the South which would give the lie to Mencken's snide comment. But curiously, the three did not resent Mencken and, for all their energy and idealism, were nearly as pessimistic as the Baltimore critic about the Atlanta region; in fact, as Woodward recalled, they all eagerly followed the newest issues of Mencken's *American Mercury* to "know what to think."[14]

In spite of Hartsock's genius for inspiring others, he did poorly by himself. Physically frail and often sick, he could be petulant and peevish, even trivial in his complaints about his fortune. Nor were his fortunes good: his family was poor even by the severe standards of the depression, and he had a number of dependents subsisting with him on the slight income generated by odd jobs about town.

He strained everyone's patience until, stricken with pernicious ane-
mia, he suddenly found his protestations congruent with his actual
circumstances; by 1931 he was truly desperate, facing a wretched
early death and with practically nobody save Woodward and Rainey
to assist him. His string ran out abruptly, and he died at 4:30 A.M.
on 14 December in a shabby apartment with Woodward at his bedside—it was the first time that Woodward would see somebody
die—and with Glenn Rainey, off at graduate school in Illinois, fran-
tically arranging by the mails to cover the expenses of illness, death,
and burial. It was gruesome business, and it left its mark on the two
who remained behind. [15]

But Hartsock continued to inspire despite his pathetic demise.
Woodward and Rainey helped to produce a collection of his poems,
and they maintained the spirit of auteurs, sharing their literary creations by mail and encouraging each other's efforts. Woodward, although he never did write his novel, produced a travel essay and
reviewed books for the *Atlanta Journal* while Rainey wrote poems,
some of which appeared in *Bozart* and several in the *New York Times*.
Perhaps more important, they lived in a small world of Hartsock's
creation in which they strained to bring truth into union with
beauty, a task which enveloped them in irony, given the truth of
their creator's physical and emotional world. [16]

This ironic commitment to truth and beauty dovetailed with
Woodward's heritage of patrician responsibility and with Rainey's
reform politics. Where Hartsock gave the trio moral impetus,
Rainey gave it political means; and Woodward fused impetus and
means with a more conservative sense of social purpose. The way the
three completed each other should not be underestimated: without
the dynamics of their dependence on each other, Hartsock might
never have printed a poem, nor would Woodward necessarily have
focused on an issue, or Rainey ever have acted on one. But the
combination was intact, and intact just as solidly after Hartsock's
death, with the result that Rainey became an activist dissident by
design and Woodward a historian as the unforeseen detritus of Rainey's design. At the time, however, neither contemplated a career in
history, and in fact both had considerable disdain for the practitioners of history at Emory.

Rainey, more mature and more stable than his friend, retained a
moral perspective engendered by the Methodist church. Around

1926, as he prepared to graduate from Emory, he began translating his Christian ethics into social action. In the fashion of the day, he sometimes styled himself radical, sometimes "advanced" liberal, but by whatever label, he was developing a set of beliefs considerably to the left of southern liberalism. A persuasive character, he insisted that southerners must search their past for the exemplary exceptions to the section's conservatism; and as corollary to the search, southerners must act by the light of the minority exemplars. He was, then, by inclination a historian, although he majored in literature and, upon graduation, began teaching English at the Georgia Institute of Technology. His study and teaching of literature were distinctly political, for he emphasized clarity and precision in writing as the best means to the end of reform. [17]

While teaching at Georgia Tech, he had brought Hartsock and Woodward to a new sensitivity to the social ills in Atlanta as the depression wore on. Curiously, however, Rainey was able to do so for a time at a conservative and pragmatic institution without rubbing the faculty or the administration the wrong way. In fact, he was fully as ingratiating with the elders there as he was with his peers at Emory; and he won such respect from William G. Perry that that man, then dean of arts and sciences at Georgia Tech, was soon hiring Rainey's friends from Druid Hills to teach freshmen at Tech. In 1930 Rainey left Atlanta to do graduate work in political science at Northwestern University, knowing that his chances of returning to teach English at Tech were very good. It was from the distance of Evanston that he learned of Hartsock's debilities and from that outpost that he shared a social vision with Woodward through the mails. At Northwestern he became a little more sophisticated, thanks to the school's proximity to Chicago, and he also deepened his commitment to reform after hearing the socialist Norman Thomas deliver a moving speech. Significantly, however, Rainey passed up the chance to become a socialist, but he pronounced himself more radical than the liberals of the *New Republic* and the *Nation,* journals which in those days were both well left of center.

That stance left of the liberals was also Woodward's in his last academic year at Emory, 1929–30. Then, in the middle of a philosophy examination, Woodward again put into practice the family prerogative of rebellion. He was trying to answer a question phrased in the old style of moral philosophy, a question designed to evoke explication of abstract principle. He had not really prepared for the test, but instead had read again in his favorite work, Goethe's *Faustus*. That play, with its theme of heroic assault on the world's knowledge, fascinated the student: there one could see abstract principle tested in human action rather than tested against yet more abstractions. Moreover, German language and culture were his avocation, and he was reading *Faustus,* and everything else he could get his hands on, in the language of Goethe. But at that particular moment literature and language took a back seat to the task at hand. To respond to the question, Woodward scrawled the words of Mephistopheles when that devil robed himself as faculty adviser to a callous student and proclaimed,

> Grau, teurer Freund, ist alle Theorie,
> Und grün das Lebens goldner Baum. [18]

Lebens, the green tree of life's experience; *Theorie,* gray and without life. This student preferred Lebens. Lebens was downtown Atlanta, where poor white and poor black jostled in the rude poverty of urban depression, a poverty different in kind from the genteel asceticism of Emory. This Lebens was already well known to the others whom Woodward joined in several political protests. The elder statesmen in a group of youth were Uncle Comer and Will W. Alexander, head of the Atlanta Interracial Commission. These two, liberal only by contrast with their fellow southerners, were characterized by the young Woodward as "paternalistic champions of black people"; they were men who sought something more and better than the conservative "justice" of segregation, but they did so without formulating a complete theory of racial equality. For their day, of course, Comer Woodward and Will Alexander were lonely rebels who seemed cautious only in the council of their small circle. Assisting them in some campaigns was John Hope of Atlanta University, a friend dear to Will and to Comer but, being unashamed of his blackness and fully convinced of his equality with whites, an ally far less disposed to work gradually. The others in this loose confederation were Mercer G. Evans, a professor of economics at Emory; Julian Harris, a correspondent for the irreverent *Time* magazine and, ironically, son of Joel Chandler Harris, who had romanticized the plantation in his popular "Uncle Remus" tales; and

Loemker, the scholar who had already survived a confrontation with Warren Candler. [19]

Of this group, Loemker exercised an influence which was intellectual as well as cultural and personal. Marking this influence, in perspective, has helped to draw the defining boundaries which show the limits of Woodward's ideology and the concomitant limits of his will to dissent. Loemker, teaching Woodward in several classes, attracted the young man into the study of philosophy, and Woodward became one of the first students seeking Emory's new degree, a baccalaureate in philosophy, Ph.B., instead of A.B., the traditional baccalaureate in the arts. The young professor served as Woodward's academic adviser and, not unlike Bola Martin at Henderson-Brown, also became a friend and soul mate who shared new books and new ideas. [20]

Woodward in later years said of Loemker that he must have been terribly conventional, and Loemker in later years said of himself that his activism was liberal, not radical, and that it was a phase in his life, not his whole life. Set against the New South skyline, Loemker's and Woodward's ideas and actions are no less remarkable; but to describe them as truly radical is to damage the meaning of radicalism (the Latin *radix,* "the root," implying a ripping up from the roots and a starting over again) and to misrepresent what both men sought. They were liberals at a time and in a place for which liberalism clearly had meaning as the pursuit of equality for black people; and their dissidence was directed at a system of economy and of society which was hierarchical in class and race. They expressed the intense passion of youth in their insistence that the abusive hierarchy be dismantled; but they were far short of genuine radicalism, a fact which both came to understand when confronted several years later by real levelers. [21]

The Loemker whose teaching, advising, and less formal discussing worked this influence on Woodward was not then the complete scholar in philosophy which he became by the Second World War. His significance, rather, lay in his relative inexperience and even intellectual incompleteness: not having fully developed a coherent philosophy yet, the Emory instructor in 1929 could insist on social action without pausing to develop a rationale for every turn in the courses of actions he sought. What he did have was the outline of an empirical justification for reform. This outline he traced around the eighteenth-century liberalism of Immanuel Kant, a variant of American pragmatism, and Weimar Republic liberalism.

Kant he used as a starting point rather than as a detailed set of guidelines to thinking. Loemker did not fully assimilate, nor did he try to pass on to his student Woodward, the complete system of the *Critique of Pure Reason.* What he did do was to take Kant's vital dictum that experience must be the testing principle for any idea, and to follow that principle through by using the Kantian concept of deduction. That word and its definition were created by Kant as a way out of the dilemma posed by David Hume when that elder Scot denied the possibility of rational theology by demolishing the Scholastics' intricate links of cause and effect. In very modern philosophical fashion, Hume both decried the meaning of *cause* and *effect* and discredited the putative relationship between them. Hume thus left eighteenth-century intellectuals without cosmology unless they chose "irrational" Scholasticism. Kant, also rejecting the latter, posited a metaphysics which was to be empirically tested by deduction, that is, by carefully marking off the lines between cause and effect, the very thing Hume said could not be done. A favorite teaching device to illustrate Kant has long been the griffin story: everyone will hunt for a griffin, having before the hunt starts a detailed set of observations which describe the griffin; there may be no such thing, but if a griffin appears, then the hunters will recognize it. With Kant, of course, the griffin would be an idea and not some unknown animal: one puts together an idea and then looks for proof or disproof of it in the experience of one's reason. Kant, then, proceeded quite oppositely from the Schoolmen painstakingly inducting the proof of a prime mover and his qualities; but Kant was not willing to abandon all metaphysics, as had Hume.

The significance of Kant for Loemker and for his student and cohort Vann Woodward was that the young instructor chose Kant and not Georg Wilhelm Friedrich Hegel, then the regnant philosopher for southern conservatism. Hegel, with his spectacular dialectical sweeps through the ideas of civilization, has generally served conservatives, and especially so in the New South.[22] On the other hand, Hegel's dialectical historicity, "stood on its head," produced the genius of Marxism, something Karl Marx was careful to point out. In taking Kant as the instructive exemplar, Loemker was thereby closing off an intellectual path to the dominant Hegelian-

ism of the region in this era. The result would be a Kantian toughness and empiricism, one perhaps not fully recognizable by Immanuel Kant, but one still shaped by him.

One thing Kant did not shape was the concept of the activism for
which Loemker called. That was a distinctly pragmatic approach to
politics often echoed by young Woodward when he would insist to
Glenn Rainey that they could define liberalism some other time; at
the moment they had to act against racism and against class oppression.[23] These components of pragmatic activism came through
Loemker from William James, the penultimate spokesman for that
belief. James's prescription for a philosophy of action grounded in
experience spoke effectively to his America at the turn of the century: every concept, to be meaningful for James, had to be verifiable
in the laboratory of experience. James's definition included interior
experience, specifically "the will to believe," a quiddity which he
thought could be tested empirically. In the decade after James's
death in 1910, many pragmatists sharpened, and consequently nar-
rowed, the mentor's perception so that only exterior actions could
qualify as experience; thus, they dismissed things such as "the will
to believe" as beyond empiricism and hence beyond the pale. By
contrast, some pragmatists went in the other direction and nar-
rowed James's perception until it became exclusively interior experience, "the stream of consciousness" which transcended exterior experiences. One such was Gordon P. Bowne, who taught Loemker at
Boston University and who gave the label of *personalism* to his tran-
scendent pragmatism. Bowne's personalism tended toward the individual and away from overarching systems of collective thought.
What it obviously did, much like the German existentialism which
inspired Bowne, was to intensify one's sense of responsibility to act
now to achieve the results demanded by one's own will to believe.
Although Loemker did not assign reading in Bowne to Woodward,
he did reiterate to him both formally in the classroom and in
friendly discussions the demand for action taken in the context of
the experiences of one's own mind. Thus informed, Woodward
could tell his friends that they could define liberalism later; *he* had
experienced a sense of injustice and he was moving now to eradicate
the injustice.

Loemker's rather dramatic cry to arms was intensified by the frequent evocation of his experience at the University of Berlin in the

Weimar Republic. There, in 1928, one Vierkundt lectured on *Geistmenschen* and *Fachmenschen,* notes of which lectures Loemker recorded in German and shared with Woodward as the student sought to master German philosophy and German language. As Loemker and his pupil "read" and translated it, Vierkundt protested depersonalization—the replacement of Geistmenschen, men defined by spirit, with Fachmenschen, men defined by work. *Das Fachmenschentum,* the process of such displacement, was the problem with contemporary Germany. In retrospect, the critique is purely Marxian, but for a crucial difference which Loemker pointed out. "It is post-Marxian criticism; there is no real class consciousness in the analysis. What we call the free cultural system of the United States—or of the Weimar Republic—is not free; big organizations or systems make the decisions. The unified sense of purpose is gone, hence the individual's loss of responsibility to self and to others. Nevertheless, the depersonalization is not what Marxists find in class oppression"; there are two significant differences: Vierkundt's Fachmenschentum is a response to conditions of the emotion and not to conditions of the economy or of the class structure of that economy; and he makes the complaint against Fachmenschentum and offers the remedy to it in Christian, not Marxist, terms. [24]

What came of these elements of Loemker's 1929 teachings, which he immediately concedes today formed a pastiche, was a powerful sense of personal responsibility to right the wrongs of the South. In fact, the very qualities of the pastiche in his lectures made Woodward's brief Emory career all the more vital, for Loemker's sense of responsibility harmonized with the controlling theme of familial prerogative and joined there with the activist signatures of Glenn Rainey and Ernest Hartsock. Thus Vann Woodward graduated from Emory in 1930 with a degree signifying at once a diffuse, but very energetic, scholarship and a social activism no less energetic—and no less diffuse. Already this newly minted Ph.B. (he was both one of the first and one of the last to earn the degree) was showing the effects of the tension between his passion for relatively disinterested and detached scholarship and his passion for particularistic reform. In fact, the small membership list of Atlanta's reformists made him just as unique as the degree did, and when his friend Rainey orchestrated a job for Woodward teaching freshman English composition at Georgia Tech, it was obvious that commencement marked neither ending nor beginning, but rather a continuo on the theme of dissidence in Atlanta.

III

If it was a continuo, then the bass dropped a full register when the scene shifted from Druid Hills to Techwood. The Georgia Institute of Technology, right downtown, was sired by New South efficacy out of postbellum industrial development. Already Georgia Tech was an excellent school, as effective a sign as any imaginable of what were regional priorities. Georgia Tech generated engineers and architects, chemists and physicists, the managers of the new economy and, as such, as fine a group as came from any contemporaneous school. But it was almost exclusively Lebens with practically nothing of art; the Fachmenschentum which Loemker descried for the Weimar Republic was also stalking this land. The task for Woodward, as for Rainey, who had preceded his friend there before going off to Northwestern, was in two parts: teaching the scientists to write effectively, thus burnishing the already gleaming armor of management; but also bringing something of the humanities to the scientists under the guise of providing them with another skill.

In the latter, subterranean task, the regnant genius was William Perry, the man who had hired Rainey and who was willing to hire Rainey's friends. Perry understood also that men like Rainey were using the composition instructorship as a subsidy to maintain themselves while pursuing the larger end of reform. Despite the school's pragmatic cast, it provided, for a time, considerable freedom with which to risk assaults on societal injustice. Such freedom obviously had its limits, for the school in the end answered to the exigencies of industry; and New South industry, in its failure in the depression years, had grown bitter and harsh with its critics. The job, then, was another tether (much like the one at Emory), with enough slack in it to permit one to protest a bit in the spirit of the day; but let a dissident proclaim a fundamental challenge to things and the tether would tauten by degrees, first pinching, finally choking. Although Woodward must have known this about the tether, he occasionally roamed about as if it did not exist.[25]

The length of his tether he immediately tested by attending the sessions of the Atlanta Forum, by traveling to the complex of black schools in town, and by joining the theater life available. The forum Loemker recalled as a copy of the institution he had seen in Boston, where "the system was elaborate, with many different speakers, with a telephone system for listeners to ask questions of the speakers." The southern version was less elaborate but fully as controversial: while there were no telephones hooked up, there was also no Jim Crow balcony for Negroes. Further, these integrated meetings began to fellow-travel with Marxists, sharing programs at a Congregational and a Methodist church with socialist and Communist groups. Loemker was elected program chairman and he accepted readily, although he realized that his new post "hurt Emory" in the eyes of many in the community.[26]

How much of a threat this forum constituted for Emory and Georgia Tech no one ever measured, because the American Legion successfully pressured the host ministers to close their parish halls to the group. Although socialist labor halls were occasionally available, "that was the end of the forum," according to its briefly reigning chairman. Having established their right as faculty members to hear socialist debate in racially integrated quarters, Loemker, Woodward, and the other dissidents thus lost their right as citizens of Atlanta.[27]

This curious achievement and failure in the forum Woodward did not pause to mark, turning instead to intellectual communion with the black schools: Atlanta University, Morehouse University, and Spellman College. These schools, each for a long time a leader in black scholarship, had been organized as the Atlanta University System in 1929 by John Hope, erstwhile member of the dissidents in town. Hope, for some time a force in the Atlanta Interracial Commission, cooperated with white liberals and moderates to earn their support for the university system. The latter was a program of collaboration among the Negro colleges, a system of backing and filling to reinforce each school where it was weak in curriculum, staff, library, or other resources. A comfort in good times, the university system was the bread of life for the difficult days of the 1930s: thanks to it, each school could offer its students and faculty the basic tools of academe. The member schools which Woodward visited were staffed with some exceptional scholars, one of whom was the dramatist, actor, and essayist J. Saunders Redding of Atlanta University.[28]

Redding, just out of Brown University after a militant black nationalist upbringing in Delaware, was then the angriest of young men in a town full of much for youthful Negroes to be angry about. Having rejected the black separatism of his father, Redding recoiled at Atlanta's Jim Crow and demanded instead integration: nor was he seeking the integration of the "white man with a black face"; his was the complete cultural and spiritual cross-pollination of historic, as opposed to genetic, gifts. Thus Redding was by temperament and circumstances more contentious than fellow scholars at Atlanta University and, as such, was immediately attractive to Woodward. More than that, he was young, and Woodward found with him "my first equal friendship with a Negro." Actually, it may not have been fully equal in Redding's eyes, since the dramatist made no note of it in his memoirs; but the brief friendship was vital for Vann Woodward because of the way it expanded his view of the racial component of social justice in the era.[29]

Specifically, the expansive qualities of Redding's social notation could be seen in the theater of the university system. This theater was well off Broadway, being a thousand miles and a dozen years off the pace, but the acting was generally of good quality, and the plays were often provocative. A specialty of Redding's was *The Emperor Jones,* the play written by Eugene O'Neill as a vehicle for the multi-talented radical Paul Robeson. In the fashion of the 1920s antihero, the main character, Brutus Jones, delivered monologues in seven scenes; and these monologues were a foretaste of the interior dialogues O'Neill would make more famous in *Strange Interlude.* This then-new device demonstrated by Redding profoundly and permanently influenced Woodward's critical reading of all literature. Furthermore, Redding's Brutus Jones expressed an intensely personal irony which his friend Woodward caught while standing in the wings listening to rehearsals or sitting in the audience. For one thing, Brutus Jones announced on stage that he was unafraid of a white lynch mob, but offstage Saunders Redding lived in active fear generated by a mob which recently had lynched an Atlanta University student. For another, Saunders Redding was also resisting the call of "progressing rationalism" expressed by his American Marxist friends at the moment that he played the role of the emperor betrayed by the "scientific plans." Paul Robeson, the original emperor, was seizing the rational dialectics of Karl Marx as his way out of the offstage dilemma of racism, but Redding was on another path, to a variant of Christian existentialism. Once again, the activism of Woodward and his friends was pulling up short of genuine radicalism. Whatever else, Redding as defeated emperor or as brooding scholar further deepened Woodward's sense of dissidence while he broadened the channels of communication across the color line.[30]

But the broadening and the deepening were not enough: Woodward wanted to be involved in more than political movements imported from abroad and more than theater delayed a decade from Broadway. He wanted to be involved in things where they started. Thus, like the protagonists of the Thomas Wolfe novels he so admired and like his friend Rainey, he set off in 1931 for the "million footed city." For Rainey that city was Chicago and the school near it, Northwestern University; but for Woodward that city was New York, the first city, and the school was Columbia University. Woodward could go to the big city and experience his intellectual responses to its challenges, and he could still return to the instructorship at Georgia Tech if nothing more glamorous developed. Moreover, the network of friends and relatives also operated at Columbia University, making the year 1931–32 one full of exciting possibilities. Will Alexander chaired the "southern fellowship committee" of the Social Science Research Council of New York and was pleased to announce that Woodward was one of two Emory graduates given a scholarship "to study economic problems of the South."[31] He went, then, with an explorer's spirit, but he went also with a security unknown to most of depression America.

The whole junket was a bit unrepresentative of the bold adventurer he intended to be, and perhaps there was the justice of poesy in its eventual failure. Dissidence hedged with security was not genuine dissidence, a fact Woodward understood after first protesting the intellectual confinement of the hedges. He tried anthropology and sociology; that is, he met with professors in those departments and attended a few classes before pronouncing the men and their work tiresome and irrelevant. Pacing the streets distractedly past apple sellers and soup queues, he crossed paths with Charles Pipkin, prominent member of that network of supporters as well as an Arkansas native overdue for the courtesy call which southern communities insist on when former neighbors find themselves in the same strange city. Very much in the ascendancy in that year, Pipkin was a visiting lecturer at Columbia, and although not the man to resolve the dilemma of dissidence and professionalism, he could at least suggest a field of study for a master's degree so that Woodward could return to Atlanta with something in hand to show for his year in New York. The field Pipkin suggested was his own, political science, and he reminded his confused and disillusioned friend that one could study the relevant events and people of recent time in political science. While that field was constricted, too, it at least offered some room for maneuver, and Woodward enrolled in the program, writing a master's thesis on the political career of Thomas Heflin, Alabama's flamboyant demagogue of the previous decade.[32]

The thesis itself was uninspired, but the research in contemporary southern politics fascinated him: he formulated a plan to write a book entitled "Seven for Demos," an examination of southern radicals including Heflin, Thomas E. Watson of Georgia, and Benjamin Ryan Tillman of South Carolina. Even as his enthusiasm for the project grew, he lost all interest in the discipline of political science, except that the master's degree could solidify his job at Georgia Tech. To Rainey he wrote letters of complaint about the curriculum, which was heavy on theories of government and constitution: much too much of Theorie. There was, however, another disappointment about which he did not tell Rainey then: up close, as his roommate, Pipkin was less than inspirational; Pipkin was drinking heavily and was both promiscuous and ambivalent in his sexual life. The source of so much excitement about scholarship and reform back in Arkansas and Louisiana was in New York essentially a playboy. Woodward might be unhappy with school, but he "got that straight" with Pipkin, that he was not interested in joining a bohemian style of life; and then he went almost cheerlessly about his business in graduate school. To Rainey he did write enthusiastically about the experiences of Lebens, New York style, with a great deal of everything to see and hear. In particular, he reveled in Broadway, with O'Neill's *Strange Interlude* at the top of his list of favorites; moreover, he thought he saw Lebens on stage, as fully present there as it was absent from the lectern of the instructor in government. He was thrilled to meet Langston Hughes and lesser members of the

Harlem Renaissance, and he even got up on stage himself, in "the only white part, a more human Simon Legree," in a Harlem Experimental Theatre production of *Uncle Tom's Cabin*. Widening the span of his social notation with these new insights, he took his degree, having failed to sharpen his vision for a life's work beyond the richly blurred scarlet impressions of the prospectus for "Seven for Demos."[33]

At commencement he signed a contract with Georgia Tech and considered attempting a second European tour for the summer before beginning his teaching duties. Pipkin, perhaps feeling a bit guilty—or a bit concerned about what Woodward had seen and heard during his New York experiences—offered to pay Woodward's way overseas, so that the graduate could again have the chance to observe contemporary Europe, but this time in more organized fashion; and Woodward, perhaps a bit embarrassed by knowing so much, accepted Pipkin's offer. This time he concentrated on the ideological flash points in Paris, Berlin, and Moscow. Paris he enjoyed the least, although he was delighted to locate and smuggle out a Black Sun edition of James Joyce's *Ulysses,* then banned in the United States. Living near the Left Bank, he could feast on the literary smorgasbord available, but one's appetite dulled as the expatriates packed up to confront problems of depression *Lebens* stateside after having struggled with the challenges of *Theorie* in the fat days of the 1920s. Berlin, by contradistinction, offered a rich feast of ideas, though some of the ideas betrayed an undertaste of poison. There he saw, instead of debate between Communist and Fascist theorizers, fights between practicing Communists and Fascists.[34]

Living with a bourgeois Jewish family, he could see the antisemitism which had always shrouded Germany: the patriarch of the family, although a well-educated jurist, was unable to find employment even in minor clerical positions. Yet he and his family insisted that the Fascists, with their more pernicious antisemitism, were only noise and would never attract enough of a following to make good their awful threats. There were, nevertheless, melodramatic scenes, scenes which gained greater power as memories after Hitler had done his work. Once Woodward went for a trip down a river on an inflated raft with a young Communist he met: the river sport, popular with Berliners, featured the spectacle of some rafts flying the red flag and other rafts flying the swastika: the combatants for the world's favor on watery parade! Another time, Woodward and a Jewish friend noticed a mutual acquaintance in a bar; this evening their friend was decked out in brown shirt, with fellow Nazis in tow, and catching Woodward's eye and the Jew's eye from across the hall, he looked coldly through them, people he no longer knew. But these instances, when each happened in 1932, seemed then examples of the variety of behavior and of experience permitted by Weimar liberalism instead of portents of the Third Reich.[35]

From Berlin he traveled for a brief but profoundly influential time to the "future" in Moscow. While not proclaiming with the unequivocal assurance of some that "the Marxist future works," he was deeply impressed by Josef Stalin's quickstep industrial development: he was enough moved by it to pick up and to use the phrase that the violence of the disruption brought with Stalin's plans was violence as viewed by the aphids in a field being sprayed by a farmer beset with pestilence. He even hinted to Rainey that he might return to teach in Moscow, having had an offer from the Soviets. But what most impressed him in Moscow was not anything produced by Josef Stalin at all: it was the news that Alabamians had railroaded eight teenaged Negroes through a sham trial and conviction for rape in Scottsboro. Everywhere he went in Moscow there was stinging criticism of southern bigotry, outrage at southern violence, fear of southern presumption; and for him, then, these criticisms rang true.[36]

He saw also a side of postrevolutionary Russia which gave him pause and which somewhat modified—though it by no means reversed—his essentially favorable judgment of the new regime. As he related it much later to a student of his: "It turned out to be a bad year for Russia in 1932. There was famine and there was oppression of kulaks. Fortunately we had a woman in the party of eight or nine who was a native and had moved to America. She could translate and did. They took us to the places selectively. I remember one incident: a man left the assembly line and came over and made a passionate speech about being a slave. I also remember a big peasant got up on a train and made an eloquent denunciation of the system. The guide sent for a soldier; but he jumped off the train. It was a confusing and sobering experience." But if these Russian experiences produced a welter of contradicting responses, there remained the more cleanly cut, starker oppression of blacks in

Alabama and Arkansas, in the Carolinas and Mississippi. And in Georgia. To Communist complaint about that oppression, he had no rejoinder to make, no defense to offer. What he did was to swear to himself that he would "get in on" the next such incident, defending Negro civil rights in his native South on his return.[37]

IV

Such an oath was more militant than the dissidence he had expressed beforehand: it was no longer protest hedged with job security, because now he was prepared not only to attend meetings of protest but also to act publicly in support of black civil rights. In 1932 he and Glenn Rainey in their political orbits swung farther left than ever before, on paths in confluence with Marxism. The succeeding fall season brought the issue to "get in on" and, in the process, drew Woodward and Rainey into cooperative action with Communists.

Where race and class met, the streams of Atlanta activism converged with the previously distant current of communism. As Rainey recollected it, the ignominy of racism combined with the most predatory capitalism to force action: "We were not dreaming some brave new world dreams; hell, we were trying to stop God-damned *lynching*. If one tries to get rid of an open sewer across the street from his home, he is not trying to make a Garden of Eden, he is trying to get rid of the stink."[38] The stink was the Atlanta economy, and the effort to clean the sewer very nearly produced a legal lynching à la Scottsboro, in this case that of a slender twenty-year-old Negro Communist named Angelo Herndon.

Herndon was born in southern Ohio and worked in the coal mines of Kentucky, occasionally traveling to Illinois to hear the Marxist labor organizers William Zebulon Foster, Bill Dunne, and Earl Browder. Moved by them, Herndon became a Communist and in 1932 went to Atlanta with several missions, all involved in the Communist party (CP) presidential campaign to elect Foster and his black running mate, James W. Ford: he was to organize Negro support for the party; he was to protest the cuts in welfare relief made by the city of Atlanta; and he was to publicize the Scottsboro case as it wended its way through appeal to the Supreme Court. To make any of the three protests in public was to flaunt Georgia's ancient defense against social protest, an insurrection law originally written against William Lloyd Garrison abolitionists and modified only slightly over the years. Plainly put, one who spoke in public about blacks' rights was "inciting to riot," and the penalty for such obversion to the public tranquility was death. By July Atlanta police had duly arrested Herndon, and the solicitor general had set his trial for a date in the following autumn.[39] Now Herndon the man disappeared, obscured by the frenetically other-created images of Herndon the Comrade, Herndon the Red, Herndon the Negro, Herndon the Nigger, Herndon the Citizen, Herndon the Apostate.

With the Scottsboro debate continuing apace, the Herndon case bodied forth as many incongruities as did any event of the Reformation, which seventeenth-century fighting it did in fact resemble. There was the prosecutorial team, dominated by John Hudson, an ordained minister out to get the Reds while protecting white women. Again and again, Hudson would ask defense witnesses how they would react if Herndon attempted to sleep with their sisters. On defense there were two able Negro lawyers, Ben Davis, Jr., and John H. Geer, who performed well enough in the abstract but who in the concrete were overwhelmed by the snide condescension of presiding judge Wyatt.[40] The combatant images in force in the courtroom did produce occasional moments of comic relief from the pathos of the obviously impending death sentence. For one, Mercer Evans of Emory attempted to testify that the materials found in Herndon's room were not subversive and in fact were available at the Candler Library. In a way he was correct, because the corpus delecti included the *Nation,* the *New Republic, The Little Red Book,* and some standard translations from Karl Marx's *Das Kapital.* Unfortunately for Evans's plan, the Candler Library did not then have these materials; but Evans, not to be outdone by circumstances, slipped into the library with the intention of putting his own books and journals on the shelves. Caught out by a diligent librarian, Evans could only concede defeat: Angelo Herndon surely did have in his possession books of unusual thought not to be found at a decent school like Emory.[41]

Actually, Evans's ploy, like Hudson's flamboyance, was secondary to the real issue in the minds of the jury: did Atlanta dare let Negro

Communists rile the masses of poor blacks? The answer was an emphatic no, and the verdict of guilty bore no surprise for anyone.[42] Immediately, however, dissidents of all sorts and conditions began organizing an appeal about which they were fairly hopeful. The old Atlanta alliance held intact: Comer Woodward and Mercer Evans from the Emory faculty, Julian and Julia Harris from the fifth estate, Vann Woodward from Tech, Will Alexander from the Interracial Commission, John Hope from the Atlanta University System, and two men named Yates and Milton from the Negro business community.[43] Now, however, this sturdy band was joined by two groups new to the scene of racial struggle in Georgia, the socialists and the Communists.

The former was mostly Mrs. Mary Raoul Millis, wealthy and strong-willed patroness of a movement which she insisted be kept distinct from communism. The latter was the International Labor Defense (ILD) coordinated by Joseph Brodsky and Alan Taub as a branch of the CP designed to make the Negro question into the entrepôt for revolution at the South. Mary Millis chaired the Angelo Herndon Defense Committee, a selection of virtue obvious to all except the ILD; the vice-chairman was Vann Woodward, but no one, least of all Woodward, took that post seriously. At an early meeting in the spring of 1933, the ILD continued to obstruct Millis, interrupting the proceedings often to deliver obiter dicta on her "fascism." Soon Millis indignantly resigned, rather than have the ILD ruin the appeal by subsuming Herndon's case under a war along the left front of ideology. Her resignation put a startled and utterly unprepared Woodward at the helm of a fellow-traveling vessel of protest.[44]

Lacking Millis's savoir faire, Woodward actually expected to preside over a successful fund raising for the process of adjudication. Taub, Brodsky, and the ILD members approached him, their very pores oozing sincerity, assuring him that the abnegation of the socialists would leave the team lighter but more efficient. Woodward agreed: after all, he had confided to Rainey that he might well move to Russia, the place he regarded as much the most interesting in the world. Flushed with the spirit of such social realism, Woodward spoke frankly with the ILD visitors. They wanted to know how helpful Will Alexander would be to the cause. Oh, replied youthful dissidence, drawing the words with precision from around his pipe, oh, Will is a dear sweet old man, but not to be relied on for this kind of politics.[45]

That statement found a prominent place on the front page of the *Daily Worker:* it was perfect for the CP's plans, since it divided the non-Communist dissidents still further, with the Communists remaining almost alone as the party championing their boy. Realization of his duping came to Woodward with sharp force when Will Alexander scrawled a note enclosing the clipping: "The cut of friends is the unkindest cut of all." Woodward hastened to make it up with the man who was both dear to Atlanta's reformists and already Woodward's benefactor at Columbia University; Alexander, for his part, readily and characteristically forgave the indiscretion, thereby keeping the moderates and the liberals on the team. Nevertheless, larger problems loomed, for the Georgia Supreme Court upheld the conviction and the Atlanta newspapers became increasingly strident both against blacks and against Reds, with the Hearst publication the *Georgian* leading the charge. Even as Vann was being reconciled with his hero Alexander, he learned that Tech president Martin Luther Brittain wanted to see him.[46]

Brittain was another kind of patriarch, tough and wily and thoroughly political. He never disclosed any particular ideology to members of the Tech faculty or administration, and he tolerated a range of political beliefs as long as no contentious thought became tendentious act. He gave Woodward a "talking to," fearsome enough in itself, but did not threaten other retribution. Woodward resigned from the committee, stung more by the CP tactics than by Brittain's thoroughly predictable reaction. He hoped that Herndon would win on appeal to the U.S. Supreme Court, but he was not going to fellow-travel with Alan Taub anymore: better to teach composition to freshmen, better to do his research on "Seven for Demos," better to confine dissidence to slower currents in more shallow channels.[47]

The edge of dissidence dulled perceptibly, and as he recalls, "I could have been happy teaching English at Tech the rest of my life." But then the vagaries of depression economics reentered, ending complacency without restoring Marxism to favor. The board of regents cut the school budget and ordered Tech to fire thirty professors at once; in addition, the board changed the pay schedule from a monthly basis to nine times per year and cavalierly disavowed its obligations to pay the fired professors the remainder of the salaries still due them for work already performed. Woodward was let go without protest from Perry, who had to dismiss the least experienced men. In later years this firing has gotten mixed up with the Herndon incident, especially since Vann Woodward himself occasionally told the story as if there were a causal link between Herndon Defense Committee and his departure. There was not a causal link, because Woodward would have been fired in any case.[48]

What there was, however, was a link of effect. Woodward departed Atlanta with no more illusions of job security inside the capitalist system of efficacy, but he left also with no more illusions about the Communist alternative. It was more than the sly trick played on Will Alexander and on himself; he and Rainey believed that the Communists were playing games with the very lives of Angelo Herndon and with the Scottsboro Boys. The cause, they felt, must need the blood of a martyr, and thus the actual strategy was not to seek acquittal at all but rather to so frustrate the liberals and the moderates in the proceedings that only the CP remained with Herndon; *then to lose* the case, thereby proving capitalism's evil; and then to shroud the body properly in the appropriate red.[49] If the agents of the cause could be as heedless of humans here as the ILD was, then what of the leadership on the raw edge of revolution? There were, he had learned, extremes of efficacy among the revolutionaries as well as among the plutocrats. Perhaps that was the stuff of pure radicalism; perhaps, as well, the two young men misinterpreted the Communists' intent, for it is obvious that a legal victory won by the Communists—acting alone—would have furthered the cause at least as much as a carefully orchestrated martyrdom, as would be demonstrated a generation later in the Angela Davis case. At any rate, the Herndon appeal marked the line between dissidence and radicalism for Woodward, for Rainey, and for others of the day who declined to answer the call of radicalism at the crucial moments.

The same events of 1933 and 1934 also marked another line, one between research and reformism, although the remainder of Woodward's life would be taken up with a continuing effort to find a proper balance between the competing masters of political causes and of disinterested scholarship. All scholars who seek societal reform ultimately face the dilemma posed by the contradictions between the two impulses; Woodward now realized the dilemma fully, notwithstanding Pipkin's insistence that scholarship and reformism went together. Scholarship requires a degree of detachment from the concerns of the moment, while genuine activism permits little time for reflection on event and characters of the past "irrelevant" to contemporary causes. Glenn Rainey would respond to this problem by emphasizing the responsibilities of societal reform much more than the duties of research and writing; in time, Rainey's scholarly output would decline and all but disappear as result of that choice. On the other hand, Rupert Vance, by then in Chapel Hill, was resolving the same dilemma on the side of scholarship: still very active as a voice calling for reform, Vance consciously placed the duties of scholarship first, the responsibilities of reform second.

In 1934 Woodward was leaning toward Vance's resolution and away from Rainey's; but for the nonce the question appeared almost moot, for there were no academic jobs and no other employment available in the Atlanta or the New York metropolitan areas. Largely because he had nowhere to go, Woodward returned to Oxford in 1934, still dissident, but no longer youthful.

3

Discovery of Agrarian Radicalism, 1934

Chastened though hardly beaten, Vann Woodward sat in his room in Oxford. The town was Old South at its core, full of grace, suffused with the charms of its history. It was genteel and settled, thoroughly comfortable with its continuing mimesis of the Victorian English countryside. The junior college, once the leading Methodist college in the Deep South, still set the tone for the community: its Christian values were expressed in lapidarian phraseology whether the mode of expression was classroom lecture, building design, or campus landscaping. The eternal verities were well shaded from the glare of Atlanta's modern woes. In such a setting he relaxed in his high-ceilinged room, puffing on his pipe, more bemused than angered by the events of the past two years.[1]

To his friend Rainey in Atlanta he wrote extolling the Oxford life. Dissidence waned in both men: Rainey groused that he found himself grown fat around the intellectual hips like some benevolent Jehovah slouching uncritically among the decadent; Woodward noted the irony of the Angelo Herndon case, conceded his inability to write his novel, and briefly lost focus on "Seven for Demos."[2] But the waning of commitment was only temporary: Rainey was almost immediately back in the fray of activism at Tech and in downtown

Atlanta; and Woodward, while not engaging in activist protest as such, was soon exploring the sweaty Lebens of backwoods central Georgia. He found a job with the Works Progress Administration (WPA) taking a sociological survey of living conditions in the countryside around Macon, several hundred miles south of his parents' idyllic home. Sharing with Rainey what he learned, he reported the scarcely believable poverty and pliability of the families he encountered; although his task was to find statistical proof of rural impoverishment, the people he interviewed invariably presumed he was bringing them desperately needed material help, and their misconception caused first a pathetic kowtowing and then muted expressions of disappointment and even of betrayal.[3]

Sometimes the scenes he found were less pathetic than horripilating. In those days one of his favorite authors was Erskine Caldwell, a South Carolinian whose social-realism portrayals of tobacco road have been in recent years dismissed as mere gothic melodrama. But one day Woodward entered a Caldwell staging which was being played out in real life. Even as he approached an old "dog-trot cabin," he was overwhelmed by the stink of human excrement pouring from the home. Ashamed of his shame, he came onto the doorsill, where next it was his ears whose sensitivity betrayed him, as he heard children crying in hunger. Still determined to be the sociological observer above all else, he called out to the inhabitants, and his eyes were challenged by the appearance of a worn and haggard young mother with a starving child balanced on one hip. It was the eyes which surrendered when the mother accidentally stepped onto an old woman who lay on the floor nearly unconscious. Woodward turned and ran, hearing behind him the shrieks of the old woman added to those of the children. That incident, most gruesomely spectacular among many, ended any nonsense about accepting things as they were by retirement in rural Georgia.[4]

But if he could not in good conscience ignore contemporary problems, how could he face up to them and struggle with them? Certainly he had been ineffectual thus far; but it could be that the *way* he had previously approached injustice was wrongheaded. It could be that he was ineffectively and even improperly using his talents. Rather than leading protest movements and rather than laboring as a welfare agent, could he not more effectively use what remained of Ernest Hartsock's gift to him by writing about the New South? By thus writing history that mattered, by offering perspective and understanding that he hoped would make an actual difference in society's response to racism and injustice, he could perhaps resolve the nagging dilemma produced by the competing claims of reformism and scholarship. Resolve, not actually solve, for always there would remain unmistakable tension between the pull of these two forces, and often he would leave one of, and sometimes both of, the would-be masters unsatisfied; but tension can be a creative as well as a destructive force in art, and perhaps it could be so as well in the art of historical writing. It was a matter of finding his medium and using it to the best possible effect, for there could be no question about either the urgency or the extent of the societal problems, and no fundamental question about his own high level of talents—or about his own deep sense of responsibility.[5]

I

From the triptych he had not only the Hartsock imperative to seek the juncture of truth and beauty but also the Rainey imperative to seek the usable past. From Atlanta, New York, Berlin, Moscow, Macon, the countryside—from everywhere except the pleasant Oxford dwelling there was the imperative of the 1930s, the imperative to solve the economic malady of Western capitalism.[6] There was available an interpretive schema, a dialectic that brought these three imperatives together, although its accomplishment as dialectic was a curious feat; this schema was Progressivism, and it was formulated in the halcyon days of spiritual confidence before the Great Depression quashed economic well-being. Progress, as a controlling idea and as a controlling ideal, dominated the politics of a brief era, but proved even more dominant over the historical perceptions of a much longer era.

In fact, this type of historiography was so crucial for Woodward and his generation that it merits a special examination of its career and of its import for this intellectual's heritage of attitudes and assumptions. For Woodward himself, then and later, these influences were not in all cases fully understood. And even where understood in part, they were not always fully and frankly acknowledged: some were so basic to cultural value that they entered into his "starting-point assumptions" and, as such, were almost never questioned because they operated at such a deep level of the consciousness; others, discredited by the advance of events through time, eventually became something of an embarrassment. Furthermore, even as a young man he was already evolving a style of prose which involved great complexity of meaning, as well as a deeply skeptical angle of approach to the regnant "truths" of his day. Despite these qualifying caveats, it remains a fact that Woodward inherited and used to great extent the concepts of progress.

It was Thomas Babington Macaulay who had most fully developed the ideal and the idea of progress through his hortatory remarks from the floor of the British Parliament and through his energetic prose, both of which dominated Victorian historiography with an interpretation stressing the Protestant liberalism of the arriviste English businessmen. He chronicled with approval the decline of the Roman Catholic church as a center of ethical and cultural cohesiveness for the West and its replacement by a looser system of sectarian churches conjoined with secular imperatives; he praised the concomitant decline of kingly authority and its replacement by parliamentary bodies; and he celebrated the decline of mercantilist or managed feudal economy and its replacement by the untrammeled marketplace. These three tidal waves, rolling over the centuries from 1492 to 1837, had brought with them at their convergence modern liberalism, with its peculiar combinations of acquisitiveness and generosity, collective responsibility and individualism, distrust of power and grand schemes of reform. It all portended progress, with each generation improving the human condition still more by increasing human opportunities still more.[7]

Ironies abounded in the history and the historiography, for Macaulay's historian students ascended at the moment when Macaulay's politician heirs descended. As the Tory regime of Benjamin Disraeli seized control of Parliament, the Whig interpretation seized control of historiography. Of course, Disraeli's genius lay in accepting some Whig programs as a part of his Tory government; but the fact remained that a Whig doctrine of liberalism had been soundly defeated by a Tory doctrine of conservatism in the political arena even as the same Whig doctrine won the day in the intellectual arena. This Whig/Tory duality was based on a sturdy ethnocentrism which examined world history in the light of Anglo-American development, a perspective which also seemed natural enough to intellectuals in the northeastern corridor of the United States. In another irony, it came to the United States at the very moment when the northeastern corridor itself was being transmogrified from Anglo-Saxon to multiethnic.

For the Whigs themselves, there was no irony in any of this; irony was a conception largely foreign to their temperament. Ever upright, with gaze ever fastened on the next day's successes, they were not pausing for such a thing as contemplation of irony; there was the dire possibility of failure lurking behind the obvious chance for success, and the Whig who considered at length the imperfection of current action felt himself to be courting the possible disaster by reason of inactivity. Surely the elements of the Protestant ethic which Max Weber delineated in modern Western culture were essentially these: the Whigs presumed that Protestantism, capitalism, republicanism, and liberalism had by nature to exist together and that if the four came together, they were bound to produce progress. It was that secular set of ethical imperatives for worldly life and not a bowdlerized "salvation by works" that produced the behavior which Weber correctly observed but then mislabeled.[8]

In the United States, Macaulay was ably transliterated by John Lothrop Motley, whose *Rise of the Dutch Republic* (1873) established the standard for reading Western history as Whig history. Motley stated things more explicitly than other Whigs: progress was a function of parliamentarianism, liberalism, free-trade capitalism, and Protestantism; and retrogression was a function of monarchialism, conservatism, mercantilism, and Roman Catholicism. His calculus of negative and positive slopes thus charted Dutch republican achievement in relation to Spanish imperial failure. It was not only that the men of Antwerp and of Orange were so deserving of victory; it was equally important that Phillip II was so deserving of defeat. For Motley, and for Whig historiography, progress was guaranteed where Protestantism, republican parliamentarianism, liberalism, and free-market economics existed as a complete and discrete equation. Introducing even one of the retrogressive elements, such as papism or monarchialism, would ruin the set and thwart progress by invalidating the calculus. Motley's thesis was echoed by George Bancroft, who could find that progress in the United States was a result of the same function, and who could find that England suffered defeat in the Revolutionary War because it had retained elements of monarchialism and mercantilism in its otherwise progressive culture.[9]

With these English Whigs and their American successors in mind, one can bring some later developments in American historiography into a clearer, more logical focus than they appear in otherwise. Motley and Bancroft were gentlemen historians and have usually been considered distant cousins to the first professional historians emerging in the 1870s under the banner of science. Woodward himself has expressed great admiration for the narrative powers of these earlier, avocational historians; and he has criticized what he considers the overly specialized profession which subsequently displaced them, because in the process of that displacement, the once-large audience of the intelligent laity was lost. In fact, however, the intellectual relationship between Whigs and scientists—in terms of the controlling assumptions which guided their studies—was quite close: the latter, directed by Herbert Baxter Adams at Johns Hopkins University and by William Archibald Dunning at Columbia University, fashioned and employed the same equation as had Motley and Bancroft. Moreover, Leopold von Ranke, their original Prussian inspiration, emphasized the same functional association between progress and liberalism-plus-Protestantism-plus-capitalism-plus-parliamentarianism.[10]

What worked to obscure the lines of relationship between Whigs and scientists was the insistence of the latter that they were laboratory technicians painstakingly amassing evidence with dispassionate disregard for the effect worked on that evidence by national ideology, political orientation, or cultural aspiration.[11] Obviously, no Whig could assert any such thing, since to do so would be to abnegate responsibility for what Macaulay considered to be the mission of life itself; and for Woodward in 1934, such abnegation still constituted what his friend Pipkin had termed the "last refuge of the scoundrel." Furthermore, the scientists' proclamation of impartiality was actually unjustifiable in light of their personal investment in the processes they studied; and in fact, the scientists' assertion of a clinical disengagement made the least sense of all, considering the nature of ideas and the way scientific investigation occurs in the laboratory: one who starts an investigation by literally assuming nothing proves nothing. The scientists, of course, had assumed plenty, and in their way, they proved plenty.

Ranke himself was eminently Prussian, Lutheran, and liberal, and those elements of his identity clearly directed his research. Noting his partiality does not damn him as a hypocrite but serves instead to underscore his normality. He was sincere when he declared that his research pulled him along to his conclusions, that he was patiently building blocks of monographs, that *wie es eigentlich gewessen* or, in other words, history is *how* instead of *why*. What he omitted to say, because it was obvious to him, was that the *how* questions he asked came from the special perspective of a Berliner describing the development of nationalism in his land. He failed to remind his reader that this careful research was bound to lead him in a particular direction which he never questioned. Components of German history—how did an administrator function? how did a general fight? how did a council govern? how did a constitution work?—these components were constituent parts of a development which Ranke presumed to be necessary and proper. He never asked why, then, simply because he *believed;* and believing, he served the mission by meticulously demonstrating the answers to the myriad questions of how one believed.

The most prominent American among those who believed was Herbert Baxter Adams, who studied with Ranke and then developed science in the United States. Adams, like Ranke, fastened on politics, and really on political form, as the subject for analysis of how. His "seminary room" at Johns Hopkins featured a banner with Edward August Freeman's slogan "History is past politics, politics is present history"; and his students all but recited, "Thou shalt not ask why." Compared with the gentlemen historians, Adams's minions were more "objective" in their prudential amassment of fact and figure and in the wide range of human events—all those things outside politics—which they refused to consider as proper history. All the same, Adams and Dunning and the many scientists who made history a profession instead of an avocation were quite clearminded about the why of history. Like Ranke, they did not have to ask, for they already knew. [12]

As a result, these scientists wrote a series of studies which proved how Germanic was the nature of American institutions; and in that proving, science reaffirmed the idea that democracy grew from a spore in the forests of Deutschland, whence it was cross-pollinated successfully with the forests of the New World. Adams very much reflected the nationalistic concern of his era: it was no accident that his seminary was first offered in the year 1877, when Reconstruction ended and the United States sought to bind North and South in national unity after the schism of Civil War. Nor was it accidental that Dunning threw open the doors of the Columbia graduate hall to a number of scientists from the South who proclaimed national identity by denigrating the "folly" of Reconstruction. The victorious North, having abandoned the former slaves to southern white "home rule," gained willing peacetime allies among the ex-Confederates; and the first professional students of history in the country were thus participating in the moral and intellectual quid pro quo in which black civil rights were exchanged for white political unity.[13] These early historians, then, were both recording a political accomplishment and affirming it. Furthermore, they were defining the terms of study and creating many of the starting assumptions—especially about Reconstruction, economic nationalism and civil rights—against which Woodward's dissident scholarship would have to struggle.

Central to all of the scientific history remained the concept of progress, the upright belief that a special equation (Protestantism-liberalism-marketplace-capitalism-parliamentarianism) guaranteed American greatness. Science brought new intellectual weaponry to bear on the issue of the American destiny to progress; but science declined by 1900 because of the limits inherent in its domain of study. The laboratory was overcrowded with technicians proving how German tribes created constitutional forms which Americans had then perfected. This faith in progress was a curious one, for it constantly demanded proof: by the new century the scientific proof was becoming redundant and, as such, was inspiring less and less confidence. At that special moment when the tenets of progress most needed proof, Frederick Jackson Turner emerged from the status of disgruntled scientist to become the first Progressive historian, doing so for himself in 1893 and winning the republic's allegiance by 1900.[14]

Turner, in breaking with the historiography in which he was trained at Johns Hopkins University, was accomplishing a rather conservative revolution, for he spoke directly to progress, the element of American culture dearest to its intellectuals. In fact, Turner was proving again belief in the existence of the special equation of progress; but his genius lay in his unique ability to delineate American uniqueness. In that respect, addressing his national culture, he was more like Ranke than were the scientists or the neo-Whigs: where Bancroft echoed Macaulay and Adams echoed Ranke, Turner could offer something which was at once consistent with Western progress and yet definitively American. Specifically, what Turner did was to examine American history in terms of the environment, geographic regionalism, and economic structure. Moreover, he also kicked free from the methodological restrictions imposed by science, for as he proclaimed: "History is past literature; it is past politics; it is past religion; it is past economics. . . . all in society's endeavor to understand itself by understanding the past."[15]

With this enlarged outlook he brought the discipline of history into line with the Progressive political movement just then coming to the fore. The state of Wisconsin was becoming the laboratory of Progressive democracy, and the state university in Wisconsin a brain trust in service to Governor Robert LaFollette. LaFollette and his compeers proceeded from the same set of assumptions about the nature of American progress as did Turner; the former may have expressed the matter a bit differently while operating a political machine, but the faith of "Battling Bob" LaFollette in the equation was just as strong as Turner's. And LaFollette had more than history graduate students in his corner: Richard T. Ely and John R. Commons in labor studies, Claude Van Hise in education, Stephen M. Babcock in modern agricultural studies, and Harry L. Russell in chemistry were all staunch advocates of progress as a cultural and as a political way of life. Perhaps all that Turner and the Wisconsin intellectuals and politicos were doing was best symbolized by one particular week in 1907 when the campus and the town played host to a myriad of conferences on socioeconomic problems with such politicians as LaFollette and Gov. William U'Ren of Oregon joining such scholars and activists as Jane Addams, Lester Frank Ward, Ely, and Commons.[16]

Although this particular conference obviously brought together a cast of stars in a special performance, it still caught the flavor of all Progressivism; that is, the conference was a fair representation of the kind and character of people involved in the movement. These activities were well known to the handful of reform-minded southerners, and they were the brand of politicized academic service which inspired Woodward's elders Will Alexander, Comer Woodward,

Rupert Vance, and Howard Odum. Further, this Progressivism, as Henry F. May has demonstrated, was a late phase of Victorianism, and as such, it emphasized belief in a triptych of progress, moralism, and culture, still another expression of the basic equation. No wonder, then, that Progressives sought reform at once socially mild and economically faithful to modern capitalism: what Progressives, whether LaFollette, Theodore Roosevelt, or Woodrow Wilson, wanted was to preserve in good order a free-enterprise system while guaranteeing a moral check on excesses in other behavior. Hence the special character of American Progressivism, with its activist stewardship over social life and its gentle sway over the marketplace—a sway which, during the severe economic crisis Woodward was seeing in 1934, was much too gentle to mitigate the ravages of what he called "unrestrained capitalism." To achieve these limited ends, Progressives, again true to the larger Victorian movement, used the shield of law and the sword of science as they "stood at Armageddon and did battle for the Lord." In American politics, this process resulted in a revival of moralism second only to the fervor with which antislavery forces entered the Civil War. As for American historiography, those in service to Clio were only a little less restrained in their enthusiasm and were identical in the nature of their concern for the triptych.[17]

These qualities of enthusiasm and of concern produced a charming anomaly in Progressive historians: while focusing on economic issues to locate "real" motivation, these historians wrote with a verve and dash that displayed a deep, even Romantic, faith in the American future. Turner certainly had faith, although he abandoned systematic, overarching synthesis for increasingly detailed, increasingly unrelated topics of economic and political and geographical research. But what he had started others carried on, whether in the dialectic architectonics of Vernon Louis Parrington performed for the reforming intellectual or in the dialectical melodrama performed by David Saville Muzzey in textbooks for the nation's youth. Parrington could explain all of American history from colonial era to early depression days as an ongoing struggle between radicals who sought to implement the equation for the benefit of the masses and reactionaries who defended privilege and property; it worked so specifically for Parrington's era that he has been dismissed in the judgments of the succeeding, less moralistic, generations, but in his day he stood at the top of the heap. Well below the heights of Parrington's dialectic, Muzzey played out American history as republican melodrama too vivid for any schoolboy or schoolgirl ever to forget. Neither was by any means Woodward's cup of tea, Parrington's history being devoid of a sense of irony and Muzzey's being innocent of complexity; but he nevertheless began his career as a historian with these traditions, because the broad area which lay between the Parrington level and the Muzzey level of social criticism was the purview of our country's greatest historian, Charles Austin Beard. Beard would work very special influences on Woodward at multiple levels, both intellectual and personal; and these influences—always acknowledged by Woodward, even at times when Beard's reputation had fallen in the opinions of historians and of fellow citizens—must be marked with some care. [18]

Beard was magnificent, and even his errors, which were large in size, had style. True to the era, he could be intensely moralistic, and when he located the devil he pursued the evil with more of passion than of good sense. Late in life he became obsessed with the notion that Beelzebub was Franklin Delano Roosevelt, and he expended the last of his great energies trying to prove that FDR was tricking Americans into the Second World War and that that war was of no concern to the republic; he was sadly and utterly wrong on that score, but the error should not affect appreciation for the bulk of his work. Fortunately, in the majority of his studies Beard had no clear sense of the locus of sin, so that he suspended the moralizing impulse of his generation, choosing instead to think. In fact, he changed the Whig's cast of demons and angels, eliminating the personalized angels and replacing the forces of light with some solid republican tenets, tenets no less inspiring in their way but scarcely prescriptions for sainthood. These tenets of republican conduct could have been written by Plutarch, but what distinguished Beard's handling of them was his sturdy belief in republicanism because it worked. The equation that others before him had written out was correct because of its economic variables; and he considered the competing equation which Karl Marx had written to be accurate in its economic variables even though inaccurate, even ludicrous, in its final sum. In short, Beard's "open-ended" dialectic operated to reaffirm the government which Macaulay and Bancroft and Turner had supported;[19] the explanation was the same at base, but with much more respect for those who were mowed down by the workings of progress.

Beard's special qualities of discernment not only let him cut through the layers of Whig nonsense; they also made him as vital for the next generation—that is, for Vann Woodward's generation—as his Progressive cohorts were for the preceding one. In fact, escaping Whiggism and entering the 1930s were the same act, for the Progressives were one kind of people and the New Dealers another. Since the Progressives reformed economic struggle as the liberals of the day and since the New Dealers did the same thing as the liberals of another day, many have concluded that Progressivism and New Dealism lie along one ideological plane; in Whig fashion one could align the two movements with the angels. But there are problems with such an artifice: above all else, Herbert Clark Hoover was a great Progressive, and his responses to the Great Depression were of a piece with anything Woodrow Wilson or Theodore Roosevelt would have attempted. Moreover, as Otis Graham has successfully demonstrated, the overwhelming majority of Progressives who lived to see the New Deal were unhappy with it. While some have dismissed Graham's evidence with the observation that age generally makes one conservative, that disclaimer holds little water in this particular instance.[20] There was, rather, a difference in *tone* which came from the difference in spirit between the two movements, and Beard embodied the crucial difference.

Although Beard could make the grand gesture and strike the pose as nobly as anyone, the occasions when he did so were rare. Essentially he was as practical as they come, never forgetting the Indiana boyhood experiences of hearing his father and neighbors in the family parlor discussing the most important things of life, all of which involved economics. From that environment he developed what a Marxist would recognize as a clear sense of self-interest, and it was this sense of self-interest, exponentially grown to encompass the entire country, which he sought for the republic. Thus he searched the documents of the past for the economic causations of events, not to castigate the actors on stage but to make sense of them; it was the not knowing, the ignorance spawned of obfuscatory rhetoric, which endangered everyone. Yet, again, the Whig faith in republican form and in capitalist substance prevailed, though not for Beard as divine inspiration; republicanism, exactly because it put a minimum of trust in individual capacity and because it leaned on form rather than on human will, was the choice among a set of poor possibilities. As Beard exulted in his most famous monograph, the very republican constitution which he supported was not the organic end result of cultural process; no, although it was "natural" enough, the organism from which it grew was the specific material interests of a class of entrepreneurs who seized the moment when it came their way.[21] Following the implications of what he wrote, then, the constitution was a good functional piece of machinery, but for it to serve the interests of other classes, as it would have to do because of unfolding events, it would need to undergo considerable retooling.

Nor did Beard stop with the constitution; he pressed on instead to that most Whiggish of crusades, the American Civil War. He drove his point home with relentless pressure, even employing abolitionist language: this conflict was "irrepressible" all right; there was no stopping it, indeed; and the result was surely the Second American Revolution. But where the Whiggish dynamics told of still another struggle between the forces of light and the forces of darkness, Beardian dynamics depicted a struggle of interests; the farm community, whose ethos was codified by Thomas Jefferson, stood abreast of the up-and-coming industrial city; and the city, "marching in seven-league boots," was not to be denied by the village. Slavery was a casualty but only because this peculiar institution was of the farm and not of the factory; it was the plantation as competing economic unit which the Second American Revolution destroyed, and it was the planter as member of a rural nonindustrial class which the same war displaced. The slave of the planter, in Beard's eye, was not terribly important to the real interests of the nineteenth century. In the middle of the war, of course, the slave gained symbolic importance as the veil for the real interests of the North and West, but with the war won, the ex-slave mattered not a whit to the victorious entrepreneur. After all, if the moral outcry over slavery was genuine and reflective of true spiritual concern, then why ignore the freedman? For Beard, that seeming inconsistency disappeared when the class interests of Massachusetts factory owner, Minnesota railroad builder, Pennsylvania merchant, and New York banker were recognized as the marching tune for the Grand Army of the Republic. None of this made Abraham Lincoln any less significant, but it certainly made him different from the icon crafted by Whiggish celebrants; Lincoln's greatness, for Beard, was not vision but rather ability to make things work when they had to work, during a crisis. Besides greatly qualifying the nature of the northern victory, Beard was reminding all that revolutions break many things, and not all of the things broken are bad.[22]

In accomplishing this tour de force, in so dramatically finishing what Turner had started, Beard was also separating himself from the mainstream Progressive movement of his day. The essence of Progressivism has been captured perfectly by Richard Hofstadter as "traffic in moral absolutes, [with] its exalted moral tone." None of that for Beard: he, too, wanted government processes cleaned up, monopoly regulated, city services made efficient, general education offered to all—the era's panoply of reform legislation. But he invested few of those very practical things with the ethical imperative of a crusade. The city-manager form of government, for example, was not a battle plan for Armageddon; it merely worked and deserved support because it worked. Not surprisingly, then, Beard ushered in the New Deal for historians with a significant address in 1933 in which he emphasized the relativistic, contemporaneous nature of his craft and conceded that the historian saw largely what other people of his time saw, ignoring what his generation would not see, that history was an act of written faith. He still espoused economic determinism, but now he acknowledged the special circumstances which led him to class analysis. In that way Beard showed the path from Progressivism to New Dealism by preserving the concept of progress divested of its moralism. Again Hofstadter said it best: "The New Deal . . . showed a strong and candid awareness that what was happening was not so much moral reformation as economic experimentation."[23]

It was thus the unique qualities in Charles Beard which explained the fact that Progressivism and New Dealism could be utterly distinct as social and political movements while historians of both eras could follow Charles Beard and could continue to speak seriously of the possibility of progress in the midst of economic depression. Vann Woodward was scarcely being original in responding to the depression by "doing class analysis" in the manner of Charles Beard.[24] But even Beard had not interested himself in the New

South, and Woodward, in choosing that topic, came before a surprisingly wide vista of possibilities for study.

II

Despite retaining the novelist's sense for a good story and despite further developing the novelist's tools of dramatic, ironic, and comedic characterizations, Woodward abandoned his novel in its planning stages. He turned instead to history, thereby affirming at last an intrinsic tendency, for he was always acutely sensitive to the concrete particularities of time and place.[25] He would be the historian of the New South who would explain the processes of development behind the story going on around him in 1933: the racism, the regional sense of inferiority and resentment at having that inferiority pointed out, the extreme poverty, the gawdy politicos, the tall tales, the persistent romancing of lost causes, the courthouse honeyfuggling, the feed-store, seed-store realism—the works.

As for his subject matter, it could not have come from Oxford any more than he could have written about it in Oxford. Demagoguery, the rabble-stirring, boisterously bullying, unconscionably misrepresenting, buckboard-podium brand, was the subject. It was not only the good stories involved, though that element was undeniably part of the lure; rather, it was the vitality of the demagogue and the way he could at once perfectly misrepresent the truth while perfectly representing the real issues which nicer folk in Oxford or at Emory left unremarked. The sad thing about a demagogue was not just that he could mass a crowd to kill a black man or a Catholic or a Jew; the sad thing was also that the demagogue talked about low wages and bad schools, differential freight rates and lack of credit, racial conflict and class tensions—exactly the dirty things which gentlemen politicians kept from their discussions and exactly the dirty things which Woodward saw all around him in his fieldwork in central Georgia and in his student-day wanderings through city streets.

He had in mind then a thoroughly rebellious book, one that would take the flaws of the demagogues seriously while berating their conservative opponents for not taking the issues seriously. The title he chose, "Seven for Demos," "implied a classical training I did not have," but was a sound analogue since the Athenian rule of the Demos marked the clearest expression of faith in the citizens even as those citizens chose to execute Socrates. These later and southern Demos needed more than British-style prosopography, and there was no question that the formal needs of biography would be subsumed under the grander need for a usable past which Glenn Rainey had urged on the triumvirate; on the other hand, the legacy of Ernest Hartsock would never let Woodward drift into the kind of superior and egoistic moralizing which marred pre-Beardian Progressive historiography. Even the negative elements of the characters who were principals in the story deserved more than that: the careers of Georgia's Tom Watson, Alabama's Tom Heflin, Louisiana's Huey Long, South Carolina's Ben Tillman, Mississippi's James Vardaman were especially instructive for an understanding of their land—too instructive to dismiss them parenthetically during a Progressive sermon.[26]

Each of these men had accomplished some good by addressing the economic needs of the bottom strata of southern white society. The hardest to figure was the contemporaneous kingfish, Long, who bid fair to surpass the New Deal in serving the poor with a full social program but who implemented that program with a Latin disdain for due process and with his own delight in perversity. Since Woodward was disappointed in the New Deal and doubted its intention to change the social order in any fundamental way, he found much laudable in Long's activist program of road and school and dam building. But there was also that damnable quality which impelled the kingfish to build a personal empire and to use it with obvious relish to bully everybody else.[27] If Long were hardest to figure, however, it was only a matter of degree, for each of the Demos shared in the paradox of reform and racism. Since the 1880s, conservatives had insisted that Negrophobia went hand in glove with radical reform, that radical reform came along inevitably with any other radicalism.[28] Woodward was having none of that argument, and "Seven for Demos" faced the tall order of demolishing at once the conservative apologia for economic injustice and the icons of extreme racism.

At times it seemed too tall an order. The achival and other primary sources for the Demos were widely scattered, disorganized, and not generally available to scholars. For southern history it was an era when historians kept their own collections of manuscripts and shared them in an "old-boy" network; the great university repositories at Durham, Charlottesville, and Chapel Hill were then just being established, and the state and regional collections in Columbia, Charleston, Raleigh, Richmond, Montgomery, Nashville, and elsewhere were in need of reorganization. More vexing was the problem caused by the nearness of Woodward's subject; some of the Demos still stalked the section, and relatives and close friends abounded. Since the Demos had created plenty of enemies during the era of their sway, the current time of their diminished political power was permitting severe criticism, and the families were keeping the private records under close guard. An individual with a record of dissidence such as Woodward had was not welcome to search the personal correspondence still housed in the residences of surviving Tillmans, Vardamans, and Heflins. [29]

To pursue those elusive sources Woodward bought an old Model T Ford from one of the few Communist friends he was still speaking to. The car "leaked"—its tires, fuel line, radiator, and crankcase could not seem to hold air, gasoline, water, and oil—and Woodward drove the contraption inexpertly, tipping it over on country roads where he would be stuck until local farmers could help him manhandle it back into upright position. Usually it all seemed humorous enough, the unauthorized biographer stranded on some backwoods path not doing either his official WPA fieldwork or his personal research; but there were also days of deep funk when nothing worked and those who saw him reported him "with no humor." Just when things looked most bleak he got help from an unlikely source, from staid and comfortable Oxford. [30]

He had returned home for a weekend and had decided to seek help from the Odum family, of whom the Jack Woodwards were new neighbors in Oxford, though old friends in that preexisting network of relatives and coworkers. One of the Odums, Howard Washington, had mastered Uncle Comer's field of sociology and combined Comer's clear eye for social ills with unmatched skills of research. Howard Odum created the Institute for Research in the Social Sciences at Chapel Hill and founded the originally dissident journal *Social Forces,* as well as helping to create Atlanta's Interracial Commission. By this spring day of 1934 he was visiting the family home as a man at the top of his profession and at the top of the small heap of southern dissidents.[31]

Although Woodward did not realize it at the time, he was already well known to Odum, for Odum had been indignant when he read in the *Daily Worker* of the "Woodward attack" on Will Alexander. Since Woodward and Alexander had so quickly and effectively restored their friendship, Alexander saw to it that Odum was assured of the young man's soundness of character. And later, in 1934, Alexander had arranged for Woodward to meet Odum in a disarmingly casual interview the full meaning of which Woodward would decipher only years later. Accepted thus as "sound," Woodward now paid a call on the great man for advice and counsel. After all, this neighbor had important things to say about who was awarded grants from the Institute for Research in the Social Sciences, Rockefeller Foundation grants, and graduate fellowships and stipends at several research universities. What he found on this visit was plain Howard, native Georgian, out back in the barnyard weaning a calf. Without intending to, Odum was teaching Woodward a great leasson: at all levels, the living have to get on with life.[32]

Fortunately, Odum offered more than rustic affirmation of eternal verities. When Woodward spoke with enthusiasm about his Demos project, Odum went into action and soon produced a fellowship award from the Rockefeller Foundation, one that would finance graduate study at any school in the country. There remained the problem of the unwieldy nature of a prosopography involving the cooperation of people who understandably acted like hostile witnesses on trial. But that problem shrank to more manageable size when one could find complete financial support in a decade of frayed coats and threadbare trousers. Shielded with newfound security and inspired again, Woodward got his creaky, leaky Model T back on its wobbly path through the South.[33]

He and the car chugged into a lucky encounter with a member of the Demos family which had produced Tom Watson, in many ways the most fearsome of the demagogues. Watson's papers, which were an immense collection, had been deposited at the University of North Carolina, but were under seal and guarded by two granddaughters, Georgia Lee and Georgia Watson. The former was utterly unsympathetic to anyone poking into her beloved grandfather's life, but Georgia Watson was a dissident whose unhappiness with southern injustice would eventually lead to a self-imposed exile on the great shifting dunes of the southern shore of Lake Michigan. Knowing nothing of either granddaughter, Woodward visited Georgia Watson at Salem Academy, a traditional woman's finishing school in Winston-Salem, North Carolina. She was delighted with his plans: she was herself studying history and preparing to attend graduate school at the University of Chicago. Not only did she open up the papers to him, but she also offered priceless personal recollections of her grandfather and of the Watson family and some sound historical insights. She secured the cooperation of the other heirs, and equally important, she was so bravely enthusiastic about his project that her attitude of confidence and commitment virtually ignited the man previously so ambivalent about his direction.[34]

The Model T made its quickest trip home. In a few months Woodward had gone from brooding confusion to renewed sense of purpose. For one thing he was now purposeful enough to sharpen focus on his project; Tom Watson alone was large enough and awesome enough to stand as the "horrible example" for all the Demos, in lieu of the more cumbersome group portrait.[35] The method, Beardian Progressivism, the means, Rockefeller lucre, the subject, Tom Watson, and the man, Vann Woodward, had at last converged.

4

The Hill

The Myth of Vann Woodward, Graduate Rebel

The odd quality already marked in Woodward's career is his dual status as outsider and insider and his willingness to use the advantages of one at the center to help him press toward the periphery. He was like that at Arkadelphia, where he was the beneficiary of the college's most influential trustee, but participated in a student and faculty revolt against the administration, and again in Druid Hills, where he was the son of an academic dean, doted-upon nephew of another academic dean, and select pupil of the new star on the faculty, but nonetheless pressed relentlessly into the very realm of civil strife whose mere mention lay on the border of good taste for the insider. He was like that at Morningside Heights, rooming with an academic's academic who knew all the right people, but showing up at an all-black Harlem dramatic production, and also when he visited the regnant scholars of liberal rationalism in the Weimar Republic and then immediately visited the practitioners of Bolshevik radicalism in Moscow. And at Georgia Tech he enjoyed the austere beneficence of friends connected with the staff while he vigorously pursued a campaign sure to distance him from that department.

This duality was the most striking at the University of North

Carolina (UNC), so much so that it created the stuff of graduate school and historian myth. If myth involves a narrative which has both a story line and an ethical imperative drawn from the conclusion of that story, then the historian must treat a myth with respect as well as curiosity. Of course, it matters whether the myth is congruent with what actually happened; but it also matters very much that people believe a myth, cherishing it and passing it on. And furthermore, if people cherish and use a myth which is different from what happened, which leaves out, blurs, and even denies some events, then that myth and its informing values become even more significant. Such a perspective can help in comprehending Woodward's days on the Hill, especially when it is remembered that duality is the very stuff of the man, and thus it is merely repeated in a different way in the graduate school myth.

This particular myth has become a comfort to those who have studied southern history since Woodward's graduate days—oddly, because the myth holds that Woodward was an indifferent student who came near failure on his comprehensive examinations and nearer still to failure in his teaching assignments. But it has been a special, if curious, comfort to the erstwhile student lost in the morass of school to "know" that even Vann Woodward once found these things overwhelming. Moreover, the myth has served quite well Woodward's own penchant for self-deprecation and for tweaking Clio's nose: he has enjoyed telling people that he went to school "hooked on a book" and that he studied history primarily because that course took the quickest route to the book on Tom Watson.[1]

This myth of the indifferent and ineffectual student with the unrecognized talent who blossomed later as a professor has a certain innate charm, partly because it is a comforting reaffirmation of Woodward's self-selected role. The Chapel Hill part of the story deserves a closer reading, one which takes the myth itself seriously but which also considers the actual events and personalities and which finally probes the discrepancies between myth and actuality. Pressing behind the myth is a little less than inspiring, for it shows that the profession basically was responding to his duality: its members recognized clearly enough his talent but at the same time recognized his reluctance to use that talent in the classroom—on either side of the lectern. That rubs away some of the charm, but it also tells plenty about the intellectual life in which he existed. Furthermore, one is again struck by the "deep reciprocities" between the personal life he lived and the history he wrote. And there remains a persisting attractiveness even in the bit of mild yarn spinning in which he indulged.

I

The 1930s were the time of Chapel Hill's approach to greatness, a decade when Frank Porter Graham and Howard Washington Odum and Louis Round Wilson and William Terry Couch and Paul Green by concerted effort pushed the community and the institution into modernity. At that moment it appeared that Chapel Hill and the university were about to meld the charm of the past with the promise of the future into a new South of grace and courage, retaining the best of conservatism, with its organic balance of individual desiderata and community need, and adding to that ancient organicism a modern conception of economic justice for those oppressed by the regime. As one contemporaneous would-be novelist put it, "Nestled in the heart of the South, the University was famous for its ultra-liberalism, world-wide reputation, and varied alumni[;] . . . its influence stretched completely over its native state, shadowed the entire Southern region and spread its tentacles around the globe."[2]

Such was the language typical of the descriptions which the community evoked among its enthusiasts in that day; but this particular artist set the phrases as an ironic counter to his own judgment. In fact, the acid observations of this fellow, Weldon A. Brown, were codified into an unpublished novel entitled "Upward" which he wrote in 1936 while attending graduate school in history. Although "Upward" has its serious flaws as art, it was remarkably clear-eyed as sociology; and as sociology, it has recorded a saddening account of promises unfulfilled. Yet neither the enthusiasm of the school's supporters nor the pessimism of its critics (and Brown was both at once) has caught the fullness of the story. In fact, despite the promise for the university's future in 1934, it never firmly grasped the greatness which once seemed fully possible. Instead, the institution fell progressively farther and farther away from its potential, describing the downslope of a gradual parabola.

In the 1930s, of course, no one could foresee the day when UNC would enjoy the wealth and, more important, the solvency which it would gain after the Second World War. Those striving for greatness on the Hill in 1934 naturally expected the biggest continuing challenge to be posed by tiny budgets and tinier student bodies and staffs. The dampening irony lay in the fact that UNC after the 1930s had all the material things that UNC lacked in the 1930s; but the modern community lost the spiritual impetus of its less opulent predecessor. Over the next three decades the leavening elements of bureaucratic mediocrity slowed and finally halted the school's rise, so that it, like other southern institutions, never managed to equal the achievement of the University of California or of the University of Wisconsin. Thus Woodward's recollection that UNC "was appealing beyond any southern school" was a recollection freighted with important reservations.[3]

Having granted the genuine potential that Chapel Hill exhibited in the 1930s and having granted its failure, one is compelled to consider Weldon Brown's criticisms further, especially since he was looking at the community from a graduate student's office inside the history department. What he recorded of the department during Chapel Hill's time of challenge was quite unflattering: "There was no logical sequence, no organized approach, and no departmental attempt to synchronize the work of closely related fields." Worse, "red tape, inefficiency, and the green-eyed monster paralyzed the system while time and money vanished and the students went begging." To drive home his disdain for the program, Brown struck a semantic blow, replacing the name *Chapel Hill* with the inelegant *Dugtown*. Nor would Brown accept the picture-postcard image of the pleasant tree-lined lanes and the lush arboretum of the village which others recalled. Instead he depicted narrow roadways the color and consistency of tomato soup and housing by ordinary drab, drafty, and forbidding. Above football, culture was nonexistent; and generally, Dugtown's indistinguishability from any nondescript Carolina burg made more striking the pretentiousness of its claims.[4]

Turning from these sharp jibes, Brown offered the more generic, and more radical, opinion that all bourgeois institutions were basically of this type and that the hypocrisy of Dugtown and the thin fare of its academy were no worse than those of any other town or school. Moreover, the work one did at Dugtown U. was no less worthy than work done elsewhere; and the main thing was the subsequent application of knowledge gained there to the economic malady of the rural South. Thus the novelist's protagonist, having endured an Iroquois line of "active indifference" from his instructors, took degree in hand and transformed a heretofore sleepy junior college into an instrument of reform in its locale.[5] In short, an eccentric but shrewd sociologist of life in Chapel Hill has left an image in double exposure: in the traditional curriculum where it promised much, it produced little; but in the tools of dissidence where it promised little, it produced much.

Woodward's own observations of Chapel Hill were not as harshly critical nor as keenly analytical as Brown's, but they were much the same. In spite of the intellectual ferment then obvious throughout the South and in spite of the always exciting and often informing debate developing between the Vanderbilt Agrarians and the Chapel Hill Regionalists, he did not find much of the emerging southern cultural renaissance in the history department at Carolina. He did, nevertheless, insist that UNC made him a scholar, by contrast with Emory, which had largely failed at that task.[6] However, it is likely that what really set Chapel Hill apart from Druid Hills was less the actual difference between the two communities than the difference in Woodward's responses to the communities. Reverting to Mephistopheles' distinction, both forests were a bit sparse in *Theorie*, the tree of knowledge; but both were thick with *Lebens*, the tree of experience. When Woodward had been at Emory, he had had only vague notions of what he expected from his instructors, and not surprisingly, this indifferent approach to the classroom produced memories of the boredom borne of this perceived irrelevance. At UNC he was equally put off by the average professor, but his own sharp focus on the Tom Watson research enabled him to discern relevance which he had missed in analogous situations at Emory. In other words, the softening of dissidence which came with the end of youth actually permitted a more effective scholarship of dissidence because Woodward now was alerted to a range of resources—a range considerably wider than he had noticed before. The change in attitude was not readily apparent in all cases, because he continued to study what he wanted to study while neglecting other things. Still, the change was there all the same, for at Emory he had learned from LeRoy Loemker and Comer Woodward, good scholars and good fellows; but at Chapel Hill he learned just as much from Joseph Gregoire de Roulhac Hamilton and Howard Kennedy Beale, good scholars but difficult and occasionally unpleasant personalities.

Hamilton in particular was a challenge. Short and stockily built, he was a product of Columbia University's southerners, those scholars who used the techniques of Rankean science under the tutelage of William Archibald Dunning to denigrate the Reconstruction experiment as a useless exercise in trying to remove the spots from the Negro leopard. Hamilton, affecting a string tie and white suit, could play the nineteenth-century role demanded by his own conception of noblesse oblige; but he was also fond of "holding forth in the old-time way" in lecture hall about "niggers" for the benefit of appreciative Carolina undergraduates. Woodward, the man who counted J. Saunders Redding as an "equal" friend and who considered John Hope a superior friend (by virtue of age and attainment), squirmed in his seat in the hall as Hamilton played up to the most profound emotions resident in the youthful male classroom. This was a campus with no black faces save for the kitchen and maintenance staffs, and there was no visible symbol of black achievement to stand in opposition to the professor's assertions of racial superiority.[7]

It was exactly that kind of behavior and that kind of attitude which the Atlanta triumvirate of Hartsock, Rainey, and Woodward had bitterly decried. Now, however, Woodward tolerated Hamilton's racism because of another characteristic "the old gentleman" possessed: he was an excellent scholar actively engaged in the heroic processes of creating the Southern Historical Collection. He was, then, more than a charming collector of memorabilia and more than an efficient curator of manuscripts; he was fundamentally a professional who knew what he was doing in a region dominated by half-focused amateurish scholarship. Although by 1934 Hamilton had stepped down from active teaching to devote his energies more fully to the Southern Historical Collection, his occasional instruction and his professional advice on research made him more valuable to Woodward than were the more moderate instructors. The graduate student might grit his teeth at Hamilton's race baiting, but he could also walk away from a given session with a new knowledge of an important cache of papers on politics in Thompson, Georgia, in 1894. The other history instructors, by contradistinction, could be moderate to liberal on race relations, but their teaching involved "too much old American Nation Series," an emphasis on unanalytical narrative history which often left Woodward pondering, "My God, is this what I'm dedicating my life to?"[8]

The frustration and doubt were the more poignant now that Woodward had a sharply defined purpose for study. Fellow graduate students knew him as the man who came to town with the half-completed dissertation in his suitcase, as the cosmopolite with the handcrafted Spanish stilleto on his dresser, as the member of the avant-garde literati with the illegal Black Sun edition of James Joyce's *Ulysses,* and most of all as the man with boxes and boxes of carefully organized research notes. But he was also a man who had never worked in a research seminar environment. Hamilton no longer offered such formal sessions, and those who did were not very professional about it, not really requiring the students to perform much primary, archival research. Instead, the graduate student found essentially the same experience in the seminar as in the reading course, that is, a heavy emphasis on secondary readings with the resultant workmanlike "research" papers derivative of someone else's research. For Woodward, as for others, it was a "chore; something I had to do."[9]

This drayman quality of instruction, at least in Woodward's eyes, marked every class which he took in preparation for his preliminary comprehensive examinations. Briefly, he perked up at the rumor that Avery Odelle Craven, then arguably the very best of southern historians, might be lured to the Hill from Chicago; but that proved infeasible in a department with relatively low salaries and heavy teaching loads. Eventually, Chairman Albert Ray Newsome's happy combination of percipience, charm, work, and luck brought Howard Beale to campus; but by then Woodward had finished classwork and was studying for the comprehensive examinations. Again, none of this is to imply that the student failed to learn in Chapel Hill: on the contrary, he was an avid student of Lebens as taught by a cordon of activists, but these activists were not historians. And he learned Theorie as taught by Regionalist scholars of the first rank; but these, too, were scholars who labored at disciplines other than history.[10]

The convolutions of these graduate study days accounted for the ambivalent record he left in Chapel Hill. Where fellow students and supervising instructors often sensed indifference in his mien,[11] others in town considered him fully engaged, a partner in excitement. As in all things, he was neither of these extremes, but rather an intensely private man drawn to the most intensely public issues. Even with the help of the sharpened focus imposed by the simple and straightforward constraints of dissertation writing, Woodward had yet to fit together the component parts of his character and mentality; no longer the green kid of the previous decade, he remained intellectually unmatured in this one.

But the Chapel Hill life outside the history department in Saunders Hall greatly speeded that process of maturation. Aside from the historians, there were good scholars who were activists as well as townspeople who were activists; and one could learn a great deal from the justly celebrated Frank Graham, Howard Odum, Louis Wilson, Bill Couch, Rupert Vance, and Paul Green. First among these, Graham was ironically a trained historian who had departed the profession for administration. He was a compact bundle of energy and enthusiasm who believed profoundly, albeit simply, in the Presbyterian church and in liberalism. Rising to the position of president of the university, he eventually oversaw the statewide consolidation of North Carolina's public colleges into one relatively unified system of fairly uniform standards.

While that in itself was a conquest of dubious worth, Graham's undeniable accomplishment resulted from his long-running struggle to preserve the Chapel Hill campus as an enclave of Western rational inquiry. Despite persisting notions to the contrary, North Carolina in that day was filled with vehement antiintellectualism accompanied by powerful racism in the east and a milder but pernicious racism everywhere else; and even Harry Woodburn Chase, Graham's predecessor as president and a man memorably celebrated by journalists Gerald W. Johnson and Wilbur J. Cash, had occasionally succumbed to such racists and religionists and, in the process, somewhat damaged both academic freedom on the campus and rational discourse in the community. That Graham and his allies could withstand these same pressures and ultimately prevail was an ennobling story, notwithstanding the fact that the unfettered college then failed to achieve the greatness which Graham sought for it. How could he do it? Politics of personalism, the hoariest of southern mementos, played some role, for Graham could be very tough and yet, in the words of a respectful adversary, "He's a sweet son of a bitch, ain't he?" As Presbyterian, as Scots-Irish, as eastern down-to-earth as he was liberal, Graham effectively gave the lie to those who made geographical and political equations which defined away the possibility of native southern dissidence. The most approachable of men, he set the tone for the Chapel Hill activists: self-effacing, almost plain, sturdily optimistic, vigorous, and undaunted. He was known to Woodward, as he was known to most students, as the engaging man with whom one chatted on the way to and from classes: he might be wandering about with last evening's dinner napkin still tucked in his belt; but he kept the know-nothings off the backs of the scholars. [12]

The scholar most often besieged was Howard Odum, the Oxford neighbor who had reminded Woodward of the eternal verity that life's daily demands persist no matter what spiritual reversals the individual is suffering. Even Graham's best efforts could not fully shield Odum from blows aimed at him, now by racists, now by reactionary businessmen, now by fanatic religionists; but Odum was resilient enough and Graham was active enough to permit the development of a first-rate school of sociology at Chapel Hill despite the state's political weather. Odum established the Institute for Research in the Social Sciences (IRSS) and published *Social Forces,* running both on capital resources so slender that one is forced to concede the occasional power of ideas. He lured to Chapel Hill such excellent scholars as Guy and Guion Johnson, Arthur Raper, and Rupert Vance, and then he turned them loose in the backlands to do their research. These young investigators asked about lynchings in towns where the victims were only recently interred; they asked textile magnates for details about "stretch-outs" and "goon squads"; and they asked teachers and librarians what books children were forbidden to read. What they were asking and reporting was laid out in the southern mind on a spectrum marked at one end "bad manners" and at the other, "sedition." In most cases, the institute's scholar combined the positivist's dedication to detail with the dissident's sense of mission, with the result that *Social Forces* in the early 1920s was a lively, argumentative, often enlightening guest at the homes of the region's thinkers. [13]

Despite the boldness of the initial effort and despite the high level of goodwill and of talent in the people who served that effort, events in the years between 1924 and 1927 transformed *Social Forces*, the IRSS, and even to some extent Odum himself until journal, institute, and man had become rather cautious; and whatever else—in the words of Odum's biographer, Wayne D. Brazil—the lingua franca of Regionalism became "the increasingly inaccessible and abstract terms of academic social sciences." Twin blows from reactionaries did the damage as fundamentalist ministers and extremely anti-labor textile businessmen, in separate and uncoordinated attacks, brought an almost unbearable pressure on the Chapel Hill academics because of studies conducted by the IRSS and essays written in *Social Forces*. Fundamentalist Protestants were enraged over a modernist sociological essay which treated religion as if it were beneath contempt; but it was the mainline Presbyterian State Synod which in formal action in 1925 made the loudest and most vehement protest against the journal, attempting to have it and Odum censured by the university. Simultaneously, David Clark, businessman and editor of the reactionary *Southern Textile Bulletin*, was so incensed by some of the institute studies of labor conditions that he applied an even more effective pressure—that is, the threat of the loss of corporate and individual taxes and gifts—on then-president Harry Woodburn Chase. The latter, despite earlier strong and principled stands on behalf of free speech and academic prerogative, was in these cases timid and evasive; and Odum eventually struck a tacit moral compromise with the reactionaries, markedly changing the magazine by defusing its blatant reformism and transforming its language into the safely exclusivist lingo of the professional sociologist while limiting its circulation to an academic audience. On the other hand, the institute remained a haven for the committed dissident who was permitted to study intensively—though perhaps not to discuss publicly—southern economic injustice.[14]

Where Odum's influence bulked largest on the Woodward mind was in his concept of Regionalism. In a schema derivative of Frederick Jackson Turner's frontier-and-section theories, Odum refused to take the South as one lumpy mass but instead considered the distinctive regions of the section, thereby laying the basis for geopolitical inquiry into the structure of southern economics. His Regionalist school was in part Progressive history, with its class analysis and its optimism, and in part the emerging New Deal fascination with southern social problems, but mostly it was Odum's personal insight into the great variety of people in his corner of the world. His belief in the capacities of the much-maligned blacks and poor whites was tied to his belief that Chesapeake Bay, Sandhill, Blue Grass, Piedmont, Appalachia, and Delta were peopled with humans who might well change themselves—and change things—for the better. [15]

Odum's fledgling institute and its journal were buttressed by the university library, which, like most things on campus in those days, was a person rather than an institution, in this case Louis Wilson. A native of Alamance County, Wilson returned to North Carolina after completing a distinguished tenure at the University of Chicago, the allocation of whose vast library resources he had directed for a decade. He may have come back to the Hill with some notion of easing into retirement in a pleasant burg, since he was approaching a traditional age for taking one's leisure and since the town and the school were at first glance sleepy and uninspiring. In fact, however, he soon became one of the most active of a very active coterie, accepting control of the university's library and of its press. Although a strong personality operating in a region immersed in the tradition of the prima donna, Wilson did not try to bring both the library and the press to national prominence by his efforts alone; instead, he looked about, often in seemingly unlikely places, for bright and energetic people to direct the component parts of the greater design. Once he found someone he trusted, Wilson turned his attentions to other problems. For instance, at the library—or actually out on the byways of the South where the primary sources of history lay—Roulhac Hamilton was already building what would become a magnificent archival collection, and Wilson gave the historian his head rather than hobbling him with gratuitous directives. Results for the library were gratifying as Wilson presided over a smoothly functioning confederation of library specialists who, in the aggregate process, built a great resource center where before there had been precious little. Wilson remained the very embodiment of a library complex; when it expanded to new quarters, he continued in its upper reaches to keep an unspectacularly steady but productive pace of work for five decades of "easing into retirement." [16]

Despite his unportentous provenance in the Carolina Piedmont,

William Terry Couch had an endowment of intelligence and a knack for operating successfully at the margin. Perhaps Couch inherited the former, for his brother was a scientist of the first rank, but the latter, the knack, was his by achievement. After a brief trial, Wilson recognized Couch's abilities and characteristically let him have his head with the publishing program. [17] What Couch's knack produced was strength where there had been weakness: if the UNC Press was backwater and backwoods, then it might for those very reasons attract scholarship of high quality but of unfashionable perspective. Thus Couch risked printing a Marxist analysis of slavery by Eric Williams and a scientific defense of Darwin's theory of evolution by Edwin McNeill Poteat of Wake Forest College; and he printed both in the 1930s, when mainstream Carolinians were fearful and resentful of that godless duo of Karl Marx and Charles Darwin. Moreover, he had the brass to reject inferior scholarship by beloved sons, turning down a poorly written and sentimental manuscript by Horace Williams, the philosopher memorably celebrated by Thomas Wolfe and a shining one in the estimation of most Tar Heels. Alongside such courage Couch could put a native craftiness that led him to cut expenses by eliminating some of the intermediary costs of publishing: his author's copy went directly to the printer, and a scholar plagued by sloppiness was simply precluded from the press's scholarship. [18]

In addition to his contributions to the press, Couch affected his friends, and particularly Woodward, with his "down home seed-store, feed-store" shrewdness. [19] The cultural renaissance in the South was obviously reaching a peak in the middle of the economic depression, and at that time the Chapel Hill Regionalists were always rivaled, and often surpassed, by the Agrarians, also called the Fugitives, in Nashville. These poets and critics sang beautiful songs indeed; but Couch had the capacity and the will to deflate them. And with good reason, for the intellectuals enshrined at Vanderbilt University were adrift in a world of past dreams in which the sun shone perpetually on congenial seigneurs and their complaisant serfs, but Couch knew the reality of the miserable shacks housing the miserable peasantry, such as Woodward had encountered in his social work survey days. Woodward was among those appreciatively present at a convention where Couch so discommoded the Agrarian Allan Tate that the fuming chevalier sputtered, "I shall withdraw my presence," and thereupon exited stage right with fellow professional southerners in tow.[20]

What the Agrarians were really marching away from was exemplified best not by Couch but by Rupert Vance, the Arkansan already an inspiration to Woodward because of his principled dissidence, which was still remembered back in Arkadelphia. Bearer of the most noble of North Carolina surnames, he was a gentle and diminutive man much like Homer's Philoktetes, the lame archer who successfully served the Greek armies long after the full-bodied Achilleus and Telemonian Aias had fallen; so too Vance, in a regional culture which gloried in physical appearance and in physical strength, overcame those twin motes in the eyes of his beholders by the power of his mind and soul. Along with the profound insight which told him that the racial difficulties of his land could be resolved by steady application of effort in favor of civil rights—an insight which he shared in such well-aimed shafts as *Human Geography of the South*—Vance possessed an encyclopedic knowledge of modern southern history. He took novitiates like Woodward into his confidence and provided them with informal tutorials which nourished young minds with the fruits of the elder's wisdom; in time what ensued was that many historians could point to this Philoktetes of sociology as the man who not only showed them the target but also kept them in supply of arrows.[21]

But none of this Chapel Hill group was quite the equal of Paul Green. The playwright, originally from rural Harnett County, hardly looked the part of the artist: a big man hewn roughly from farming stock, he was tempered by hard work and play, with arms elongated from heavy lifting and right hand turned palm inward from the trick pitches he threw on the baseball field. Despite this rugged and even calloused appearance, Green was the most sensitive of chroniclers, already by 1934 recipient of the Pulitzer Prize for his 1927 play *In Abraham's Bosom* and the translator for presentation in the American theater of Henrik Ibsen's *Peer Gynt*. Obsessed with "those guys"—the impoverished of both races in field and factory— Green had both an ear keen enough to write realistic dialogue and judgment sensible enough to take his characters as he found them, unembellished with the contemporaneous nonsense which often glorified the working classes beyond credulity.[22] What he produced, then, in those days before he turned to outdoor melodrama, was a social portraiture in art as accurate as Vance's or Odum's, but lifted to the more memorable form of expression in poesy.

In sharing his poetic vision with the dissidents of Chapel Hill, Green also actively dissented and did so on the tough issues of the day: he brought the black novelist Richard Wright onto the white campus to collaborate on a production; and he directly challenged in print and aloud to their faces mill owners in squalid company towns. Green bargained hard on these issues, bringing in his friends in high literary and journalistic places to wield the carrot of favorable publicity and the stick of opprobrium at the heads of the small but growing number of politicians and promoters who sensed, at least a little, the divergence between the dictates of equity and Carolina's treatment of the poor, of the Negro, of the disadvantaged. He seemed to be everywhere, this fellow with Ernest Hartsock's gifts and Glenn Rainey's reformist energy, and it was all but inevitable that he should touch Woodward. Thanks in large part to Green, Woodward soon "got in with the wrong crowd," in particular the dissident eccentrics who coalesced around the unlikely Communist character of Milton Abernathy, known to all as "Ab."[23]

Ab was still another Chapel Hill institution, the proprietor of Ab's, a kind of bookstore, salon, and clearinghouse. In New South gothic, the old store sat in the middle of Franklin Street and featured a dissident presence along with its odd library of books and periodicals and its resident hound dogs, lazing on the worn floors. Ab himself had declared for the Communists after falling in love with Rose, who came to the village from New York City to win brothers to the cause and ended up wooing a husband. The depth of the Abernathys' commitment to Marx was hard to plumb, and today, on the other side of McCarthyism and with Milton Abernathy a respected Wall Street figure, one may never mark it correctly. They professed the faith in the 1930s and the 1940s, as did at least one other Chapel Hillian, an artist and sometime IRSS researcher named Olive Stone who made her home proletariat-style in a spare garret, whither she occasionally summoned bewildered Piedmont textile workers and farmers to hear of revolution. Beyond them, incipient Communist organization was far to seek, and the dominating tone at Ab's was less Marxist than eccentric, less ideological than artistic, less, finally, substantive than stylistic.[24]

But style there surely was: Ab presided over lively repartee in his peculiar little bookstore, and with one-time graduate student Tony Buttitta he printed a literary journal, *Contempo,* which called to mind Hartsock's *Bozart.* More concerned with current politics than *Bozart* had been, *Contempo* was less solidly innovative than Hartsock's magazine; but it was true to the spirit of innovation and it drew both attention and appreciation. Buttitta in his memoirs exaggerates the importance of Ab's and of *Contempo,* but evidently Faulkner visited to pay his respects, and whatever friendship Buttitta forged with F. Scott Fitzgerald, then far down on his own luck, would be traced to the magazine. More easily substantiated is the fact that on a given day, there could be quite a lively and engaging crowd at Ab's: Gertrude Stein had once showed up, and there were frequent appearances by journalist Jonathan Worth Daniels, a tough iconoclast from the *Raleigh News and Observer,* by Bill Couch, and by Paul Green. Likely, many graduate students came by essentially for the show, lured there by Buttitta's tales, true or not, of Fitzgerald and Faulkner; and there usually was a show available, with someone on hand to recite an experimental poem or to read off a social manifesto. In retrospect, it was hardly the stuff of true revolution fit for Victor Hugo, but it made the perfect counter to the staid mediocrity which so incensed Weldon Brown, who spoke for many in "Upward."[25]

Woodward was certainly among those who sought refuge at Ab's, a place much to his liking. With his prized Black Sun book, his reputation as one "fired from Georgia Tech," and his tales from the Soviet experiment and the Berlin marches, he was a minor gargoyle expertly cut for its available perches. Defying Howard Odum's explicit warnings, he showed up often at Ab's, in escape from the hated lectures, to energize for assaults on the large Watson collection or for assaults on the even larger, living collection which was Rupert Vance. At least once, however, he was so charged with the juices of dissidence that he publicly took on an issue of labor controversy right in North Carolina.

The depression and the mean reaction to it seen in Atlanta's city government were of course replicated throughout the South. In the Carolina Piedmont, the 1920s had been the scene of labor activism as the United Textile Workers Union (UTWU) attempted to organize the country's last bastion of antiunionism; but the little company towns, often deceptively placid and even pretty on the surface, were in fact a formidable last bastion. The labor union putsch of the 1920s was halted, reversed, and followed by vigorous counterattack primarily from the textile mill owners. In 1929 Gastonia, actually a collection of mill villages southwest of Charlotte, was one such place transformed into labor activists' folklore by the blood and the beatings with which the bosses maintained the laborers' "right to work." By 1935 the combination of economic upheaval, international radicalism, and Franklin Roosevelt's avowed sympathy for unions was inspiring renewed campaigns despite the thoroughgoing setbacks of the previous era. The campaigns even reached the Piedmont, with a big organization drive launched in the textile mills around Burlington; in that year the textile workers went out on strike at the mill.[26]

This time it was a more complicated story, with the laborers as willing as the management to use force in the effort. Given the political climate, the owners were not quite as free to bludgeon the union out of existence; at least now the owners faced much more extensive press coverage and a reading public generally more sympathetic to labor. In fact, the university campus served as the site for a labor organization drive and for the kind of group discussions and public lectures which a later generation of college students would describe as "consciousness raising." Still, most North Carolina dailies treated the story as an attack upon civilization by the Ostrogothic unionists. Picking up this cue, the *Tar Heel,* the campus student newspaper, editorialized on the side of civilization, as civilization revealed itself in the boardrooms of hosiery and bed-sheet producers; its editors bemoaned the presence of such labor rebels on their fair campus. Woodward read the editorial with disgust and sent in this letter: "If you young gentlemen believe you are doing the University a good turn by writing such stuff as this for the consumption of timid legislators and mill owners, may I suggest that you take a look at the current William Randolph Hearst editorials in his right wing chain of papers and you will find your own President Graham and his predecessor [Harry Woodburn Chase] pilloried in about the same tone as you adopt toward this little meeting on campus. . . . Yet you also quote Graham describing the traditions of academic freedom. Need I add that this tradition was not won, nor can it be defended, by truckling? . . . It ought to be worth a better defense than it is getting."[27]

As for the *Tar Heel,* its editorial staff said in rebuttal that this was merely a case where "a liberal takes us to task" about an episode best left to the Burlington people to resolve. In a perverse, rather self-serving, way, the paper's response pleased Woodward, who noted to his friends that the undergraduates were uniformly conservative or apolitical, as were the school's historians. But he was too good a person to engage in such emotional one-upmanship, and he tried to match his words with deeds. To reaffirm his own commitment to dissent, Woodward traveled several times to Burlington to see things at first hand; and he helped Green and Couch to organize some "mass protests," though none actually attained any size. As he told Glenn Rainey, the workers—accused of dynamiting a mill—were receiving a treatment in court which was a "pretty raw sort of thing, with not even a half-hearted regard for the formalities of legal decorum."[28]

At this time, much as in Atlanta, he fellow-traveled with Communists, working closely with Don West (alias Don Weaver) of the CP on the organization of protest rallies. However, as before, he showed ambivalence toward Marxist ideology, and especially toward its practitioners: witnessing the great socialist Norman Thomas in Durham, Woodward wrote him off as one who "employed pretty sissy tactics"; yet he seemed most upset that the Burlington authorities were not following the formalities of jurisprudence in the trial—hardly a genuinely Marxist position. And he insisted that the CP, which earlier had exercised a real influence on the UTWU, no longer had any connection with that union. Even as he experienced difficulty with his history instructors, so did he experience difficulty with the specific ideals of dissidence. Where the injustice was egregious, he worked alongside Communists, but he found them distasteful; socialists he thought often uninteresting and occasionally "sissy"; the Roosevelt liberals he judged vaguely disappointing, in some way not going far enough, evidently because the National Recovery Administration truckled to industrialists. In correspondence, he labeled himself liberal or radical, complained of labels, and expressed disdain for most exemplars of any recognizable party. As before, he remained a tough critic, rather generally though somewhat amorphously dissident, attaching himself from time to time to specific issues and to particular people. Although well left of center, his dissent was not informed by a coherent ideology.[29]

I I

What distinguished Woodward's curious brand of dissidence by
1935 was the way he kept plugging away on the Watson biography.
He did not talk much to fellow graduate students, sharing his ideas
only with two, Joseph Carlyle Sitterson (himself a fine scholar and
later chancellor of the university) and Joseph R. Caldwell. These
two sensed that he must be quite far along on the dissertation; but
he did not tell even them that a first draft of it was finished as early
as March of 1935. Only to the distant Rainey did he confide that he
had taken a completed draft to Hamilton; and to his great delight,
Hamilton the archetypal conservative liked it![30] This success impelled Woodward to focus on scholarship rather than politics; it
seemed ample reinforcement of his hope to make a difference in the
southern world, to make things better through scholarship which
awoke intelligent readers to the reality of social problems and which
at least pointed the way to resolution of those problems. Moreover,
Hamilton's favorable response even convinced him that enough
study to pass the doctoral examination was in order.

This decision to study for examination ran into the difficulty that
he had not really taken very seriously the lecture notes or the parallel readings in the American Nation Series. Just by having been
around, by having seen Berlin and Paris and Moscow, even by having seen New York, and even more by having studied at Columbia
University and by having taught at Georgia Tech, he enjoyed advantages over his fellows in any general testing; but failing was a very
real possibility. Surviving village myth has it that he nearly failed
one question; and although those records have been safely sealed
away, it seems likely. Shortly after the questions, he wrote to a
friend that he had bollixed the entire Hanoverian dynasty, an error
sure to drop the score on any discussion about the eighteenth century! Fellow students recall him as quite knowledgeable, but as
capable of poor performance on the comprehensive oral examinations because of the great weight he placed on his own research at
the expense of course study.[31]

But failing the session would postpone the day of freedom to do
his research and writing on his own as a professor with that office's
perquisite of self-managed time. This put the neglected lecture
notes in a different light, and he sought out Caldwell, a meticulous

notetaker and able student. Caldwell, nicknamed "Spec," came from the hardest-working of hardworking rural Carolinians. With few monetary resources, he had gone through tough little Davidson College and earned top honors; and then he came to the Hill, where he would be a dutiful servant to the university for four decades. All he knew of life was hard work, and although he had a bright and supple mind, the short, square-shouldered soldier never blanched at the mundane chore of the lectures which so offended Vann Woodward. The two boarded together and talked often over meals, over coffee, and over more spirited beverages, with Woodward unabashedly cribbing Spec's once-despised but now indispensable notes.[32]

On the appointed day of examination, all members of the graduate faculty were invited to participate, and there was among the questioners a scholar new to the scene, Howard Beale, recently lured down from New York University by Ray Newsome. Although Woodward did embarrass himself on at least one question and was rather lackluster on others, Beale considered the response to a question about Reconstruction to be brilliant. Beale, solidly within the Progressive tradition and a political activist, admired what he saw of Woodward, not only in style but also in substantive knowledge. That day Woodward, having cleared this examination hurdle rather clumsily, went out, got drunk, and came back with uneasy step to deposit Spec's notes with their rightful owner. By contrast, Beale, the urbane sophisticate, went home full of hope for the bright intellect he had just encountered. In their different ways, the two were both expressing the same fact, that Woodward was now unleashed to complete the Watson project; and more than being unleashed, he was now empowered with an academic adviser, a historian, of congenial spirit.[33]

That is, a part of Beale was a spirit congenial with Woodward's; there were many spirits in Beale, and in the end his internal contradictions pushed him to the nether region between eccentricity and madness. He was at once a battler (in one student's apt phrase, "a crusader" who was already very active on behalf of black civil rights) and a mama's boy (many noted how his mother dominated both his successful business-executive father and the successful academic son). He had the zeal of the moralist in attacking sin and had already served in bold campaigns to integrate certain northern hotels and other accommodations and to assert academic freedom for historians; but he might cave in, almost whining, in the face of life's more rudimentary demands. A diligent and meticulous scholar, he broke from the Ph.D.'s starting gate with a book-a-year pace, but by his mature years, he evidently forgot how to write, instead compiling a cache of memoranda on the trivial and an imposing set of file cabinets crammed with index card notes on Theodore Roosevelt. He was the kind of man who sent a blank check to the Library of Congress for the purpose of setting up his own personalized mahogany filing case in a study; but who then dickered with a headwaiter about the price of an inexpensive pie in a restaurant. Understandably, all of those contradictions affected students in a wide variety of ways; Woodward, Lyle Sitterson, and Guion Johnson found him to be a stimulating lecturer, but the stomping majority, including many thoughtful students, considered him a disorganized and confusing boor.[34]

A basic thing to remember in considering such a welter of spirits is that Beale possessed an excellent mind which had been well served by his studies at the University of Chicago and at Harvard University. Moreover, he came to the Hill because of his respect and affection for Newsome, and he was kept there for some time for the same reason despite offers from Smith College and Brooklyn College, both in many ways more attractive in that era to a Chicagoan/New Englander. Whatever he felt toward Carolina later in life, he came there full of enthusiasm, all but gushing to a friend, "The South is old, but very young in its outlook . . . with a marvelous possibility for the future if the right kind of leadership can be provided." Profoundly impressed by Graham, Couch, Green, and others, Beale felt that the teachers capable of fitting youth for leadership were already on hand. And young people like Woodward and Sitterson and Guion Johnson were to be the first of many waves of young leaders to serve "the young South" of the depression.[35] In time, Beale's hopes soured. It has often been so for the missionary: no matter how promising the start, in the end the natives fail to measure up to the standards of civilization. Unfortunately, in this instance, when Beale's hopes soured, he also soured.

But in 1936 and 1937, Beale and his hopes had yet to sour; quite the contrary, Beale was then sweet-to-bursting with his expectations of the youthful South. To Yale's president James R. Angel, he wrote a letter chiding the Eli for their alleged neglect of academic freedom; and to drive home the point, he held up Frank Graham as the example of what a college president should be. With the Carolina moon so comforting at this point, Beale went to work for Woodward. Dozens of letters clacked out of his typewriter: recommendations for possible vacancies were sent around the circuit; editors were told of the young scholar's availability for reviewing books; and historians who might be able to help Woodward were sought out for personal conferences at future conventions.[36]

The most effective help Beale provided was nevertheless more prosaic, and it consumed energy at a less frenetic pace; it was the thorough tutelage in the ins and outs of historical scholarship. Hamilton, of course, had carried this tutelage a long way, but he had not worked at close hand on the specifics, and in his chosen role of the elder, he had been rather genteel. Beale, who still had a world to conquer, was uninterested in gentility: "He gave me a sense of the demands and rigor of historical scholarship," Woodward recalled. And, significantly, "he made demands on me." Choosing to be discriminating as well as encouraging, Beale steadily pushed Woodward to tighten up the logic of his argument, to document yet more thoroughly, to express himself yet more clearly.[37]

Above all, Woodward set himself the task of telling a good story: he had to avoid Odum's prose, with its occasional opaqueness and unsteady story line. Yet he aimed at much more than the "good read" of the conventional history; there must be straightforward class analysis and frank treatment of the racial issue. He sought to take the sharp analytical insights of the Chapel Hill sociologists and to express them in the superb expository style fashioned by the historians, whether Progressives like Beard and Beale or conservatives like Allan Nevins and Avery Craven, who were writing in the 1930s. Although he had yet to develop a full and mature sense of irony, he had caught something significant in the inconsistencies and ambivalences of Watson's character and career. Where others saw hypocrisy in Watson's biracial Populist campaigns of the 1890s and his race baiting of the twentieth century, Woodward saw something much more significant as well as much deeper than mere hypocrisy. Watson was nothing less than a special type, almost an archetype, of reformer-gone-bad; he was the particular representative of a trend in the South. Woodward was convinced of Watson's greatness in his capacities for good or for evil. Watson's story, then, as Woodward chose to handle it, amounted to a tragedy both for one man and for an entire people. Central to the tragedy was this: the

demagogue was made, not born; and for all the fiery redhead's or-
atorical power over the people, Tom Watson was more influenced
than influencing. Basically, Watson was a good man who reached for
greatness and nearly attained it; he was stopped by his own personal
flaw, and therefore he fitted the classic mold of the tragic hero. The
flaw which ran so deep was a refusal to accept full responsibility for
his actions, especially those which failed. Under great stress, he was
apt to eschew his responsibilities; and under very great stress, he
would blame scapegoats for his woes—and then punish those
scapegoats. This flaw, in its particular and peculiar expression of
Negrophobia, was seen in many southern characters, perhaps in
most of the political spokesmen on the scene from 1893 to 1898.
Because of Watson's status as the heroic representative of the lower
class, his rise as reformer, his flaw of character, the resultant scapegoating, and his descent into desuetude became a virtual syn-
echdoche for the southern political man at the turn of the century.

As Woodward developed this story, surprises were compounded by
surprises. Earlier authorities claimed that extreme racism was the
excrescence of Populist emotionalism, that is, that extreme economics
and extreme politics produced an equally extreme racism. Even those
favorably disposed toward the Populists of the Midwest tended to
accept that line of analysis. Sadly, historians, without investigating
the primary sources, were accepting the conservative politicians' version of their archenemies the Populists. In fact, Watson's Negrophobic tactics were products of his later, conservative career, after
1900, when his service to railroad interests of Georgia won him
election to the U.S. Senate. His Populist days, surprisingly, were
marked by rather liberal racial attitudes, with the vox populi a
biracial chorus. But Watson's Populists were defeated by conservatives who used fraud and intimidation against Negro voters. It was
the gentlemen Bourbons, nominally the party of memory beholden
to honor and honesty, who cheated at the polling place and who first
bruited about the Negro. Nor was that all: these Victorian patriarchs
were not the detached, shambling romantics of legend: they were
tough-minded businessmen out to make a buck and pretty successful
at it, thanks in large part to their political expertise. Thus a great deal
of Woodward's dissertation is less a book about Watson than a sobering estimate of the conservatives against whom Watson strove until,
broken, he went over to their side.[38]

Other revelations concerned the characterization of the Populist

platform and the life of the Watson mind. As to the former, Woodward followed the lead of John Hicks in reading the national Populist movement as a pragmatic, rational, workable, and forward-
looking response to severe economic challenges. Like many another,
he found analogies between the Populists and the radical agrarians
in the left wing of the New Deal. But he broke new ground in
extending these claims to the southern Populists; Hicks had concentrated on the midwesterners, and his *Populist Revolt* did little to
break the mold of tradition that pronounced southern Populists to
be emotional hayseeds. Woodward, however, was emphatic in drawing the line of the Hicksian interpretation down south, and he made
his point by careful exegesis of the Georgia People's party platform.
In doing this, he also proved his point about Watson's mind, for the
platform was largely Watson's thinking, and Woodward pronounced the quality of both product and author to be high. Watson
was an intellectual, and Woodward went so far as to entitle his
thesis "The Political and *Literary* Career." None of this was to deny
that intellectuals could do terrible things; but something from the
old *Bozart* days must have been at play as Woodward insisted that
southern politicians were intimately and significantly involved with
ideas. H. L. Mencken, Frank Tannenbaum—all of those who said
otherwise were wrong.[39]

There it was: the hybrid novel finally between covers and accepted as a dissertation. But its completion brought more than the
typical postpartum doubts which graduate schools have always created among their students. If the thesis could not be published and
if the job-search team could not turn up a teaching position, then
the dissertation would come to mock what the dissident sought.
Without an audience to be moved to act, the Tom Watson research
would be the kind of ineffectual exercise which Charles Pipkin and
Ernest Hartsock had taught him to avoid. Woodward felt that he
deserved publication and a teaching position; he felt that his insights and investigations were both sound and seminal. Yet the
spring of 1937 and the summer to follow hulked in front of him
menacingly. Unlike Weldon Brown, he did not enjoy the author's
power simply to write that the protagonist successfully escaped
Dugtown, whence he came to inspire the entire South.

5

Two Kinds of Travel

The Quest for the Origins of the New South, 1937–1946

As Howard Beale searched for a position for Vann Woodward the newly minted Ph.D., he became strident in his insistence: Woodward would serve the profession and all of society, but first he *had* to be placed. Beale searched high and low, sometimes improbably high and low: Woodward, he said, was fully qualified for a chair in European history at New York University; or he could fill a chair vacated at a preparatory school which made unreasonable demands on its faculty—the very kinds of demands against which Beale was fulminating in his recently completed monograph about academic freedom and working conditions for teachers in American education. Beneath the comedy, and occasional pathos, of Beale's vigorous campaign was the reality of a generally depressed labor market with especially slim pickings in the academic disciplines; even after witnessing the disastrous circumstances of academic employment in the 1970s, Woodward still considered the late 1930s to be the worst time he had seen for historians. Given such conditions, Woodward expressed very limited objectives for the short term: all he wanted was a way to pay his bills while he started on his journey of investigations, his mental travel to the origins of the New South into which he had been born. [1]

He also knew he would be doing another kind of traveling, from temporary post to temporary post, until he had published enough to gain a secure tenure with major archival resources close to hand; and he knew, further, that he would not be making either journey alone, for he had met and had fallen in love with Glenn Boyd Macleod. Glenn Macleod was a native of Greensboro who had earned a graduate degree from Columbia University in 1932, when Woodward had earned his, although they actually met in Chapel Hill, where she served as a secretary for the university. In those years a strong and independent woman, she was attractive and sprightly; her traits of character were in almost every case vital complements to Woodward's, and especially so in those days of uncertainty. They planned to marry, but knew they would have to wait a year or two while she put aside savings—and established a file of personal references— from her job at UNC. Thus Woodward got himself ready for a great deal of traveling of two kinds, knowing that inevitably both trips were likely to be lonely; however, even his dark realism and occasional cynicism could not prepare him fully for the lengthy and circuitous route of his physical travel from 1937 to 1946. [2]

I

The first way station on the two journeys was Gainesville, Florida, and there was rich irony in the fact that this opportunity was prepared not by Beale or Rupert Vance or Howard Odum but by the traditionalists at Chapel Hill, the exemplars of the very things which had put him off as a graduate student. It developed that the University of Florida was creating a general-college curriculum for which it sought traditional humanists who could teach in several fields. The university was not after the historian in Beale's mold or the sociologist in Howard Odum's mold; but instead it was after scholars in the mold of Carolina's William Watkins Pierson, a man who could teach both literature and political science. Florida's first choice was evidently Woodward's good friend Lyle Sitterson, who passed up this opportunity in favor of a more generous offer of full-time teaching and research at Carolina; but one of Sitterson's references, the aforementioned Pierson, then suggested Woodward's name. Pierson had taught Woodward; Woodward had a collection of degrees in philosophy, political science, and history; and Woodward had a curriculum vitae which listed English instruction. In other words, on paper he seemed to be exactly what the school wanted. In fact, of course, someone so committed to search work in the original sources and someone so indifferent to undergraduate teaching was exactly what the newly formed general college did *not* want. But Woodward had learned plenty from the Great Depression, and if a school needed a generalist to teach freshmen, then he could certainly do that work and "be damned glad to get the job." He signed a contract in midsummer 1937, with duties to start in a few weeks.[3]

By a happy spin of Fortuna's wheel, he soon became fast friends with political scientists William G. Carleton and Manning J. Dauer, two tough dissidents alongside whom he would campaign during the next six decades. Neither had had anything to do with hiring Woodward, and in fact, both were initially leery of this newcomer, whom Carleton ruefully recalled being introduced to as if the Chapel Hillian "were a *prize.*" But Carleton's father was a radical Indiana journalist who had raised his son on a diet of Tom Watson—1890s Populist version of Watson—and Bill Carleton could recite long passages from the Georgian's *History of the French Revolution.* This of course delighted Woodward, who wrote approvingly to his old-time companion Glenn Rainey that he had finally found someone "really radical" in his approach to scholarship. Dauer, while less iconoclastic, also pleased him with an emphasis on first-rate scholarship dedicated to improving social, namely, race, relations in the South. Moreover, Woodward even found himself enthusiastic about the University of Florida and the community of Gainesville because of the rapid and thoroughgoing change which seemed imminent in a place until recently as backwater and parochial as his own Ouachita region of Arkansas.[4]

In 1934 the university had been a student body of a few thousand instructed by a faculty of a few hundred; very few in either group harbored aspirations to national prominence. That was understandable, for the vast peninsula supported an overwhelmingly rural citizenry barely numbering a million people; incredibly, considering what has since happened, Florida was then perhaps the least developed, least populated, and least wealthy section of the union. Despite the short-lived experience of rapid growth in the 1920s, the collapse of the Miami real estate market and the national stock market crash which followed combined to restore Florida to the norm of southern poverty and economic backwardness. The community of Gainesville thus nestled itself deeply into the peninsula, feeling more affined to south Georgia and to south Alabama than to any other cultural and social patterns.[5]

But there was a force, President John J. Tigert, who intended for the university to burst the cake of Gainesville custom and to become a bold and innovative national leader in curriculum development. When Woodward arrived in 1937, Tigert was in full sway, engineering one of the plans for a general-education core of instruction which marked that decade. Despite the nation's grim economic ambience, Yale University, Amherst College (fresh from a rebuff from the town's Young Men's Christian Association, which had been offered the school's main building in a desperate effort to raise funds), the University of Chicago, and the University of Minnesota were busily refashioning their programs of instruction to provide a comprehensive core of general education in the liberal arts.[6]

Tigert, who had served as commissioner of education for Presidents Calvin Coolidge and Herbert Clark Hoover, knew of this trend and realized that his campus was in a unique position to follow suit, since most of the faculty were by training and inclination generalists. Changing the shape of the curriculum would turn a weakness into a strength, for that political scientist, that botanist, that historian who had quit doing research in his field of specific training would be called on to teach general introductory courses. More, the team teaching of interdisciplinary courses in plenary sessions of the freshman or sophomore class would inject a healthy competition into lecture performances, stirring the juices which might otherwise dry up. Meanwhile, an upper division, for the research scholars, could be established and supported by the labor of the general college. But the plan had this weakness: the research positions were cushy in comparison to the heavy teaching loads which characterized duties below decks; preserving the upper division as an enclave for serious scholarship could only be done by forcibly drafting some senior professors into the general college. Exciting to administrators and to recognized researchers, the plan was a great threat to the ninety and nine of college professors on campus. Knowing this, Tigert gave the faculty a chance to vote, lost the vote, and then in 1935 summarily imposed his will.[7]

Some young scholars benefited from Tigert's aggressive pursuit of curricular innovation. For one, Bill Carleton, just out of the University of Indiana, received a choice research position in political science in the upper division. On the other hand, his good friend Manning Dauer, also just out of the University of Indiana and no less committed to his scholarship and publication, was shouldering the burden of teaching in the general college. Dauer was joined there by Woodward, who was instructed to help plan the teaching of the Western heritage and was set to work composing multiple-choice questions on Aristotelian ethics and Platonist ideals while preparing lectures on St. Augustine and St. Anselm. For Woodward, the door upstairs to the senior division was firmly closed when the history chairman, James Miller Leake, announced emphatically that only the chairman would teach upper-level courses in southern or U.S. history.[8]

But if the door upstairs was closed, at least the outer door was also shut against unemployment. Long accustomed to "stealing time" for his book, he soon found that one could finagle chances for research and writing out of the odd moments of freedom permitted by the crevices of the general-college structure. He managed a trip or two to Thompson to restore his soulful communion with Watson; and he maintained his more mundane communion with the surviving Watsons as he tidied up his facts for the manuscript, which sat on an editor's desk in the New York offices of Macmillan publishers. When not at these labors he even professed admiration for the Tigert plan, writing to Glenn Rainey to let the boys at Tech know that the University of Florida had a real liberal arts school. "I am really enjoying the teaching much. I dash in my office from a lecture on anthropology, jerk off my false whiskers, and then off to one on architecture."[9]

The only hitch was that he was not very good at this teaching: his new friends and his enthusiastic superiors alike regretfully conceded that he lectured poorly, mumbling at such a low pitch that only those in the front row could hear at all, and even they missed the point since it was invariably made without inflection. Although he was successful in his small and informal weekly discussion groups, by and large his lecture performances fit the pattern traced by fellow historian Bennett Harrison Wall when he said dyspeptically of a Woodward speech: "We heard it. *Then* we learned it was great!"[10]

Students, of course, did not have the opportunity to read Woodward's lecture notes and thus did not perceive their true quality; but the overall program in those days of its inception was appreciated, and Woodward benefited from the more skillful presentation of others on his team. In any case, these were happy times as he, Carleton, and Dauer formed what they called the Three Musketeers, swearing oaths of fealty to a reform politics and to an economic development, both of which were to include the poor of both races; they also had much sport in cocktail-hour mimicking of the campus administrators, most of whom they disdained as a vastly inferior species. But this happiness was obviously uncompleted, for Woodward increasingly realized that he needed Glenn Macleod with him in this new life. If only he could feel secure enough to marry in these least secure of days! He pondered the kind encouragement from his senior colleagues, but he doubted that these mere words ensured a future salary if his great work failed of publication.[11]

Earlier, in the charmed atmosphere created by Beale, he had sent the dissertation off to Macmillan, assuming that he also had a good chance of publication with the UNC Press. He could play for the big marbles in New York; and if that attempt failed, he could still pick up the lesser marbles in Chapel Hill. But actually Couch, for all his bravery and innovation, was not about to print "The Political and Literary Career of Thomas E. Watson" until it had been cut considerably in size. Learning of the extensive reconstruction chores ahead just to merit serious consideration from the politically and personally sympathetic Couch greatly altered Woodward's perception of his chances elsewhere. The long wait for a verdict from New York bred depression and made a mockery of Beale's optimism: probably, he reasoned, Macmillan was uninterested in yet another bulky biography of yet another politician. With sadness, Woodward wrote to Macmillan asking for the return of his manuscript.[12]

In this confusion about his future, Woodward had to attend one of the lengthy September conferences about the introductory course. On the way in to the session he checked his mail, finding a letter from Macmillan; not having time to open what he "knew" was a rejection notice, he carried it with him, resting it in his lap. But, he realized with desperate hope, the letter *could* be good news. He squirmed under the weight of conflicting emotions and tried to look attentive. "Then I had to sit there an hour and a half pretending that I was listening to what the ass was saying about the course Man and the other World or something. I didn't hear a thing he said for an hour and a half and then when I did get a chance to read it before I was out of the hall I guess the guy thought I was completely nuts. . . . I met dozens of people without knowing what they said or remembering their names. Of course I couldn't very well blurt out that Macmillan was going to publish Tom, so all I could do was go out on the campus and yell and walk half the night and drink beer—the only thing available."[13]

As he learned more from Macmillan, he did less walking and less drinking, but the impulse to yell remained. Allan Nevins, the very archetype of conservative and narrative historiography, had been the publisher's outside reader or referee for "Tom," and a very enthusiastic one at that. Moreover, Nevins was to review the eventual publication for one of the New York dailies, quite a christening for any vessel. Happily caught up in the details of selecting illustrative photographs and subscribing to review-clipping services, Woodward could safely make plans for a real future, in Gainesville if he wanted it, perhaps elsewhere with a little luck. If not yet a true "prize" in Carleton's wry sense and if not yet entrusted with southern history, he was at least assured of work in his profession. Perhaps now he could write the kind of history he wanted to without asking Glenn to endure a straitened life of transient employment.[14]

Enjoying this much security, he journeyed back to the Hill during the 1938 summer break in classes to make Glenn Macleod his wife. As ever eschewing formality, he arrived by train hours before dawn and insisted that she marry him immediately in a civil, not a religious, ceremony. Glenn, accustomed to such mannerisms and no more enthusiastic than he about the formalities of organized religion, agreed readily enough to the civil wedding, and the two looked up a notary authorized to oversee a service. But the fellow operated a hardware store and intended to perform the offices there, which was too much for Glenn: disdain for bourgeois formality need not produce a storeroom wedding, at least not for her. Instead, the two visited the local justice of the peace, and with Milton Abernathy as witness, they tied the knot. Having the resident village Communist for a witness, Vann's taste for the unusual could be tempered with Glenn's greater good sense. [15]

They honeymooned in Miami, with persisting legend holding that the scholar, preoccupied with his author's task, lay on the beach proofreading *Tom Watson: Agrarian Rebel* (as the dissertation was felicitously retitled). In actuality, the couple enjoyed a rather typical honeymoon, but there was this kernel of truth in the legend: Woodward did carry the typescript with him, and Glenn had to endure a long moment of frantic but ultimately successful search through the hotel trash bin after a zealous maid cleared their room of the untidy pile of papers. Returning from such light farce, the Woodwards eased into life at Gainesville, with emotional prosperity reigning at their little home near the campus. She took instantly to the bachelors Dauer and Carleton, and the Three Musketeers became Four who could share trips to the nearby beaches and to the juke joints of the college town. They made an enthusiastic little band, one whose members punctured each other's egoistic balloons as the three scholars grew in power and prestige; but also one whose members constantly reminded each other about the enormity of the injustice of the South and, even more important, about their accountability to the challenges posed by that injustice. Thanks in large part to the atmosphere engendered by the Four Musketeers, Woodward remained true to his mission of writing history that mattered: he still burned with the intent to produce the kind of meaningful, usable, and yet artistic scholarship first and most forcefully urged on him by Ernest Hartsock. [16]

In the small but growing pond of Gainesville, each of the Musketeers was becoming a duck of some size: Dauer was starting to make a name as a fine teacher and as an authority on second president John Adams; Carleton (having become an administrator notwithstanding all his jibes at "those careerists") was combining in a rare way good scholarship with wise administration; but it was Woodward who was splashing about most noisily and who consequently drew the sharpest barbs from his friends. After one visit to Tom Watson's mansion in Thompson, a visit orchestrated with uncharacteristic care by Woodward, Carleton issued the deflating verdict on Watson: "He never really made it, he never really made it." Moreover, both Dauer and Carleton teased Woodward about his ambivalence, about his dissident calls for thoroughgoing reform in the midst of an inclination to celebrate the patricians of the ancien régime. And both could poke fun at their successful friend as he tried to find a suitable topic for his "next book"; the man who had once been rebuffed, even as unauthorized biographer, by *the* black radical William Edward Burghardt Du Bois, now sought out other topics: perhaps a biography of Alabama's moderate Oscar K. Underwood? or perhaps a study of Georgia's quixotic antebellum intellectual and politico Alexander Hamilton Stephens? Did he cast the net of his ambition that far, or was he merely confused?[17]

But the jokes were grounded in great expectations; they were laughing with someone on his way to the top. Woodward's unique biography was becoming an instant success, with some predicting correctly that it would become a classic against which future political biographies would be measured. Nevins, as was by now expected, produced a glowing review, and the Sunday *New York Times Book Review* gave it a lavish front-page treatment; Woodward's elders in the profession presented the book the Charles Sydnor Award for historical scholarship. As he would do often in his career, Woodward had sensed a potential change of mood in the nation's intellectual makeup, and he had moved boldly to the front with a book which drew together in a complete way many thoughts then only partially formed, only hinted at, in the scholarship of others. Even as a great social revolution in race relations seemed to be forming because of forces unleashed, however unwittingly, by New Deal economic experimentation, there was Woodward with his story which demonstrated that it had almost happened before, in the 1890s. Soon the profession would follow his trail, examining the Farmers' Alliance and the People's party to see if other men in other southern regions were also part of an initially rational, biracial radical agrarianism; the whole process he set in motion created much dispute which by its nature can never be fully resolved; but the significant thing is the way in which Woodward's questions, Woodward's starting assumptions, and Woodward's terminology became the lingua franca of such studies, even, and especially, among those who disagreed with his conclusions.[18]

Three highly controversial aspects of the biography have been established as a virtual trinity of debating points for New South scholarship ever since: the economic rationalism or irrationalism of the Populist platform; the putative racial liberalism or illiberalism of the party leaders and members; and the characterization of the William Jennings Bryan free-silver campaign of 1896 as the "cowbird" which dislodged the "real" Populist concerns. Basically, Woodward's Populists were said to believe in a managed (or command) economy more than they did in a pure market economy; they bid farewell to perfect competition and accepted monopoly where it could be regulated while calling for nationalization in a few cases where regulation was ineffective. With the exception of their simplistic ideas about monetary policy, their economic plans were rational, and one's response to them really depends on one's ideological preferences for pure market, command, or a mixture of market and command economics. Woodward's personal preference for a mixture of market and command economics—his oft-repeated disdain for "unrestrained capitalism"—was certainly not calculated to endear him to the many scholars who prefer a market economy with minimal government interference; and he did not expect such mentalities to *like* the Ocala platform or Tom Watson's speeches and essays. But he did try hard to persuade all comers of the internal consistency of Populist economic logic, for he was convinced that the agrarians pursued—in a suitably modern and materialist fashion—their own rationally conceived self-interests.

As the years came and went and the spirit of the New Deal lost its appeal, Richard Hofstadter's *Age of Reform* (1955) protested Woodward's depiction of a class-conscious agrarian radicalism responding to market failure and inequities with a carefully thought-out program of regulation and restraint. In fact, Hofstadter himself emphasized the emotionalist and nonrational elements of the Populists, treating their economic theories as strictly secondary to their larger concern, or "anxiety," over their loss of status in the national culture and their corresponding political fall from grace. Following his cue, but moving without his sense of restraint, Daniel Bell, Peter Viereck, and other scholars influenced by Hofstadter began to describe the Populists as wild-eyed protosocialists, or even protofascists, for whom economic policy was not so much secondary as it was a smokescreen to hide an ill-conceived agenda of social revolution. By the 1960s, what with the ferment of the Kennedy-Johnson economic experimentation, New Left scholars began to resuscitate Tom Watson and the Populists, and when they did so, Woodward's biography was back in fashion with a vengeance. In particular, Norman Pollack celebrated the "Populist mind," whose "response to industrialism" he found to be eminently workable as well as far more humane than the responses of the alternatives to the People's party. Furthermore, Pollack exhibited a bracing spirit, almost teleological in aspirations, as he described their ideological soundness; Bell's and Viereck's accusations of protosocialism in one generation had become another's commendation. Populists were "hot" items on campuses, the images of their plainness and their simplicity a kind of reverse chronological reflection of the emerging style of the modern radicals who sought grass-roots reform; and these men and women of the Left were then well pleased with Woodward, largely because of his version of Watson.[19]

By the mid-1970s, however, a more self-consciously "cool" mentality prevailed among scholars grown wise and a bit reserved after the Watergate scandal and the failure of U.S. policy in Indochina. Initially, Woodward's description of Populist economics fared well with this group, too, despite the telling disclaimer by his own student Sheldon Hackney that, at least in Alabama, the individual Populist assemblymen were more concerned with being elected and with staying in office than with a concentrated effort across the broad path of macroeconomic reform. More representative was Lawrence Goodwyn, who drew inspiration from Woodward to paint his own picture of less ideologically charged, very result-oriented Populist party organizations with their varying agendas of shrewd, viable answers to significant economic questions at the levels of the many local communities spread from Wilmington to Waco.[20]

The 1980s have revealed, however, that the Woodward Watson, with regard to economic thinking, was not destined to be a man for all seasons. James Hunt has demonstrated that North Carolina's Marion Butler, not Watson, was the real thinker behind the Populist economic proposals; and Hunt has also demonstrated that Butler's Populists were simply much, much less radical and far more accepting of industrialism and urbanization than Woodward assumed. More dramatically, Steven Hahn and Barton C. Shaw have tramped back over Woodward's very stomping grounds in Georgia, and in different ways, each has weakened the image of the *agrarian rebel:* Hahn casting doubt on the *rebel* part of that memorable subtitle by showing that traditional peasant values exercised considerable power over Populist thought and action; and Shaw successfully plotting the close parallel lines which almost converge when one traces the economic policies of conservative southern Democrats and their Populist rivals, so that Watson emerges as "hardly a radical . . . challenge to commercial values or to national and local exploitation." Thus, unless someone should discover an unseen fatal flaw in the meticulous research of Hackney, Shaw, Hunt, or others, Woodward's portrayal of Watson's pragmatic economic radicalism has been fundamentally damaged, although there seems little chance that the profession will again embrace the 1950s descriptions of Watson as an emotional protofascist.[21]

As for the racial attitudes of the Populists, and specifically of Tom Watson, Woodward's evaluation now appears much too generous. Even when he originally wrote, a number of his friends cautioned him that his passion for interracial reform in his own day might make him read a similar liberalism back into the Populists' era, so that his hopes for his era might seem to have been "realized" in an earlier decade. Subsequently, scholars retracing Woodward's manuscript searches have found considerable racism in the Populist ranks, and Charles R. Crowe and Barton Shaw have even found Watson and other leaders Negrophobic *before* the collapse of agrarian radical reformism in 1896. In addition, Shaw has noted that many blacks in Georgia supported the Democratic party there because, for a time, it did offer them legitimate political opportunities. On the other hand, Joel Randolph Williamson has painted a fittingly lurid landscape of the 1890s—his metaphor of the "crucible" thus lending a moral direction lacking in Eugene Genovese's earlier piquant phrase, "orgy of extreme racism"—and against that backdrop, the Populists' racism seems rather mild by comparison. And in this much-altered context, Lawrence Goodwyn's many and deeply affecting examples of cooperation between whites and blacks in Populist campaigns have indicated that such activities were fully as remarkable as Woodward claimed. The most accurate picture now available would describe the Populists as people who shared the racism which permeated their respective regions of the South but who laid to one side their most extreme prejudices long enough to attempt a major economic reconstruction through the political processes. In some ways, white Populists attempted to manipulate black votes, but many blacks were politically shrewd enough to gain real opportunities, and most blacks successfully eluded manipulation. This brings the profession back to Woodward's original claim, with the difference that his 1938 tone of enthusiasm must be modulated, for in race relations, the Populists now seem not so much the best hope as the best of a bad lot.[22]

A more fundamental criticism leveled at Woodward's story of Watson involved the issue of the 1896 election campaign platform. In Woodward's version, Watson and the Populists had always represented not only biracial radical protest but also an extensive set of concrete proposals for reform; then Bryan, the "boy wonder" who was "hurling his thunderbolts" at the eastern bankers, came along with a single issue, an extremely simplistic plan for bimetallic currency, and in very duplicitous maneuvering, convinced Watson to be his vice-president on the national Democratic ticket. The Populists, falling for this trick—since Bryan in fact had no intention of letting Watson serve as his vice-president if elected—thus saw most of their "eggs" of reform proposals rudely cast out from the nest by the "cowbird" Bryanites, who left the single "egg" of coinage of silver at sixteen to one. Most notably, Robert F. Durden has written that Woodward missed the point of this issue: as Durden reads the same events and personalities, the silver issue was always vital to the Populists, and most of them supported the one-issue campaign readily enough. While Durden's critique underplays the extensive range of Populist proposals which Bryan discarded, he has forever modified Woodward's rather naive claim that Bryan fooled the innocents with his sly ruses. Since the mid-1960s, a host of students initially inspired by Woodward and urged on later by Pollack have reexamined the ideological underpinnings of Populism, and most of that group have ended up by crediting the movement with a remarkably full slate of reform proposals, a slate sacrificed, to their subsequent regret, to the cowbird of bimetallic currency, much as Woodward had contended. In particular, Bruce Palmer, still another Woodward student, garnered the Sydnor Award by examining the Populist ideology in speeches, pamphlets, and editorials to show that the People's party was most concerned to maintain the dignity of mankind in the changing circumstances of the new industrialism; as he quoted them aptly, "man over money." What Durden has done, however, remains important despite the work of Palmer and others: he has emphatically reminded Woodward and those who follow his lead that Watson and the Populists were free and independent men and women who willfully *chose* to cast their lot with the one-issue politics of Bryanism. The cowbird issue thus becomes deeply suspect, not because Bryan must be reassessed as a good leader and not because the Ocala and the Omaha platforms were less than rational and just visions of future possibilities, but because the Populists themselves—not the devious, devising cowbird Bryan—pitched their eggs, however attractive, out of their own nest.[23]

The larger implications behind each of the trinity of research questions concern the dilemma of Watson's character, and this, oddly, has seldom been addressed directly. Watson is not really the stuff of greatness, and it is hard to concede that he possessed a tragic flaw which led to his downfall and the downfall of a radical movement. Instead, the larger agrarian movement itself has gained in stature and in respect as scholars have continued to investigate it,[24] and Watson increasingly appears to be a clever opportunist possessed of great charisma who arrived at the right moment to lead the movement into national prominence; later, the frightening Negrophobic movement would present him with still another opportunity, one which he seized to gain even greater notoriety. The tragedy inherent in Woodward's depiction is not expressed outright, but the tone is tragic, and that is one of the things which makes the story so compelling a drama. However, Woodward's portrayal of a reform leader "gone sour" is much more than drama: it suggests a profound insight into the motivations of southern leaders at the turn of the century.

II

These debates over a man's dissertation and first book, debates persisting in intensity nearly fifty years after publication, underscore the magnitude of Woodward's achievement, even if scholars ultimately decide that he was wrong on each of the specific counts of his thesis. In the late 1930s the significance of *Tom Watson* was not as readily apparent as today, but the leaders of the University of Florida shared Nevins's admiration for the biographer, and when the school initiated a Phi Beta Kappa ceremony, Woodward was selected to address the group even though that decision passed over prominent senior members of the faculty. Nor was the choice any mistake, for Woodward took the occasion to lay down the lines of several major interpretations which he would develop over his career. Progressivism, as in his dissertation, remained the mode of interpretation, but he was demonstrating how flexible were the pneumatic walls of that analysis in the hands of a master. Obvious debts to Charles Beard were expressed when Woodward described the Civil War as the Second American Revolution and when he labeled as colonial the postbellum economy of the South; but there was also that profound respect and even warmer affection for the Populists, something the Progressive historians seldom demonstrated. Further, there were deep regrets about some of the changes brought by the passage of time, and this lingering sympathy for much which had been worthy in the displaced aristocracy of the old order was hardly a Progressive attitude. Moreover, having yet to develop a way to interpret history ironically, Woodward in this speech still floundered somewhat: a kind of Progressive with second thoughts and reservations but with no effective way to express those ambiguities except for a rather overstated tragedy and a sometimes clumsy sarcasm.[25]

One problem was that, in 1938, Woodward had yet to read William Faulkner with any real understanding; in fact, in his address he chided the Mississippian for "pulling his characters out of a well," and he generally disparaged the novelist's efforts. Furthermore, his distaste for the Fugitives from Vanderbilt University, while understandable to large degree, shut him off from some of their valid insights into the injustices spawned of the rapid industrialization, urbanization, and commercialization of a formerly agrarian culture. In fact, Woodward shared both Faulknerian attitudes and Fugitive attitudes toward the crass materialism of the postbellum southern city; and as he would discover later, Faulkner's ideas about race relations, while a complex jumble of seeming and real contradictions, were certainly more liberal than those of most southerners. Perhaps he could develop some alternative way of expressing the irony of what he found in the South; or perhaps he could assimilate a part of the Fugitives and a part of Faulkner, making them his own and using them for his Beardian purposes. But until he could do one or more of those things, his interpretation would remain more suggestive than informative, with only the Populist part of the story cogent and internally consistent, and even that marred by his occasional excesses of enthusiasm.[26]

Despite these interpretive and stylistic problems, his research already was leading him along some very interesting intellectual pathways, and those hearing the speech were struck by its seminal nature. Starting with the Beardian assumption that the antebellum South was not only agricultural in the main but also a farming middle class, Woodward pronounced the Civil War a defeat "at all levels," including the "surrender of a point of view." By 1876, "the industrialist was now in the saddle and the reins were in his hands. The farmer had been crowded out." While some of the old leaders retained power, they did so in the manner of Georgia's Joseph Brown, described as a pragmatist who cut his politics to fit his economic frame: before the war, agrarian; after, industrialist. Woodward peppered this explanation with examples, such as John Caldwell Calhoun's grandson Patrick Calhoun deserting the cause of the old States' Righter for the cause of Jay Gould's railroad empire; or Kentucky's journalist Henry Watterson discerning a "taste of money" on palates which had tasted too much blood; or North Carolina's Walter Hines Page, also in the service of Jay Gould, calling for several first-class funerals for the southern old guard. This set of ideas the historian called the New South Movement, and Atlanta journalist Henry Woodfin Grady he denoted as the movement's premier spokesman.[27]

Although the very nature of such a movement must jar a traditional land once governed by soil and season, in the 1880s southerners "generally quite lost their hearts" to Grady and to his cohort Joel Chandler Harris, "the tenderest chronicler of the Old South," but a chronicler celebrating a day now done. However much Harris's readers might thrill to the plantation yarns of Uncle Remus and Br'er Rabbit, they were to understand that the city now held sway and that that was good. Of course, Woodward himself knew that Harris's own descendants were even then in active revolt against Grady's doctrine; for his son Julian was in league with Glenn Rainey and other Atlanta dissidents. And so he turned to a consideration of those who rejected "Grady's Reconciliation"; and here Woodward suddenly dropped his formerly playful tone to strike a very hard blow: "Grady preached the reconciliation of all classes, that is, the

reconciliation of farmers and laborers to a continuation of the businessman's regime, the reconciliation of the races, that is, the reconciliation of the Negro race to the unquestioned domination of the
white race; reconciliation between sections, that is, an alliance—
cultural, financial, and political—between the Industrial East and
the New South; and finally, a type of reconciliation about which
Grady had nothing to say, reconciliation of labor to its lot—whatever that might be."[28]

Was Woodward's 1938 distaste for Grady's values matched by any
southerners of the 1880s? It was, in degree, but the kind of dissent
he unearthed was reactionary, even neo-Confederate, the romance of
the Lost Cause. Instead, it was in the next decade, the 1890s, that
Woodward found his kind of rebel, the Populist who had a "tough-
minded realism, a fact-encrusted hardness that was modern. It was
not afraid of soiling its sleeves in a catch-as-catch-can tussle." Even
more enticing, the Populist displayed "a half-joking fighting spirit
born of an undaunted consciousness of rags and tatters, a consciousness of nothing to lose and something to gain." Prototype of
this Populist was Tom Watson, the "real reconciler" of race and
class, who asked that the poor of both colors unite against the oppression of poverty. Moreover, "in their political platform the Populists made demands that one associates more with the 1930s than
with the 1830s—except that the New Deal blinked before the
harsh gaze of local racism and thus acquiesced to Democracy "for
whites only," while Populism, "reversing the Southern tradition,"
strove for political equality of the races.[29]

Courageous and tough-minded, these Populists gained the support of many southerners, their influence peaking in the years 1893
and 1894. It so stirred spirits and minds that it battled on equal
terms with the "romanticism of the Southern middle class," especially since Grady had died in 1889. But, though Tom Watson
received a hamper-full of laudatory prose and poetry, his biographer
the former English professor had to concede that the establishment
retained a monopoly over the literati, for the things Watson's correspondents wrote were inferior in style. And in the final voting at the
polls the Populists also lost, but only after "the conservatives were
compelled to use fraud, violence, terrorism, and actual murder to
turn back the great tide of rebellion." Following those close nominal
defeats at the polling places, the Populists saw the great tide flow in

the other direction as the facile orator William Jennings Bryan stole their show in 1896 with the free-silver campaign. As in his biography, he again employed Watson's "cowbird" critique of Bryan, and he again faulted the national Democratic leadership for denuding the Populist programs. But with Bryan's defeat, followed by the stirring adventurism in empire of the Spanish-American War in 1898 and the resultant wartime prosperity, the Populists were routed: no conservatives had to stuff any ballot boxes after 1898.[30]

Not long afterward in the upper Midwest and in the Far West, Progressivism appeared, a movement which was the political expression of the ruling mentality, the mentality which Beard, Parrington, and Turner possessed and which, blasted of its excessive moralism, the lecturer Woodward still professed. By the twentieth century, Progressivism had swept southward, into the Corn Belt and the Cotton Belt, raising the possibility that the agrarian South and the agrarian West could unite for a reform campaign. Moreover, he quoted a former Populist who said of the Progressive in the abstract, "He is doing what we want done, and cannot do ourselves." But it was not to be, for the South repeated its experience of the antebellum era when it failed to form a bond with the "natural ally" in the West. In Beardian terms the first failure was explained by industrialism and urbanism, economic ways of life "bought by" the West; but Woodward explained the second failure, the twentieth-century one, as a matter of class antagonism in the South. And this class antagonism—in which "the old agrarian following" was split between tenant and owner—subsequently became a racial antagonism: "Certain of the old leaders of the Populist Type on finding the split began to resort to new and sensational devices to attract support from the unorganized mass of voters." Thus Hoke Smith's 1906 gubernatorial campaign in Georgia, while "truly progressive" in some respects, also promised disfranchisement of the Negro "in behalf of White Supremacy."[31]

At this point Woodward made a bold pronouncement: it was the peculiar *nature* of the defeat of the Populists which made the South of his day so backward. Reform having lost in the 1890s, the old Populists had adopted the technique of racist demagogy which had defeated Tom Watson and thereafter combined economic reform with racial extremism. "In this manner progressive social thought in the South became identified with disreputable political methods.

In this manner such men as Watson, Benjamin Ryan Tillman, James Kimble Vardaman, and later Huey Long, are remembered and despised as 'demagogues,' while their progressive social ideas are forgotten." This "confusion," peculiar in its provenance, became "tragic" in its results, for economic reform could always be blocked thereafter by principled conservatives repelled by demagogy.[32]

As he hoped, Woodward was making an analysis of remarkable power in bringing Progressive concepts and questions to bear on the morass of southern politics, 1889–1914. He was leaving much unexplained—namely, why did the Populists who were putatively liberal about race in 1894 become so extremist, and violently extremist, about the same question by 1906? Somehow, the class analysis failed to catch the profundity of the change from "Colored and whites in the ditch unite!" to "Lynch the nigger!" But in taking seriously the demagogues of this century, Woodward was asking questions not asked before by historians of the section: that was because, before him, the reform elements in the New South countryside were ignored. Having established this new angle of approach, he was careful to kick himself free from any possible ties with the Vanderbilt Fugitives, who used the same term, *southern agrarian,* in a positive sense. He could still see the Vandy cordon in pious retreat before W. T. Couch's attack, and he spoke of them with sarcasm: "On the Boulevard de Montparnasse, Southern esthetes of the Fugitive school sat around the same sidewalk cafe tables with Northern esthetes of the Humanist school—both convivial in a self-imposed exile—as long as their stocks and bonds returned dividends. When the dividends began to fail in 1929 the Northern expatriots returned to New York to find themselves sudden converts to communism, while the Southern expatriots returned to Louisiana and Tennessee to find themselves sudden converts to agrarianism." The members of this contemporaneous movement, which was never in fact so cohesive as he then imagined, he labeled romantics "with faces fixed on a never-never land of the past."[33]

Much as he sneered at them, however, Woodward shared the modern agrarians' rejection of the "boosterism" employed by self-satisfied Main Streeters. The only acceptable response, however, was Howard Odum's and Rupert Vance's: "the relentless pursuit of facts, facts, facts dug out, tabulated and analyzed by professional students of society." By 1935 the New Deal was calling on the Regionalists for data and, the reformer hoped, for some direction in policy as well. Certainly neither Vance nor Odum was shy about offering opinion about social policy; and so Woodward had thought that southerners might take to the "hard, narrow path of realism" after all. For instance, Will Alexander had relocated his reform efforts, moving from Atlanta to Washington to work with Rexford Guy Tugwell's Resettlement Agency; and there was the possibility that that department would address more fundamental questions of economic structure in the South as a result of Alexander's influence and the search work of Odum's students. By the time of this address, however, the agency had abandoned any radical plans of economic reconstruction, and Alexander returned to Atlanta to devote full time to regional civil rights campaigns, which seemed more productive than did the stalled New Deal. There were thus only a few men seeking the narrow path, and Woodward could not express either the moralism or the optimism of the 1914 Progressive from Oregon or New York. He closed his speech, therefore, with the warning that many southerners, as before, were "deceiving themselves" in the self-created "maze of romance."[34]

This address bespoke a hard-edged class analysis of reform tainted by demagogy: it extended the biography's theme of racially tolerant and economically pragmatic Populists; and it introduced the concept of the colonial New South. Even his signal contribution, explaining the provenance and progress of Jim Crow segregation, was there in confused, uncompleted, and disorderly, but no less real, form. Absent was real depth, even in his language, which was, that day, not so much ironic as comic and sometimes harshly didactic, where in later years it would be superbly effective because so gentle. Primarily, the speech served to introduce a range of important new questions, with answers only hinted at; by contradistinction, the nature of the speech did clearly answer the seriocomic questions of his friends: no, he could not stay in Gainesville and accomplish what he intended; instead he must be traveling on.[35]

III

Even as he read the proofs of the manuscript for the Phi Beta Kappa printers, he was closing in on a major publication project, thanks to his own persistence, but also thanks to Rupert Vance and to a bit of good luck. Woodward, corresponding with Vance and briefly visiting the Chapel Hill-Durham area to search through manuscript sources, shared with the Regionalist several of his possible projects. One was a rather improbable coauthorship with the aptly named Texas liberal Maury Maverick; the idea was that the politician and the professor would team up to produce "Symbols for the South," a series of sketches of interesting characters from across the political spectrum. Another plan, urged on him by Vance as being far more practicable, was a major study of Virginia's Carter Glass; Vance felt that Glass could be characterized usefully as a southern Cato, a liberal who "went bad," the financial expert with the immature sociology. These two projects were soon abandoned, however, and were replaced by a plan for a study of Eugene Victor Debs, the socialist who had so much influenced Woodward's friend Rainey, although he had not much impressed Woodward in a Durham speech (the occasion when the graduate student observer had dismissed Debs as one practicing "sissy tactics"). For this project Vance prepared generous letters of support to the Social Sciences Research Council and also to the Rockefeller Foundation, both sources of funding which had often benefited the Regionalists and their students. Vance further suggested that if no funding developed, Woodward could work on Alabama's Oscar Underwood, whose papers would be more centrally located than Debs's and whose biography would require less travel.[36]

All of this was sound advice, but Vance was also doing another favor, one which in some ways made Woodward's career: he was in communication with the directors of the ambitious History of the South series, a multivolume excursion through the periods of southern history. While it was still in the planning stages, the original editor, Charles Ramsdell, had signed on Vance for the final volume, about the modern South, and Burton Kendrick for the penultimate volume, which had to bridge the gap between Reconstruction and the First World War (the starting point for the modern South in 1938 historiography). However, Kendrick had withdrawn, suggesting Woodward's name for the ninth volume, and Vance had enthusiastically affirmed the nomination. This series was itself like something that Woodward might have made up about the New South: Texas money comprising the Littlefield Fund made publication possible, and Huey Long's prized state college, Louisiana State University, provided the editing, printing, and other publishing services at its presses. Moreover, Wendell Holmes Stephenson and Ellis Merton Coulter, the men who edited the series after Ramsdell's own retirement from the project, were a curious pair, both talented but in very different ways, and thus themselves reflective of the diversity which Woodward always insisted characterized southerners. Coulter, a meticulous scholar, had established himself happily at the University of Georgia, where he remained throughout his very long career; deeply conservative on all issues and a white supremacist of the genteel school, he eschewed ideas for facts and, while a fine "blue-pencil editor," often lost the point in the web of complex issues such as race relations. On the other hand, Stephenson traveled around on several teaching assignments, never very happily, but always excited by ideas; politically more moderate than Coulter, he was also by nature far more receptive to challenging ideas. These two, different as they were, sometimes in spite of themselves, worked successfully with Woodward, although Coulter persisted in his complaint that "Woodward can't write" and only late in life came to acknowledge the accomplishments in this volume.[37]

For all that, the History of the South series presented a special kind of opportunity, one that might make Woodward very attractive to a number of campuses with major research facilities. The then-extant multivolume sectional history, *The South in the Building of the Nation,* was the product of the fine conservative scholarship of Hamilton, Ulrich Bonnell Phillips, Walter Lynwood Fleming, and others; dated in its facts and out-of-date in its ideological perspective, it needed a replacement, but that replacement had to be of top quality, so solid and so graceful was their synthesis. Woodward's volume was to cover the years 1877 to 1914, when these predecessors came to maturity, and to beat them at the task of chronicling their own era would be an accomplishment indeed. To seize that opportunity and to use it successfully, however, it seemed propitious to leave Gainesville and thus trade the security of the moment for the chance of eventual prominence. Whatever else, Woodward would never be able to devote the time and energy needed for this task while laboring under Tigert's system of the general-college staff; and despite the administrators' professed happiness with his work, he seemed fated for service at the introductory level of instruction for years to come. Nor was there any hope that history chairman Leake would permit him to work with the senior staff: a summer session of teaching New South history to high school teachers was as close as Woodward would get to that status. To compound these difficulties, Glenn Woodward was unable to adjust to the climate, her skin reacting unfavorably to the humidity and the vegetation of Florida. Without rancor but with studied determination, the Woodwards began looking for another home at another school.[38]

They found a fine one, the University of Virginia, attractive not only because of its quality but also because of its proximity to the major manuscript depositories of the National Archives in Washington. Glenn Rainey had already reported to him about the excellence of the William Chandler Papers, the archives' huge collection for the northern political and economic figure who played a role vital to the development of the New South Movement; and of course, the political saints and sinners of the era had left both official and personal records of their doings here. With all of its attractiveness, the position did have this drawback: the appointment was strictly a one-year replacement.[39] Abandoning the known quantity at Gainesville for the promise of opportunity at Charlottesville, the Woodwards made their move during America's Indian summer of 1939, when peace and prosperity were putatively to be wed, the golden days when world war was an affliction confined to the Poles and the depression seemed about to end.

On such an assignment, Woodward did not fret over finding or not finding a new group of friends, particularly since he still corresponded constantly and visited occasionally with Rainey, Carleton, and Dauer. Nor did he trouble himself over his teaching performance: though still not entrusted with southern history, he was no longer party to any schemes of interdisciplinary lecturing. Instead, he flung himself into the research available in the Alderman Library on campus and in nearby Washington. As often happens with historians, he made his strike of oil: the depository was big enough to sustain his production for most of his career, and he established, starting in 1939, what would be his life's work. After his year in Charlottesville, he would return to the same sources again and again, that is, the urban industrial figures and the resistance they spawned among intellectuals and among poor farmers. Using the frame of analysis built for the Phi Beta Kappa speech, he pushed along the writing, determined to deepen Beard's and Turner's profound insights into the sectional political economy. Life at the University of Virginia was thus everything he could hope for. Occasionally he did feel a "stuffiness" reminiscent of Emory, but when he did, as he wrote, "I lift up mine eyes to Monticello and reflect that these colonnades were not constructed on the proceeds of coca-cola stock." His students must have been lifting their eyes for inspiration, too, for he described his teaching as a "miserable job" despite having a provocative Beardian text by Curtis P. Nettles. But if students also looked away for a moment of Jeffersonian inspiration, they might well miss the lecturer, who escaped campus often to work in Washington. Once, on such a trip, he met and became friends with Hugo Black, the Alabamian recently appointed Supreme Court justice; it developed, as others would see soon enough, that the New Deal Democrat was fairly open-minded about racial issues and, even better, that Black and his family were enthusiastic readers of Woodward. Enthusiastic himself, Woodward told friends, "We ought to be damn glad he is where he is."[40]

But, of course, Black had a long-term appointment where he was and Woodward did not, however happy he was at the moment. He kept an eye out for another job and for what he really wanted, another research grant. Making the appropriate "bows and scrapes to the foundations" and obtaining help from men such as Bruce Bliven of the *New Republic,* Odum, Vance, Black, and others, he won a Rosenwald Fellowship and he found, as Frederick Jackson Turner himself would have willed it, a job in the Golden West, at Scripps College in Claremont, near Los Angeles. This time when the Woodwards moved, in 1940, the Indian summer was obviously ending even in the California clime, and it carried an undertaste of bitter winter. Writing to Rainey, Woodward could see no way for the United States to avoid involvement in the war, even as he could see no reason to join the fray. Unlike the young Woodward who once excused Stalin's excesses, he now detested the Georgian's regime; moreover, he continued to despise British and French colonialism in their decay, and he could thus find no real distinction between the injustice of Hitler's cause and the injustice of the imperialistic opposition. Not by any means a thoroughgoing pacifist, he would eventually change these 1940 views as Hitler came to threaten much more than the British Empire and as he came to know more about the nature of German wartime fascism.[41]

At the time of his move, he was apprehensive about other things more immediately threatening than the great international crisis; he was apprehensive instead about scholarship in this "California atmosphere since, as represented in their picture prospectus and described by real estate salesman's pen, the campus looks like an abandoned movie set representing the Garden of Allah." Still, this job certainly had its appealing aspects, for it gave him an initial semester's leave to use Rosenwald money in the East and then gave him two summers off to complete that research; and his chair in history and biography was endowed. The school's location also gave him access to the vast archival treasury of the Huntington Library, one hour's drive away; and if he tired of research, the deep-sea fishing and swimming in which he reveled were available to the west of the campus. In some ways, too, the school's location was doubly good for him, in the sense of being utterly removed from the South: while he missed the intimate contact with southern dissidents, he benefited from the perspective which great distance provided him. This has happened to many southern intellectuals who have left home physically but have then written much more convincingly about Dixie than before. Three decades later Mississippi essayist Willie Morris would describe this phenomenon, in which distance and difference produced less fondness than perspective, as "going north toward home"; and with Woodward the concept "west toward home" seemed to be at play, for he completed the bulk of *Origins of the New South* and *Reunion and Reaction* in his first years out there.[42]

During his first months of service at Scripps, Woodward pursued a rather dreamlike version of his own Indian summer: coming off his period of intensive search work in the Library of Congress and the National Archives, he fashioned a teaching schedule which left Tuesdays and Thursdays completely devoted to research and writing, and he fashioned a teaching style which made minimal demands on him for lesson preparation. Abandoning lectures, he built his courses around great books and relied on lively discussion of the big issues—in those days he was quite good at the Socratic method as long as the group was a small one—to move his classes along. The students were bright and, despite his apprehensions that their wealth and their climate would make them lethargic, as energetic as any he had encountered. Glenn Woodward flourished in this environment, and the two felt secure enough to bring a child into the world; Peter Vincent Woodward was born in February of 1943 with a future which seemed as vast and as golden as California itself. Perhaps the family's personal Indian summer really could go on and on; certainly that winter it still appeared so, for as ignorant armies clashed by night his Wednesdays were filled with students talking energetically about Vernon Louis Parrington's architectonics of class struggle and his Thursdays were spent pulling together the themes of his Phi Beta Kappa speech into a brilliant introduction to the History of the South volume. As he shared it with a few students and with a few correspondents, the focus of the thesis was sharpened: not only had the South been reduced to colonial economic status as a result of the Second American Revolution; but the entire nation had also relinquished its commitment to freedom and equality by giving up on Reconstruction. The "reunion" of 1877, brought about by a series of regional economic trades among the major politicos, was actually a major diplomatic compromise which redefined the United States as a republic founded on trusts and dedicated to the proposition that Negroes should not vote. The boldness of the thesis underscored again his creativity, and the massive spadework—he ultimately published *Reunion and Reaction* as a separate volume to unwind the intricacies of what he was saying in this one chapter—solidified his reputation for mastery of the primary sources in addition to reinforcing his renown for developing a provocative thesis.[43]

Still, this nonpareil artistry, this blending of search work and of interpretive sway, was soon subsumed under the crush of the international crisis, which he found deeply saddening in its meaninglessness. The felicitous schedule of pondering the South, 1880s, from California, 1940s, was burst apart by the pressures of world war. In early 1942 a dispute developed involving the academic rights of Fascists on the Scripps campus, and for one devoted to the scholarly search for the usable past, this controversy posed a very special kind of dilemma. A handful of Scripps professors were sympathetic to the Fascist cause, and a larger contingent, including Woodward, were then neutral concerning the war; but war fever was running high in the community, and the faculty ranks included several French academics recently exiled by the Vichy regime of occupied France. The French exiles were vocal and effective, and they enjoyed the support of the local American Legion in calling for the removal of the Nazi sympathizers from the campus. The threat to colleagues with Fascist views was a classic test of Woodward's commitment to the John Stuart Mill principles of tolerance for the expression of the minority view, and Woodward came down with all his weight on the side of the prerogative of academic freedom. No reasonable person could believe that a Nazi scholar was going to contribute meaningfully to the quest for the usable past, and in fact, the youthful covenant with meaningful scholarship was here at odds with Woodward's evolving sense of the freedom necessary to the academy. The dilemma was simplified, however, by the sweeping nature of the indictment against the Germans: in words which echoed the excesses of World War I, the Francophiles spoke against *everything* German, including the language, the art, the philosophy. The Scripps administration was in no mood to resist the American Legion, and soon "President Jogrea precipitated a crisis" by trying to remove the Germanic scholars and the supporters of academic privilege.[44]

As Woodward interpreted Jogrea's actions and words, "he was bent on firing us if we did not fire him first." And once again, repeating acts taken at Henderson-Brown and at Georgia Tech, Woodward thrust himself into the maelstrom of an administrative and faculty power struggle in which issues of academic freedom and of academic standards were paramount. The opinion that this soft-spoken man is actually at heart "a controversialist" who thrives on such disputes is strongly upheld by these incidents, about which he has spoken only occasionally since they happened. Through the summer the disputes roiled, ending with the resignation of the college president, the retreat of the legionnaires, the discrediting of the Gallicists, and the reaffirmation of academic privilege. By October, Woodward found "the fog lifted," and he was back to simpler tasks, paying more attention to his students by providing them real instruction, and still writing insightfully about the distant South; more, he was promoted to associate professor and generally given considerable encouragement in his scholarship.[45]

But if the fog of oppression had lifted, the Indian summer was completely gone too: the war was on in earnest, and Woodward, although now a father and at thirty-five a little long in the teeth for combat duty, was marked for the draft. Moreover, the Gallicist threats to campus freedom of expression were as nothing compared to the forced relocation and detention of thousands of Japanese, and

even some Chinese, which began in California at this time. Franklin
Roosevelt had succumbed to the dangerous combination wrought
by the country's jingoism of the moment and the region's long-
simmering prejudice against Orientals; federal policy had established detention camps according to national and racial identities,
and the government had in fact seized property and destroyed careers as racism marched haughtily under the banner of the Four
Freedoms. Gov. Earl Warren enthusiastically supported the national
policy and did nothing to indicate that he would one day be associated with the culmination of a judicial revolution in civil rights for
minorities. Woodward's old adviser and confidante Howard Beale
came out west to work with displaced and dispossessed Oriental
families; and while Woodward did none of this kind of counseling
and assisting, he signed petitions which protested the policies of
confiscation, relocation, and detention, and he involved himself in
public demonstrations against these actions.[46]

Mostly what he did was to buy time from the draft, maneuvering
through temporary deferments while awaiting an opening with navy
intelligence. For a term during school year 1942–43, he taught
American history to two hundred army meteorology cadets sta-
tioned at Pomona; but finally, in 1943, he received a commission
with the Office of Naval Intelligence and the Naval Office of Public
Information and was off to Washington, D.C., to serve the war
effort. His distrust of the simplistic moralism of the Four Freedoms
was undiminished even as he came to concede the necessity of the
conflict against fascism. Nor was he unaffected by his own ambivalent role in the day's action: as a classmate from Chapel Hill put
it, "Vann *wrote* about the battle of Leyte Gulf; others were *in* the
battle of Leyte Gulf!"[47]

Yet his experiences of intelligence work in the war were in many
ways rewarding, not least because of the way his historian's mind
was challenged to discern meaningful patterns in the complexities
of such a war, and especially because the degree of this challenge was
aggravated by the technological revolutions in warfare and in the
study of warfare. Two of his studies of battles—*Kolombangara and
Vella Lavella* and *The Bougainville Landing and the Battle of Empress
Augusta Bay*—were circulated strictly in-house by the navy. In producing them, albeit as an anonymous bureaucrat-scholar, he found
that "the strenuous exercise of mind in a completely strange and

highly technical field of history induced a new respect for precise and reliable information, exact timing, and the infinite complexity of events with large consequences." Even as the exigencies of his new tasks forced new expertise, however, he saw that his historian's tools were also quite useful, for despite the new weaponry and the new rules and the new rhetoric, "the historian soon found himself dealing with such familiar categories as personality, accident, luck, ambition, stupidity, and human error, even national character— factors that often proved more important than weaponry, fire power, and numbers. . . . it was a gratifying part of the naval experience to learn that the historian, with his old-fashioned compass, could find his way in deep blue waters—surface, subsurface, or air—as well as on dry land."[48]

Another result of his military tenure was a publication, *The Battle for Leyte Gulf,* which uniquely encapsulated his attitudes and experiences. Dedicated to his son, Peter, it fairly vibrated with the descriptive force produced by one who had been there, "in the drink" of the Philippines, during the largest and most calamitous naval engagement in history. Of course, he had not been there, any more than he had taken the stump with Tom Watson. It was rather that marvelous faculty of his imagination, in combination with painstaking research, which allowed him to write in this way:

Radar search, air reconnaissance, and radio communication have not eliminated from naval warfare two of its oldest characteristics—confusion and misapprehension. Both were present on each side of the Battle off Cape Engano. Our overestimation of the enemy force, both its gun power and air power, is matched by the enemy's underestimation of our strength. A few of the numerous ironies of the Third Fleet strategy have been suggested. The most ironical plight, however, was that in which Admiral Ozawa found himself. For while his luring mission had succeeded beyond his expectation, the wholesale sacrifice of ships which it entailed proved in the end to have been futile for the simple reason that he was completely unable to put through . . . the report that he had succeeded in diverting the Third Fleet northward. It is not known why a sixteenth-century Spaniard should have named as he did the obscure point of land from which this battle took its name.

Engano is a Spanish word translated variously as "mistake, deception, lure, hoax, misunderstanding, misapprehension, misconception"—in about that order of preference.[49]

And thus did he explain the story, emphasizing the twists and turns of fate and circumstances which made "the failure of the Japanese plan seem less remarkable than the relatively narrow margin by which it missed success." Woodward's way of reading history in *The Battle for Leyte Gulf* is markedly different from his procedures and practices in *Tom Watson*. The difference is a richer sense of irony, one which he would develop even further over the next years until the sword of ironic interpretation would become fully as important a weapon in his arsenal as the aegis of Beardian economics. In California and in the District of Columbia, he renewed acquaintance with Robert Penn Warren; as the years slipped by in the midst of the chaos of war, the two became fast friends, though neither has any clear sense of when they moved from being respectful and polite adversaries to intimate comradeship. Warren, no longer a Fugitive save in the brilliance of his style, was becoming quite liberal on racial issues and was coming to develop themes about time and sin and the intertwining inevitability of evil and necessity of struggling to resist that evil. These thematic developments in his thought deeply influenced Woodward, for Warren was now really probing history itself. Moreover, Warren the poet began to visit archival repositories and to "do history" even as Woodward the historian began to deepen his already profound knowledge of literature; between them, they created a conversation, both public and private, which was dynamic indeed. Finally, and also possibly owing to Warren's influence, it was during these last two years of the war that Woodward began to read William Faulkner with real comprehension and began to peel back the onion-skin layers of meaning in the novels, especially *Absalom, Absalom!* with its Woodwardian description of déclassé aristocrats and peasants, the enduring but dispossessed Negroes, the dominance of a new order of business, and the decadence of the ruined plantation. By the end of the world war, Woodward had come to a new and much deeper level of understanding about the South at the end of its Civil War.[50]

Mustered out, he hurried home to be with his little family, returning also to the kind of activist and committed scholarship with which he intended to help improve a world so ill served by militarist solutions. The writing and the research moved smoothly now, and the work he had already done in combination with the profession's expectations of the work to come vaulted him into national prominence with all historians, not just historians of the South. This was all the more remarkable, for the postwar historiography led by Richard Hofstadter and Louis Hartz was taking leave of Progressivism, eschewing class analysis and themes of conflict for what they termed a "consensus" interpretation of the American past. Beard himself was out of favor, partly because his last book belabored an untenable "devil thesis" for FDR's conduct of the war, but more especially because the world war created a distinct generational break between historians, with a new cadre in active rebellion against the giants of Progressivism. Yet Woodward's historiography remained unabashedly a class analysis of conflict in the shrewd, clever, and pragmatic fashion of Beard and Turner at their best, though now of course it was modulated by a new tone of irony.

Material reward came along with the respect of historians, and in 1946 he received a call to Johns Hopkins University in Baltimore: at last, here was the chance to teach southern history full time, with the nation's archives close to hand. The appointment in Baltimore would produce some remarkable episodes in his remarkable life; but above all else, it would produce the era of his boldest, and his best, scholarship.

6

Questions of Provenance

A Theory of
Conflict for the Age
of Consensus,
1946–1954

Baltimore has always been a border area as well as a transportation and communication nexus for the regions of the country which conjoin there. Not really northern in attitude or appearance, it still profits more from commerce and trade with Philadelphia, Boston, and New York than with Norfolk and Richmond and points south. Not really southern, it still betrays its kinship with the South in gestures and accents which jar the mentality of the northern urbanite. However, there are other anomalies in its collective character besides those produced by its border status: much of the city is architecturally significant, for men there have built well, and the Chesapeake Bay is lovely proof that other forces can also build well; but a great deal of the city is ugly, for men there have also built poorly, and the bay has been much victimized by the abuses of those who plan and execute poorly. Moreover, human history has played tricks on the city, which was named for nobility and which consequently finds the coat of arms of its Calverts' lordship on the flag of the state of Maryland, a situation that implies aristocracy and noblesse oblige; but Baltimore has always been as well a workingman's city, with a large labor movement and the class consciousness and political activity concomitant with that identity. It has thus taken a stance which is sui generis, at once reflective of competing traditions and scornful of both traditions. How right, then, that a man who was developing irony as an interpretive tool as well as a style should live here to explain what he would later call the "contrapuntal nature" of northern and southern attitudes and relationships.

I

When the Woodwards arrived in 1946, it was not only the citizens of Baltimore who were unsure, and a bit uneasy, about where they fitted in the scheme of things. The nation's historians, responding in part to a palpable mood among their students and among their readers, were about to rewrite American history and, in that process, fundamentally alter our definitions of the past. But the reasons for this change in historiography lay deeper than the fact that historians were writing and teaching what audiences wanted, vital as that ambience is to the process of reinterpretation; the historians themselves were new, constituting another group far removed from the great Progressives who dominated thought before World War II. This was because the lines of generations among historians, which are usually marked somewhat arbitrarily and even haphazardly, were especially clear after the war had dramatically slowed and in some cases even stopped the main efforts of historical investigations for a number of years. Stepping into this vacuum, these new historians, heirs as they were to full-blown theories of cultural relativism, regarded the moralistic historiography of the Progressives as quaint at best and nonsense at worst; as one of them put it, no one could stand to read Vernon Louis Parrington anymore.[1]

But it was not only the moralism of the Progressives which offended them: the very notions of class conflict, of materialistic dynamics, of the primacy of economics, all of which had still made sense during the early years of the New Deal, now seemed exaggerated, blown far out of proportion. *Consensus* was what these historians felt as they reinterpreted American history; they discerned a fairly smooth plane of continuity from one era to the next in a culture where only a few ideas affected politics, and where these ideas always stressed harmony and conciliation around what Richard Hofstadter labeled "a central faith" in the "sanctity of property." This "faith" was a "mute organic" one which evolved, Hofstadter said and others agreed, in a republic whose entire history was comprised of the industrial revolution. Going farther, Hofstadter observed that rhetorical conflict was "the nature of politics," but the real conflict was personal and occasionally geographical: as far as he could see, ideas of genuine dissent were entertained only by a handful of intellectuals far from the mainstream of politics. *In* the mainstream, the politicians "differ, sometimes bitterly, over current issues, but they also share a general framework of ideas which makes it possible for them to co-operate when the campaigns are over"; despite genuine material interests which are at stake, the same ideas, "which already have wide acceptance, will be adapted again and again with slight changes to new conditions," producing "shared convictions" which make the major political parties "indistinguishable."[2]

That these ideas should emerge after the war was certainly ironic, for the postbellum era was itself hardly one of continuity with its predecessors, and it was even less a time of national consensus. In fact, one suspects that the "consensus historians" were seeking in the past what they could not find in their own day; and in particular, the cold war seems the likely culprit for instilling this drive to find a placid and calming oneness in our culture and in our politics. This surely was an irony with a sharp, even a wounding, edge, for the domestic politics of the cold war, with its excesses of "scoundrel time"[3] probings into the actions, words, and even thoughts of American intellectuals, were intensely resented and stoutly resisted by the consensus historians and scholars of other disciplines, many of whom met at Columbia University to discuss a responsible course of defense from the assaults of the witch-hunter cold warriors.

Joseph McCarthy, Martin Dies, Richard Nixon, and the rest of the assailants had no regard for the pursuit of ideas and very little regard for civil liberties, and thus they were rightly castigated by Hofstadter for the "paranoid style" of their "anti-intellectualism." Of course, no one could accuse the consensus thinkers of either fault, but the source of their attitudes also seems to lie with the overwhelming challenge posed by the new military threat, suddenly aggravated by atomic weaponry, of Soviet communism, a development coterminous with the appearance of Communist revolutions around the world. Facing such a manifold challenge to fundamental values, to strategic plans, and to economic interests, many understandably sought a common front of opposition both to Soviet adventurism and to any Communist movements which might ultimately ally themselves with the Russians. That aspect of "containment policy" and the "nuclear umbrella," while in retrospect exaggerated, was at least logically consistent with American self-interest in foreign policy. But when this common front was moved deep inside the purely domestic activities of Americans, the cold war became an ugly and irrational overreaction to outside threats as well as an excuse to "contain" substantive debates about reforming at home by hiding underneath the anti-Communist "umbrella." Where some politicians attempted to legislate sameness by declaring what was legitimately American and what "un-American," the new historians honorably followed the rules of rational debate according to John Stuart Mill, trying to make their points by persuasion and not by coercion.[4]

Hardly venal, this new history simply could not conceive of radicalism in the context of American politics, since the most influential of its practitioners, Hofstadter, spoke of conflict occurring *within* rather than *between* classes. Defining political radicalism thus strictly in terms of class conflict was a remarkably Marxian approach (and Hofstadter in his youth had been very interested in Marxian ideas and evidently had been involved in some dissident politics), but the result was rather peculiar: with no political conflict of substance to explore, the consensus historians turned away from class analysis of economic rivalries to examine with more care the cultural context of the American mentality as it developed over the years. When they did so, their work was initially valuable, as well as prolific, for Progressives had indeed overdone economic issues at the expense of ideas not easily analyzed—or even incorrectly analyzed—by the "dismal science." Hence Perry Miller provided a compelling account of the Puritan mind in colonial New England; it was an account far richer in detail, and probably truer to the actual state of mind, than Parrington's exciting, but rather two-dimensional, description of the same era. Nowhere was this difference more obvious than in the way the two historians treated

Roger Williams: for Parrington, the founder of Rhode Island was a proto-Jeffersonian laying the foundations for a new republic freed of the religionists' laws and practices, which not only repressed thought but also kept the lower classes and the outsiders tucked into their appointed niches; by contradistinction, Miller held that Williams, far from showing Jefferson the way, was actually so intensely a spiritualist that he seized the concept of freedom of worship *in order to ensure the development* of a culture more dedicated to a variant of Puritanism than was the Massachusetts Bay, as well as a culture caught up in beliefs which Jefferson would have derided as a distracting chiliasm. Atheist that he was, Miller took the Puritan mind seriously enough to show where its ideas came from, how they were transformed by the wilderness, how they were adapted to cities and to commerce; and the resultant images were fetching, for he accomplished the incredible feat of making even Cotton Mather seem human. More especially, this kind of intensive and imaginative recreation of another era's way of thinking set the standard for intellectual history in America for at least the next two decades.[5]

In the same way, Hofstadter examined his own Progressive forebears, both those who taught him his history and those who went before the historians to make the Progressive history. By reading widely, and shrewdly, in other disciplines, especially social psychology and theories of collective behavior, Hofstadter could apply new techniques to old questions of motivation in the Gilded Age of the turn of the century. The result for the study of the northeastern urban aristocracy in the period 1877 to 1900 was a highly sensitive portraiture of men and women fearful of losing their place, or status, in the rapidly changing society and hence driven by their anxiety sometimes to despair but more often to a reform politics which ultimately met the challenges of industrialism and immigration with a rational, equitable, and successful program. Withal, Hofstadter was convincing as he argued the case for a politics of moderation and gradualism presided over by personalities steeped in the tradition of Anglo-American compromise. Not only was this a reassuring description of Teddy Roosevelt and his allies, but it was also comforting to the reader in the 1950s who regretted the espousal of radical programs of reform in the country's political left wing and who at the same time regretted the radical turn toward the right represented by extreme anticommunism. Although Hofstadter had too much good sense to say it explicitly, the suggestion was there: this, too, shall pass, for the political genius of American culture has always overcome radicalism in the long run.[6]

The mention of genius in such a context has inevitably recalled the most extreme of those who decried extremism: Daniel Joseph Boorstin, who, unlike Hofstadter or Miller, chose to lead cheers for his kind of consensus "heroes" and against what he saw as conflict-producing, worrisome "villains." When he wrote of the colonial culture that "America lacked enthusiasm for the man of profound, detached and 'pure' intelligence," he was making one kind of observation; but when he went on to say that "a wholesale fear of the exotic and the hieratic, of the power of the mind to raise any man above men, inspired American faith in the 'divine average,' a faith which would not have grown without American opportunity," he began to reveal his direction. And when he had to treat of the great Quaker intellectuals in Penn's woods—describing "the Quaker preoccupation with the purity of their own souls," and their "inward" vision which turned from community toward the "quest for martyrdom," especially manifest when they "refused to fight attacking Indians" and when they willingly "martyred" themselves to the immigrating non-Quakers, who often persecuted them on their own lands—he sounded his themes most clearly: the denigration of the individuated intellect, the contempt for the principled action of dissidence, and the refusal to concede the validity of any ideal. Furthermore, he delighted in the "culture without a capital," in the "decline of the book," in the "Puritan Conservatism," and above all else, in the "undifferentiated man" produced by the "higher education in place of the higher learning"; and while each witty phrase was thought-provoking, the overall effect of Boorstin's *Americans* was most unfortunate, for it glorified the sameness of the practical, marketplace community, and when his narrative simply could not ignore dissidence, such as that of the Pennsylvania Quakers or the Georgia antislavery experiment, it dealt with such experiences in a studiedly officious, disingenuously nasty manner. Where many consensus historians obviously thought that there were uniformity and homogeneity in the American culture, Boorstin went a step farther, celebrating sameness and castigating difference.[7]

Another of the great consensus figures, one who came to symbolize for Woodward the worst of the historiography's trends, was

Louis Hartz. Essentially Hartz, in a way oddly reflective of Wood-ward himself, was an iconoclast who enjoyed taking aim, with the most wittily engaging of styles, at some of the overblown images created by his Progressive predecessors. Especially devastating when he approached the antebellum "southern enlightenment," he de-clared the whole episode to be a non-event; and generally, he shrank American thought down to a few aphorisms from John Locke about property, happiness, and compromise. Hardly as malicious as Boor-stin, Hartz wrote with humor, he took European ideas seriously, and he adopted a cross-cultural vantage point for the study of ideas (thereby ironically forecasting, albeit by thirteen years, one of Woodward's own intellectual directions). Hartz's injection of humor into studies of American culture, along with his insistence on a comparative analysis within a broad-gauged perspective, did much to enliven historians' interpretations and reinterpretations after the war; but Woodward was never able to credit him with these achieve-ments and, unfortunately, was never able to benefit from any di-alogue with Hartz, despite his demonstrated ability to learn from Boorstin and Hofstadter.[8]

In any case, Woodward's unhappiness with consensus in general and with Hartz in particular was almost sui generis in the late 1940s and the 1950s, for these figures, Hofstadter, Miller, Hartz, and Boorstin, then rode the crest of enthusiasm for their work, dominating the graduate programs at Columbia, Harvard, and Chi-cago, where they taught, and at most major research centers, where they were read avidly. Nor was there any gainsaying the vitality of their contributions, for ever since, even those who have disagreed with them have surely benefited from their techniques, from Mil-ler's intense dissection of the mind, Hofstadter's and Boorstin's in-terdisciplinary syntheses, and Hartz's trans-Atlantic perspective. On the other hand, none of them was particularly insightful about the South or the Midwest, and in fact, the farther one moved from the intellectual centers of the northeastern corridor, the less useful they were. Unfortunately, their relatively light research and writing about the rest of the country did not affect their willingness to describe the rest of the country, and even more unfortunately, through much of the era, few questioned their capacity to speak authoritatively.[9]

This was the national milieu when Woodward arrived at Johns

Hopkins University (JHU) to begin training his own graduate students; and as his publications gained a countrywide audience, this was the milieu in which his books and essays were read and reread. Thus there would be much close questioning by historians about the style of history that he wrote, in which class conflict, racial disharmony, material deprivation, and the aspirations of the disadvantaged were all taken seriously. This questioning he reveled in, preparing for conference and symposium debates by establishing on his own campus dissertation discussion seminars known to participants as "head-cracking sessions." These occasional sessions—ostensibly providing a chance for young scholars to try out their ideas before completing their dissertations—in actuality pitted the Woodward graduate students against one another in extempore debates by turns rancorous and good-natured, but always lively. Some of the exchanges were memorable for the students, and all of them were memorable for Woodward, who encouraged his charges to defend themselves against all comers by preparing ahead of time through meticulous primary research and extensive review of secondary sources. Even, and especially, in the so-called extempore context of debate, Woodward insisted that a scholar who was serious about his or her business would be ready for anything. He consciously set himself up as an example, courteous and witty in defense of his own work, but also nearly invincible, demonstrating his other real millieu—besides the obvious fit of his personality to the written forms of argument—in groups of fewer then twenty where each member of the group was already apprised of the lines of debate on some given issue.[10]

Despite the rather formidable reputation of the discussion seminars and despite his own developing reputation as an extremely demanding graduate adviser, Woodward began to attract some of the very finest young talents in the country to study with him at JHU. Although the Yale students who would work with him after 1961 were, generally, more talented—much of the difference, he always suspected, had to do with the lavish scholarship funds available at New Haven in the 1960s—he has always regarded the JHU students, as a group, as his best; and certainly he felt a special kind of kinship with these men and women who were training along with him for the grand assault on the consensus historiography. At the same time, Glenn Woodward was likely happier than at any other time in her married life, still enjoying fine health and positively in love with the neighborhood where they lived in Baltimore; and Peter was growing in all senses, an intrepid outdoorsman, steady athlete, and capable student; not a great sports star, nor a brilliant scholar, but obviously gifted and with an infectious energy and optimism about each thing that he did. The Woodwards, then, had found their own niche: the place and the people around them all seemed right. For all of his iconoclasm, Woodward was actually intensely loyal to certain institutions, and especially to this one, where his ideas took center stage with the potentiality for a national audience.[11]

Perhaps surprisingly, his "older" history held up well not only under this era's scrutiny at JHU but under scrutiny in environs far from his home base; and in fact, Woodward deserves a fair share of the credit for the supplanting of consensus history in the 1960s. But if Woodward was beginning to prevail in choosing appropriate questions—namely, what kinds of things should historians ask?—there persisted doubts about the answers he was finding. Even more than the Tom Watson biography, his *Origins of the New South,* from its appearance in 1951, has established the order of debate for southern topics, and thus an assessment of the state of historians' discussions about a number of controversies which Woodward raised seems merited.

I I

Most persisting as a debating point has been Woodward's insistence that the Civil War produced a sharp break with the past, tumbling down a majority of those who had stood in prominent places, and fully as significant, that those who succeeded in regaining power and wealth were transformed by the process. Thus, when Wade Hampton moved to the city of Columbia and began to focus on railroads and factories, he was then a man different in kind from the planter who had focused his energies on Millwood and Linwood. In the course of his own life, Woodward had seen this, for it was one of the "deep reciprocities" between experiences and belief. First, in Arkadelphia, the idealism and aristocracy of the antebellum days were preserved in monumental, that is, *dead,* fashion in a Greek

Revival planter's house which presided over a view of a banker's late-Victorian house that was pragmatic and middle class—and *alive.* Later, in Atlanta, he had marked the Old South families of Brown and Calhoun, whom he found busily constructing railroads and banks, as well as constructing a political machinery for the new industries. Moving northward in the Piedmont, there were the Clemson and the Calhoun families, leaving a bequest for a state college in South Carolina, but the resultant Clemson A&M was by its very name as much mechanical as agricultural; and even the agricultural training was studiedly middle class, a captive farming in service to regnant industry. Finally, there was Durham, a railway crossroads for planters and farmers before the war and afterward a thriving city and host to the Duke family tobacco-manufacturing and -sales concerns. In each case the mighty plantation had fallen, even if the planters themselves, or their families, endured by becoming industrialists or financiers.

Like so much else, Woodward owed the basic concept of a Second American Revolution to Beard; and in fact, the notion was so deeply ingrained in his mind that he realized he was not even crediting Beard in the footnotes, an omission he more than compensated for in his introduction to *Reunion and Reaction,* which spelled out the details of the argument encapsulated in the first chapter of *Origins.*[12] But there were differences in the conclusions which Beard and his "student" reached after they made the class analysis of the revolution. For one, Beard's antebellum planters were rather Parringtonian, that is, followers of Jefferson and more physiocratic than aristocratic; by contrast, Woodward's planters by the 1850s were a long way from the departed philosophe of Monticello and had become consciously aristocratic, proud of their elitism. Thus Woodward's aristocrats fell a greater economic distance after Appomattox Court House than did Beard's. For another, Woodward's postbellum southern leaders were clearly second-class citizens in the republic, bit players directed by northerners; Beard may have implied as much in his *Rise of American Civilization,* but he certainly had not developed this conclusion as extensively as Woodward did. Finally, there are the Faulknerian influences, and probably something of Penn Warren as well: these postbellum leaders had done more than change roles—they were soul-drained. Some, like Jason Compson, became thuggish capitalist automatons, with little more sentience than zombies; others, far more sensitive, like Quentin Compson, were rendered morally impotent by their awareness of their sin, fall, and subsequent inability to fit in the new world. According to Woodward, then, the old aristocracy was removed from leadership, most dead or déclassé, the remainder warped beyond recognition, even beyond self-recognition.

Most historians of the South had seen it quite otherwise: they had noted the reappearance of Confederate figures such as Hampton or Lucius Quintus Cincinnatus Lamar in positions of leadership after Reconstruction. Also many had observed the celebration in the 1890s of the Lost Cause—a celebration in which the names of Jefferson Davis and Joseph Johnston enjoyed respect and even affection, in contradistinction to the pillorying which they endured during the years of their actual service—and thus had concluded that antebellum values continued to hold sway. Ulrich Bonnell Phillips in 1929 had insisted on this continuity, claiming that a white will to dominate, a "central theme," linked up southerners on either side of the Civil War interregnum; and his research was so thorough, his writing so felicitous, and his students so numerous and influential that while he died in 1934, his depiction of a continuous South remained in the 1950s almost an academic commonplace. More, Phillips in his later writing had discarded many of the Progressive assumptions of his training to focus instead on social motivation, that is, genteel racism; and this made Phillips's story of continuity appealing to the consensus era which preferred social to economic analysis, even as it made him repellant to the rapidly growing civil rights movement. [13]

To Phillips's work could be added the studies by Broadus Mitchell and George Sinclair Mitchell which buttressed this concept, ironically with the Progressive tool of economic analysis. But in 1939 came the most dramatic statement of the continuous South, from Wilbur J. Cash, whose *cri de coeur, The Mind of the South,* among many other things left an unforgettable image of captains of artillery and cavalry who became New South captains of industry, and saw both eras as dedicated to a stifling and antiintellectual racism, sexual chauvinism, and aristocratic class tyranny. Cash's message, in stirring and affecting prose, appealed to those who felt that the South could never reform itself; and while Phillips appealed to apologists for segregation, Cash appealed to radicals who proclaimed the South hopelessly reactionary. This conclusion was reinforced by Cash's subsequent suicide, which to many a mind was a case of life imitating art, but which to other minds was the reification of the South's intellectual self-destruction.[14]

In the teeth of Cash's life and thought and of Phillips's scholarship, Woodward never entirely won the day in the 1950s and the 1960s on this issue; and in the 1970s, Carl Degler, Jay Mandle, Dwight Billings, and Jonathan Wiener have all made much the same point in major presentations and books, while the eminent historian David Herbert Donald has weighed in with a very public approval of Cash's version of the South, and a very public disapproval of Woodward's. To some degree, unfortunately, all of these historians have talked past each other by setting up and then demolishing straw-man caricatures of the opposition. For instance, Phillips both participated in and welcomed the appearance of the New South industrialization, the railroad financing, the growth of cities, and a modern bourgeois mentality, most of which Woodward disliked, but all of which certainly constituted the elements of the Second American Revolution. Phillips's central theme, of course, was racial and not economic, and Woodward should not have blurred the distinction: to disprove Phillips's theme or Degler's, Woodward needed to deal directly with the issue of racial attitudes—and this he would attempt to do in future years by examining the cultural institutions of Jim Crow segregation.[15]

If the racial aspect of continuity is laid aside for address later, then one can intelligibly pick up the threads of the issues involved in the continuity or discontinuity of economic institutions and of sociopolitical elites. Most provocative of recent interpreters of the institutional dynamics has been Wiener, who adapted Barrington Moore's concept of the "Prussian Road" to industrial development in an effort to show that the plantation remained dominant by subsuming the new manufacturing businesses and, concomitantly, that the planter elite maintained command by presiding over the economic transformation, by directing the new factories, by orchestrating the development and extension of credit at bank and banklike institutions, and by controlling the lines of communication and transportation so that the infrastructure of roads served the planter-owned factories in the countryside and in the little towns rather than serving the smaller number of more classically bourgeois factories of the cities. [16]

The analogy with Prussia seems more than a bit strained, since the Prussian story is one of a powerful agrarian elite in the process of uniting the regions of German-speaking peoples into a nation and also in the process of sweeping its way to a stunning military defeat of the French, and furthermore, since the Prussians had to contend with a powerful and well-organized labor class which was actually stronger than the still-emerging middle class. By contrast with this Prussian power, the southern postbellum planters seem a poor lot: the elite, victim of crushing military defeat inside its own borders, was hardly capable of sweeping to victory over another nation and certainly did not displace much water in the national domestic politics; and the South's weakly organized laboring class, divided by racial antagonisms and frequently the object of vicious purges directed by the bourgeois managerial elite, scarcely constituted a threat to the emerging southern middle class. On the other hand, if the historical particularities of experience are ignored, then Wiener has made a point sociologically: the planters, at least in the Alabama counties he has studied, do seem to have been the same kinds of men as their antebellum forerunners, and they did exercise remarkable control over the processes of industrial growth and development in their region. [17]

Another recent study, by Woodward's student David Carlton, of his native South Carolina Piedmont, has indicated quite the reverse: in the upcountry textile communities, Carlton has found an essentially new class of men rising to business leadership, that is, both a new elite of textile entrepreneurs and a new institution, the textile factory, and neither elite nor institution is beholden to planter or to plantation. Given what Odum and Vance have demonstrated about regional diversity, it could be that Carlton has taken the measure of Piedmont South Carolina and that Wiener has done the same for a part of Alabama; and this could well imply that nothing can be known substantively about the persistence of institutions or about the endurance of elites until more of the richly variegated regions of Dixie have been examined in detail. [18]

There has developed, however, still another level of meaning for this debate, one that can best be described as cultural and can be characterized by study of the attitudes toward society, rather than by close study of the institutions or of the elites. At this level, Carl Degler has discussed in a meaningful way an intricate and thick web of values and beliefs which have vouchsafed to southerners a self-conscious sense of *place over time:* and this has been both a geographic sense of specific identity with a place in the region and a hierarchic sense of role and duty endowing a place for each individual in society. Building on the work of the Annales School created by Marc Leopold Benjamin Bloch and maintained by Leroi Ladurie, Degler has suggested that the *durée* of such regionally distinctive cultural attitudes was essentially unbroken, and perhaps not even bent, by the Civil War. In a related fashion, James Charles Cobb has examined the attitudes toward industrialization and toward modern capitalism and has found a curiously illiberal and even "backward" response to the challenges of economic development; for Cobb this backwardness—attributed by Aleksandr Gerschenkron to persisting agrarian and elitist values in relatively underdeveloped areas which have yet to realize the potentiality of industrial growth—could be traced to the plantation system, which had effected traditions of slow growth, low wages, a repressive social order, and a weak and "unprogressive" middle class. In that sense, Cobb's thesis has been well supported by the work of Jay Mandle, who has demonstrated that the persisting availability of surplus labor has prevented both the growth of a strong labor class and the growth of innovative entrepreneurial use of capital and machine resources, since the "rational" incentive would always be to rely on the low-priced labor rather than bearing the initially high costs of other resources—this, of course, an obvious birthright of the slave system. [19] By this point, given the impressive, though widely diverging, work of Cobb, Degler, Wiener, Billings, Mandle, and others, one could begin to regret the dominance of Woodward's questions about continuity and discontinuity because of the way he phrased them: perhaps Woodward's dramatic language in the first statement of his thesis and, subsequently, in his defenses of his work has created a falsely bipolar debate in which scholars feel compelled to answer either/or questions; perhaps some future, more fruitful, debate could center on the question of a gradual evolution in economic development, one whose most dramatic element is the extreme regional poverty brought largely by the self-induced destruction of the planter elite which insisted on fighting the Civil War.

Whatever historians eventually conclude about institutions, elites, and economic development, there remains a different kind of cultural question about the lingering southern attachment to the Lost Cause. Woodward originally dismissed it as a combination of hypocrisy and sentimentality, implying that the celebration of the old plantation was essentially diversionary noise to draw attention away from what the new elite was really doing, which was building factories, laying rail lines, and developing urban economics to serve new markets; the few industrialists or bankers who used such language sincerely were deluding themselves. Thus he characterized the situation in his speech in Florida, and while the *Origins* description of the phenomena is far more subtle and gentle, there seems to be no serious consideration of the possibility that large numbers of intelligent and honorable people actually believed, and believed intensely, in the values rather awkwardly encompassed as the Lost Cause. Although Woodward was insightful about the transformation of leaders and about the new directions of their economic policy, his treatment of the ideas of these new leaders was far less satisfactory. In 1970 Paul Gaston slipped this Gordian knot with *The New South Creed,* a handsomely turned essay which demonstrated that the New South leaders consciously seized on the plantation values to legitimize what Woodward said they were doing; in particular, they appealed to existing racism as well as cavalier charm to validate their claims to continuity with the honored past. Perhaps this was a kind of self-delusion, but if so, it lay at a level far deeper than Woodward acknowledged. It was indeed, as Woodward said, a rationale for actions they would have taken in any case, but he had underestimated the effort and the will which went into that rationalization as he also underestimated the effort and the will which went into speaking and hearing the rationale. As Gaston caught it perfectly with his phrase, this was a *creed*—hardly one that he liked any more than did Woodward, but all the same a sincere statement of beliefs which justified actions. Actually, as Sheldon Hackney has shown, Gaston ultimately reinforced Woodward's contention of discontinuity in leadership, roles, and modes of operating, because it is that break with past authority which necessitates the very quest for legitimacy which Gaston has so gracefully chronicled.[20]

Whether these leaders were new or old, sincere in their professions or Catoists, a set of significant questions involves the way in which they functioned in national concert with a postbellum northern leadership which was new in its own composition and new in economic directions it was taking. *Origins* assessed three major campaigns, all closely related, which these southern leaders undertook: the Compromise of 1877, which ended Reconstruction and reestablished home rule; the political response to economic dislocation and poverty wrought by monetary deflation and agricultural recession in the 1880s; and the Jim Crow movement for racial segregation after 1894. In each case Woodward was the iconoclast stripping away what he regarded as the dangerous delusions in the existing regional galleries where apologists had reverentially gathered to remember the services of Hampton and Lamar and Charles Brantley Aycock and Hoke Smith. Furthermore, in each case his iconoclasm also affected the national galleries where stood images of Rutherford B. Hayes, Grover Cleveland, William McKinley, and Theodore Roosevelt, all now implicated for cooperating to some degree with schemes bringing injustice to the emancipated blacks and to the rural poor of both races. And in each case, the day's prevailing consensus interpretations, few of which had intended to establish any marble statuary, were also damaged by Woodward's icon smashing.

The first of these campaigns, the Reconstruction-ending compromise, was a discovery of Woodward's, one about which he was "enormously excited" when he first made it and one which still excites discussion among historians. Prior to *Origins,* the end of Reconstruction had been described memorably by Paul Buck in *Road to Reunion* as a fairly simple, relatively painless process of achieving again a harmonious union, which had been broken apart by mistakes. The South had come to its senses by recognizing the wrongness of slavery, and the North, in a nearly perfect counterbalance, had recognized the wrongness of its own Reconstruction experiment in social engineering. Each section, by owning up to its errors, was able to forgive the other and reunite in 1877, with the former Confederacy accepting the former Union general Rutherford B. Hayes as its president, and the Grand Army of the Republic accepting conservative native whites as the home-rule governors and assemblymen of the South. Buck's story was charmingly told, beginning with a nicely counterpoised description of a Confederate veteran and a Federal veteran at war's end; moreover, it became an especially appealing message for the consensus mentality of most historians in the 1950s, for it said that the one great, "atypical" conflict in American history had been resolved quickly because both sides so deeply regretted the hostilities that they subsequently chose the "road" of rational debate and cooperation. Woodward's search work, particularly in the National Archives, told a quite different story, one which he pieced together painstakingly out of the correspondence of political officers and businessmen whose actions had beforehand seemed unrelated. Hence he provided a new description: severe conflict over material interests, conflict sporadically violent and capable of erupting into much more extensive bloodshed, was resolved only after Herculean diplomacy—between what were in effect two separate nations—and the course of this diplomacy revealed much about the values and goals of the nation's leaders in both the public and the private sectors of the American economy.[21]

Far from being dedicated to the triumph of sweet reason, Woodward's "road to reunion" was "twisted," for it ran a tortuous route through regional aspirations for economic development, individual claims on high offices, national parties' efforts to control government porkbarrel patronage, and a great class struggle between the elite business leaders and the impecunious freedmen. Southern economic interests were united in calling for a rail route to the golden markets of the West, while northern economic interests were united in seeking to retain their virtual monopoly over federal moneys for such internal improvements. Southern commercial interests, hoping to replicate northern successes by adopting the Republican strategy in which the federal government became a helpmate in the much-trammeled marketplace, sought a cabinet-level position for one of their own to ensure a voice in the inner councils of the White House, regardless of which party was given the presidency; and northern commercial interests, remembering how the business downturn of 1873 had reversed the postbellum pattern of economic growth, resisted giving up a cabinet position to a southerner when the potential markets might well be shrinking instead of expanding. The Democratic party, though still victimized by the "bloody shirt" tactics of the Grand Old Party, was rapidly restoring itself to real power, especially in big northeastern cities, and it was jealous of its opportunity to hang onto the presidency, which Samuel J. Tilden appeared to have won after the first electoral-ballot counting; the Republicans, sensing their own grip faltering, were fully as anxious to retain the chief executive's seat. There was also a commitment made to the Negro men, who were constitutionally guaranteed freedom, citizenship, and the vote. These ethical claims affected both parties, with Democrats insisting that their quest for dominance at home was not racially motivated but rather was a matter of politics and economics, and with Republicans sworn to protect black rights won by the sacrifice of a million casualties. Moreover, the moral commitment was borne home to the Republican party by the active voting and officeholding of the highly politicized southern blacks. Lastly, beneath the sectional wrestling over things of matter and of spirit, there was still more conflict, between regions inside the northern and the southern sections, and even more among individual personalities.[22]

In the fast-moving and complex horse trading which ensued— very little of which Woodward found occurring in the famed Wormley Hotel previously thought to be the scene of all negotiations—no single item in the above agenda was completely guaranteed, but none was completely eliminated either. Rather, sectional economic issues were pressed hardest by southern Democrats, and continuity in the White House was pressed hardest by northern Republicans. At first blush, the southerners would seem to have had very few good cards in the momentous gambling session; but the trump card of continuing violence was always there in the northern mind: Woodward was not by any means saying that southern Democrats actually threatened a new attack on Fort Sumter, but he was struck by the palpability of the largely unspoken threat of intermittent, almost guerilla, violence all over the vast stretches of the former C.S.A. Moreover, there was already apparent slackening of will among the Republicans, North and South, to uphold the hard-won black suffrage, and this slackening of will had as much to do with northern racism as with fears of violence. Although civil rights thus took a back seat to the accrual of power and wealth, blacks were by no means completely abandoned, for there were the most solemn assurances from southern white leaders that the freedmen's citizenship would be honored, and there were equally solemn assurances from northern white leaders that they would keep close watch on developments in the South. For all that, however, it is significant that enforcement of such rights shifted from the national level to the local level and that even the federal troops—after the mid-1870s both inadequate in number and indifferent in attitude—were to be removed by the new administration.[23]

When the cigar smoke had at last cleared, white southerners had their cabinet representative in Tennessee's David Key, the new postmaster general, and some prospect for a Texas and Pacific Railroad linkage to California, as well as home rule for statehouses and assembly halls in South Carolina and Louisiana; the Republicans had held onto the White House; northern troops were doing what all soldiers always want to do, which is to come home; and the southern blacks had been told to give up the guarantee of their rights by political allies and to accept instead the guarantees proffered by their political rivals. Heroism and harmony were conspicuously absent from this intricately woven tale, and there was a dramatic sense of groups engaging in conspiracies which moved with the irresistible gathering force of a modernist playwright's centrifuge.

So meticulously had Woodward tracked down his sources, so compellingly had he told his story, that there was no frontal assault on the basic thesis of the compromise until 1973. Prior to that time, the best one-liner of friendly criticism came from colonial historian Wesley Frank Craven, author of the first volume of the History of the South series, who said that Vann Woodward considered membership in the Whig party to be *the* original sin; and following that vein, it was a fair question how the much-needed economic development could have taken place in the postbellum South except with the measures adopted by these neo-Whigs. Nevertheless, this kind of criticism has not touched the essence of Woodward's thesis of the compromise; instead, it has reminded him that he may have no better remedy for southern economic maladies in 1877. Eventually, Woodward's own chapter in the widely used textbook *The National Experience*[24] spread the idea of the compromise much farther among the general audience than either *Origins* or *Reunion and Reaction,* and by the early 1970s it had become so commonly accepted that Woodward was occasionally scolded for belaboring the obvious. Of course, his story was hardly so commonplace in 1951, when the JHU professor first unveiled it before a consensus audience largely unsympathetic to his methodology and his message and already happy with Paul Buck.

However, in 1973, Allan Peskin attacked the whole concept of a compromise, pointing out that many of the quid pro quo agreements so artfully traced out by Woodward never actually were put into effect: the southern cabinet member, David Key, was not especially effective in arranging patronage appointments or internal improvements in the South; in fact, very little was done in the way of internal improvement in the South by any federal agent in Hayes's administration; and the railroad connection for the Texas and Pacific southern route to California did not materialize. Although Peskin's critique caused many historians to modify their sense of a compromise, Woodward's rebuttal at the time appeared effective: he emphasized the process of negotiation, saying that the quid pro quo trades were discussed seriously and that such political and diplomatic negotiations often end in disappointment for some of the parties—he dryly noted that the Compromise of 1850 could not meet "the test of fulfillment and good faith" suggested by Peskin for 1877; and finally, he insisted again that contemporaneous documents indicate a genuine fear of violence by southern Redeemers, and thus the very real threat of such violence necessitated the talks leading to the settlement.[25]

Almost immediately thereafter, however, Woodward's thesis was again attacked—by Michael Les Benedict, who said that fear of violence itself was almost the sole motivating factor in the negotiations and that the whole process was not legitimately compromise in Woodward's sense of political resolution of economic conflict; and by Keith Ian Polakoff, who said, conversely, that violence was never a real threat and that the plural compromises were actually the results of the "politics of inertia." Benedict used the correspondence which formed the basis of *Reunion and Reaction,* along with a sophisticated roll-call analysis of congressional voting behavior, and concluded that economic considerations, while not absent, were distinctly secondary to the fear of violence in the South and that there was virtually no sense of bargaining for favors or concessions beyond a fairly straightforward swap of Hayes-for-president for Hampton-for-governor. In a mirror image of this critique, Polakoff examined in greater detail the correspondence of the contemporaneous northern politicians, as he put it, out of a fascination with the question of what the northern Democrats were doing while the southerners were bargaining away Tilden's presidency for southern economic and social needs. Discerning a "tremendous inertia" in the politics because of extreme intraparty factionalism, Polakoff questioned the crisis language of *Reunion and Reaction*, claiming that none of the politicians evinced much fear of violence and in fact that each faction in the two parties felt secure enough to insist on serving a relatively small and highly particularized constituency without fear of allowing the nation to slide into violent strife in the interim of discussions. Far from Woodward's depiction of major negotiations at the national level concerning the broadest concepts of economic and social policies, Polakoff's depiction was of smaller men with smaller ends in view: "In the final analysis, the electoral dispute ended as it did because Hayes worked harder to hold the jealous factions of his party together in the crisis than did his Democratic adversary and because Tilden, after being outgeneraled, had the courage and the grace to accept defeat." Even the abandonment of the Republican gubernatorial nominees Daniel H. Chamberlain and Stephen B. Packard was something Hayes had already determined to do, so that all the "discussions" by "friends of Hayes" and by "representatives of the South" were "largely irrelevant to the settlement of the dispute." And finally, Polakoff wrote off the withdrawal of the troops as less a "Hayes concession" to southern Redeemers than the logical outcome of policy irresistibly set in motion by Grant when the military had avoided intervention to stop the barbaric white violence of the successful Mississippi Plan of Redemption in 1875.[26] There were some mutually exclusive aspects of Benedict's and Polakoff's works, but the cumulative effect of the two in concert was to cast the gravest doubts on the very idea of a broad-scale Compromise of 1877 which focused on economic policy.

The era of the 1970s would eventually spread these grave doubts even farther, until the basic Beardian assumptions of economic primacy were questioned not only for the end of Reconstruction but for the entire period. William Gillette's *Retreat from Reconstruction*, as August Meier noted, almost militantly refused to consider economics at all. Instead, Gillette examined the reasons why Republicans abandoned the quest for racial justice in Reconstruction and concluded that economic considerations had almost nothing to do with the political actions. After announcing in his introduction that unmitigated racism was not the cause for the abandonment of racial justice, Gillette then chronicled chronic racism in northern and southern politicians which blended disastrously with the Grant administration's acute lack of resolve in the policies of civil rights. But the rather odd line of Gillette's argument was less the issue than the fact that a good scholar could successfully marshal such an array of distinctly noneconomic determinants of political behavior in the context of Reconstruction. As Meier also noted, with a tone of regret, Gillette's book was the culmination of a process of revision which usually aimed at William Archibald Dunning and his Columbia southern apologists; but in actuality, these shafts did not hit Dunning, Fleming, or Hamilton: they hit Beard and Beale and Woodward. By the 1980s, very little was left in the way of a viable economic interpretation of Reconstruction, beginning, end, or middle.[27]

As for the second campaign, the one to meet the challenges of the 1880s, Woodward's 1951 verdict on the new elite was severely negative: do-nothing politics promising truth and peace while producing dishonesty and violence. On top of all that, the "ruling" elite constituted no more than a set of figureheads in a colonial economy directed elsewhere. Once this postbellum elite was left in charge of the South by the retreating northern troops, it had to face extreme shortages of liquid capital and of credit, and it also faced major difficulties in developing an effective network of transportation and communication despite the compromise measures. The federal government enforced tight-money policies in pursuit of the gold standard, and the rural areas of the nation—primarily the Corn Belt Midwest and the Cotton Belt South—found themselves hard up for cash (too little money chasing too many goods, as the monetarist Milton Friedman might put it). In addition, the concentration of banking in the populous Northeast also caused regional shortages in the supply of money created privately through credit. The upshot was a dark joke played on the conservative business leaders whom Woodward labeled the Redeemers: freed from titular military occupation, they found their land so deeply in debt to northern creditors that the states amounted to mere colonial possessions of New York, Philadelphia, and Boston.[28]

To pay off these loans, southern farmers were forced to rely on the cash crop of cotton during a time when world markets demanded less of that staple from the South, thus creating a perpetual-motion spiral of self-destruction: needing cash, they produced more cotton, thereby lowering its price still further and consequently needing still more credit, which could be obtained only by the promise to grow still more cotton, which would in turn further swell the world's stock in markets where the South was now only one supplier among many. Thus the Redeemers' own schemes to industrialize and urbanize were stymied by monetary and credit policies which they supported. The only remedy Redeemers could find was to work with the national railroad lines, the sole organizations of the private sector which were large enough to generate the surplus capital that could be reinvested; and so the land-rich and credit-poor South handed over precious acreage for a pittance, eschewed taxes on the railroad corporations, and accepted severe regional differentials in charges for hauling freight, in addition to opening the councils of government to railroad entrepreneurs and their agents.[29]

This, told now in a more subtle fashion and supported by more documentation, was Parrington's saga of the Great Barbecue in which the new-style business interests of the Gilded Age gorged themselves on the natural resources of the land. And like Parrington, Woodward felt that by the time the southerners and the heartland midwesterners arrived at this barbecue, little was left for them other than the scraps. The political result was a protest movement which eventually damaged the southern Democratic party and by the 1890s created the Populist party already celebrated in *Tom Watson*. In a relatively short time, then, the New South Movement was deeply in debt to northern rail corporations and was pressed hard for political leadership at home. Moreover, the biracial characteristics of the Populist movement gave the party an especially potent consciousness of class interests, and the hard times on the farm gave the party an especially concrete set of reform proposals for its platform. Again, as in the Watson story, Woodward laid into the Redeemers, excoriating them for their insensitivity to the poor, their malleability in the hands of unprincipled entrepreneurs, and their lack of a vision of justice. With the most sophisticated and gentle malice aforethought, he reported how the conservatives finally resorted to fraud and violence to forestall what seemed an inevitable victory—if it were a fair fight—for the hard-charging People's party. And even their chicanery was not sufficient alone to hold off the

Populists: there were also the romance of the Spanish-American War and the prosperity unleashed by this imperialism; only with all these forces in combination was the agrarian revolt quashed.[30]

These Parringtonian elements of *Origins* were hardly de rigeur in the 1950s, but the activist excitement and the frequently anti-business attitudes of the 1960s later provided Woodward a powerful force moving in confluence with his critique of neo-Whig policies. The Great Society campaign to attack poverty in the South, a campaign only slowed rather than stopped by the Nixon administration, brought the attention of a generation of scholars to the very problems Woodward's New Deal perspective caused him to label colonialism. These features of *Origins* have remained attractive to scholars as late as the 1980s, but recent trends could be going in another direction as historians of economic development express considerable sympathy for the policies of growth essayed by bourgeois entrepreneurs. In addition, students of the Populist and agrarian opposition to those business leaders have begun to question in a serious way the differences between the economic policies of conservative industrialists such as Gordon, Brown, and Thompkins and those of Populists such as Watson and Marion Butler—in several cases, it appears that Woodward and those inspired by him have overstated the extent of these differences in attitudes and plans.[31]

By contrast with the compromise and with questions of economic planning, the conduct of race relations—the third challenge Woodward discerned for the Redeemers—immediately drew the attention of scholars and activists, many of whom were ready by 1951 to hear what Woodward had to say concerning the course taken by the conservative Redeemers once they had regained power. And as the civil rights movement seized the attention and eventually the devotion of the country's intellectuals during the decade, Woodward's discussion of this third challenge to leadership found an enthusiastic readership. He said that conservatives and demagogues cooperated for once in a social movement, Jim Crow segregation, which was closely interwoven with Progressive reform in education and in city management, and in regulation of public utilities, public transportation, and financial institutions. Woodward could not resist pointing out that much of the "practical reform" of the Progressive agenda was essentially the proposal of the Populists accused by the consensus historians of "emotionalism and impracticality"; but more to the point was the question of racial justice and societal peace. The rigid de jure segregation of basic services and offices was crucial, and often foremost, in the southern Progressive platforms; and most Progressive politicians winked at Negrophobic violence, while some actually encouraged it and a few even participated in it. Moreover, the Progressive era failed to bring racial harmony with its discriminatory laws, although many had agreed with historian apologists for the system, such as U. B. Phillips, who contended that the fetters on blacks would ease tensions between the poor whites and the poor blacks. What Woodward was demonstrating instead was that the extreme racism beginning in 1889 and still intensifying at the outbreak of World War I was a more complicated story than a case of "red-necked" or "po-buckra" or "one-gallused" bigotry. It was, in fact, part of the entire New South fabric, and if poor whites committed the lynchings, rich whites both approved and also actively encouraged the violence.[32] Thus, in responding to each of the three great challenges posed for political leadership between 1877 and 1913, the conservatives, in Woodward's view, not only failed to produce a better world but in many cases made things worse.

The way in which he told this story fundamentally altered what in other hands would have been a happy ending, since his volume was concluded by the election of Woodrow Wilson to the presidency and his appointment to executive positions of fellow southerners such as Georgia-born William Gibbs McAdoo, North Carolina's Josephus Daniels, and Texans Edward House and Albert S. Burleson. Here were sons of the South constituting fully half of the cabinet and exercising power in the White House after two full generations of virtual exile from such positions of responsibility as a result of the formation of the Confederacy. Furthermore, these Wilsonian southerners were Progressives, men proudly associated not only with the high-toned idealism of Wilsonian diplomacy but also with the domestic reform program of New Freedom. Woodward by no means slighted the significance of their arrival on the national stage in these penultimate years of the Progressive movement; they were winners, and as he aptly put it, it was hard to say no to the section's politicians in this era. Still, he was not out to celebrate this kind of success, for these were the Progressives who had disfranchised Negroes, who had withdrawn vital public services from Negroes through the institutions of Jim Crow with their practices of "separate and unequal," who had defrauded poor whites of their votes, and who, for all their nominal relationship to the managers of national economic development, were presiding over a southern economy marked by colonial dependency on northeastern credit, backwardness in techniques, maldistribution of wealth, and inefficient production. These were, finally, the kind of men whose flatly stated intent was to transform graceful Charleston into Pittsburgh's contemporaneous brand of hardscrabble, grimy industrialism. At the very moment of their greatest recognition by the Wilsonian Progressives, then, Woodward had these leaders come across as a signally unworthy bunch of knaves and fools.

As Sheldon Hackney wryly noted, *Origins* did not endure as a classic because of its optimistic and inspirational qualities in Woodward's characterizations of his personae. Rather, said Hackney, the work's dominance over subsequent studies must be explained by the fact that it was essentially right, since some twenty years of hard work by other historians failed to disprove—and in fact generally reinforced—most of his conclusions.[33] Since Hackney himself wrote, more than a baker's dozen of years have elapsed, during which time major revisionist scholarship has indeed dislodged some of the very foundation stones of *Origins;* but the significance of the work for the things it began by inspiration and its enduring stylistic qualities have remained unquestioned. Furthermore, the complexity of the subjects addressed in the volume and the fluid nature of historical scholarship itself both militate against a final judgment of rightness or wrongness for any of the points Woodward made, so that some of Hackney's insights into the attractiveness of the thesis have retained a certain validity.

As vital as were Hackney's observations, however, he likely exaggerated the downbeat tone in the Woodward of 1951. This tone, while scornful of bad leadership and skeptical of the glib rhetoric of the real estate agent, is one of a resolute determination to find out the truth and then to act on that knowledge. What he discovers goes down hard, for he finds that conditions have been bad and might well get worse. Yet there remain a few examples of noble struggle, what the ancients called arete, and these, despite their failing in the face of overwhelming odds, are worthy both of celebration and of emulation. *Origins,* then, is also a call to arms in the cause of social reform, but it is not a call to arms issued by the happy warriors of liberalism. Rather, it is a call to join a long and difficult struggle whose outcome is very much in doubt. In this paean to such struggles of arete, there is also the ancient's concept of the *aurea mediocritas,* or the golden mean, for Woodward here struck and held a precise balance between the delusions of easy victory and the impotence of fatalism. On the one side lay the dangers of underestimating the immense problems of the South, and that way lay the path to defeat and self-destruction traveled by those who would slight the challenges of racism and poverty. On the other side lay the equal danger of overestimating these problems, which led to resignation in the face of challenges so great that one simply had to surrender to them; and this kind of flight from responsibility produced not only defeat but also destruction of the soul itself. Not lightly optimistic or cheery, this; but all the same a message about duty is quite clear and, in its own way, inspiring.

III

Woodward and everyone else needed inspiration of some kind to meet the difficult challenges of the era, since both the domestic and the diplomatic problems were of a kind and of a degree which could daunt the most stouthearted. His research and his experiences told him that the injustices done to black people were the proper focus of reform energies; and his Beardian perceptions told him further that the chronic economic distress of the South and the acute economic maladies of the urban ghetto must be cured simultaneously with the treatment of racism, for these were surely major contributors to the disease. But the nation from 1947 to at least 1953 was preoccupied with the threat of Soviet communism, and especially with the threat from the Russian agents allegedly infiltrating governmental services in great numbers and in high places. At few times has the aurea mediocritas been as difficult to strike and to hold as in the 1950s; of course, Woodward's mastery of the golden mean in an essay was more sure than his, or anybody else's, mastery of it in the day's political disputes. The consensus historians, he felt, were deluding everyone about the nature and the magnitude of the country's problems by underestimating these conflicts. But at the same time, the anti-Communist right wing, by overestimating the Russian internal menace to our domestic security, was diverting precious energies away from the major flaws and strains in the economy and in the society. Only by burning away the shrouding mist created by the witch-hunting investigations could one even see the pathway of the very long trek to racial equality and economic justice.

Soon, however, Woodward found that scoundrel-time politics were posing a much more direct threat to his circle of intimate friends. His JHU colleague Owen Lattimore, a foreign policy expert and a gentle soul who, with his brother, the classicist Richmond Lattimore, delighted in sharing with Woodward the literature of the ancients, was fingered by congressional investigators as one of the putative "Communist sympathizers" whose governmental service had been dedicated to betraying the national security. In Lattimore's case, this was the second occasion on which Woodward had had to bring bad news to his family. Once, earlier, Woodward had been driving home from the campus across a bridge when he saw a Baltimore city bus strike a bicyclist, who was nearly thrown over the bridge railing into the bay; rushing to the victim's side, he discovered that the unconscious man was his friend Lattimore and, after getting him into a hospital for treatment, had to call the family to explain what had happened. Now, on 26 September 1951, while Lattimore was conducting research overseas, Woodward was tipped off by a journalist friend that the next day's headlines would feature the foreign policy analyst as the object of a major investigation by the U.S. Senate Internal Security Committee; and as before, he took on the task of telling the Lattimore family the devastating news.[34]

As important as was that painful but necessary task of friendship, the larger duty involved him in the issues of academic freedom, much as he had been compelled to join those issues earlier at Georgia Tech and then at Scripps. This time the issues concerned Lattimore's service as an "occasional consultant" to the State Department; his membership in the Institute for Pacific Research (IPR), a private research group operated by left-wing Democrats of the Roosevelt-Truman era, including Phillip Jessup, Edward C. Carter, and John Carter Vincent; and his participation in a State Department roundtable of confidential discussions conducted with some IPR figures and other academicians in 1949. The IPR also included a number of fine scholars and career diplomatists, and some of its members, weighing the probability of Mao Tse-Tung's victory in China, had discussed the feasibility of the American government's establishing diplomatic ties with the Communists. In the 1949 roundtable, Lattimore and others expressed skepticism about the policy of containment in Asia and expressed considerable doubt about the efficacy and the justice of continued American support for the Kuomintang anti-Communists of China; these discussions were labeled confidential, and the scholars and officials were encouraged to speak candidly. However, in this 1951 testimony before the Senate committee, Northwestern University political scientist Kenneth W. Colgrove publicized Lattimore's roundtable ideas, which he characterized as "contemptible" and "almost revolting." Furthermore, Colgrove described the IPR as "nothing more than a propaganda organization following a line—in this case the Communist line."[35]

Writing to Rainey, Woodward said that Colgrove "brackets John K. Fairbanks and Edwin O. Reischauer of Harvard and Nathaniel Peffer of Columbia," as well as Lattimore, with this alleged conspiracy to overthrow Chiang Kai-shek and establish communism in mainland China. Almost scolding Rainey for even having studied at Northwestern, Woodward told his friend:

> I recall that you were a student and admirer of Colgrove. And I remember a delightful conversation with the man at a cocktail party in Washington during the war. I am the more deeply shocked at his testimony. It strikes me as irresponsible and hysterical. Nobody in the academic community who commands respect has joined up with this sort of thing. . . . I need not preach you any sermons on the meaning of the episode—how it makes the free expression of unpopular views of governmental advisors dangerous and closes to the government the access of expert advice from the universities and encourages government by dopes. But apart from that we are on the firing line up here. It's deadly serious business. And to be sniped at from within our own academic ranks is demoralizing.[36]

Lattimore received important support from many sources, including a lengthy statement from former vice-president Henry Agar Wallace in which he emphatically disassociated Lattimore from his own formerly "soft" position concerning the spread of communism.

And the administration and faculty at JHU were perhaps less susceptible to such "sniping" and may have been farther removed from the "firing line" than Woodward thought during the heat of the controversy. But the important thing for Woodward was the way in which members of the faculty closed ranks around the scholar, successfully defending both Lattimore's professional reputation and his job tenure. Neither defense was accomplished without considerable emotional injury to Lattimore, of course, and Woodward would rue the memory of the incident after the testimony was over and the academic was reaffirmed in his status at Hopkins: "The damage is done."[37]

Since many of the extreme Right were militantly opposed to the civil rights movement, this episode also morally empowered Woodward to take a much more active part in the unfolding story of the campaign for racial equity. By 1952 he was acting on behalf of the movement on at least three levels: first, as an investigator providing specific historical data and perspective for the research team of the legal staff of the National Association for the Advancement of Colored People (NAACP) headed by chief counsel Thurgood Marshall; second, as an officer in professional history associations using his power and influence to open up opportunities in those national groups; and, as before, as an inspirational writer—albeit one still locked in his lifetime struggle to find the balance between the demands of scholarship and the demands of activism—whose research and prose aspired to awaken the national conscience to its rightful mission.[38]

The work for the NAACP paid dividends all around: it let Woodward see in action the energetic and insightful Marshall, in that era virtually unbeatable in a courtroom contest and behind the scenes thoroughgoing in preparation and a rigorous taskmaster for his historian and political scientist research assistants; it reunited Woodward with Gainesville "musketeers" Dauer and Carleton, both of whom were also on Marshall's team and who helped to draft what would ultimately become the basic plan for school integration in Florida; it brought him into spirited partnership with scholars and activists of both races from all over the country, thereby giving him a better sense of the size and strength of the movement; and above all else, it immersed him in the legal questions of civil rights, both in the documents from the 1890s and in the ongoing campaigns of the present. Research conducted by Woodward, Dauer, Carleton, and black historian John Hope Franklin was employed with telling effect by Marshall in the most famous case of the era, *Brown* v. *Board of Education of Topeka, Kansas,* in 1954. On no other issue than the NAACP's drive for racial integration did Woodward so completely involve himself in moral and material, as well as scholarly, commitments.[39]

The research and the writing and the campaigning flowed with no perceptible break into the activities of the professional historical organizations, especially the Southern Historical Association (SHA), which was founded in 1934, the year Woodward entered graduate school at Carolina. As his tenure among historians of the South became secure, he found himself on various program committees and even on the inside track to the eventual presidency of the SHA. Increasingly, he became aware of the things which he could do in an even more direct and personal way to provide opportunities for black scholars. Entire sessions at association meetings could be dedicated to the study of civil rights, and the meetings themselves could become scenes of less formal but equally valuable chances for interested scholars to share their findings and to encourage each other. Furthermore, these meetings were the occasion for the apprentice scholars to demonstrate their wares before the pastmasters by reading papers and by participating in discussions; and they were the places where the first vital professional contacts were made for the young historians. Those, such as Woodward himself, who harbored aspirations for high office in the profession could also demonstrate competence in the administrative work of the organizations and thereby begin the climb to prominence.[40]

Woodward, like most good historians, consciously used the organization to help his students, introducing them to senior scholars with related research interests, to editors looking for worthy and salable manuscripts, and to university and college administrators who anticipated staff openings on their campuses; perhaps more important, he showed his graduate students by quiet example how they could begin to make these kinds of opportunities for themselves. But it was obvious that a great deal of the conference life, with its myriad opportunities, was in actuality closed off to such promising black scholars as John Hope Franklin, Alonzo Theodore Stephens, Elsie (Lewis) Mitchell, Charles Wesley, and Clarence

Bacote, who were stymied in their work by the various restrictions of the racist laws imposed at the sites of most of the historians' meetings. Although these blacks were dues-paying subscribers to the national organizations, their exclusion from the speaker's dais, from the banquet tables, from the hotel lobbies, and from the restaurants nearby the host hotels—and sometimes even from the very meeting rooms of the program sessions—kept them from being full-fledged de facto members.[41]

A number of reform-minded activists, of whom the then-relatively unknown Howard Zinn and August Meier were especially outspoken, had determined by 1949 that the SHA must be genuinely integrated; and Woodward came to cooperate with these men in several actions which would greatly improve conditions of professional life for the Negro historians, although only the passage of the Civil Rights Act of 1965 would meaningfully integrate the SHA. They chose the SHA, though for many the name itself must have seemed ominous, because it was in many ways more important to black historians than the American Historical Association or the Mississippi Valley Historical Association: for three centuries, black history had occurred within a context which was primarily southern; and the manuscript sources as well as the preponderance of black scholars were in the South. To open this door, Woodward and the liberal Tennessean Bell Irvin Wiley (himself a student of U. B. Phillips's), selected John Hope Franklin for the exposure of reading a paper at the SHA, for they agreed that Franklin was the man with the right combination of talent, spirit, and character to establish this precedent of black participation.[42]

They began to plot, Woodward and Franklin and Wiley. Wiley, who was in charge of a panel for the 1949 convention, said he wanted to offer a program so attractive that scholars would attend regardless of the color of the participants. More, there was good luck in the sites already selected for the meetings: the Williamsburg Inn and the campus of the College of William and Mary. While Virginia seemed committed to the practices of segregation, there was less reason for Franklin to fear bodily harm; as Woodward put it to Franklin, "The insults . . . would not be too crude." The team went into action, with a then-obscure Professor Franklin scheduled to read a paper at the 1949 convention.[43]

Those who looked through the program prospectus with care

noted that the little-known scholar taught at Howard University, the distinguished black school in Washington, D.C. In time, attention focused on Woodward, the acknowledged perpetrator of the deed. By the peculiar workings of southern racial manners, those who objected to an integrated program blamed Woodward more than they blamed Franklin. Thus the mesh of details—"Where am I gonna eat? where am I gonna sleep?" as Franklin recalled—this mesh of details fell over the larger convention plans, at least in some minds. There was less talk about the subject matter of the panels and more talk about the mundane affairs of eating, sleeping, and traveling. Even if southern historians accepted a black scholar on the speaker's dais, would the convention not become a scene of confrontation between the black man and segregated hotels, restaurants, cars? Under the questioning, Woodward was cool and dispassionate, only occasionally stirred to gentle sardonicism, never to visible anger. When asked where Franklin would sleep, Woodward answered, "In a pup tent"; when asked where Franklin would eat, Woodward answered, "Oh, he's very resourceful, he'll probably bring K-rations." The whimsical replies masked his knowledge that there would be no confrontations with the town itself: Franklin would stay with the family of historian Douglas Adair, sleeping and taking his meals in seclusion from the other conference delegates.[44]

Howard Beale, someone who had not lost his taste for such breakthroughs, drove Franklin in his car down to Williamsburg. The short trip was a beautiful one, for the Virginia countryside sparkled with autumn. After an evening with the Adairs, Franklin made his appearance at the sessions. A tall and very dignified man, the lone Negro was imposing as he walked to the dais to be introduced by Henry Steele Commager, a famed liberal who had eagerly sought the task. Tension ran through the hall and even outside—many historians, students, and the curious from town peered through windows, probably hearing little but watching with keen eyes. The speech, a distillation of his forthcoming book, *The Militant South,* went well, being received with an encouraging combination of approbation and intellectual respect.

When it was done, there was considerable relief for all concerned. Professional historians had proven themselves capable of attending a racially integrated session in a quiet college town. Later, Franklin was permitted to dine at the Williamsburg Inn with his fellow historians, although it was in obvious defiance of city law and community practice; and this, too, was accepted. All things, after all, start small.[45] In retrospect, the excitement of anticipation seemed a wonder, since the act itself went smoothly, even went without excitement. It was another in a series of confrontations with the monster Jim Crow in which the monster had proved to be the most reluctant of dragons.

One thing about this dragon, however, was its caprice: in a twinkling, Jim Crow could transform itself from a state of reluctance to a state of militance. Only a few years after the success at Williamsburg, Woodward and Franklin found themselves simply unable to share a Saturday meal together in the nation's capitol. The two men were both doing research at the Library of Congress and regularly dined together at the Supreme Court Restaurant. On Saturdays, however, government business shut down and there were no official facilities available. Then Washington reverted to the norms of the largely segregated Virginia and Maryland communities which surrounded it. The whole experience educated Woodward about another side of the life of the black scholar.[46]

As Franklin remembered it, Woodward came around and asked worriedly, "What will you do?" His friend replied, "I eat a big breakfast, I come late [to the archives], I bring a piece of candy, and, when I can't stand it, I go home." It was this kind of mundane thing which continued to bear in on the handful of black scholars in the republic: things concomitant with daily life for the white historian were privileges denied Negroes. Mulling it over that day, Woodward told Franklin, "I don't think I could *be* a historian if I couldn't eat dinner!"[47]

Then, both men laughed, but they and others soon swung back into action. In 1952 the *Thompson* decision ended mandatory segregation in the cafeterias, hotels, and other accommodations in Washington. Things were loosening up across the border states and the upper South; but the very loosening across the northern fringe by comparison made the bonds on the former Confederacy seem tighter. That fall, Woodward again confronted Jim Crow inside the profession of history. Honored as the president of the Southern Historical Association, he was to deliver his executive address to the organization at the Knoxville meeting that session. For the occasion, he had prepared an intricate examination of the peculiar relationship of the South to the rest of the republic, an examination which emphasized the special perspectives which the South could bring to bear on national history because of being the only part of the United States which had experienced military defeat and occupation and had openly participated in an obvious evil by creating and developing the institution of slavery. The point was that the South thus had solid historical reasons for avoiding the dangers of national presumptions of innocence and invincibility. But as Woodward readied his address, the program chairman, LeRoy Graf, learned that the host hotel, the Farragut, would segregate the keynote dinner address: in other words, black historians Franklin, Bacote, Mitchell, Wesley, and Sherman Savage could not hear Woodward's speech. Graf, an Ohioan newly arrived at the University of Tennessee, was outraged, since the hotel had earlier promised an integrated session.[48]

The whole incident perfectly illustrated the convolutions which Jim Crow could take in a given instant. The association was integrated, for Franklin had established that fact by delivering a paper three years earlier. Moreover, the association purported to welcome its black members to participation in the annual meetings. Nevertheless, the Farragut exercised its legal right to segregate the dining facilities inside its walls. And as usually happened in such cases, the hotel management was unctuous in its insistence that it was not prejudiced but was only responding to the economic realities reflected by the cultural norms of eastern Tennessee: namely, the hotel feared it would lose customers if it integrated its dining room. Otherwise, the managers pointed out, Negroes were perfectly free to attend sessions in the hotel. Of course, this was the kind of specious reasoning which had kept the historical profession essentially white. The dinner which the hotel insisted was a private affair was the forum for the presidential address; not attending dinner deprived black historians of full membership in the SHA by keeping them from the main attraction of the weekend. Beyond the professional issues—which were troubling enough—there were the continuing realities of the layered insults of persisting segregation, the accumulated weight of little insults and minor deprivations being almost unbearable. Here was still more proof that a black scholar was not really a normal professional with access to the full range of the historian's perquisites.[49]

By this time, Woodward and Franklin found that there were many others who were unwilling to put up with this kind of segregation. Graf, who had come onto the scene as program chairman unexpectedly when a senior colleague won sabbatical to study abroad, decided to take a swing at Jim Crow. He won immediate support from the young secretary of the SHA, none other than Woodward's loquacious graduate student friend Ben Wall, whom Graf thankfully called "one of the beautiful young men of the South." Graf and Wall set in motion the plan, which Woodward readily approved: the entire SHA would abandon the Farragut for an outlying clubhouse restaurant, the Whittle Springs, which was integrated. The racial, cultural, and economic rationale which the Farragut had employed would be turned back on itself. Let the management suffer the embarrassment of an entire professional organization of historians leaving its facilities en masse. Bad manners to a few black guests would cost dearly: all the guests would seek hospitality elsewhere.[50]

Later, it seemed an amusing spectacle. Graf and Wall put most of the historians on a bus which drove them to the suburbs, while Graf had to use his own car to shuttle a late-arriving black historian, Elsie (Lewis) Mitchell, when he learned that the local white taxi drivers refused to give her a ride. It went off all right, although Woodward delivered the speech in his ineffective, halting style, which belied its actual eloquence. The excitement of the long day overwhelmed the moment of the evening address, since few men and women had either the remaining psychic energy or the hypersensitive hearing necessary to follow what the president was saying. But a principle had been established; if southern white members harbored any grudges against the black members for the relocation of the session, said Woodward later, "they didn't tell me that."[51]

Following these episodes, Woodward became less active in the continuing administrative processes of integrating the SHA and less active in research work for the NAACP legal staff, because he was turning his attention to the other level of his campaign, the inspirational scholarship of the kind which was becoming his hallmark. By 1954 he and those who had worked to help Marshall prepare for the appeal of the *Brown* case were highly optimistic about the outcome of that hearing; and when the Earl Warren Supreme Court went beyond Woodward's hopes with a sweeping indictment of segregation, he was pleased as a researcher whose homework had been rewarded and moved deeply as a committed reformist who sought a better life for his black friends and coworkers. But he also understood that the decision itself represented a scholar's unique opportunity, especially after he received an invitation from the University of Virginia to deliver the Richard Lecture on campus in that eventful year.[52] The problem of integration was on the southern mind as never before, and now, he realized, was the time to encapsulate the very mood and tone of racial reform in the country through a work of supremely usable history within the context of his ironic discussion of continuity and discontinuity.

7

The Strange Career of Jim Crow, 1954–1955

Unfettered spirits will aspire in vain to the pure heights of
   perfection.
He who wills great things must gird up his loins;
Only in limitation is mastery revealed,
And law alone can give us freedom.
   —Goethe, *The Sorrows of Young Werther*

Law alone can give us freedom. Only in limitation is mastery revealed. The language and the logic of Johann von Goethe were ever
inspirational to Woodward, the man who as a youth had quoted the
German playwright's character Mephistopheles as an "answer" to a
philosophy examination question which the student deemed overly
Romantic. Of course Goethe passed through several phases of intellectual and moral development and, in fact, as a youth had himself
given the world the character of Werther, the supremely suffering
egoist. But by the nineteenth century, Goethe had no use for young
Werther, save as an example of what he found wrong with the
world. The excesses of putative great men with putative great souls
had nearly wrecked Europe, and with no recognizable benefit to
Western culture; it was blood shed for nought. The Romanticism

which characterized his own creature Werther the poet later labeled sick, pronouncing that which is Romantic wrong and even unhealthy, critical angles of approach very congenial with Woodward's mentality.

Others, too, have sensed this twentieth-century duty to tend to the needs of the collectivity with a concomitant deemphasis of individual desires. In this sense, Michael Kammen could read the history of the nineteenth century in the United States as a struggle between liberty and equality and that of the twentieth century as a struggle between equality and justice. Both phrases illustrate the dilemma of choosing between what an individual wants and what society deserves. The nineteenth century had many Werthers of all ages and of all stations from Napoleon to the lowliest slaveowner, each of these people claiming the liberty to direct others' lives and each denouncing equality by the act of seizing such liberty. By the twentieth century, the concept of equality had been firmly set in the value system of American culture, but the cry for justice to the poor and to the persecuted had risen up to confound the harmony theoretically achieved in the equality of groups in pluralistic society.[1] By whatever labels, the struggle was persisting without apparent resolution: perhaps the turn to law, taking up the option of legal limitation of freedom, perhaps the limiting structure of law, would reveal the mastery of racial justice.

At any rate, Woodward was convinced by 1954 that the limiting structure of law had revealed the mastery of racial *injustice* in the past and the present. His own research conducted for Thurgood Marshall and the NAACP legal campaign in the *Brown* case had just reaffirmed the significance of law, for layers of such law, laid across the body of the South, had altered the body's growth; no matter that "organicist" theories of sociology denied the possibility of such alteration. Inorganic, even unnatural, laws had been used, and used with telling effect, to alter the organic growth of an entire section of the country.

Oddly, the harm done by law also implied a great deal about the potential for good in law. It certainly was the case that local and regional laws had guaranteed slavery and racist oppression; and it certainly was the case that the absence of federal law—or, more precisely, the loss of the federal will to enforce the laws affirming civil rights—had guaranteed a continuing racist oppression. "Resisting" bad laws with the absence of law certainly provided black southerners what two scholars have scathingly called "one kind of freedom."[2] But Thurgood Marshall's work and the whole concept of the NAACP were demonstrating convincingly that law could protect blacks too. Perhaps, after all, the master had said it correctly: "And law alone can give us freedom."

If so, then the historian-student would essay a major examination of that freedom-giving law.

I

Thomas F. Pettigrew has described the *Brown* decision as giving blacks "heart to fight." As conservative critics often complained for different reasons, the decision asked as much as it answered: it gave rather vague directions toward a goal of fully integrated public education. The qualifying phrase "with all deliberate speed" made it possible for obstructionists to thwart integration by delay instead of attempting the futility of outright resistance. It would take years of judicial and administrative clarification of language to establish lines of commitment. What the ruling did immediately was to fix blacks with a sense of purpose: a tribunal voice had decried segregation and had proclaimed integration.[3] The Delphic qualities of the tribunal's pronouncements were secondary to the spiritual power of the message which affirmed integration.

Moreover, the most conservative institution in the republic had made the new directive. In 1803 John Marshall had begun to counter Jeffersonian liberalism with a conservative judiciary; the first powerful chief justice succeeded over the next three decades in demonstrating the ability of the courts to protect the elite from the competition of the lower classes occasionally threatened by Congress or by the president. With the notable exception of the Civil War era, the court maintained this role until the middle of the twentieth century. Of course, the Supreme Court did much more than preserve an economic stasis by looking to the interests of a business elite; and certainly the societal and political equilibrium thus created had its positive elements. Nevertheless, the Supreme Court had come to symbolize class interests which in the South were also racial interests. Most notably, in 1896 the court had ruled in *Plessy*

v. *Ferguson* that public facilities should be "separate but equal." That judicial defense of Jim Crow gave southern segregationists what they wanted: the burden of proving inequality, something difficult to prove, lay with blacks.

In retrospect, the traditional reading of the court's judgment on civil rights has been almost backward: *Plessy* v. *Ferguson* represented not the beginning of a new policy but rather the culmination of a policy. The principle of white supremacy was ringingly reaffirmed by a court which, for a decade, had affirmed oppression by its inaction. But in the wake of that ruling, the NAACP began to erode the edifice by patient digging at its subterranean foundations. In the 1930s, even before Thurgood Marshall scored his first victories before the bar, his teacher Charles Hamilton Houston won precedent-setting cases which weakened Jim Crow. By 1954, then, astute legal minds could see the direction that Earl Warren's court would take; the heartening surprise was the unanimity and the strength of the statement it issued.[4]

But the possibility remained that law would move independently of practice; in fact, a solid body of Western thought had always maintained that law was a superficial, almost passive, reflection of societal mores. The words of the poet Oliver Goldsmith,

> How small, of all that human hearts endure
> that part which laws and kings can cause or cure,[5]

continued to speak for many in the social sciences, which until the Second World War were largely positivistic, organicist, and conservative. At Yale, William Graham Sumner had iterated and reiterated the point that mores bodied forth law and that laws which defied mores were doomed to be dead letters. Southern apologists for segregation grasped at Sumner's proclamation throughout the twentieth century and especially in 1954: many northerners presumed that segregationists were right, that Jim Crow predated the Supreme Court and was thus organic, natural to the southern way of life, indispensable, and ineradicable save by violence. Much the same thing was announced in 1929 by U. B. Phillips in "The Central Theme of Southern History." Thus many of those most deeply committed to racial reform assumed that the drive to integrate was in fact destroying the South, an attitude proving the persisting relevance and importance of Sumner's conservative and organicist views.[6] Liberals in the South endured a combination of emotional pressures: subject to overt criticism by their peers for "unsouthern" and disloyal behavior, they also suffered from the nagging self-doubts which came from the contemplation of a perhaps radically different South, altered beyond recognition by integration.

At least at the conscious level, Woodward had not fretted overmuch about the charge of being disloyal, of threatening the South with the juggernaut of integration. Frankly, he said often and often restated, if the South actually stood for segregation, if Jim Crow were the virtual essence of southernness, then the South merited destruction. Human values, the claims of justice, more than outweighed the claims of sectional identity. On the other hand, Woodward simply doubted that Jim Crow was the essence of southernness. His own life and his own research had turned up cases in point which disproved a thesis of unbroken, unvarying Jim Crow. Moreover, Sumner was a poor shield for the segregationist and a poorer tool of social analysis. With forty-four words Woodward threw down the gauntlet for a fight: "When a scientific theory ceases to account for the observed facts of common experience, . . . it would seem to be time to discard the theory. In lieu of another to offer in its place, we can at least try to understand what has happened."[7]

What had happened, in Woodward's personal experiences and in his research experiences, was that the "organically sealed" system displayed telltale cracks. In those cracks could be seen the many patterns of race relationships he and black friends such as J. Saunders Redding and John Hope Franklin had witnessed since the 1930s. In those cracks could be seen his uncle Comer Woodward, who experienced just as much variety in the 1920s. In those cracks could be seen the exceptions of the 1880s and the 1890s whom he had already studied—the young Tom Watson, Louis Blair, George Washington Cable. In those cracks could be seen the sweeping urbanism, cosmopolitanism, and industrialism which the Second World War and its aftermath were bringing to a South once rural, parochial, and agricultural. In those cracks could be seen the increasing numbers of southern blacks who were successfully defying the racial presumptions which justified Jim Crow.

Along with the internal inconsistencies of Jim Crow, there was a special perspective of comparative history with which one could examine its institutions. South Africa, defiantly independent of worldwide patterns, lay at the bottom of an African continent which was struggling out of colonial vassalage. But the white minority (really a plurality inside the minority, since the Dutch Afrikaners were more militant than the British-African whites on this score) had thwarted British plans to exchange colonialism for majority rule: South Africa, in fact, retained the nineteenth-century principle of rule by white men as justification for apartheid.

Oddly, South Africa itself had only recently become the extremist in the realm of race relations: before the period 1945–49, race relations there had been relatively fluid, with some privileges for all blacks and a share of citizenship rights for mixed-blood "coloreds"; and the Western world generally shared the Afrikaners' guilt of racist oppression. But rapidly after the conclusion of World War II disrupted colonialism, South Africa froze its system into a hardened, unmoving, unbending pattern complete with forced removal of blacks into "homelands" reservations, located on poor soil far from gainful employment in urban industrial centers; and this freezing of attitudes and stiffening of policies came at exactly the moment when the Western world began to move rapidly and self-consciously down the long route to racial equality. The resulting contrast in perception may have been even greater than the undoubtedly real contrast, but white South Africans set their faces like flint, for apartheid guaranteed an economic and political world of "white over black" by socially mandating segregated living and working quarters and by forcefully excluding the black masses from citizenship. This system guaranteed to the Afrikaners a plush material life, and in some inchoate way it satisfied profound emotional needs; but it was surely time borrowed—at heavy moral interest—in a continent overwhelmingly black and in a world overwhelmingly "colored." South Africa, in a metaphor Woodward borrowed, was a man on a cliff, a man doomed, and a man watched with dismay by the rest of the world at the bottom of the cliff.[8] By theory, apartheid was the logical extension of Jim Crow; if southerners were defining themselves by Jim Crow, then the South, too, clung to the sheer side of a cliff. But was Jim Crow integral to the South in the way that apartheid was integral to South Africa? Much in contemporary southern life said no, decidedly not.

For one thing, South Africa was truly alone, but the South was attached to the republic of the United States, and the fearful beating inflicted by the battles of the Civil War made subsequent talk of rebellion suspect. Southerners, in other words, were always distinctive and were often cantankerous in expressing that distinctiveness, but they generally respected the dominant cultural practices of the nation. The fact of the matter was that until recently, the entire country had practiced various forms of Jim Crow, so that the South, dimly reflecting the South African experience, only in the 1940s began to look dramatically different, in its segregationist practices, from the rest of the nation. If the entire nation were genuinely commited to integration, then the South would most likely submit again to the national will. The final question lay with the force and with the staying power of national policy on race; would the government push hard and would it keep pushing?

The willpower and the wisdom of that emerging policy could easily be doubted, especially during the infancy of the Dwight David Eisenhower administration. A look at the electoral strength of Eisenhower and a glance through his policy statements made it obvious that the war hero owed few favors to blacks or to social activism. But those were the perceptions of a subject examined at close range. There was a longer-range view: the Eisenhower years were also a part of a continuing American adjustment to power and responsibility newly found after two world wars. In the world arena, the turf was crowded with "colored" people, and the United States had to acknowledge rudimentary tenets of racial equality at home if it expected to be heard abroad. Jim Crow was a liability in foreign policy; if Americans hoped to benefit from the momentum of the World War II campaign for the Four Freedoms—much as Woodward disliked the hypocrisies of those expressions—then they could not tolerate Jim Crow in the southeastern quarter of their land. Indeed, diplomatists fully intended to keep their hold on the Four Freedoms as a forceful symbol, and the global needs of American strategy thus pressed hard on social policy at home.

The immediate expression of this policy came in the days of the cold war, in the struggle between Western capitalism and its Marxist antagonists. The former insisted on competitive free enterprise, due process, government by law, and the indirect representation of republican politics; the latter disclaimed those values as obstacles to the grander tasks of feeding the masses, educating the masses, and some day letting the masses govern directly. The best of both worlds was conspicuously absent from the verbal and physical battles of the era; after all, the Soviet Union and the United States were both quite new to the business of world leadership, and each by turn showed its inexperience by playing the knave and the fool.

Whatever the eventual shape of things in world policy, the Russian superpower found in southern racism an issue it could use in its strivings for global mastery. One comic incident demonstrated the very real negative weight of southern racism in the scales of world opinion. Russian spokesmen were showing American news correspondents a gleaming new subway station. Unfortunately for all concerned, the train was late; for hours, the spokesmen camouflaged the obvious by pointing out the beauties of the station and by talking about Other Things. Finally, an exasperated correspondent asked, "Isn't the train late?" One guide's face flushed, and then he blustered, "Yes, so what? What about Mississippi?"9

"What about Mississippi?" was a question for political leaders at home as well as for diplomats. At one time it had been a question largely confined to idealists, but the political muscle which black voters had flexed in Harry S. Truman's surprising reelection in 1948 made blacks a concern for the pragmatists who wanted to win votes. The cities and industrial centers of the northeast corridor, of the upper Midwest, and of the growing West were filling up with black populations who were politically active. These blacks were from the South, they kept up with affairs "way back home," and they constituted a source of internal pressures for domestic politicians to end Jim Crow. Of course, millions of blacks still in the South were largely denied the vote, but their potential strength attracted ambitious politicians to the plight of Mississippi, much as the Russians were attracted to it.

To these inner and outer pressures for social reform were added powerful economic forces; for the experiences of the multinational corporation mirrored those of the diplomatic corps: that is, it was impracticable to do business the Jim Crow way in other hemispheres. Thus the worldly-wise men of the corporation let it be known that they would not be coming south if they had to bend their business practices around the peculiarities of local Jim Crow. Moreover, the latter complaint traveling from the conference room to the chambers of commerce underscored something Woodward had learned from the Regionalists: there was not one southern Jim

Crow but a number of regional Jim Crow practices, and a multinational corporation would not just have to change its otherwise universal practices for *the* South; instead, it would have to set individualized policies for Tennessee and for Alabama and even for north Louisiana and for New Orleans.

In short, the institutions of Jim Crow were ground by the nether wheels of economics and politics, and those wheels were driven by momentum generated by the cold war. There were good reasons to assume that Jim Crow, or really, the Jim Crows, would crack under the rapidly increasing tension from within and from without. But that left unresolved the question of the South's relationship to Jim Crow: would the best of the South perish along with the worst? Without here denying the significance of racism, Woodward sought to demonstrate the marginality of Jim Crow. Although his entire oeuvre does, in fact, underestimate the destructive power of southern racism, that perceptual flaw was not in this book. The *Strange Career of Jim Crow* focused a brilliant light on a particular aspect of racism, on the life and times of segregation.

I I

At least two men had preceded Woodward down the path of the investigations which resulted in his theme of the strange career. These, Vernon Lane Wharton and George Brown Tindall, were friends and contemporaries of Woodward's and were also products of the Hill, although they were directed in their studies by Fletcher Melvin Green instead of Howard Kennedy Beale. Both Wharton and Tindall produced astute monographs on patterns of race relations in the Deep South, both monographs became minor classics, and both offered an interpretive trend as well as solid documentation to fuel the course of that trend. In fact, the work of Wharton and Tindall, in retrospect, was practically designed to support Woodward's emergent thesis: Wharton refuted the claims of a monolithic and time-out-of-mind Jim Crow for Mississippi in the decade after the Civil War; and Tindall did the same for South Carolina from the end of Reconstruction to the twentieth century. Each man had examined a state which was heavily black, which was known for racial violence, which was infamous for fierce southernness, and which boasted a white citizenry which claimed to trace its Jim Crow practices back to antebellum days. Thus whatever could be shown about these two sister states—customarily grouped together at the bottom of the nation's socioeconomic heap—would have telling significance for the entire section. If Mississippi and South Carolina had ever been different, then perhaps there was real hope for the South and for the United States. [10]

In Mississippi, Wharton had chosen quite a threatening territory. It was the state whose violent reaction to the reforms of Reconstruction had set a pattern for the eventual overthrow of all black and radical governments in the South. In 1875 white Mississippians had begun to organize into paramilitary units which used force and fraud to drive blacks from their offices and from the polls. This policy, which relied on the original Ku Klux Klan for effect, became known as the "Mississippi Plan," which was copied in South Carolina, Florida, and Louisiana in the centennial year. When Wharton started his graduate research in the 1940s, the scholarly presumption had been that the Mississippi Plan represented immutable white values, values temporarily suppressed by northern military force for less than a decade. In fact, Carolina's Joseph Gregoire de Roulhac Hamilton had glorified such schemes and practices in Reconstruction Alabama, and his colleague Hugh Talmadge Lefler had glorified such violent expressions of "values" in North Carolina. Chapel Hill, then, had quite a history of upholding Jim Crow by the labors of the scholar. Even Fletcher Green—who dominated southern history in the 1940s and 1950s with an insistence on "bread and butter" monographs and a deemphasis of interpretation—even he was prone to defend Jim Crow practices of the day, although he seldom pressed these views on his students. [11]

Nevertheless, Wharton was not completely alone in disliking the Mississippi Plan and in doubting its status as an immutable expression of societal mores. In the middle of the depression, Francis Butler Simkins and Robert Hilliard Woody had published a different view of Reconstruction in South Carolina, one that while still flawed by genteel racism, took seriously some of the black aspirations for societal achievement; and although Simkins and Woody exhibited little sympathy with the effort of Reconstruction, they at least conceded that much of the problem was caused by forces considerably larger and more powerful than the negative "traits" supposedly inherent in black people or in northern carpetbaggers.[12] As such, their investigations helped to prepare the way for major revisions of Reconstruction historiography, of which the earliest and one of the best was Wharton's.

In fact, Wharton, given his head by Green in the dissertation which became a book, went much farther than had Simkins and Woody. Where his predecessors described failure in a nonracial context, Wharton described accomplishment: whatever else, "many gates had been opened to the Negro that never would be closed again." Moreover, many of the white "cooperationists" of Mississippi included men from the leading families; and these men had worked successfully with idealistic northerners and with efficient, honest Negro leaders to build the state's first good public school system. Since Negroes never controlled the state general assembly, nor any county government, nor any town government, the things done in Reconstruction for blacks took on a new significance: native white leaders had for a time been willing to treat blacks as mature adults and as a political constituency with needs worth attention. Such a statement was quite a contribution to historical research, and as such its weight counterbalanced any shortcomings in the rest of Wharton's thesis. In addition to this new perspective on the attitudes of white leaders toward blacks in Reconstruction, Wharton offered a reason for the disappearance in the 1890s of that former willingness to help. He located the forces of change in class structure: the lower stratum of whites, increasingly gaining power after Reconstruction ended in 1877, never had developed any sympathy for black political dreams. In fact, the poor white, beset with severe economic problems, insisted on some reaffirmation of white dignity; and the aristocracy gave it to him with Jim Crow, with political disfranchisement of blacks, and with an understanding wink at the violence of the Ku Klux Klan. Thus Wharton wrote that "by 1890 almost all white men in Mississippi agreed that the Negro was in his place, and that, at all costs, he should be kept there. That place, like the place of the slave, was carefully defined, and theoretically, unalterable." His words thus underscored Woodward's growing suspicion that once it had been different and that social change was only "theoretically unalterable," not genuinely immutable.[13]

Beside Wharton's book on the shelf of excellent state/era monographs went George Tindall's *South Carolina Negroes*. Tindall, also given his head by Green in a dissertation which became a book, attacked the problem of what happened to the blacks in that state after the restoration of racist home rule. It was a question that transcended ideological orientation: that is, whether one was "for" or "against" black participation in politics, what was the nature of the Negro's fall from power between 1877, when hundreds of blacks held office, and 1900, when most blacks could not even vote? Before Tindall made his study, liberals and conservatives alike presumed that the fall from power was both precipitous and complete. It was thought that the loss of social privilege and prerogative, especially access to public facilities, had paralleled the loss of political strength in 1877—that one disappeared alongside the other as a matter of course.

Tindall, nevertheless, moved behind those presumptions to look at what actually happened. What he found was a very intricate set of patterns with significant variations by region and by class. The 1880s were not a period of uniform Jim Crow social practices, nor a period of statewide political disfranchisement. A black elite continued to rub shoulders with at least some of the white elite; and the heavily black areas of the coastal low country continued to vote and to send a black representative to the U.S. Congress. Moreover, trains, restaurants, and other quasi-public facilities were available to blacks in at least a few counties of the state. Summing up, Tindall found the term *fluidity* the most apt description of race relations in the 1880s; things were flowing, but there was no real proof that events had to flow inevitably into the specific patterns of Jim Crow segregation. What happened in the 1890s mirrored Wharton's picture of Mississippi: poor whites, losing more and more economically, were placated socially by Jim Crow and politically by disfranchisement of blacks. Yet even with the "white revolt" of the 1890s, there remained blacks in South Carolina who exercised power and enjoyed privileges, as there remained some whites who defied the segregationist law and the prophets.

Between Tindall and Wharton there were indeed the lines of a new direction. Both deserved immense credit for assisting in what Woodward eventually achieved; but neither man had fully realized the potential of his own research findings. Someone had to seize the moment offered by the renewed attention of the 1950s era to the history of Jim Crow. It was Woodward's genius that he looked at fragmentary evidence and discerned there a direction, a shape, something worth demonstrating to others immediately; to wait for complete support from all sources was to miss the moment—not the moment for fame, but the moment for effect with usable history.

Thus he staked out survey lines, lines which ran directly from his own research, from his friends' and his family's experiences, and from the Tindall and Wharton research in two states. All of the lines converged in the 1890s when the varied practices and the varied attitudes became simplified and almost unified; in Tindall's terminology, the fluidity ceased and patterns of race relations froze or solidified. The assumptions which young Woodward had made while studying Tom Watson dovetailed with the conclusions of Tindall and Wharton: after 1896, conservative politicians had acted to placate the poor whites who were beset by the oppressions of a faltering economy. What no one had done was to show linkages between perceived cause and identifiable effect: what was the relationship between the Jim Crow that came at the beginning of the twentieth century and the economic reversals that came at the end of the nineteenth century?

For the answer, Woodward offered something old and something new: from the old came the class analysis and the material dynamics of Progressivism; from the new came the regnant sociopsychological theories of the 1950s, especially the concept of the frustration-aggression nexus. The old fit neatly with the evidence; clearly a world-wide depression, crop disasters, deflation of money, and other economic woes had forced confrontation between rich and poor, confrontation dramatically symbolized by the Populist campaign of economic and political reform; clearly an elite group had defeated the Populists by employing a racial stratagem, Jim Crow; and clearly the masses of the white have-nots had eventually settled on the Negro as the scapegoat for all the woes of the day. That alone would have been straight Progressivism, the message of Beard and Beale, of Parrington and Turner. But Woodward pressed beyond that economic model of interpretation: he found sociopsychological reasons for the Negro to become the scapegoat, those reasons which, in combination with economic privation, had produced the odd beast Jim Crow.

III

Although the elder statesman Goethe, the nineteenth-century Goethe, can fittingly serve Woodward's thesis about law and freedom, it was the Sturm und Drang dramatist of the eighteenth century whose Geist suffused the Woodward thesis on the emotions of the impulse to segregate. Woodward orchestrated sociopsychological voices, especially those of Gordon Allport and Konrad Lorenz, into one lilting movement of color and excitement. As he said, Marxist economic determinism left out too much of the human emotions of racism. On the other hand, Progressivism had room for a dialectic of the emotions, and he took full advantage of that opening to incorporate the latest available social science research. [14]

Much as he might disdain the message of the consensus historians, Woodward was certainly learning from their methods: Hofstadter, Boorstin, Hartz, and others were reading deeply and wisely in the era's social sciences and then using those tools of analysis to demonstrate the sameness and homogeneity of American culture; now Woodward, in order to show the conflict and the heterogeneity of American culture, was reading such theories and finding applications of his own. To use in this way Allport's humane, lucid, and inspiring essays concerning prejudice was natural for any liberal scholar of race relations in the 1950s; Lorenz's work, by marked contrast, was always far more problematical because of its implications and because of his political background and allegiances. In spite of any unhappiness with the nature of the sources of a scholar's inspirations, however, the thesis of *The Strange Career* certainly involved the quixotic theorist of frustration-aggression, for without Lorenz's studies and analyses, Allport's subsequent work on prejudice becomes almost inconceivable.

Over the years, Lorenz vacillated between the measured observations of the technician in the laboratory and the extremism of the monocausalist. At his best Lorenz succeeded in demonstrating an undeniable relationship between acts of aggression and the frustration which came when goals sought were thwarted; what he had noted with painstaking care among his beloved ducks and geese had its parallel among his fellow humans. The difference he noted was that most animals never attacked members of their own species except for defense of turf or in seeking a mate. Considering that difference between homo sapiens and other animals, Lorenz thought that he had found the secret of the distinction. He then proceeded to develop a soul-defeating explication of the nature of human life: life itself was basically a series of aggressive acts to "save one" from a series of frustrations; life was reduced to a grim series of games in which survival turned on the ability of some players to shift the burden of real defeats onto the shoulders of scapegoats, scapegoats who had had little to do with the thwarting of the real goals, scapegoats whose chief characteristics were vulnerability and inability to fight back. Such bullying was not only instinctual but also beneficent, for it constituted the chief mechanism of survival in a strife-filled world.[15]

Lorenz's system was an odd parallel to, and at first blush not much better than, the early behaviorist theories which insisted that life was a series of responses to stimuli: both systems gave short shrift to will, choice, and morality, emphasizing instead an almost reflexive reaction to external pressures. Worse, Lorenz during World War II had been honored by the Nazis, and his subsequent career was always shadowed by that association, especially since his theory, carried to extremes, could serve so well the goals of German fascism. In his case, too, there were objections besides the humanist's rejection of the frustration-aggression nexus: investigators following up his studies began to doubt the efficacy of his theory: laying aside the question of free will, did aggressive responses to frustration of goals actually solve problems or otherwise help the individual in question? Some investigations showed that aggression bred aggression; instead of bringing cathartic relief, aggression only led to more aggression. Other investigators revealed that many animals, not just humans, responded aggressively against their own species after frustration of goals. What remained, then, of Lorenz's research and ideas was the establishment of some relationship between frustration and aggression.

But on second thought, what remained was quite useful for the study of race. Scapegoating had certainly had its moment on the stage of southern history, for how else could one describe the physical brutishness of the 1890s and the early twentieth century? Doubtless, white southerners were acting with extreme aggression against blacks. Was there not enough in Lorenz's theory and in his clinical observations to make a link between frustration and aggression? Surely there was; and there existed already ample contemporary testimony to the high level of frustration operating in the South of that era. But did one have to accept the entire Lorenz thesis, including its glorification of aggression as a positive instinct which guaranteed survival?

To that the answer was no, for Gordon Allport had already thought his way through to an explanation which included the frustration-aggression linkage without making it the essence of survival. Defining frustration much more broadly than did Lorenz, Allport considered a panoply of emotional reactions to the negative events in life, noting that there was frustration in such feelings as the desire to conform, the attempt to enhance one's self by identification with society's fair-haired ones, anxiety over anticipation of vague threats, and guilt over the omission or commission of certain acts.

It was the latter sense of guilt which actually proved most useful for the study of race relations. Allport had succeeded in taking the modern concepts of transference to others of one's sense of guilt and projection of one's doubts about self onto others and linking them with the biblical idea of scapegoating: "And the goat shall bear upon him all their iniquities." In that passage from Leviticus, the ancient tribe on the Day of Atonement had ritualistically laid its collective sin on a sacrificial goat which was then abandoned in the wilderness. In the same way, the moderns "coped" with frustration by locating surrogate goats to bear the community's sin, or at least its collective culpability. Thus far, Allport sounded much like Lorenz, except that the former wrote with a grace of sensitivity and sensibility unavailable to the latter. Yet at exactly this point Allport made a clear break with Lorenz: scapegoating ritual or subconscious projection, the transference of responsibility for a personal defeat or defect was a "primitive" act and an act which must cease. What Lorenz celebrated as the instinct for survival, Allport denigrated as a device for destruction.

Focusing narrowly on scapegoating as a racial or ethnic expression of the frustration-aggression nexus, Allport found the seeds of genocide: "The Nazis were, in reality, trying to shift a burden of intolerable shame, guilt and frustration from the German people to a convenient goat, in this case selected not by lot but by the macabre course of history."[16] For Allport, then, the advanced civilization would face up to its shortcomings by conceding them for what they were, choosing as the action of courage not aggression but restraint. Without denying the universality of scapegoating, Allport called for a higher response from present civilizations facing challenge from the future. Curiously, then, the real world for both scholars was much the same, a landscape of aggression against the weak scapegoats. What differed so dramatically was the desired world, for the ideal of Lorenz was glorified instinct, but Allport's ideal was learned patience.

Reverting to the real world which he hoped to change, Allport was especially troubled by the scapegoating of those groups with a history of being the outsiders. The norm in any collectivity is a predilection for the familiar; from that predilection comes prejudice against the unfamiliar. With prejudice—a "rigid, inflexible, exaggerated pre-dilection"—begins the long, fearful slide from a celebration of oneself to aggression against others. Prejudice as a mentality does damage only to the mind and soul of the prejudiced; but prejudice acted upon, prejudice in kinesis, is discrimination, "an act of exclusion prompted by prejudice." And "note well, it is not *we* who move out, prompted by our predilections, but *they* whom we forcefully exclude from intruding into 'our domain.'" The movement toward prejudice picks up its own speed, and "if conditions are ripe—if frustration, ignorance, and propaganda combine in proper proportions—discrimination breaks over into scapegoating."[17] That "breakover" may end in the camps at Auschwitz or Andersonville, in the courtrooms of Boston or Scottsboro, in the streets of Berlin or Atlanta.

Woodward was aware of the slide up and down the southern continuum: of the breakover of the 1890s violence of the lynch mob and the city riot, but also of the more peaceful, institutionalized discrimination embodied in Jim Crow. From Allport's perspective, Jim Crow was the specific act of a predilection to disapprove the "strange" black other, while the lynching bee was the specific act of scapegoating. The unique historical position of the Negro in the South was almost beyond remark, as Woodward noted: "Looking back, way back, it seems to me that I took racism as the 'given' in the Southern condition, so pervasive and oppressive and obvious as to be assumed and require no proof or demonstration. Same was true about segregation."[18] But the specific acts of segregation and of oppression, the ghastly expressions of prejudice—what conditions had brought them to the point of the breakover, and what could southerners learn from the context of those past conditions?

Thus Woodward began with the presumption of prejudice and concerned himself with the peculiarities of scapegoating which took shape as forms of violence and as forms of extreme discrimination in every conceivable service, good, or other quiddity from birth to burial. Deeply indebted to Beard and Beale, Woodward again revealed Progressivism as his form of explanation: the frustration which white southerners felt in the 1890s was economic at base, and the greatness of Progressivism was its ability to hold together an economic argument of some complexity. Where Marxism, for Woodward, took insufficient account of the powers of racism, Progressivism had room within the workings of its internal logic for a system that described that preexisting social force of Negrophobia being called into discriminatory operation by the severities of an economy gone bad. After all, Progressivism was open-ended where Marxism was a closed system: Progressivism started with economic determinism and then proceeded down any of several possible paths.

I V

Now Woodward could return to a theme which had troubled him since he began his graduate research: the politicians of the early twentieth century, Watson, Tillman, and Vardaman,

> are remembered and despised as 'demagogues,' while their progressive social ideas are forgotten. In this manner conservative leaders could discredit reform leaders in the eyes of liberal opinion by denouncing them as demagogues. This confusion . . . is as full of tragic consequences for Southern thinking and living . . . as the tragic confusion of the 1850s—I mean the inexorable identification of the defense of human slavery with the defense of the whole Southern cause—its economy, its point of view, its soil, its very livelihood. Just as in 1860 slavery drove the West away from the South, its natural ally, into the arms of the East, and supplied an embattled industrial capitalism with a humanitarian war slogan, so the demagogues' treatment of the

Negro and other minorities in a later day has prevented reconciliation with the West and offended men of good will everywhere, driving them away from the cause of social progressivism. I do not say that the demagogue was justified in
using the methods he used any more than I think slavery was
justified in 1860. I do say that the fortuitous identification of
social revolt with demagogic tactics was heavy with tragic consequences for the South. [19]

That fortuitous identification was the reason for his investigation
of Tom Watson and earlier had been the inspiration for his original
plan for graduate school, to write the dissertation "Seven for Demos."
Before 1954, Woodward had offered a compelling specific rationale
for the tragic linkage between radical politics of economic reform and
racist demagoguery: that had been the case of Tom Watson, the man
with the preexisting flaw of personality who cracked under the extreme economic and psychological tensions which came with the
defeat of Populism. By now, however, Woodward had note cards to
show that Watson was an individual case of a generic development:
most of a society had reacted as had Watson, not to the same degree,
but in the same way, to the reversals of the 1890s. Fusing Beard with
Lorenz and Allport, Woodward produced one part of his Jim Crow
thesis, namely, that the masses had responded to economic adversity
by designating the Negro as the scapegoat in this time and place.
What Woodward was doing was producing under the aegis of Progressivism a two-part argument at once subtle and inspiring: it was,
first, that Jim Crow lacked a tradition of unbroken, uniform application in the South; and second, that there were alternatives which had
long been forgotten.

These alternatives Woodward traced back to the 1880s, a decade
marked by relatively "cool" race relations, especially in comparison
with the urban race riots and paramilitary struggles of the preceding
and of the following eras, those of the 1870s which ended Reconstruction in the Deep South and those of the 1890s which introduced calamitous Negrophobia of an intensity not imagined even in
the 1870s. The 1880s had usually been ignored, or noted as an
aberrant exception to a broad pattern; Woodward, instead, traced
lines of continuity from this era back to the antebellum South and
forward into the twentieth century. In the tracing he outlined three

clear lines, all existing in his own experience, and he labeled these three in traditional political language, Liberal, Radical, and Conservative.

In that very special and not always fully conscious sense of deep reciprocities, Woodward himself embodied the three southern traditions which were the alternatives his fellows had forgotten. The slaveholding Vanns who left North Carolina to found a community in Arkansas were themselves exemplars of the patrician Conservatism for which he relied on Wade Hampton as the historic symbol. His beloved uncle Comer and his near-relative advisers Vance, Odum, and Will Alexander were the expressions of rather traditional Liberalism. And Tom Watson, the red-haired orator of the early agrarian campaigns, was young Vann himself, the Radical who sought economic and social reform.

Turning such political categorizations to use in describing racial policy has always been difficult, because racial politics long ago established independent existence; Liberals who worked to ameliorate other societal ills were often unabashedly racist; and even Radicals who intended to change society drastically were often intensely racist. Woodward's solution to this recurring problem was to search for a certain time, a day when political labels were relatively in line with racial practices; and then to chart the two courses, the development of racial attitudes and the development of political attitudes. What he insisted on was that in the 1880s southern politics and southern race relations were in near-alignment; there were Liberals who could apply Jeffersonian tenets of equality to blacks as well as to whites, and there were Radicals who could push class rebellion right across the dreaded line of color. As Woodward said of Conservatism, Liberalism, and Radicalism: "All three of these alternative philosophies rejected the doctrines of extreme racism and all three were indigenously and thoroughly Southern in origin."[20]

Looking at the Conservative legacy of his own family and of his own community, he noted the lack of a fully developed social philosophy but instead picked his way among "fragmentary formulations" and "policies pursued" to reach what was "clearly an aristocratic philosophy of paternalism and *noblesse oblige*."[21] A nearly perfect model for this attitude was Wade Hampton, patrician of the Old South, gallant cavalry leader for the Cause, Redeemer of South Carolina from Reconstruction, and voice for moderation and reconciliation in the New South. Despite Woodward's disdain for Hampton, the man fit into the groove of Conservatism which was emerging from the pile of index cards. Clearly he considered Negroes to be inferior, and he had coordinated a campaign in 1876 which included the use of violence and fraud to break the political power of the black Republicans in South Carolina. But Hampton's presumptions of superiority did not extend either to lynch-mob violence or to Jim Crow separation. In fact, Hampton appreciated physical and even spiritual closeness to blacks exactly *because* the race was said to be inferior: he loved them, in part, because they were beneath him. After all, he considered his class to be fit to rule as fathers over the children of the world, that is, blacks, poor people, women. His racial philosophy was an insult of real magnitude, but it was not Jim Crow.

The broader social philosophy of Hampton Conservatism involved a duty to preserve order and harmony while shaking up the ancient economic system through rapid industrialization and urbanization. Hampton, builder of railroads and benefactor to factories, was tearing apart the agrarian order; and he had no specific answer, no program, with which to respond to the dislocations he wrought. The one general response he could always make was the promise of honesty: Conservative government would seldom act to help the impoverished, but it would never act to harm anyone. Scrupulous attention to right conduct was his hallmark, one intended to comfort the spirit during the material distress. The spirit comforted was actually Hampton's own, and that of the members of the league of industrialists, entrepreneurs, and planters in the elite of the New South. Throughout the 1880s, then, Hampton had done real damage to the entire lower class, but he had also permitted some racial integration and a modicum of social freedom for Negroes.

The crisis for the Hampton spirit came with the Populist challenge of the 1890s. Not only did Populism offer a concrete program directed at the actual ills of the southern economy, but it also damaged the Conservative image of self. Populism could not be defeated except by fraud and violence: in the words of Hamptonian governor William Calvin Oates of Alabama, "Count 'em out!" What Populism had done to Hampton Conservatism was to expose the emptiness of its spiritual presents as well as its inability to tend

the body. Conservatives, in cheating the Populists, had almost destroyed their own illusion of respectability, that of the fair fighters,
the men of character. This meant that Conservatives, to regain face
in their own eyes, had to find something worse than themselves,
some entity which uniquely embodied their worst fears about their
own identity. What they did then was to seize again on the racial
scapegoat: it was the black man who was sent into the wilderness
damned for dishonesty, obfuscation, chicanery, misrepresentation,
improvidence, and general irresponsibility—projections of exactly
the traits which Conservatives found themselves exhibiting in the
campaigns of 1873–77 and 1894–98.[22]

At last Woodward was able to resolve one of the more vexing
problems of explaining Conservative actions: he had a sociopsychological rationale for the Conservatives' support of scapegoating by
Jim Crow. They did it not primarily by reason of economic privation, which would have been a ridiculous argument considering
their relative wealth; nor by reason of political conflict, also
ridiculous because they had already won their fights in that arena;
but rather because of their own nagging doubts about their own
worth. And they were seized with these doubts in the very midst of
transforming the South, which made Jim Crow not at all part of
traditional Conservatism, but instead an excrescence of change.

With this problem untied, Woodward had the entire exegesis and
explication at hand. The lower classes he presumed to be more susceptible to racism than were the upper classes, a presumption suggested by the research of Wharton and Tindall. Thus he was not
surprised by the popular embrace of Jim Crow, the institution of
extreme racism. Tom Watson had persuaded the poor whites to sacrifice color identity for the sake of economic reform. That reform
failing of achievement, why not strike at the Negro, given the
lengthy tradition of bad blood between the races? Woodward, of
course, was always aware of that lengthy tradition of racism, and he
viewed the Populist "era" of the 1880s and the early 1890s as an
experimental time, a day of testing out reform theories. Conservative acumen, fraudulently expressed, had "disproved" the theory
of "brothers united in the ditch"; and the poor white, never fully
convinced by the "ditch" symbolism, responded with rage, rage
that invested with new power the once-neglected color identity. For
the poor, then, the response to the frustration was a terrible level of

physical aggression and an equally terrible level of mental aggression, the former expressed by lynching, the latter by Jim Crow.[23]

This interpretation has been hard on the lower classes, for it makes them bear more than a fair share of culpability for the sins of a section. The rough handling in Woodward's treatment of the wool-hats reflected more than the research of the day: it also reflected the deep disappointment felt by the aristocrat about the performance of the masses. Those seeking radical economic change, after the 1896 election, had to couch their appeals in radically racist language, the very stratagem which, to repeat, had created the tragedy which "has prevented reconciliation with the West and offended men of good will everywhere." For all of Woodward's own youthful radicalism and for all of his mature desire for fundamental economic reform, the author of *The Strange Career of Jim Crow* felt some real disdain for Watson's hordes. The best he could say of them was that for one shining moment, they had considered a higher path.[24]

There remained the much smaller group, the Liberals, who along with the mass of blacks were the recipients of racist aggression. He never fully marked off Liberals, like George Washington Cable, from Radicals, like Tom Watson, but presumably the difference was in two parts, both style and the degree of change sought. Cable, Lewis Harvie Blair, and the others in this tiny band were racially more progressive than the 1890s Radicals, but their Radical ethos was not informed by the Populist economic program; nor were these aristocrats communicant for good or ill with the plain folk. At any rate, with the coming of Jim Crow, Liberals failed to voice alternatives to the dominant practices of the new institution.[25]

V

Those were the lines of argument Vann Woodward laid out for his friend John Hope Franklin as the two discussed the course of the civil rights movement after 1954. Franklin immediately liked the interpretation. It seemed to catch up his personal experiences, Woodward's, the region's, and such pieces of historical research as had been accomplished by 1954. Franklin encouraged his friend to press on with the work, something Woodward would probably have done anyway.[26]

He offered it as the public address in the fall at Charlottesville, accepting the invitation to deliver the Richard Lecture. There, in that most southern of environs, he told a biracial (but separated) audience that one could be distinctly southern without being a segregationist. Immediate response was hard to gauge, since the Virginia way was politic and mannerly; and his halting, uninflected, occasionally mumbling delivery may have left unheard certain crucial elements of his address. There were, of course, some signs which Woodward himself picked up as he was reading: "Oh, it was favorable. I do remember a friend, a lawyer with an awfully old Virginia name. I knew him to be interested professionally in segregation. During the speech I caught his eye—and I saw him afterward—he was awfully quiet, which was probably a negative reaction."[27]

More remarkable was the uncavalier reaction of the reading public to the book which he released in 1955. Most were overwhelmed, buying it and talking about it. It caught the attention of the literate public outside the field of history just as Frederick Jackson Turner drew people to the frontier thesis or Charles Austin Beard drew them to the economic interpretation of the Constitution. In this reaching beyond professional historians, Woodward did create a problem for himself, a phenomenon which one observer labeled the "two *Strange Careers of Jim Crow;* for there was the book he wrote and there was the book people read."[28] For many, the book they read became a tract, a polemic which made the 1880s into a goldern era of race relations, which made the South perpetually liberal and tolerant, which ignored racism by studying only legal formalism, and which created a morality play out of historical events.

The nature of the offering left it open to such readings; and that nature troubled Woodward's friends. As it left the presses, crusty Bill Carleton scolded him in a letter which anticipated later scholarly criticisms: it was excessively legalistic and thus overlooked less formal, de facto, arrangements to accomplish the same ends; the analogy with South Africa was weakly developed and inaccurate; and it was overly popularized. Of a broader philosophical nature was David Potter's question: "What has the historian to do with hope?" by which Woodward understood his friend to be saying that historians must understand the past by its own light instead of using it to rearrange the future. This notation by Potter described the perpetual dilemma in all of Woodward's "committed" scholarship, for it was this quality of presentism which made his earlier work most tellingly relevant for a particular era, but it was this same quality which would also make that work most obviously dated in later years. In the 1950s, however, this was not even a recognized debating point for Woodward, who then continued to give full credence to the old injunctions of Hartsock and Pipkin and Vance that scholars owed the public "usable" research and writing.[29]

As less friendly critics entered the discussions in the 1960s, new data, far more detailed than what Woodward had found available in 1954, came to the front. Some fashioned careers out of Woodward's thesis, either by defending it or by attacking it, and Woodward was himself caught up in the second *Strange Career,* the one people were reading. At times he, too, seemed to be reading some other book in his efforts to defend his thesis. He brought out revised editions and he became defensive, in the 1960s claiming that it was his greatest work, but in the 1970s discounting it as historical contribution and emphasizing the limited nature of what he sought to prove in 1954.[30] Briefly in the middle-1970s he was at his least attractive, narrowing the vision of the original thesis to answer criticism, while simultaneously denying the significance of the work. Yet the debate certainly went on, ultimately to everyone's benefit, both because of and in spite of Woodward, for there was another side of the man, a warmly encouraging side; and the nature of scholarly debate—that is, the way that young historians are urged to "take on" their elders—in combination with Woodward's efforts of encouragement eventually produced some of the recent era's most interesting social history.

In particular, Joel Williamson did much to shape the contours of this discussion, in the process experiencing a wide range of responses from Woodward. Completing in 1965 a study of Reconstruction in South Carolina, Williamson provided a considerable proof that de facto segregation was so prevalent during and immediately after the period 1865–77 that it vitiated Tindall's concept of fluidity, which was, in turn, vital to Woodward's thesis. Further, Williamson, in subsequent research and writing, began to blame the upper class for most of the racial discrimination, including the violence, thus reversing Tindall's and Wharton's contentions that the aristocracy was responding with some reluctance to demands from the poor whites. And Williamson insisted that Conservatism was much more fully developed as a distinctive southern philosophy than Woodward understood, and that Liberalism was practically nonexistent even as a "forgotten alternative"; he implied, too, that the Populists were not Woodwardian Radicals of the *Strange Career* mold. Finally, Williamson questioned the primacy of economic forces in determining race relations, and he sometimes appeared to say that racism not only could move independently of economics but also could alter the shape of economics. All of this was the most fundamental kind of challenge to Woodward's work, but Williamson, since his graduate days "as a young whippersnapper on the research trail," has enjoyed warm personal support from his elder. At the same time, however, Williamson has also witnessed an occasional bit of condescension from that source, most notably in an important essay on Jim Crow scholarship which Woodward published in his collection entitled *American Counterpoint.* And in the dialogue with other scholars influenced by Williamson, Woodward sometimes exhibited, by turns, a rather testy defensiveness and a frustrating evasiveness. By 1978, however, he had developed a much healthier attitude: "I could revise it, but no more: it can stand."[31]

In fact, the way toward a far more interesting and ultimately far more valuable perspective began to appear in that year of 1978 with the work of Howard Rabinowitz and after him, in 1982, that of John W. Cell. Rabinowitz had the advantage of studying at Chicago with John Hope Franklin and thus learning about Jim Crow from one who knew the phenomena thoroughly and from one who knew Woodward's early thinking about segregation. Perhaps more important, Rabinowitz, by writing about the issues in 1978, could benefit from the development of the historians' debates which had already gone before, and since much of the passion was gone from the discourse, he was assured an audience if he could suggest a fresh approach. For one thing, Rabinowitz recognized that there were plural institutions and plural practices which were created by racism: he was able to show that disfranchisement and segregation and Negrophobic violence and denial of access to public services were different actions which occurred at different times and not in one mass of undifferentiated motion. For another, he looked again at the talismanic and emblematic quality of Jim Crow—at the way Conservatives were said to use the threat of violence as an excuse for creating the institutions to keep whites and blacks apart "for their own good"—and he noted that this contemporaneous argument actually had some merit. Jim Crow, he found, was not the worst aspect of extreme racism, and while reprehensible enough, it was preferable if one were reduced to bad choices between Jim Crow and the lynch mob, as people likely were by the period 1898–1912. Along the same line of thought, segregation was in some ways an advance in that "for colored only" at least provided access to services, especially to services completely closed to Negroes before Jim Crow offered segregated facilities. Thus, in Rabinowitz's perspective, the interesting question was not so much when de jure segregation began "but what it replaced." And what it replaced was "exclusion," the outright denial of any services at all; given this background, Jim Crow was in this special sense an improvement, since it was better to have a chance separately and with prejudice than not to have the opportunity at all. According to Rabinowitz, de facto segregation emerged during Reconstruction to replace antebellum exclusion, and it was "initiated by radical white Republicans" and "supported" and sometimes even requested by their black allies. After 1890, the de jure institutions of Jim Crow completed the transformation.[32]

Most useful of all has been the ripe wisdom evinced by John W. Cell, whose *The Highest Stage of White Supremacy* has drawn on decades of research in South African history and on a lengthy tenure in the Carolina Piedmont. Like George Fredrickson before him, Cell made the point that contrasts between South Africa and the American South can be overdrawn; that is, both places bear long traditions of racism and discrimination; but both have experienced extreme racism as a "discontinuous" and "revolutionary" expression of white dominance—Pretoria after 1948, Atlanta after 1889. But Cell was most insightful when he turned to a consideration of the dramatic shift in the political rhetoric and the laws in the South: like Rabinowitz, and unlike Woodward, Cell took seriously the idea that Jim Crow did provide physical protection for blacks. It was not the awful symbol of the worst policies available in this grisly time when white riots decimated the black populations in Wilmington, Atlanta, and New Orleans and when, in each of the years 1893 and 1894, over 120 Negroes were lynched; rather, in that time the most awful symbol was the mob's rope. Moreover, the new patterns of rigid separation were most evident in the textile mill village, which prompted Cell to note that *The Strange Career,* with all its sophisticated sociopsychology, was really not explaining the reasons for segregation. In fact, Cell said, *Origins of the New South* was the one publication among all of the things written about Jim Crow which had correctly located the genesis of the new laws: they were produced in the processes of industrialization and urbanization.[33]

Once scholarship has reached this stage, one could well ask what actually remains of *The Strange Career,* since historians in different ways have rejected large portions of it; and with so much of it now rejected, one could equally well question the claim that it is a great work. To some degree, Woodward himself has been embarrassed in later years by the obvious commitment and intensity which reside in the text. As he entered a more conservative political and less experimental academic phase of his career in 1969, he lost for a time any controlling sense of commitment to a social program, and he expressed a sense of distance, almost an estrangement, from the energies which surged through *The Strange Career* and which moved no less than Martin Luther King, Jr., to proclaim the book "the Bible of the civil rights movement." But Woodward would not remain for long in this phase, which his friend and former student William McFeely calls ruefully "his Tory period"; and besides, an author's subsequent judgment on his or her work is seldom the point. Rather, considering the question of influence in cultural and political life, King seems to have been right: Woodward's thesis, like the *Brown* decision itself, gave integrationists "heart to fight" with a work whose mythic qualities of inspiration were indispensably a part of a social movement. Without *The Strange Career,* some who worked for reform might have hung back from the fray in the indecisiveness of immobilized ambivalence.[34]

Shifting to another kind of question, Woodward's inspiration was also indisputably a part of the ongoing study of social history, for without *The Strange Career* as an "impertinent first question," other scholars might never have moved toward the "pertinent" answers.[35] The genius in Woodward was orchestration: his sense of timing and of arrangement, of colorature and of range. Perhaps others were on their way to the same thesis, but no other expressed it with the symphonic brilliance of Woodward's first edition. By writing it as he did, when he did, he created a new debate and thus has shared in every amendment which any scholar has made to the first work, and even in the refutations. Had he not produced the first bold statement of thesis out of fragmentary evidence, the more mature clarifying monographs would have been postponed for decades—if written at all.

Moreover, there is a special characteristic of this work which will endure as an insight into the very nature of race relations and of the institutions of Jim Crow, although it is the kind of insight which can never be effectively proved or disproved by scholars' research. This is the insistence that segregation will ultimately be defeated by the human identity itself: that basic impulses, both positive and negative, in soul and flesh, will simply overwhelm the strictures of racial separation. After all, the antebellum plantation, where the vast majority of blacks lived their experiences, was certainly a place of cultural integration, as has been demonstrated redundantly in the superb scholarship of historians with such differing perspectives as Eugene Genovese, Peter Wood, Leon Litwack, and Charles Joyner. In Ralph Waldo Ellison's perfect phrase, the syncretic nature of the black experience in slavery and afterward has made it "a culture of cultures." The physical integration was there too, often in brutal form, but there unmistakably in the miscegenation and the growing mulatto population. And the palpable physicality of the mixing was caught by William Faulkner, describing the moment when an embittered old white woman brushes against her exiled black counterpart: "There is something in the touch of flesh with flesh which abrogates, cuts sharp and straight across the devious intricate channels of decorous ordering, which makes enemies as well as lovers know because it makes them both—touch and touch of that which is the central I-Am's private own: not spirit, soul; the liquorish and ungirdled mind is anyone's to take in any darkened hallway of this earthly tenement. But let flesh touch with flesh, and watch the fall of all the egg shell shibboleths of caste and color too."[36]

In other words, Jim Crow expressed racism, a force Woodward underestimated in other places. But it also expressed a kind of separation known to the South only briefly: the syncretic qualities of the southern subculture would not have developed if the Old South had really kept apart white from black as Jim Crow in theory demanded they be kept apart. Free blacks were segregated, but the ninety and nine, the slaves, had whiteness pressed on them even as they pressed blackness on their masters. This insight of Woodward's has been seized on with telling effect by Albert Murray, who made it one of the themes of his intellectual and emotional excursion, *South to a Very Old Place*.[37] What Jim Crow marked, then, was properly considered an aberration, not in extreme racism (which really came as early as 1889 before the institutions were set in legal place), but in cultural patterns: only in the few decades starting this century have white and black moved along truly separate wavelengths.

Finally, there is a reasonable answer to the skeptical question of Woodward's friend Potter: the hope that Jim Crow would die without killing the South infuses the book; and that hope has been subsequently realized. In the years since 1954, the South has rid itself of Jim Crow, albeit without ridding itself of racism, and it has remained the distinctive section of the country. Blame for those things which have changed for the worse in the South is as well laid on the head of grasping materialism as on the death of Jim Crow. And those things which have changed for the better about the South are often directly traceable to the Supreme Court decision and its implementation.

In reflecting on this individual piece of work, one can see much the same embroidery as in all of Woodward's scholarship. All of the embroidery is fascinating, most of it is good, but *The Strange Career of Jim Crow* is his best artistry. Here he has succeeded in weaving class studies with race studies without losing sight of either; and here he has managed to express most meaningfully his love for the South without crafting for it an apologia. Furthermore, the cry for racial justice was the very definition of Woodward's contemporary liberalism; after the civil rights movement was fragmented by the myriad events culminating in 1968, Woodward could no longer define either liberalism or his own ideological stance. This work of 1955 is both self-definition for an era's liberals and a prescription for societal change; it is so charged with moral energy that once he began to doubt its significance, he lost for a time his moorings. But when he recovered his ironic reformism—in part by responding again to the profound challenges of racism—he was able to present the nation's thinkers with a gift of very special value.

8

The Burden of Southern History

Ironic Perceptions, Ironic Commitments, 1955–1965

A work of art is a corner of creation seen through a temperament.
   —Emile Zola, quoted and discussed in
   Josephson, *Zola and His Time*

Ironies of all kinds characterize the temperament of modern art, and great art has always revealed the thoughts and feelings of an age. It is not metaphorical to describe Woodward as an artist, for his preoccupations since his youth have been with artists and with works of art; and it is a commonplace that his writing demonstrates in its sensitivity to the nuance of expression both a knowledge and a mastery of the techniques of the creative stylist. This characteristic has posed a special dilemma, however, because of his commitment to a usable past: artists, after all, need some detachment from their creations, and it seems contradictory to call simultaneously for the artist's emotional distance and the reformist's emotional engagement. Such contradiction exposes several layers of the possible meaning and applications of irony, and particularly the kind of irony to which Woodward committed his scholarly artistry in the years between 1955 and 1965.

I

By and large, historians have used irony only at its most basic levels of meaning and application, to describe the unintended consequences in which even the best-laid plans of men "gang aft agley." For example, David Levering Lewis has noted the irony in President Dwight David Eisenhower's refusal to help Negroes in the civil rights movement: it so exacerbated conditions that a confrontation ensued, and as a result of that confrontation, the movement was in fact speeded along considerably. The eventual consequences of these executive actions could not have been Eisenhower's intent, and thus Lewis marked, with much wit and just a little malice, the way in which the executive inactivity and lethargy actually contributed to great activity and a new sense of energy. But as subtle as is this usage of irony, there are other and deeper levels of it as a methodology. Two levels of application are especially significant for Woodward in his work between 1955 and 1965: one, adapted from theologian Reinhold Niebuhr, concerns ideological action and choice within the context of irony; the other, learned from the poets and critics Robert Penn Warren and Cleanth Brooks, concerns the relationship of style and substance within that context.[1]

That Niebuhr could work such an influence on him was itself an unintended and largely unacknowledged product of Woodward's intellectual development. Since his arrival at Emory in Atlanta, Woodward had expressed cynicism about the leaders of his former faith of Methodism; during the Great Depression years he was agnostic about all organized religions; and by World War II he characteristically expressed atheism. Niebuhr was a neoorthodox Protestant standing in the pulpit of a church in then-prospering Detroit and wrestling with the demons of a liberalism whose programs Woodward supported heartily. But it was the *target* of Niebuhr's attacks—the assumptions of innocence—which first drew Woodward's attention and which eventually informed his thinking. Theologian of neoorthodoxy notwithstanding, here was a man expressing skepticism while most academicians and politicians proclaimed optimism in an unreflective style which the poet W. H. Auden once decried as "the tearless chirping of birds." The claim to a singular innocence and a singular invincibility for America had angered Woodward since the Four Freedoms campaign, which he considered fallacious. And now the thing to say was that everyone believed in this odd combination of purity and power and that it had always been this way, with no one—save for "bigoted" and "emotional" Populists—questioning the revelations of received wisdom. Yet there had been Thomas Jefferson in the dusk of his long day writing that slavery could not be legislated away but also that the republic could not survive without resolving this issue of freedom; and there had been Jefferson in that same fading light scorning the "monks" of New England for substituting a false religiosity for true reason.[2]

Niebuhr deserves quoting at length:

The confidence of modern secular idealism in the possibility of an easy resolution of the tension between individual and community, or between classes, races and nations is derived from a too optimistic view of human nature. This too generous estimate of human virtue is intimately related to an erroneous estimate of the dimensions of the human stature. The conception of human nature which underlies the social and political attitudes of a liberal democratic culture is that of an essentially harmless individual. The survival impulse, which man shares with the animals, is regarded as the normative form of his egoistic drive. If this were a true picture of the human situation man might be, or might become, as harmless as seventeenth- or eighteenth-century thought assumed. Unfortunately for the validity of this picture of man, the most significant distinction between the human and the animal world is that the impulses of the former are "spiritualized" in the human world. Human capacities for evil as well as for good are derived from this spiritualization. The one form is the desire to fulfill the potentialities of life and not merely to maintain its existence. Man is the kind of animal who cannot merely live. If he lives at all he is bound to seek the realization of his true nature; and to his true nature belongs his fulfillment in the lives of others. The will to live is thus transmuted into the will to self-realization; and self-realization involves self-giving in relation to others. When this desire for self-realization is fully explored it becomes apparent that it is subject to the paradox that the highest form of self-realization is the consequence of self-giving, but that it cannot be the intended consequence without being prematurely limited. Thus the will to live is fully transmuted into its opposite in the sense that only in self-giving can the self be fulfilled, for: "He that findeth his life shall lose it: and he that loseth his life for my sake shall find it" [Matt. 10:39].[3]

Obviously by 1944, when Niebuhr quoted the words of St. Matthew which were surely the most important to the theologian, this concept of giving up his life for Jesus Christ no longer spoke to Woodward's values; but there was still in Niebuhr that uncompromising toughness, that idealism without illusion, which had drawn the Arkansas adolescent to Bola Martin and Charles Pipkin and had pulled the newly arrived Atlantan to Ernest Hartsock and Glenn Rainey. It was also the quality which had drawn the graduate student to Rupert Vance and Howard Beale and the young professor to Charles Beard. Working through Niebuhr's essay, he discerned a profound reaffirmation of some very secular, very Beardian values; and more than that, he found some insights which gave the lie to the regnant politics and the regnant historiography of this day. In particular, he appreciated Niebuhr's explanation of the way in which choices for action are limited both by the very nature of humanity and by the decisions reached by one's predecessors.[4]

If the intended consequences of the highest form of self-realization are in fact limited by the very nature of self-giving, then there must be considerable limitation of the moral choices presented to people for decision and action. Furthermore, it is obvious that many people seek self-realization through *taking* instead of giving, and Niebuhr also said that the term *original sin* was best formulated as self-aggrandizement at the expense of others. The selfishness which often characterizes the instinct for survival limits the kind and degree of moral choices open to man. In this perspective, Niebuhr defined pathos as the complete absence of any choice except to let evil happen, a condition which might describe a woman awaiting the execution of her death sentence in a totalitarian concentration camp. Following that vein, he described tragedy as a choice between two evils, both undeniably malevolent, but one clearly more awful than the other; in his example, the decision to commit the evil of world war was not as awful as the decision to permit the greater evil of global fascism. But the choices for action most often confronting people in a democratic society are usually less confining than tragedy: they express *irony,* that is, the choice among a range of actions, none truly good but some clearly more awful than others. Niebuhr insisted that democracies live on the edge of such ironic choices. If so, the citizen's duty is clear, to choose and to act even if the decision is between "bad" and "worse." Avoiding decision and delaying actions in difficult circumstances will only proscribe future choices, perhaps producing tragic or even pathetic choices for later generations.[5]

But for all that Niebuhr wrote about ironic choice and for all his notation about unintended consequences, he told little about the writing style of irony and nothing about the relationship of such a style to the substance of irony. About these elements of irony Woodward learned much through discussion with Robert Penn Warren and through his own careful reading of essays suggested by Warren, including those of Cleanth Brooks. In time, Brooks, Warren, and Woodward would all serve together at Yale University, where Woodward came to influence the literary men; but in the 1950s the influence essentially flowed in the other direction, from the Louisiana State University poets toward the historian. Brooks was especially masterly in explaining that the modern artist so frequently chooses the ironic style because other styles have become morally and intellectually bankrupt: "There is the breakdown of a common symbolism; there is the general scepticism as to universals; not least important, there is the depletion and corruption of the very language itself, by advertising and by the mass-produced arts of radio, the moving picture, and pulp fiction. The modern poet has the task of rehabilitating a tired and drained language so that it can convey meanings once more with force and with exactitude. This task of qualifying and modifying language is perennial; but it is imposed on the modern poet as a special burden."[6]

As important as were these insights into style, however, the most profound motivation for Woodward came from Brooks's insisting on the duty to use irony to strip away delusion and to expose sham, noting that "the irony is not that of a narrow and acerb satire; rather it is an irony which accords with a wise recognition of the total situation." Going on to state the case even more strongly, Brooks celebrated the commitments and the occasional successes of some modern ironists: "To the honor of the modern poet be it said that he has frequently succeeded in using his ironic technique to win through to clarity and passion." What Brooks was calling for and what Woodward attempted to do between 1955 and 1965 was nothing less than to wage war on the language of obscurantism and of defeatism by adapting a style which would "win through" to truth and beauty.[7]

Equally compelling was Robert Penn Warren's image of truth and beauty, which the historian-ironist was attempting to gain in the style of his own matured essays. This image Warren derived from William Faulkner's novels about the struggle of the human soul and from Eric Voegelin's philosophy of the history of order. Faulkner's texts Warren studied with close attention, and Voegelin the man— one of the European immigrants swept in by the "sea change" of Hitler's rise to dominance—Warren studied up close in Baton Rouge as a coworker while the modern metaphysicist labored over his magnum opus for the Louisiana State University Press. Although Warren and Brooks in their own ways had already thought through some of Voegelin's concepts, there is little question that each man learned from and used the newcomer's full statement of the necessity of the fall, the experience of judgment for the arrogant, and the alternatives of restoration and catastrophic punishment.[8]

To Voegelin, innocence was a bad thing and invincibility only a temporary illusion. In terms of Jewish history, the glories of Solomon were not the full height of justice, since the very presumptions of being uniquely apart from and above the rest of the world were fundamentally unhealthy. Instead, the Jews' great accomplishment was the subsequent patient treading of the "hard line" *back* to the rest of the world, for the way of justice lay in engagement with the potentiality of the whole universe. During the Enlightenment, when rationalism destroyed old superstition, the triumph of the "just polis" remained unrealized despite this dramatic "leap in being," because the "break with the order of myth" did not guarantee success: it guaranteed only the opportunity to act—which opportunity included the very real chance of failure. Disabusing mankind of the dangerous notions of innocence and invincibility was one of the most important tasks in life, and "amiable" language was decidedly not the proper and effective means of awakening spiritually and intellectually slumbering men. Rather, "it must be a critical study of the authoritative structure in the history of mankind."[9]

Such concepts Warren applied to understanding and to employing Faulkner's themes, both as a critical exercise and as a part of his own life's mission to wake up the intelligent and sensitive citizen. Obviously echoing Voegelin, Warren showed that in Faulkner's work, "the human effort is what is important, the capacity to make the effort to rise above the mechanical process of life, the pride to endure, for in endurance there is a kind of self-conquest." Thinking specifically of Faulkner's *The Bear,* Warren suggested that God asked for pity and humility from men because men held the earth in a moral trust. "It is the failure of the pity which curses the earth," said Warren; and the "lust for power over nature is associated with the lust for power over other men."[10] Perhaps irony both as an attitude and as a means of expression provided the chance to resolve the considerable dilemma posed for the historian by the competing goals of the usable past and the artist's duty to art itself.

II

In thus turning toward the interpretive essay, Woodward took a new direction in his career, one foreshadowed unconsciously by *The Strange Career of Jim Crow.* After 1955, he would not again produce a research monograph, although he would certainly stay close to the primary sources in the manuscript collections of New South financial and literary leaders. Even *The Strange Career* is more an extended reflection on research already conducted than it is a research monograph, but over the next thirty years he would not produce another "book"; rather, he would write ironic essays; edit "diaries," papers, and reprinted editions of earlier New South essays; lead investigative teams in historical research for political ends; work on a college textbook; direct, with Richard Hofstadter, the ambitious multivolume interpretive *Oxford University History of the United States;* and pen a charming extended essay "thinking back" over the processes of writing history. He would attempt to write a major book concerning racism, another concerning Reconstruction, and a minor book concerning European travelers to the United States and their changing images of America; but he would fail to complete, or even to get very far along with, the research monographs on Reconstruction and on racism. Instead, his essays in collected form and his editing projects, along with the textbook, the *Oxford History,* and *Thinking Back,* would reveal the new phase of his career: much more consciously trying to speak to the readers who were literate and educated, and who cared, by providing them with distillations of specialized historical research. He also used the essays and his increasing activism in the professional historical associations, as well as his obvious influence over his very fine Johns Hopkins graduate students, to speak to the profession, to offer direction to the specialists by taking the measure of the generalist audience.

Bearing in mind the multiple meanings of irony, it is significant that Woodward became more prominent after World War II as he became more unlike the nation's consensus historians. Again, it was Cleanth Brooks who caught the image beautifully: "The kite properly loaded, tension maintained along the kite string, rises steadily against the thrust of the wind." Brooks's image was especially apt because Woodward was not being particularly original or even fundamentally rebellious; rather, like the kite, he needed the starting point of string provided by other scholars, and again like the kite, he needed the opposing winds for his ascent. Thus supported by the opposition, Woodward rode the currents to write a series of essays which raised vital questions and provided some fascinating answers about his own time as well as about the southern past. Recognition of his contribution became more widespread as a growing audience began to seek the Woodward opinion on a given social or political issue; and in 1961 Yale University signaled the extent of the national change of mood when it recruited Woodward to fill the generously endowed Sterling Professorship of History, thus endorsing dissidence where once the distinguished conservative U. B. Phillips had defended and even celebrated southern racism from his own special chair associated with the Jonathan Edwards College.[11]

As the decade of Woodward's ascendancy began, the currents of political wind and the currents of historiographical wind were producing an unexamined irony already marked in the consideration of *Origins of the New South:* the damage done by Wisconsin senator Joseph McCarthy not only threatened intellectual and artistic expression; in the process he created a confrontation between intellectuals and the body politic, a confrontation essentially unresolved except by a kind of segregation of the two. In insisting on a stark bipolarity between Communist world and free world, cold warriors adduced a politics of conflict at two levels: at the higher level, a unified and self-contained communism assaulted a similarly homogeneous capitalism called freedom; and at a lower level, communism won adherents among the treasonous and the naive in a process which threatened the requisite unity behind the walls in the great fight to come. Again, as noted before, the mainstream of the historians in that era rejected this cold-war description of conflict and instead insisted on a basic consensus among all Americans. Yet consensus historians, in making such claims in resistance to McCarthyism unfortunately only reinforced a notion central to Joe McCarthy's message: the notion of an undifferentiated, uniform, national way of thinking distinct from any way of thinking which existed outside the walls of freedom.

Such concepts remained anathema to Woodward, what with his Progressive emphasis on class and sectional conflict and with his lessons from the Chapel Hill Regionalists, who dwelt on differentiation even within the boundaries of a given state. In many ways he reacted to postwar intellectual and political trends with a prewar mentality made up of equal parts of Howard Odum and Charles Beard. To review, there were certainly oversimplifications which needed correcting by the likes of Perry Miller, who plumbed the depths of the Puritan mind which Vernon Parrington had underestimated and oversimplified, or of Richard Hofstadter, who showed that the reform impulse in American politics was as much a product of mainstream as of dissident values. Nevertheless, the homogenized historiography which blended with liberal politics after Joe

McCarthy's demise was not particularly insightful or useful. In resisting both Joe McCarthy's explanation of the Communist menace and Louis Hartz's interpretation of consensus, Woodward brought historiography into focus on valuable and exciting trends in other disciplines.

Although the first presentation of the ironic essay form had actually come at the Knoxville (or Whittle Springs) meeting of the Southern Historical Association in 1952, the nuances of that evening's speech had gone unnoticed because of the disputes over integration of the dinner session. "The Irony of Southern History" gained more attention in 1953 when historians could read it in the *Journal of Southern History;* and it gained even wider acclaim when his *Harper's* and *New Republic* and *New York Review of Books* audiences could read it in the collection *The Burden of Southern History.* The latter was a graceful set of Woodwardiana made available by Louisiana State University Press in 1960, and the essays in toto became in that year as significant for the laity as the volume's individual constituent parts had already become for the profession. "The Irony of Southern History" began disingenuously, with Woodward saying that "nationalism sweeps all before it," and therefore regional and sectional historians must justify their endeavor. And then he went on to say that historians of the South in particular had much to explain, for the South was a guilty loser in a nation which celebrated innocence and invincibility. Therefore "as a standpoint from which to write American history it is regarded as eccentric and, as a background for an historian, something of a handicap to be overcome." Nevertheless, as he dropped the disingenuity, "Of the eccentric position of the South in the nation there are admittedly many remaining indications. I do not think, however, that this eccentricity need be regarded entirely as a handicap. In fact, I think that it could possibly be turned to advantage by the Southern historian, both in understanding American history and in interpreting it to non-Americans."[12]

Going to the heart of the irony which he observed for the South in the United States, "from a broader point of view it is not the South but America that is unique among the peoples of the world." The South, not being able to participate as a full partner in this national legend, was just like the rest of the world: southerners, having perpetuated slavery, had a very tangible skeleton in the closet which rattled noisily whenever the words *innocence* or *purity* were mentioned; and as for invincibility, every little burgh had its monument raised in honor of those who fell in defeat, and a score of good-sized cities preserved the pockmarks of defeat on the faces of otherwise stately buildings. Everybody knew this and the South was accordingly treated as an embarrassing distant cousin kept in the corner at the family reunion. But Woodward was devoting his life to the study of this embarrassment, and he insisted that this South could instruct the entire nation, and not just by negative example.[13]

What the South had learned, or had certainly had the chance to learn, was something about the limitations of human attainment. No doubt, important leaders of the antebellum South were fully convinced of their own invincibility, having crafted a "positive good" defense for the slavery which characterized their society and, from those inspiring words, having drawn the conclusion that their economy alone could defeat any foe by force of "cotton diplomacy." While many southerners doubted the soundness of the slavery cause and many more doubted the efficacy of the cotton diplomacy, war at full scale produced the kind of dealing in absolutes which tested the Confederate claims; and of course, for the South the results were unambiguous and unequivocal in exposing the sham of cotton diplomacy. Even the concerted efforts of various romancers to salvage the name of the Confederacy invariably faced up to the fact of defeat: the Cause was a Lost Cause. For the sectional mentality, the nexus of invincibility and rightness was broken; even those who proclaimed the justice of the antebellum way of life had to acknowledge Appomattox Court House.[14]

By contradistinction, the same Civil War was the vital element of U. S. righteousness, for what could be more wrong than slavery and what could be more obvious than the victories won over the evil by the Grand Army of the Republic? Compound that experience with the Four Freedoms, where the evil was even more stark and the victories over it even more spectacular, and one had produced stuff of real potency. Surely the walls of all future Jerichos would tumble wherever the chosen tribe needed to go. And so it seemed in the early days of the American nuclear monopoly, for the Greeks and the Turks both bearded the lion of the Communist menace, Western Europe was rebuilt with U.S. aid, and in the otherwise inscrutable

East, Chiang Kai-shek guaranteed that China would be a stable ally of freedom. Yet how quickly that sense of security disappeared! In short order, the backward Russians had their own nuclear weapon, and even as the Gulag Archipelago was being revealed in definitive and unmistakable detail, Eastern Europe was sealed off by the Communists, Chiang Kai-shek was guaranteeing a mere island as an ally of freedom, and the rebuilt Western Europe was experimenting with variants of Marxism.

What could Americans say by way of explanation for these reversals? That the world was not their oyster? That, like the Confederacy, the United States could be defeated because it was not really innocent, not really chosen? Or was it that something had happened to the leaders, that some persons had betrayed a trust to a tribe which itself remained innocent? Mystics of every era have dealt in conspiracies because of the greater effort demanded by rational examination of unpleasant and unflattering facts; and thus it was that even a skilled logician such as the conservative William Frank Buckley, Jr., could be heard chanting for an examination of the American leadership. It was claimed that some men in high places lacked the faith required to govern the chosen ones and thus it became necessary to test the loyalty of all leaders.[15] That such unquestioning champions of capitalism as Dean Acheson and John Foster Dulles were suspected of being "soft" on communism was a measure of the comic miscalculations of the era.

But these miscalculations could produce even more catastrophic results should Americans turn from the pursuit of devils within the walls of freedom to the pursuit of devils outside: "Driven by these provocations and frustrations, there is the danger that America may be tempted to exert all the terrible power she possesses to compel history to conform to her own illusions. The extreme, but by no means the only, expression, would be the so-called preventive war. This would be to commit the worst heresy of the Marxists, with whom it is dogma that they can compel history to conform to the pattern of their dreams by the ruthless use of force."[16]

For all the value of Niebuhr's political prescription, he had missed one thing: the South, the embarrassment which was not permitted a full role in the national myth. If Niebuhr were correct, then the supposedly benighted regions actually had an advantage over the rest of the country because the South, participating in the antebellum evil of slavery, the wartime fact of defeat, and the postbellum experience of poverty and racism, had long ago entered into history. Thus the South shouldered a burden all right, but it was not the burden of evil: it was instead the burden of irony, the burden of having available a set of experiences which could instruct the rest of the nation; what the South actually had was the burden of responsibility, the responsibility to share its painfully learned lessons of irony.[17]

Left unaddressed in this essay were two questions which Woodward would ponder for the next three decades: did southerners themselves understand their ironic past? and if so, would they accept the burden of instruction? Initially, Woodward was optimistic, for his earlier research in the sources of the 1880s and the 1890s had produced an image of the Populists as tough and pragmatic types able to learn from the mistakes of the past; moreover, even the Woodward label for the conservative opposition—the Bourbons, by implication those who had forgotten nothing but also those who had learned nothing—reinforced the idea that it was the Populists virtually alone who had established the useful precedents. As long as some dissident voices—those of Populists in the 1890s, those of Atlantans in the early 1920, those of Chapel Hillians in the late 1920s—were raised on behalf of ironic reform, Woodward could be hopeful that his reading of irony was accurate. In the 1950s, the consensus wisdom to the contrary, many southerners were actively dissenting from segregation, but the important question for Woodward concerned the quality of that dissent: was it suffused with what Niebuhr called the bourgeois optimism of innocence and invincibility, or was it more solid stuff? This was a vital question, for the sentimentalist, encountering defeat, could always turn sour and look for scapegoats to carry the blame for his own failures; only a proper sense of irony was good for the long haul. Looking at a tough and unsentimental nut like Georgia's Glenn Rainey, Florida's Manning Dauer, Tennessee's Bell Wiley, or Mississippi's Willie Morris, Woodward was reassured that this latter-day movement was sufficiently informed with irony to go the distance in what would be a very long and arduous campaign.

To answer these questions in another essay, he turned to literary sources to see if sensitive novelists had also noted this ironic perception among southerners in the past; if so, then perhaps there was a genuine tradition of irony for the section; but if no one except Woodward had noticed this southern tradition, then he could easily be dismissed as an eccentric. Casting about, he considered the literary idols of his youth, Thomas Wolfe and Erskine Caldwell, as well as the more recently appreciated William Faulkner. But these choices did not work in support of his idea, because Caldwell exhibited very little ironic sensibility; and Faulkner's and Wolfe's protagonists were ironic in a subtle and rather introverted vein, seldom breaking into events with action. Wolfe's Eugene Gant and Faulkner's Gavin Stevens stripped away delusion, but usually in the privacy of their own chambers. Attractive as they were, they were thin reeds to support the weight of a consciousness which was at once ironic and *active*. Curiously, better sources to corroborate his belief were the northern writers of the Gilded Age, Herman Melville, Henry Adams, and Henry James. Each, it developed, had created southern characters as the vehicles to critique the ills of the republic, and in each case, the sensibility was appropriately ironic-activist.[18]

The blackest of these assessments was penned by the man who wrote of the white, white whale, for Melville late in life produced *Clarel* (1876). After a decade of subsisting on a meager wage as outside inspector for the Port of New York, Melville had picked the scab of American capitalism: all around him was bribery and collusion, yet market forces were said to guarantee efficiency in a time of unmatched growth and development. Clarel is the character of contemporaneous American youth in search of ethical standards; rather unsophisticated, he is exposed to the blandishments of the apostles of liberal progress, but he remains skeptical of American claims to invincibility. To counter effectively the seductive voice of progress, Melville created Ungar, a half-Indian veteran of the Confederate army. As Woodward marked it, "Ungar is an American who has suffered two rejections, two defeats, and a double estrangement from his native land." This doubly estranged man detests the hypocrisy of putative equality proclaimed by free enterprise in the face of de facto servitude: "Your arts advance in faith's decay." And this strange fellow also rejects the "flattering unction of nationalism," convinced instead that this land is only "slumberous combustible / sure to explode" at the touch of the demagoguery to come.[19] It is a dark and twisted but not inaccurate description of the Gilded Age, with some ominous hint of the McCarthy era which came three generations later.

Where Melville used Ungar the half-breed to score the soulless capitalist, Henry Adams made the same points about what he called the Chromo Civilization through a blue blood, John Carrington, in *Democracy* (1880). An aristocratic lawyer fallen on hard times during the heyday of President Ulysses Grant, Carrington is a distant relative of the Lees, and although his suit for the novel's female lead, Madeleine, is ultimately rejected, "he gained dignity in his rebel isolation." While Adams caricatured the northeastern politico through Senator Ratcliffe, a soulless, scurrilous opportunist who "talked about virtue and vice as a man who is colour-blind talks about red and green," the novel "deliberately associates valor, honor, dignity, and the heroic traditions of the past—of whichever side—with Virginia soil and name and place." Adams was profoundly alienated from all things in this era, since his labor as a Washington journalist exposing the ills of the republic had produced disdain for the prevailing culture, but he had not yet discovered what became for him the restoring and reinvigorating elements of Roman Catholicism. Unwilling to let Dixie get the girl in this novel, Adams settled for Ratcliffe's defeat in his quest for Madeleine: so much for the blast on the American horn before the walls of that Jericho! Instead, Adams removed Madeleine to Europe, a trip she takes with a feeling of good riddance for the District of Columbia, but with warm memories of the cool Virginian who has learned from defeat.[20]

For *The Bostonians* (1884), Henry James went deeper south to locate his ironic critic, and when he found his Mississippian, the matchless stylist chose to breathe into Basil Ransom a temperament warmer than Carrington's and more urbane than Ungar's. In his unlikely courtship of Verena, a Back Bay reformist in the cause of women's rights, Basil is the principled conservative resisting the glib palaver about progress: it is not that he disbelieves in progress, but only that "I never saw any." "Ransom's defense of marriage, family, tradition, and chivalry is a merciless onslaught upon the cant of the age, the cant about progress, equality, universal education, and the emancipation of women." Nor is Ransom caught up in any ambivalence about the place of a man and a woman in the proper sexual order of things: "The whole generation is womanized; the masculine tone is passing out of the world; it's a feminine, a nervous, hysterical, challenging canting age, an age of hollow phrases and false delicacy and exaggerated solicitudes and coddled sensibilities which, if we don't soon look out, will usher in the reign of the feeblest and flattest and the most pretentious that has ever been." With such unrestrained masculinity crackling across the pages, James simply *had* to let Basil run off with Verena, even arranging a late-moment escape from the rear of the stage where Verena is set to speak more "feminist cant" before a Boston liberal audience.[21]

With this triptych of northern criticism of the North, Woodward was being very clever, noting that "the taste for irony could hardly have been better served, in fact, than by the belated Yankee deference implicit in the selection of Confederate censors for Yankee morals."[22] But he was very nearly too clever, for these ironic activists were acting on the right side of the stage when Woodward himself was positioned on the left. For one thing, it was simply not enough to show that principled conservatism could emerge from the southern experience, since an experience of defeat and disillusionment which taught no more than conservatism would vitiate Populism and the civil rights movement. For another, it was not enough to show that northern sensibilities could benefit from this southern experience, since an experience which instructed only northerners would likely return things to Mencken's "Saharra of the Bozarts," where northern seers guided the southern fools. No, having fortified himself with proof that others could learn from the South, Woodward was off on two new missions: one a glorification of southern radicalism and the other a destruction of northern radicalism. For whatever reasons, he did not attempt the former without also attempting the latter; and the chip on his shoulder as he went after the abolitionists became a different kind of burden for his historiography.

In "John Brown's Private War" (1952), he started by attacking Brown but finished by assaulting no less than the "American Renaissance" of the vaunted Ralph Waldo Emerson. Brown he dismissed as an unworthy psychopath who rose to power at a moment when those of strong emotions seemed "sublime in their wisdom" to masses of confused people. Kansas became a free state despite Brown's massacre at Pottawatomie; farmers more rational than he in calculating their self-interest did the effective politicking and, where necessary, the effective fighting to keep slavery out in 1856. Brown's bloodlust and his horse thieving discredited the cause of abolition, but not enough to force midwesterners into the camp of proslavery. After that, Brown's raid on Harper's Ferry was a bloody opera bouffe which attracted none of the slaves in the area, because they, like the Jayhawk farmers, had common sense. This much on Brown, while a rather severe judgment, could be supported by a great deal of evidence from the abolitionist's odd career, which was indeed marred by excesses of violence and by instances of dishonesty in prior business; but Woodward intended to fry much bigger fish in American antebellum culture—the Transcendentalists themselves.[23]

The problem with Transcendentalism, as Woodward saw it, was that unlike the Virginia field hands, its adherents lacked the common sense to discern the folly in John Brown's plans, even though the "Secret Six" of Gerrit Smith, George L. Stearns, Theodore Parker, Samuel Gridley Howe, Franklin S. Sanborn, and Thomas Wentworth Higginson—"capitalist, philanthropist, philosopher, surgeon, professor, minister," men of "reputability and learning"—who financially backed Brown's raid, "far from being horse thieves and petty traders . . . came from the cream of Northern society." These men clandestinely diverted money from abolitionists to Brown's raid, but upon Brown's capture, they exhibited "a very unheroic panic" about their roles in support of the Harper's Ferry scheme. Yet instead of the censure each man feared, the "experience contributed greatly to his moral prestige, if little to his political sophistication." The misperception, Woodward claimed, was partly their own doing but largely the illusion imposed by Emerson's "Over-soul," which could not understand that "Southern zealots of secession had no better ally than John Brown." To Woodward the "cultural and moral aristocracy" of New England and New York which produced a celebration of John Brown's raid was no Renaissance of letters or of anything else. On this issue, he implied, Emerson was so wrong that one must question his accomplishments in general, including his previously much-esteemed influence on others.[24]

This essay was the weakest of the lot which he produced in this era; significantly, it was the only major essay which departed from his ironic insights about consensus historiography and the politics behind it. Appearing first as a contribution to a volume edited by humanist Daniel Aaron, the essay exhibited greater ironies in the production and distribution of "John Brown's Private War" than in the actual writing itself, for both editor Aaron and the treatment of the topic were compatible with consensus attitudes toward radicalism. While Woodward's assessment was made without the benefit of the extensive research into abolition which came in the 1960s, it was a disappointing one because it dodged the crying question *why* the abolitionists seemed so impractical and so irresolute, then and now. While one could certainly go either way, for them or against them, in assessing the abolitionists, here Woodward went nowhere, being content to reaffirm the era's wisdom about the mentality of the radical dissident. In his own raid on reputations, he was scarcely more effective than John Brown was at Harper's Ferry.

But fortunately, Woodward retained his basic ironic disposition for the study of the South, and while he misread some things, it was not necessary to lay Emerson low to develop an appreciation of the rich complexity of southern minds and actions. Thus alongside the failure of the one essay there was the bright achievement of two others, "Equality: The Deferred Commitment" and "The Political Legacy of Reconstruction." Each of these essays presaged a decade of revisionist writing about the Reconstruction era, about the very basic issue of racial equality in this culture. In both of them he stubbornly insisted that the original Reconstruction could have worked, that it did not because Americans reneged on a commitment, and that northerners as well as southerners shared culpability for its eventual failure. In his gentle but dogged manner he stripped away the illusory garments of consensus liberalism: other courtiers could proclaim a hundred years of racial progress, a hundred years of steady effort on behalf of civil rights; this essayist said quietly but unrelentingly that the emperor of American race relations was quite naked indeed.[25]

Writing for the *Journal of Negro Education* in 1957, he was Parrington with soul, again invoking that Progressive's "great barbecue" imagery, but this time with a profound racial consciousness. Why had Negroes been granted a political legacy of suffrage and officeholding in the first place? Carefully he picked his way among the records left by the most ardent abolitionists, finding that as late as 1864 William Lloyd Garrison, Charles Sumner, Horace Greeley, and Thaddeus Stevens were all opposed to unlimited black suffrage, most preferring some kind of educational qualification, although no such barrier was erected for illiterate whites. But by 1867 things had changed rapidly, so rapidly that these very men were in 1868 fervently in support of the Negro voting and officeholding which were then widespread in the states of the late Confederacy. The change of heart was in part philanthropic, and in the essay Woodward emphasized that philanthropy persisted in at least a few Reconstruction leaders; but it was essentially a political realization that the business allies of the Republican party needed votes, even black votes, for tariffs and for other legislation to protect industrial interests against any challenge from southern farming interests. Parrington again! Except that Woodward added, "This ulterior motivation, then, is the incubus with which the Negro was burdened before he was awakened into public life. The operation and effective motives of his political genesis were extraneous to his own interests and calculated to serve other ends."[26]

This meant that when something other than Negro suffrage could effect "party advantage and sectional business interests," then the only remaining support for Negro suffrage—philanthropy—would likely be too weak to bear the weight of racist pressures for Negro disfranchisement. What, then, of those blacks who had been permitted political powers? Given the incubus, what did they produce? As he had done with *The Strange Career of Jim Crow,* he again drew attention to the monograph by Vernon Lane Wharton on Mississippi Reconstruction, a work which showed the black political record to be perfectly respectable. Putting Wharton's perspective in his own words, Woodward said, "Moral pigsties undoubtedly developed, but they were oftener than not the creation of the other race, and more of them were to be found outside the South than within." If this was so, then what of the decision in 1877 to abandon black voters to the machinations of home rule in the South? The act of reneging became an especially horrid thing seen in this light, for qualified and competent people were disfranchised; and the fault was national, rather than strictly southern, since the Northeast and Midwest weighed in with a clear majority in Congress. Thus the republic could have, and should have, protected the right of the Negro man to vote in the nineteenth century.[27]

The republic failed in its duty in this case because it failed in a more fundamental sense to honor a commitment to equality. This commitment was clearly there in the Declaration of Independence and in the rhetoric under which the moral crusade of the Civil War proceeded; it was clearly there in the postbellum constitutional amendments thirteen, fourteen, and fifteen that each rebellious state had to ratify to rejoin the Union. "Every device of emphasis, repetition, re-enactment, and reiteration" was employed, and "America would seem to have firmly committed to the principle of equality . . . so far as it was humanly possible to do so by statute and constitutional amendment." Unfortunately, such devices did not guarantee radical change, for there was a "moral lag" between constitutional commitment and actual practice:

> Equality was a far more revolutionary aim than freedom, though it may not have seemed so at first. Slavery seemed so formidable, so powerfully entrenched in law and property, and so fiercely defended by arms that it appeared far the greater obstacle. Yet slavery was property based on law. The law could be changed and the property expropriated. Not so inequality. Its entrenchments were deeper and subtler. The attainment of equality involved many more relationships than those between master and slave. It was a revolution that was not confined to the boundaries of the defeated and discredited South, as emancipation largely was. It was a revolution for the North as well. It involved such unpredictable and biased people as hotel clerks, railroad conductors, steamboat stewards, theatre ushers, real estate agents, and policemen. In fact, it could involve almost anybody. It was clear from the start that this revolution was going to require enthusiastic and widespread support in the North to make it work.[28]

It did not work because the requisite support was not forthcoming, and support was not forthcoming because there was racism in the hearts of the agents of enforcement, starting with the chief executive, Ulysses S. Grant, running through the Republican party and the Union army, and extending to the white citizens who rioted in the streets to protest against equality in Cleveland, Cincinnati, Chicago, Detroit, Buffalo, Albany, Brooklyn, and New York. This lag he also termed "borrowed moral capital" and a "moral debt that was soon found to be beyond the country's capacity to pay." In time, specifically between 1889 and 1896, the Supreme Court declared the debt nonexistent, but Woodward dismissed these decisions as nominal injunctions which fooled no one; and he noted instead that over the next eight decades, "interest on the debt accumulated." By the time Woodward spoke at Gettysburg College in 1958, the country was at last owning up to its moral obligations, the time was at last at hand; but again, there was a lag between conviction and constitutional commitment. This time, however, the lag was reversed, and it was the judicial system which until 1954 was outpaced by "popular commitment." Finally, the Supreme Court's ruling in *Brown* v. *Board of Education* rationalized things and recognized the long-standing and by now enormous debt. Just as Woodward was absolute in his conviction that the debt must be paid, so was he convinced that the process of payment would be exceedingly long and painful—and best undertaken without the kind of moral fervor which could only exhaust itself after a few setbacks. Southerners must be held to the task, but perhaps the lessons of the burden would permit the South to face its responsibilities "with better grace" and "with forbearance and humility" this time.[29]

Woodward was not one to express such hope without some previous example for validity, and for him the southern Populists remained exactly that example, exactly that group which had demonstrated the uses of ironic activism. In his feistiest response to the consensus school, he wrote "The Populist Heritage and the Intellectual," thereby closing out the 1950s with a piece which set the tone for a new generation of activist scholarship deeply appreciative, at times even celebratory, of the agrarian radical movement. As noted before, the Populists had enjoyed favor in the 1930s, with Parrington linking them to Jeffersonian radicalism in *Main Currents in American Thought* and with John D. Hicks chronicling their exploits with real sympathy in *The Populist Revolt.* But again, these two were examining the Populist movement primarily in the midwestern Corn Belt, and thus neither paid much attention to the southern side of agrarian reform. Then had come Richard Hofstadter's brilliant dismantling of the American reform tradition, in which the Populists were dismissed as so many emotionalists, rhetoricians crying from the heart for a return to a past which never was: having suffered a loss of status as the country urbanized and industrialized, the American farmer clamored for a glorified Physiocracy which he had never believed in himself. In the wake of Hofstadter's *Age of Reform* came a fleet of consensus vessels, few of which were floating on any major research in the primary sources, but all of which trained their guns on Populist targets. As the criticism grew nastier, some of the scholars began to identify the Populists with the Nazis, an extreme oversimplification almost as unfair as the one Woodward himself had made about some of John Brown's supporters.[30]

Hearing those whom one esteems being labeled Nazi has always struck a special nerve with the American liberal, and Woodward responded sharply, among other things questioning whether these fellows had done their homework—after all, one of their number had actually described Tom Watson of "ole Georgia" as one of the "apostles of thought-control" coming out "of the western Populist movement" in America![31] In response, Woodward took the occasion to cite again the vital flaw in consensus liberalism: its tendency to regard anything other than mainstream moderation as radical right wing. It was the same complaint he had registered in his essay on the irony of southern history; but now he offered specific rebuttals from his search work concerning the Populists. First, a review of the Ocala and the Omaha platforms and other party pronouncements and state legislation revealed a left-wing—hardly a right-wing— orientation, for how else to describe popular election of senators, the Australian Ballot, a postal savings service, railroad regulation, relief from deflated currency, and government ownership and operation of all transportation and communication lines? Second, whether left or right, those plans were practical and effective as well as forward-looking, precursors of New Deal pragmatism. And third and most important, the Populists were not the racist demagogues portrayed in consensus essays; in fact, in contrast to the racism and antisemitism of the era, their political cooperation with the Negro made the Populists the actual progressives and their opponents, many of whom became nominal Progressives, the reactionaries. Moreover, the persisting claim that the Populist was antisemitic simply fell apart on examination of the correspondence sources and of the contemporaneous newspapers, broadsides, bulletins, and circulars.[32]

Now Woodward pushed things farther, insisting that there was a positive legacy from the Populists because the South was less responsive to Joe McCarthy than any other American section. Many who lived in the Deep South in the 1950s found this claim doubtful, but Woodward cited an opinion poll by Seymour Martin Lipset and Nathan Glazer to support his contention. In any case, the contemporary national audience very much needed to learn about the southern Populist tradition, but this opportunity had been denied by the dominant intellectuals of the northeastern corridor who had created and spread consensus liberalism:

> One must expect and even hope that there will be future upheavals to shock the seats of power and privilege and furnish the periodic therapy that seems necessary to the health of our democracy. But one cannot expect them to be any more decorous or seemly or rational than their predecessors. One can reasonably hope, however, that they will not fall under the sway of the Huey Longs and Father Coughlins who will be ready to take charge. . . . For the tradition to endure, for the way to remain open, however, the intellectual must not be alienated from the sources of revolt. It was one of the glories of the New Deal that it won the support of the intellectuals and one of the tragedies of Populism that it did not. The intellectual must resist the impulse to identify all the irrational and evil forces he detests with such movements because some of them, or the aftermath of some of them, have proved so utterly repulsive. He will learn all he can from the new criticism about the irrational and illiberal side of Populism and other reform movements, but he cannot afford to repudiate the heritage.[33]

Where the intellectual of the 1950s repudiated the heritage of the Populists, the intellectual of the 1960s practically worshiped Populism's memory, and Woodward's essay thus forecast accurately a direction which the national mood would take. Woodward destroyed the simplistic use of the word *Populist* to denote protofascism, racism, antisemitism, and any other form of mass persuasion by emotional appeal to prejudice. On the other hand, he himself occasionally used the term to describe a kind of generic reformism, and many of those inspired by Woodward came to use the word *Populist* just as simplistically to denote any mass movement of almost any kind and in almost any place: this usage reached its illogical conclusion one evening when the television news feature "Sixty Minutes" described the late New York governor Nelson Aldrich Rockefeller as having a "Populist" exchange of opinion with the citizenry in a town meeting. That the name Rockefeller could ever be used in conjunction with the word *Populist* was proof that a new oversimplification had developed and proof that stripping away delusion is a difficult business yet to be completed.[34]

If his best efforts occasionally confused the issue of Populism, the same cannot be said of his essays on the tangle of issues which was the civil rights movement. Writing an article for the *Reporter* and another for *Harper's,* he reached larger audiences with some simple but profound generalizations about the sources and the direction of the movement which he had served so willingly and so well. The former piece concerned the legitimacy of past and present southern dissent, and the latter concerned the future of national dissent; both were distinguished by his sure sense of what was, what could be, and what should be. He would never again write with the authority granted by such confidence in his own perceptions, and the two essays, taken together, marked the height of his scholarly and personal achievement.[35]

The *Reporter* was in its own glory in 1964 when Woodward brought to it an essay on Lewis Harvie Blair; its editor, Max Ascoli, had built a tough, argumentative, and effective journal on the supposition that the liberal was "always on assignment," and the assignment in those days was dual: support the Vietnam War and support the civil rights movement. They were still popular stances in that year, though very shortly a wholesale defection of liberals from the ranks of war supporters would leave Ascoli with a suddenly inadequate subscription list. But all of that was still to come when Woodward wrote a tribute to dissidence past in honor of reformism present. Without overtly mentioning it, his essay on Lewis Harvie Blair—born in 1834, died in 1916 in Richmond—gave the lie to the claim that 1890s reform came from outsiders and primarily from those recently thrust outside who were thus acutely aware of their fall from societal grace (the famed "status anxiety" thesis propounded by Hofstadter and his followers).[36] And also without overtly mentioning it, he gave the lie to the segregationist claim that support for civil rights came only from "outside agitators." The case of Blair, when combined with what Woodward had shown of Tom Watson and George Washington Cable, simultaneously contested the faiths of consensus at Morningside Heights and of segregationism at Pleasantburg.

Blair was old-line Virginia, with a colonial ancestry, and even better, he had distinguished himself in gray during the Civil War. He was a wounded hero of unquestionable valor despite his belief that his service was "more than three years wasted in the vain effort to maintain that most monstrous institution, African slavery, the real, tho' States Rights were the ostensible, cause of the War." With the war over and both real and ostensible causes well lost, Blair turned to the pursuit of his daily bread, quickly rebuilding the family fortune, which, fittingly, had been decimated by the conflict. In fact, "it is doubtful if any of the three preceding generations of American Blairs lived in finer style or occupied higher social position in that city. Whatever may explain the rebellion of the Richmond aristocrat, it was hardly the loss of status."[37]

But rebel he certainly did, producing in 1889 a book which made a "blistering and iconoclastic attack on the dogma of white supremacy and Negro inferiority, the plantation legend of slavery, the paternalistic tradition of race relations, the black-dominated picture of Reconstruction, and the complacent optimism of the New South school of economists." With a compelling argument, Woodward used Blair for comparison both with the slavery debates of the 1830s and with the contemporary civil rights struggles. In each case, Woodward's crucial point was that time matters, that attitudes changed because of events and personalities, that the southern mentality was not fixed for all time but was instead fluid in some eras, fixed in others. Without claiming an unbelievable level of liberalism for the South of any day, Woodward marked the relative openness of discussion in the 1830s and the 1880s as he marked the contrasting "rigidity" of attitudes in the 1840s and the 1890s, when the "South had reached a consensus on race policy. Its mind was closed. The debate was frowned down or smashed. Conformity was demanded of all."[38]

It was Blair's message, issued in the last hour before debate ended and the door was barred, which fascinated Woodward. That was because Blair himself understood the ebbings and flowings of southern history and thus refused to subscribe to the notion of a solid South. Moreover, Blair had about him that tough pragmatism which Woodward celebrated in the Populists, for Blair insisted that the reason for the South's extreme poverty was primarily racism. Arguing from Benthamite presumptions of self-interest, Blair described racism as the dominant factor keeping this section backward: only by "elevating" the entire Negro population could the South escape its economic trough. His program included continuation of Negro suffrage, integrated public schools, and full economic opportunities for both races. In addition, Blair made the point that northern self-interest in a national economy which functioned efficiently also demanded a federal policy of full civil rights: without integration "at the South," the southern section would continue to slow the progress of the rest of the United States. Most important of all, Blair would have no halfway measures of partial civil rights which were gradually doled out; justice had to come in full and swiftly—*or not at all!*[39]

That all-or-nothing mentality made Blair's prophecy especially ironic, since the twentieth century found the aristocrat himself "swept up in the wave of [racist] hysteria." By temperament, Blair rejected partial measures, and when the white South rejected the full measure of racial equality, Blair came to reject *any* rights for blacks. While there was evidence that Blair regretted and at least privately retracted his Negrophobia of the new century, the real story for Woodward was that Blair had written the prophecy in 1889 in terms "clear and relevant and challenging" for 1964. As in the nineteenth century, modern southern racial injustice impeded national progress in a way that made mockery of the halfway measures of gradualism; but that injustice could be overcome by a consistent and aggressive federal policy. To the consensus liberal, Woodward insisted that the time for vigorous action was now. And to the southern segregationist, he said, "At least no one could call [Blair] an outsider."[40]

Besides introducing Blair to the *Reporter* "liberals on assignment," Woodward brought out a new edition of the Virginian's 1889 manifesto, *Prosperity of the South Dependent upon the Elevation of the Negro.* The *Reporter* essay served as the core of his editorial introduction, and significantly, he dedicated the entire volume to Lyndon Johnson, citing LBJ as the man who had done the most for the cause of civil rights in the modern era. Already Johnson was expanding the Vietnamese campaign, and already Woodward was complaining about the war; and friends such as Bill Carleton were quick to point out to him the possibility of future embarrassment by this dedication: after all, Tom Watson himself had warned that the blare of the war bugle could drown out the call for reform, and it could happen in 1965 as easily as it had in 1898. But Woodward stuck by his dedication, for he felt that only Johnson's political knack had made practicable Blair's prophecy, and he wanted the Texan to receive his fair measure of credit.[41]

For *Harper's* centennial supplement on the South one hundred years after Appomattox Court House, Woodward presented to the lay intellectual the concept of two Reconstructions, thereby popularizing revisionist scholarship, which, although bright with insight, had been heretofore confined to the cloisters of the monograph writer. As he had before, Woodward asserted that the first Reconstruction should have worked and could have worked, but failed because of a lack of will at the national level. Moreover, the nation's complaisant racism, which in combination with the more extreme southern bigotry had thwarted the attempted revolution with the Compromise of 1877, could well thwart this second Reconstruction with a twentieth-century "Compromise of Tokenism." He broke off the phrase with some malice—Voegelin had said this was no time for amiable language—and he evinced his contempt for the cocktail liberal who "pointed with pride" to his maps, which listed as successfully integrated those county school systems that enrolled one Negro at a "previously segregated" school. As difficult as it was to drag Mississippi up to the national norm of race relations, one must not underestimate the distance which stretched onward from that point to genuine equality. In 1965 racial justice thus continued to elude the halfhearted grasp of the republic's white citizens.[42]

But this time there was a difference, for it was not simply left up to the white citizens alone: Negroes were enfranchised, "less fully but more strategically" than in the first Reconstruction. Lyndon Johnson was attuned to this new electorate, which had become pivotal in the urban Northeast and in the upper Midwest during the day of Harry S. Truman. And Johnson's appeal to the South was in direct proportion to Negro voting: where blacks were still kept from the polls in precincts in South Carolina, Alabama, Mississippi, Louisiana, and Georgia, Johnson had been soundly defeated in the 1964 presidential race. To Woodward this was proof both that the solid South had been splintered under the blows of the modern civil rights movement and that it remained divided. It was important that the rest of the nation understand and acknowledge the diversity of opinion in the South, for at this period the section was closing the once-yawning economic gap between it and the rest of the nation; but the barbarity of "Bull" Connor's response to the plea for civil rights had produced in the national media an image of a homogeneous reactionary land. In fact, however, Bull Connor's police dogs were the desperate outlash of the already defeated; and most southerners were now like most northerners—that is, they were reconciled to the modicum of racial justice forced on them by a vocal minority with effective political representation locally and nationally.[43]

Thus, despite the Sturm und Drang of the campaigns throughout the lower South, the "corner was turned" already on the second Reconstruction, and southern race relations were no longer distinct from the American pattern. Yet if this was true, then what made the South distinct? From Right to Left, and from past to present, there was an operating assumption that a unique racism was what marked the South off from the rest of the country. Since early in the century, conservatives had pointed to the graceful apologia for paternalistic racism crafted by U. B. Phillips, who proclaimed that the effort to make the white man predominant was the central theme of southern history. By 1964, in the middle of the civil rights movement, and from the middle of it, Howard Zinn, the neoabolitionist then based in Atlanta, had said much the same thing, but with a provocative twist. Racism, Zinn declared, certainly characterized the South, but it also characterized the rest of the nation; or as he put it, there was no mystique in the South, just plain garden-variety American racism gussied up in pretentious garb and speaking with a stage accent. Zinn was a tireless and courageous worker on behalf of the movement, and he, with Augie Meier, had been especially effective in the difficult and dangerous, although less dramatic, work of opening up more opportunities for black scholars in the Southern Historical Association after John Hope Franklin's speech at Williamsburg and after the integration of Woodward's presidential dinner address at Whittle Springs. In Warren's terminology, Zinn had certainly "earned his ironies" with action, but for all that, his acerbic style in describing the southern identity encompassed much less than a comprehension of "the total situation."[44]

From the Left, Zinn was asserting the evil of southern racism while denying its uniqueness as southern identity; and from the Right, Phillips was asserting the virtue of southern racism while upholding it as the distinctive element of southern identity. Different as Zinn and Phillips were, and much as one might disagree with each historian, both were making a point, both were saying something which had to be answered. Was there anything to the South other than racism? Woodward, of course, had already told historians that there was, that the South bore the burden of an irony with which it could instruct the rest of the nation. Now he told this to a larger audience of intellectuals, and he added a considerable change of emphasis: Negroes also shouldered this burden of a duty to share with and enlighten an entire culture through their southern experiences. That was hardly the kind of burden described for Negroes by most writers in 1965, who spoke instead of laying burdens down; but for black as well as for white, Woodward argued, the past had to be used, not forgotten. Understanding the lessons of the past was essential to the present task of understanding oneself and one's responsibilities and prerogatives. "In this new search for identity the Negro is fully engaged. In fact, he has taken the initiative and the white man reacts to him. Their discovery of each other will define a distinctively new period of Southern history and a new Southern identity." And Woodward was without doubt that this new identity would remain distinct from the nation's even as he hoped that the new identity would be better than the old.[45]

This was Woodward at full flow, the very force of his ideas sweeping almost everything before him. Graduate students at major research centers called *The Origins of the New South* their Old Testament, and his own former graduate students—such as Willie Lee Rose, James McPherson, Sheldon Hackney, Thomas Holt, William McFeely, Bertram Wyatt-Brown, and John Blassingame—in their own different ways began to be heard in the profession. The combination of Yale's institutional reputation with his own personal reputation attracted plenty of excellent graduate students; and the Yale endowment for its graduate program was so vast that virtually no qualified scholar was kept away for financial reasons. Flush with superb students and virtually guaranteed a supply of more, Woodward was emerging as the dominant force in southern historiography and as one of the major forces in American historiography. Fellow historians bestowed on him both the Sydnor and the Bancroft awards for his books, and it became apparent that in time he would inherit the presidency of either the American Historical Association or the Organization of American Historians, and perhaps of both. Besides the Sterling chair at Yale, he had twice received appointments at Oxford University, first in 1954–55, an especially propitious time, for he was able to witness the formalization of a major rapprochement between town and gown at Oxford, and again in 1961–62, prior to assuming his duties in New Haven. So popular was he with British scholars then turning to their first genuinely serious examination of American history that he formed long-lived friendships while becoming the established American figure of historiographical authority for them—and therefore the target for revisionism.[46]

But his appeal went well beyond the historical profession: Willie Morris, author of the poignant and apt *North toward Home,* saw to it that readers of his *Harper's* magazine enjoyed exposure to Woodward; Gilbert Harrison's *New Republic* and Ascoli's *Reporter* could hardly get enough of him; and as previously noted, Martin Luther King, Jr., during the Montgomery march, pronounced *The Strange Career of Jim Crow* the Bible of the civil rights movement. Woodward even became the friend of some of the intellectuals from whom he dissented, most notably the consensus historian Richard Hofstadter, who still doubted both the practicality and the rationalism of the Populists, and the conservative Yale jurist Alexander Mordecai Bickel, who remained deeply skeptical of the Earl Warren Court's judicial activism. Nor was the swell of good fortune confined to himself alone, since his son, Peter, a bold athlete who delighted in hiking and canoeing, had become an excellent scholar with a bright future in political science; after distinguishing himself at his undergraduate college at Yale, he entered the graduate program at Princeton. And Glenn Woodward remained the loving source of emotional reassurance for the historian as well as the boon companion to his friends; she enjoyed the Yale campus, reveling in Peter's development and in the increased opportunities for travel which came along with Woodward's increased renown.

Despite Woodward's hardheaded realism and habitual skepticism, he fairly glowed with the personal triumphs of friends and family and with the solid prospect of fundamental economic and social reform in the South. Furthermore, the national goals of the

Great Society, especially in 1964 and 1965, seemed to him fully attainable, as it appeared that at long last the previously unaddressed items of reform's real agenda would be taken up.[47] Of course, the nagging voice of his ironic disposition was reminding him that so many triumphs could not, and perhaps even should not, endure for long; but he felt prepared both for a modicum of life's expected personal problems and for the usual reversals dealt out by the complexities of collective politics. After 1965, however, he would slowly and painfully learn that it would not be his fortune to endure a modicum of problems at either the personal or the societal level.

9

Irony in a Centrifuge

The Waning of Commitments, 1965–1974

Woodward's ironic interpretation of the past had already given intellectuals plenty to think about, and he certainly continued to make contributions to American thought after 1965. But over the next nine years, the once-glowing light of personal well-being illuminating his friends and family flickered and nearly went out altogether. It was a period of death and disease for loved ones, and while Woodward himself emerged physically hale, he was disheartened by the fate spun for those dearest to him. Along with crushing personal losses came the societal reversals after 1968, during which time the formerly cohering elements of American liberalism "spun out" with an increasingly centrifugal force: once united in the cause of racial justice, now reformers waged individuated campaigns concerning the Vietnam War, poverty, hunger, the environment, and advocacies of rights for self-consciously identified minorities, although justice for blacks remained in Woodward's term "the deferred commitment." Even graduate schools and the professional study of history were altered for the worse as the discipline was called upon to defend its existence because of its putative "irrelevance" both to the spiritual resolution of social problems and to the material rewards for individual talent. The defense before this jury was unconvincing and, when combined with overall reduction in enrollments on campuses, resulted in the cancellation of courses and the collapsing of chairs of instruction. Even Woodward's Yale students, despite their undeniable comparative advantages over other applicants in the historians' job market, found themselves competing for salaries, security, and prestige, all of which were diminished.

That these questions of relevance and irrelevance would cause such problems for historians and for the profession of history was itself an ironic result for men like Woodward. This development appeared to bear out the warning of his old friends Bill Carleton and David Potter that the presentism of Woodward's "usable past" could produce a contempt for those areas of history less obviously relevant to contemporary concerns. [1] Of course, Woodward's own concept of a usable past was always a richly layered thing: his penchant for the classics, his fascination with the unpopular, and his compassion for the powerless added considerable depth and complexity to his words when he talked of relevance and utility. Yet the fact was that his advocacy of the kind of historical scholarship represented by *The Strange Career of Jim Crow* and by the civil rights essays, carried to its logical conclusion, could indeed damage the study of the past as a *thing* deserving study in and of its own right and on its own terms. During this era, Woodward not only acknowledged the problems inherent in his earlier scholarship but also virtually disowned the informing vision of Ernest Hartsock, Glenn Rainey, Charles Pipkin, and Rupert Vance, all but turning his back on their kind of committed scholarship.

His ironic perceptions also continued to develop. As noted, irony can take many forms, and there is nothing in its nature which insists that the ironist commit himself to reform of society's wrongs; in fact, a great deal of modernist irony militates against action. Once again, Woodward's ironic temperament reflected both personal conditions and much broader societal changes of mood, and his ironic essays in this era were different in kind from those of the period 1952–65. Now, in many cases, he seemed to think that inaction was preferable to wrong action; and sometimes he appeared intimidated by his own sharp sense of the way in which unintended consequences emerged from the best of intentions.

As A. Alvarez has noted, irony as an interpretation can "turn against" the ironist himself, rendering him powerless; and exactly this odd turn of events may have affected the historian-ironist at this time. In this new atmosphere, Woodward's scholarship was indeed different in tone from his previous work: still ironic, still witty, still tough, but now with a chalky undertaste of deep pessimism and occasional defeatism. Wiser than ever, he rightly scorned the admittedly shallow optimism prevalent between 1965 and 1968; but in some of his writing and discussion he became disingenuous and overly clever. Although he remained generally dependable as a voice in dissent against injustice and illusion concerning the important issues, his work during what he called his "times of trouble" was often disappointing to others and, one suspects, disappointing to himself as well.[2]

I

The disappointment with Woodward's work was tangible, although it can only be marked impressionistically. In fact, from the perspective afforded by the passage of a full generation since he departed Johns Hopkins University, such disappointment seems odd and even a bit unfair: after all, between 1960 and 1974 he would certainly produce superb essays, insightful editing, leadership in the profession, guidance for educated generalists, and sound training for graduate scholars who would become significant historians in their own right. Perhaps expectations at Yale were simply unrealistic: there was the hope that he would write those major research monographs on Reconstruction and on racism, even though he was obviously dedicated to crafting ironic essays; and many undergraduates eagerly enrolled for his lectures, despite the well-established fact that he was by nature a terrible public speaker and a shambling lecturer.[3]

But these feelings of disappointment were not sensed nor were they expressed by men and women who enjoyed the vantage point of such a long view. Instead, in the optimism of 1961, there seemed few limits to Woodward's capacities—despite his own efforts in "The Irony of Southern History" to warn about the limited performance of any man. Even to Woodward himself, such limits may have appeared almost irrelevant to his own career, since it would be so difficult for anyone to predict the chain of circumstances which developed to sadden his personal life and since he was then quite hopeful about the great potentialities of social reform in the country. Furthermore, the campaign to bring Woodward to Yale had been a vigorous one, marked by promises of special privileges, including the chance to take the first year off so that he could study, teach, reflect, and write at Oxford. Back on the New Haven campus, however, there was obviously no concomitant arrangement to quell the gathering excitement over the civil rights movement and its spectacular confrontation with southern laws and practices. Many of the students committed to activist reform sought out courses on racism and on the South; and who would have more to offer about these subjects than Woodward?[4]

Yet when these undergraduates actually heard Woodward lecturing, they were usually greatly disappointed, although many retained an attachment to his books and essays about civil rights, racism, and poverty. More striking was the response of graduate students, since his teaching at Johns Hopkins had been effective in the seminar and since he had always relished the spirited exchanges between young scholars who had already mastered the secondary literature and who were learning how to use the primary research materials. Yet even here there was some dissatisfaction. In Baltimore these sessions, especially involving dissertation research, were occasions "to knock heads together," and the spirit and vigor of the discussions were recalled fondly by Woodward; but in New Haven things never really worked out, although "head knocking" sessions were certainly characterized by student vigor, energy, and talent. Something was missing, Woodward and the students knew; and the otherwise sympathetic observer Bill McFeely agreed with those who thought that what was missing was Woodward's own willingness to use the seminar discussions to "tease out" the full implications of student hunches and other imperfectly formed ideas.[5]

Of course, such descriptions can be overdrawn. The seminars and discussion sessions, if not memorable for their inspirational qualities, certainly taught students "the rigor of the discipline" and "how historians think," the vital things Woodward had learned from Howard Beale. And most graduate students cherished the occasional intensive individual conferences at which he pushed them to clarify their thoughts and to support their contentions. In his office inside the gothic confines of the Hall of Graduate Studies, Woodward was not the mumbling lecturer; there he was the self-assured pastmaster whose calm manners and quiet voice belied the stern regimen he was establishing for his students—although much of the regimen was actually self-imposed by ambitious men and women eager to earn his respect.[6]

This respect they certainly did earn from him, and students otherwise worn down by the demands of the graduate program could take solace from a special shelf behind his desk: there sat a steadily increasing number of books which had originated as dissertations under his direction. Occasionally he, too, drew solace from the achievements of his students, and he could tap the burned tobacco out of his pipe and gaze contentedly around the office with its portrait of Faulkner and the shelves of his own books and of his students'; but despite its spacious dimensions, the office was always somewhat insubstantial, a place where he met people, not a place where he felt comfortable to work. Instead, he worked at home, in nearby Hamden, in a lovely house chosen and decorated by Glenn.[7] Attractive as it was, however, that home was the scene of serious problems, problems which no scholarly achievement—not his own and not his students'—could overcome.

I I

As he grew older, Woodward almost never expressed extremes of emotion, and in particular he rarely demonstrated anger. His Yale colleague John Morton Blum—who gradually became one of his few confidantes after working with him closely in history department business and on the wildly successful *National Experience* textbook—often argued with Woodward and often saw him in the middle of impassioned debate with others, but Blum could recall only a few outbursts of temper from the obviously troubled historian. However, one day in 1984, long after the greatest trials appeared to be over, Blum mentioned the word *cancer* while the two men were having a private and, until then, subdued conversation. Woodward all but erupted. "Cancer!" he suddenly shouted. "Cancer!" Then he balled up his big hand into a fist and with surprising power and vehemence pounded the fist into his palm and shouted, "Cancer is my *enemy*!"[8]

The cancer which was so tangibly present as "my enemy" in this angry moment of old age had come to his consciousness slowly over the years as it took away his little family and as it further reduced his already small group of intimate friends. It came first to the one he loved most, his son, Peter Vincent Woodward, and it manifested itself as a bitter process of degeneration and declension when the young man seemed to be only at the beginning of a satisfying and enriching life and career. Nearing completion of his doctoral studies in political science at Princeton University, Peter was married to Susan Lampland, herself a promising scholar of Eastern European politics, and the young Woodward couple had quickly become emotionally vital to the senior Woodward couple. But these portents of a bright beginning were false, for this was actually the end for Peter, who at this point contracted a debilitating cancer which gradually made physical activity virtually impossible for him. How strange that the father who disdained sports remained vigorous enough to play handball with younger men, while the son who was enthusiastically athletic scarcely had the energy to attend a game or a match.[9]

Since the days at Johns Hopkins, the Woodwards had been vacationing in the summers at Ocean City, Maryland, where the men could indulge their passion for swimming and for deep-sea fishing in environs more congenial than the self-consciously "high-quality" New England resorts which they considered in fact quite second-rate. Often they were joined in Ocean City by Manning Dauer, companion in such activities from the days of the Three Musketeers in Gainesville; and the ageless bachelor recalled the new scene in the summer of 1968 when he came calling as he always had in the past. Peter was gaunt and so tormented by pain that he was unable to find a position in which he could endure to lie on the beach in the sun. Vann and Glenn reluctantly took him into the cottage, where father sat by son, Vann able to speak only a few words to his visitor: "I don't want to go swimming. I don't want to go deep-sea fishing, I just want to stay here with him." For Peter the pain at least was ended by death in 1969, but for his parents the pain never really left, with Glenn largely withdrawing from their once-enlivening circle of mutual friends and with Vann—though he continued to travel widely and to write with vigor—doing his work with few traces of the bounce and the spring which his oldest friends could remember. After all, Woodward had lost more than the relationship between father and son, which in any case Peter's advancing maturity would have greatly transformed; and he had lost even more than the special intimacies of maturing love. He had also lost the future, what George Santayana describes as the morningstar for those who reject, as Woodward certainly did, the simple certitudes of American Puritanism: no longer could he even dream the question unasked of Peter: "Might he come in time—and not too late—to understand America, and throw his understanding into arresting words, or better still, into contagious actions?"[10]

No pain which followed would equal this loss, and no subsequent accomplishment or new relationship would make him forget it; but new losses followed quickly in numbing succession as other cancers struck deep inside the circle of supporting friends. The disease took three men who in different ways and independently of each other had become indispensable to Woodward and his family: the historians David Morris Potter and Richard Hofstadter and the jurist Alexander Mordecai Bickel. Each man was important to him intellectually because each so consistently engaged him in public and private dialogues: each was to some degree more a man of consensus mentality than a student of conflict, none was as liberal on social issues as Woodward, and thus all forced him to sharpen his arguments. As valued as they were to him in developing his ideas, however, Potter, Hofstadter, and Bickel were even more vital as intimates with whom he shared the happinesses of the mid-1960s and the sadnesses afterward. In fact, of course, in combination they had contributed much to the earlier happiness; and the loss of each in turn—Hofstadter in 1970, Potter in 1971, Bickel in 1974—not only hurt him but also deprived him of support and comfort in his moments of grief.[11] All intellectuals had benefited from the fruits of the public conversations between Woodward and his nemesis-friends, since these dialogues were prominently displayed in periodicals or were heard at convention meetings; and the rude way in which cancer cut short these conversations produced an obvious loss for the whole community of scholars. But the private dialogues with these special friends were just as rudely cut off, producing a loss less obvious but no less real, for it palpably diminished Woodward's person and, for a time, his scholarship itself.

Potter's early death emphatically affirmed the essentially tragic quality of a life whose sadness and complexities belied the elegant simplicity of his writing style and the calm reassurance in the substance of his teaching. Although unjustifiably the model for a rather disagreeable character in a minor novel which was consumed eagerly for a time in the New Haven area, Potter was actually a warm and charming man whose friendship earned him the loyalty of his colleagues at Yale and then at Stanford much as his scholarship earned him the acclaim of his profession. However, his life in New Haven was marred by sadness and dissatisfaction, which he shared quietly with a few close friends; and then, before he could fully realize the promise of a new life in Palo Alto, he developed an incurable cancer. Nevertheless, none of these problems had any demonstrable impact on his matchless scholarship; nor did the rather conservative cast of that scholarship have any demonstrable impact on his friendship with Woodward. Where Woodward was proud to march and sing "We Shall Overcome," Potter repeated his warning that historians have nought to do with hope; and where Woodward virtually celebrated the decision in *Brown* v. *Board of Education,* Potter lamented that, of all things, the schools were not the place to start integration. Moreover, his famed essay *People of Plenty,* while sui generis and thus not properly part of any historiographical "school," certainly reinforced the consensus depiction of the nonideological sameness of American culture and politics: a people so blessed with a material plethora had little reason to engage in substantive ideological debate, since there was little of the economic deprivation that usually produced the kind of class struggle which in turn informed such debate. And Potter, as the most distinguished of the students trained by U. B. Phillips, was not sympathetic to Woodward's portrayal of a dramatically *New* South produced by a Second American Revolution: instead Potter, like his mentor, pointed to the threads of social continuity—especially racial attitudes—which bound up southern identity for all time. [12]

As a matter of fact, Potter's differing interpretation of the same history was one of the most important of the strong currents of wind against which Woodward's ironic historiography rose—and without which it might have stayed on the ground. It was Potter who showed that the Populists and then their champion Woodward had both exaggerated sectional rate differentials in the charges of railroad carriers during the Gilded Age; and it was Potter who first noted that Woodward could well be correct about the origins of Jim Crow segregation while still underestimating the racism which shot through the South in each era. In all of these exchanges of views, Potter was not only the gentlest of critics but also one of the wittiest, one who could frequently anticipate the anecdotal consequences of things. For example, when he read a draft of Woodward's essay "Clio with Soul," he immediately warned that that "mighty catchy title" would never work, since those who know who Clio was do not comprehend *soul* and those who understand soul do not talk about Clio: this prediction was immediately and hilariously realized when the traditionalist historian introducing Woodward for the occasion told the audience that Mr. Woodward would discuss "Clio with a Soul." In such little events, and in larger matters, Potter was ever Fabius the buckler to Woodward's Scipio the sword: without aggressive use of the sword, no new lands would be won, but without the restraint of the buckler, none would be held. Just as Plutarch's Rome needed both because of their differences, so did the intellectual community profit from the way the more adventurous Woodward and the more cautious Potter ultimately worked together.[13]

This kind of cooperation, this working together, was even more remarkable in the case of Hofstadter and Woodward: after all, Hofstadter was the very essence of consensus historiography, and to complicate matters further, he had little regard for the South and even less regard for the rural radicals of the 1880s and 1890s. He seldom traveled to the South or to the Corn Belt Midwest; he was always most at home in the urban Northeast; and as marked earlier, his renowned *Age of Reform* was at once a brilliant light focused on the New York and Massachussetts Progressives and a shadowy misrepresentation of the Kansas and Carolina Populists. In fact, it was primarily he who inspired the disdain of the 1950s intellectuals for the study of southern or of Populist ideas, and it was this Hofstadter message in general against which Woodward spoke and wrote until the scholars of the 1960s began to express appreciation of—and in their enthusiasm, virtual adulation of—agrarian reformers. Yet Hofstadter cannot be understood primarily as a man of consensus, despite his contributions to and inspiration for that analysis; he was, above all else, committed to the most vigorous pursuit of ideas, especially as ideas developed over time, and he was intolerant of intellectual self-satisfaction and the concomitant presumption that the big question was already answered. When he attacked the Progressive historians in the 1950s it was because he felt that their historiography had become too formulaic, too predictable, and too self-assured; and in the same way, by the end of the 1960s, he was attacking his own followers for the same attitude. Perhaps in its own way fittingly, this man who wrote so soothingly in the 1950s about consensus homogeneity in the American culture was actually a provocative personality who delighted in quick, sharp exchanges in highly charged conversations, and soon he came to include Woodward in these discussions.[14] Nor was either man unaffected by this dialogue, which was initiated in the late years of the 1940s and which gained power and substance throughout the 1960s; Woodward for his part could acknowledge the excesses of the Populists, and Hofstadter for his could return to his youthful appreciation for class analysis and for a serious consideration of economic determinants and class conflict in our history.

He and Woodward began to extend their conversation by widening its sphere significantly: after 1965 they began to plan joint projects, and they sent each other their graduate students as they developed further their own kind of dialectical process, which promised great results. Hofstadter created a plan for a series of mid-century social portraits of America; and he and Woodward planned to edit together the *Oxford History of the United States,* an ambitious project designed to meet the new challenges posed by the extreme specialization of disciplines in American academics. Both men, and the percipient Oxford editor Sheldon Meyer, were disturbed by the centrifugal nature of modern historical scholarship and even more disturbed by the way other disciplines ignored historians. What they intended, then, was a full-scale interpretive treatment of U.S. history, with each major period discussed in a clear and distinct line of historiographical analysis by scholars who used the latest techniques of analysis afforded by many disciplines, but who could still report their conclusions to the educated laity in language which was accessible and attractive. The intended audience was thus composed of the thoughtful generalists for whom both men had always written;[15] but now Hofstadter and Woodward set their sights higher, aiming at nothing less than the restoration of a historical education. With such large tasks ahead, it was vital to Woodward that Hofstadter be there to help in the struggle; it was unthinkable that Hofstadter not be there; and when the unthinkable happened again, the commitments they had made together began to seem less challenging than cumbersome and perhaps even unmanageable.

With Bickel, the effect was different, since there were no joint projects, no common scholarship which united the legal expert with the historian. Indeed, in many ways this was the least probable of all friendships, given Bickel's constitutional disinclination to dissent and his unhappiness both with the style of Earl Warren's judicial activism and with the substance of the later decisions which Warren's Court rendered on civil rights. Still, a warm friendship developed, one which melded Alexander and Joanne Bickel and Vann and Glenn Woodward into a kind of a family unit. The Bickels saw Peter dying and helped him to face it as well as helping Vann and Glenn to live without him; they also saw and understood how the subsequent losses of Potter and Hofstadter affected Woodward at multiple levels, professional and personal, of his being, and they again assisted him through these months of 1970 and 1971. But then came the day when Bickel discovered that he himself would be denied the biblical quota of years because of cancer. After that, it was the Woodwards who helped Alexander to meet his end and who helped Joanne to accept it; but of course, the Bickels' suffering was also the Woodwards' suffering, and the three who remained after 1974 very much needed the reassuring symbiosis which had resulted from their unique friendship. [16]

Also still available to Woodward in this diminished circle was Robert Penn Warren in the New Haven area and outside it his old friends Dauer and Carleton. But his chief solace remained what it had always been, the sheer work involved in the quest after what he called "the subject" of the South. With such an obvious void in his personal life, he needed his professional life more than ever, and his students became even more important to him than they had been before. He also took on even more editorial work, much of it performed gratis for scholars of "the subject" regardless of where they taught and studied or what they said. Although prodded by his colleagues and friends to "take the time to grieve"—as Blum put it, "like us other mortals"—Woodward instead immersed himself in this work, astonishing even those who thought they knew him best by the sheer volume of things he was willing to read and to critique in detail. [17]

Woodward was thus far from alone and far from inactive even by 1974; he certainly had a full and vigorous professional life which was by any standard a great success. But again, his personal life was so integrally a part of that professional life—a man like Hofstadter or Bickel was friend, critic, colleague, and rival all at the same time, and there were no clear boundary lines between their friendship and their work—that these losses inevitably affected for the worse the quality, though not the pace or the volume, of his scholarship. During this same period, the larger society was about to halt, and in some cases even to reverse, the justifiably celebrated accomplishments of the civil rights movement, and this result—in its degree and its speed of dissolution surprising even to one as skeptical as Woodward—was to a great extent also a defeat at a personal level for him, since the movement provided a significant component of his liberal identity.

It also developed that the deaths from unfathomable cancer were only a presaging of much more death, which would spring from a source more easily located, although equally irresistible. This source was war and this decade's particular version of it took place in Indochina. Woodward's reaction to the Vietnam War could be predicted after his grudging acquiescence to World War II: one who resisted the Nazis only with reluctance because of disdain for British colonialism would hardly support French colonialism when its enemy was localized communism. He wanted no part of this distant civil war, and he was fearful that prolonged American involvement in it would draw away the material and the moral resources necessary in the country's campaign for racial equity and in the newly joined struggle with structural poverty. [18]

Much as he deplored the glib proclamation of an unattainable Great Society, he appreciated Lyndon Johnson's obvious commitment to political participation for blacks, and he supported the substance, if not the style, of the War on Poverty. Even if the more grandiose schemes of economic reform eventually proved fruitless, the era seemed sure to produce opportunities for blacks and for others in the lower classes to gain and to exercise power. But the simplest calculations of the feed-store, seed-store proprietor told him that two wars were too costly for one nation and that an escalating fight with communism in the rice paddies of Vietnam would sap energies of all kinds desperately needed in the equally expensive battles with racism in the city streets of the United States; as had been the case before, enough noise from William McKinley's bugles inevitably would drown out Tom Watson's voice calling for reform. And yet there was still this hope, that Johnson could stand on McKinley's—and Watson's—shoulders; that the errors of one century need not be repeated in the next. Moreover, if Woodward's reading of southern irony was accurate, then the timing was propitious with a Texan presiding alongside a Georgia secretary of state: between Johnson and Rusk, as between the Pedernales and the Chattahoochee, flowed the knowledge that not every war can be won, that the enthusiasms of the crowd are always lessened when its ranks are thinned out by bloodshed in actual combat. Surely enough had already happened to awaken the pragmatic proprietor of the store, who was likely still tucked away somewhere inside both Johnson and Rusk.[19]

It made sense for Woodward and his friends to attempt to influence the Johnson foreign policy, since the Kennedy quest for and conduct of the presidency had been ably assisted by a number of high-voltage academics who remained close to JFK's successor in the early months of the Great Society. This group of intellectuals was later to be lambasted with some justice as the self-proclaimed "best and brightest" who induced disaster in Asia by computer-war adventurism; but in 1965 it all appeared much less sinister, merely men and women of great talent who had been attracted to Kennedy's Washington after two terms of Eisenhower's comparative lethargy. Nevertheless, by April the United States had begun the "Rolling Thunder" aerial campaign of saturation bombing in Vietnam, and the Johnson administration had more than doubled the number of ground troops there. In the same month the ascendancy of leftists in the Dominican Republic had drawn an occupying force of twenty-two thousand American troops onto the island, a force sent in without consultation of the Congress or of the Organization of American

States. One could discern the emerging pattern of massive commitment, of world policing, and at the very moment when the domestic programs were winning congressional approval. Doubts within the cabinet, within the career foreign service, and even within the army intelligence were rumored, and Woodward attempted to gain the president's ear through the network of academic and public servants which ran through Washington in those busy days.[20]

With the sharp, lurid highlighting of later developments in foreign policy, Woodward's quaintly insignificant effort may seem quite futile, but at the time it was a rational-enough gesture. Manning Dauer asked a University of Florida graduate student, Howard Wierarta, to prepare a memorandum explaining that the Dominicans were not in danger of becoming a Soviet satellite and calling for a Caribbean policy more sensitive to Latin nationalism. Then Dauer sent the precise, restrained memorandum to Woodward, who carried it over to his Yale colleague Eugene Victor Debs Rostow, who in his turn promised to get it to his brother, Walt Whitman Rostow, then serving in LBJ's administration. Such memorandum shuffling was actively encouraged as a useful exercise in the Kennedy-Johnson years of "cross-pollination of ideas," as some of the best and brightest liked to phrase it. Only this time the bee's pollen was rejected, as Dauer recalled: "I get back from Walt Rostow a five-page letter; it said that life was a set of dominoes; that Communism was taking over the world; you know that stupid line. I send a copy to Vann and we shake our heads and say, 'Well, this [Johnson's theory of foreign policy] isn't the world we actually live in.'"[21]

An irony learned much later was that the Georgia past did make an impact, that Dean Rusk in the councils of war spoke often of the danger of overcommitment in terms not unlike those of Wierarta's memorandum. But this interesting exception only probes the rule without breaking it, for Rusk persuaded no insiders and publicly affirmed the policy as enunciated by both Rostows, William Bundy, McGeorge Bundy, and Robert McNamara—and by LBJ himself, who spoke grandly of an Indochinese land-reclamation project patterned on the Tennessee Valley Authority and funded by the Asian Development Bank, capitalized at a billion dollars by the United States, a country which "could do anything" and which certainly was not about to lose a war. The bugles were loud indeed, but Woodward found that the voice of reason had reached congressional ears even as it missed Johnson's; his fellow Arkansan James William Fulbright used his Senate Foreign Relations Committee to say publicly what Rusk, unknown to the Congress, was saying privately. In fact, Fulbright gave a speech that became a book, *Arrogance of Power,* which became a catchword for the antiwar movement; in it he said, "Power tends to confuse itself with virtue and a great nation is peculiarly susceptible to the idea that its power is a sign of God's favor." Like Woodward in "The Irony of Southern History," which Fulbright later cited as an influence, the senator asked, "Can America overcome the fatal arrogance of power?"[22]

Fulbright's affirmation of Woodward's theme went far to substantiate the historian's claims, for the senator was no radical but rather the quintessential pragmatist, a man who tolerated segregation's heyday without complaint and then accepted its demise without much regret. Disdaining to join any crusades, Fulbright simply refused to support another sure-to-lose cause such as the Vietnam War; and Fulbright, unlike many antiwar spokesmen, was not hoping to direct national energies toward social programs at all. When an effective and moderate politico such as this man could swing into line with Reinhold Niebuhr's reading of irony, that phenomenon seemed solid proof that Woodward was "really *on* to something" about the lessons of the southern past. But Woodward was less impressed by the Fulbright response than he was depressed by the Johnson mentality: LBJ was simply more powerful than Fulbright, and if the Texan rejected the available lessons of irony in this crucial decade, then it had not really been worthwhile to point them out.[23]

Moreover, within a year the civil rights movement was altered beyond Woodward's recognition, to his eye damaged beyond repair by a combination of defections from the ranks: white reformists formerly concentrating on civil rights seemed to spend most of their energies trying to stop the war; and many blacks were leaving to press for black nationalism or pan-Africanism, causes which both mystified and frustrated Woodward. The latter allegiances struck Woodward as being especially incongruous, a kind of black-willed resegregation which played into the hands of the seemingly defeated white separatists. Privately, he expressed bitter sarcasm about black radicalism and about separatism: "my colored friends at each other's throats or screaming incoherently or retreating to fantasyland." In the more public forum provided by a revised edition of *The Strange*

Career of Jim Crow, he was more restrained in his language as he added a chapter which traced developments since the *Brown* v. *Board of Education* decision. However, there, too, he expressed a bafflement with black radicalism and a regret about the apparent demise of the Second Reconstruction; and that chapter, especially when read in the context of his letters and remarks to friends, implied a causal relationship between the "new" forces of radicalism and the failings of the movement.[24]

Social historians have yet to explain the reasons for the centrifugal nature of liberal reformism, although that phenomenon was evident to some as early as 1966 and was almost beyond remark after 1968. Clayborne Carson, the historian of the Student Non-Violent Coordinating Committee (SNCC), has been most effective among those who hold that black radicals never "departed" or "defected" from or otherwise "left" the liberals, but actually never were any part of the liberal reformism associated with the Urban League or with the NAACP. Thus, according to Carson, the forms and expressions of black radicalism essentially represented an entirely different movement, one coming primarily "from the bottom up." Moreover, Carson has agreed with those who note that pan-Africanism has a history of its own, a history considerably antedating the more recent legal campaigns of liberal integrationists.[25] Yet these explanations, while clarifying something Woodward misunderstood about the nature of black support for the movement, do not address the question of what did happen to the broad-based coalition of labor, clergy, professionals, academics, mainstream politicians, liberal business and civic leaders, youthful activists, and others who worked so successfully to encourage the congressional reforms of 1964 and 1965.

J. Mills Thornton, a Woodward student, has suggested a highly plausible explanation for the literal and figurative disintegration of the movement after its earlier successes, which had been marked by such real cohesion. Thornton noted that the sharply focused legal issues of rights to education, rights to vote, and rights to public accommodations, while controversial enough, made no fundamental assault on the basic system of values in the liberal and capitalist middle-class society which existed outside the South. However, when the relatively moderate Martin Luther King, Jr., echoing radicals before him, began to talk about economic issues in a way which threatened middle-class white possessions—that is, when the claim to legal justice was transformed into the more inclusive claim to economic equality—a serious and irreparable split occurred along class lines among the former allies. As Thornton marked it, freedom was one thing, but equality was another, and there were contradictions inherent in the concepts of freedom and equality which could not be obscured or ignored or otherwise fuzzed over after 1966. In thus discussing the struggle between freedom and equality, Thornton was repeating for a particular social issue what Michael Kammen has labeled *the* ongoing cultural tension in American history since the Civil War. From still another perspective, these observations tend to parallel the message from economist Lester C. Thurow, who has pointed out that the ability of the elite in the United States to hold onto its wealth forces an often bitter competition among minority interests for what remains of the "rest of the pie"; and when economic growth has slowed or even stopped, this competition in a "zero-sum game" militates against the formation of broad coalitions seeking social justice.[26]

Whatever historians finally conclude about the causes, there is little doubt about the results of these developments: by the year 1966, Woodward's world of liberal reform was cracking apart. And concomitant with this demise of coordinated liberal activism was a reinvigorated racism, gussied up as "white backlash" for its appearance in Michigan or Wisconsin but looking and sounding remarkably like prejudicial old hat. Even Atlanta, proclaimed by its energetic biracial publicists as the "city too busy to hate," revealed itself to be not unlike the place of the 1920s known all too well to Hartsock, Rainey, and Woodward, for in 1966 Lester Maddox, a fried-chicken restauranteur who has chased Negroes from his establishment with a stick, ascended to the governorship of Georgia. Woodward wrote to Rainey, "Is it really as bad as it looks? Or is that possible? Or is it some nightmare about the ghost of Tom Watson? Or can half a century roll back and Georgia suddenly revert to the Leo Frank days of howling mobs led by grinning goons? Or does history really go backward? I feel like Rip Van W. in reverse. Where have I been anyway? Maybe [southern liberals] were dreams and Tom [after 1900] the only reality." But this was not an expatriate bemoaning the sins of the South he had left behind: "Hell of it is that it does not look like a local phenomenon. West Coast,

East Coast, Midwest, All closing in fast." He ended his note by saying, "Looks much like 1877 from where I sit. Chaos and old night."[27]

The extreme categorization, "chaos and old night," he did not offer publicly; but he implied only a little less in his essays and speeches. The specter of the centrifuge of the present cried out for some historical explanation; and those hoping for a new moral direction to guide reform were casting about for something usable from the past. By this period, as noted, Woodward was much less interested in the uses of history, coming to sound now a great deal like his departed friend Potter; but again, he was uncomfortably hoist with his own petard. Irony was indeed a dangerous weapon, for in trying to use ironic language to "strip away delusion" and "win through" to truth and passion, Woodward had found a set of most discomfiting truths: perhaps nothing much in the past was usable, and perhaps nothing much in the present contained the least hope for change. Yet his own past work had inspired scholars who still hoped for a great deal, and the higher quality as well as the greater optimism of that earlier work now became an ironic burden for which he had never bargained.

In particular, this man who had said and who had done so much for the civil rights movement, this man who had so frequently and with such insight clarified issues borne of racism, was now pressed for a more meaningful analysis of the larger phenomenon of racism: what was it, where did it come from, and why? Granting that these were daunting questions, one still judges the Woodward response from 1965 to 1974 a grave disappointment: failing to address the questions himself, failing to write *the* book on Reconstruction which the profession had come to expect, failing to write *the* book on race relations which the profession had come to hope for, he also failed to learn much from those who were actively engaged with these issues. Rather than improving his work by drawing on their new research for modification of his monumental interpretations, rather than improving their work by bringing the best of his own ideas into a genuine dialogue with new and challenging interpretations, he often relied on slippery, evasive replies to fundamental questions. There were reasons for him to be less effective in this time, but he was too much the gentleman in the old style to lay these things before the public: in Virgil's description, well known to him, he was the Rutulian hero Turnus who, sensing correctly that the very gods are against him, becomes "bewildered by disaster's shifting image."[28]

The cultural historian Carl Schorske has been especially perceptive in explaining why the intellectual gods of the new era presented such shifting images. As he has remarked, contemporary scholars shifted "the premises for understanding man and society from the social to the psychological realm. And they did so under the pressure of new, uncongenial turns in the world of politics." These new conditions produced for a great many historians "a revolution of falling political expectations" and a concomitant change in perspective from the problems of structure in society to the problems of the psyche in the individual. "Among the shifts from Promethean to Epimethean culture heroes," says Schorske, "none was more striking than the turn from Marx to Freud. For here the search for and understanding of the ills that plague mankind tended to be translated from the public and sociological domain to the private and psychical one." Finally, Schorske notes that even many of those who continued to maintain a firm commitment to the reform of the collectivity changed their emphases in order to incorporate Freudian insights, thereby "redrawing the lineaments of Utopia."[29]

These trends spelled trouble for Woodward, who eschewed psychological investigation partly because he was untrained in its methods, but even more because he was essentially doubtful of its findings. Thus, for all his obvious fascination with the individual exceptions to societal patterns, he did not attempt to probe the psyche in search of the impetus for deviation. This refusal restricted his exercise of one of the things dearest to him, which was meaningful discussion and debate with younger scholars. For instance, he was superb in interpreting the previously undigested statistics on comparative slavery which Philip D. Curtin produced, for in that case he was explaining things at the grand level of the cultural and economic processes of slavery; but by contradistinction he did not join in any particularly useful way in Winthrop D. Jordan's discussion of the psychic responses to color and sex as processes of personal relationships which for each man and woman include the most fundamental understanding—or misunderstanding—of self. Thus others began to shade in the chiaroscuro of personality traits in order to define more fully the character of such leaders as Lewis Harvie

Blair, Benjamin Ryan Tillman, James Kimble Vardaman, or even, to some extent, Tom Watson, despite Woodward's earlier dominance over such topics.[30]

In the environment of such a tangle of motives and moods, he produced in 1971 a volume of interpretive essays which was a flawed gem, brilliantly articulated by a master cutter, but flawed all the same. The title, *American Counterpoint: Slavery and Racism in the North-South Dialogue,* certainly promised a great deal, and the book was pointedly dedicated in memoriam to Peter as an obvious sign of its serious intent. As a unit, the essays were intended to complete the work begun by *The Burden of Southern History,* that is, to develop the perceptions of a uniquely ironic historical temperament. Essentially, however, the essays continue the work of demolishing icons, turning now against icons abuilding on the Left; and as such, they seem as much the product of youthful spunk as of elderly sagacity. They demonstrate above all else a man beholden to no one, absolute in his refusal to suit up with anybody's team for some school of historiography. "Tags, the problem of tags!" he said, with which words he ruefully dismissed efforts to categorize, and thereby evaluate, his scholarship.[31]

The introductory essay catches the imagination, for it suggests a special perspective from which to consider both southern identity and race relations, a perspective vastly superior to the dominant trends of considering the two subjects as separate or, if unified, then unified in a way proving for good and all the hopeless degeneracy of the South. As before, Woodward's vision was not only different but also grander than others', and as before, he borrowed from some other discipline the means to express what he saw. This time he borrowed from musicology the term *counterpoint,* defined as "the technique of combining two or more melodic lines in such a way that they establish a harmonic relationship while retaining their linear individuality." And from this he concluded that "harmony is based on dissonance as well as consonance," but even so he warned that "applying the technique of counterpoint to such dissonant and prickly lines of thought and controversy as are treated here may rarely be expected to produce a perfect harmonic relationship, for the linear individualities remain strong." What Woodward sought instead of an unbelievable harmonizing was some way to put together North-South relations and black-white relations into a synthesis, a comprehensive synthesis, but one still well to this side of the hubris of Hegelian dialectics.[32]

Of race relations he wryly noted that America had produced two huge "hyphenate minorities," the black Afro-American and the white southern-American. Adapting Daniel Boorstin's description of the Negro as the "indelible immigrant," he noted that blacks were thereby given a "hyphenate" identity whether sought or not; but "the white Southerner, on the other hand, has been at least in part a hyphenate by choice." Moreover, for the two largest and longest-lived minorities in America the shared irony was that "confronting each other on their native soil for three and a half centuries, . . . [to a remarkable degree] they have shaped each other's destiny, determined each other's isolation, shared and molded a common culture. It is, in fact, impossible to imagine the one without the other and quite futile to try." Here was another patented usable irony, one with the potency for good or ill, one which had produced more of the latter than of the former, but one quite dangerous to miss as thoroughly as it was missed by many otherwise respectable experts on race.[33]

That irony supported the basis for study of North-South relations, since those two sections "have used each other, or various images and stereotypes of each other, for many purposes . . . not only to define their identity and to say what they are *not,* but to escape in fantasy from what they *are.*" The former had been said, and said well, by Willie Morris in *North toward Home,* and the latter had been said by William R. Taylor in *Cavalier and Yankee;* it was the putting together of the two insights, in combination with the perspective on race, that made the introduction enticing. As if to forewarn against too great expectations, however, Woodward modified his declaration by marking the gap between potentiality and practice: "In the main . . . North and South have served each other as inexhaustible objects of invidious comparison in the old game of regional polemics."[34]

And with the essays proper, he blunted the force of the observations he had made in the introduction. The essays were uneven, with those on the Old South being models of how a historian should proceed to define a cultural problem, but with those on the New South, where his own research was so prodigious, being imperfectly cast. Withal, his continuing refusal to deal with the psychological phenomena at the individual level left big questions not so much unanswered as never asked. This was most apparent in his treatment of Wilbur J. Cash, the Carolina journalist who had attempted the single boldest exploration of the southern psyche before committing suicide in 1941. As noted earlier, Cash's *Mind of the South,* while itself deeply flawed, has stood up as a work that demands a response by anyone attempting to explain the South. Woodward's difficulties in coming to terms with Cash were symptomatic of his even greater problem of coming to terms with the whole of southern history, despite the incredible strides toward that object he had already made before he wrote in 1969. His essay on Cash, then, is a kind of sandbar in his career as well as in *American Counterpoint:* to one side flows the current of comprehension of the New South; to the other flows a shallower—albeit swift and broad—current of comprehension of the Old South; but the two never converge and Woodward was unable to develop any sense of the continuity and contiguity of the sectional history he lived and studied.[35]

As always, his essay was sprightly, and as usual, it was sympathetic even to someone with whom he disagreed. Cash's book had never really been treated critically, perhaps, Woodward suggested, because of the author's sad end. Without being insensitive, Woodward announced that it was time to give the man his due credit by taking his ideas seriously enough to critique them. The crucial element in Cash's story was the concept of damning sameness, an ongoing and basically unchanging theme of southern history; and the unique twist he gave to this was the psychological analysis of race and sex as the final determinants of class structure, economic activity, political stratagems, social etiquette, and even food and speech. Cash's world was violently sexual and the Negro was always the victim, the human target for the frustrations released by the high-energy field which was the southern culture. The irony here, perhaps not known to Cash, was that *The Mind of the South* was a misnomer; the mind was scarcely involved at all, something Woodward was quick to point out and to challenge.[36]

Furthermore, Woodward rejected Cash's thesis of the continuing captains, the notion that the wartime captains of artillery and cavalry became the postbellum captains of industry: this was exactly what the apostles of the New South Movement had said—only they said it with approbation—and Woodward was having none of that, even if it were expressed as a radical critique. Again, as he had in *Origins of the New South,* Woodward emphasized two things: the first, that the Civil War mattered, that it radically changed, even revolutionized, the agrarian South; and the second, that the South itself was composed of regions which were distinct one from another. Cash, then, was committing the error of unwarranted generalization from the specific: the extreme sexual and racial prejudice he described may have characterized the leadership in the rapidly industrializing areas of his native Gaffney and his adoptive home, Greensboro, in the years immediately before and after the First World War; but it did not adequately describe the rest of the South, and it was too simplistic even for Cash's subregional homeplaces during other eras. Although Woodward was largely correct in these assessments, he would have it that Cash contributed precious little to understanding the South; and that was not so. Cash's genius, as the ancients would put it, was as narrow and as brilliant as a high note forced from a flute: he did exaggerate and he did miss a great deal, but his Freudian analysis of racism held profound insight, insight which in the hands of the later analysts Winthrop Jordan and Joel Williamson, explained something about the persisting racism of Woodward's land.[37]

These two historians, and others, have recognized that Cash was employing a rather static Freudian interpretation which provided considerable insight into the Carolina Piedmont mentality during a given era. If Cash's thesis could be infused with some dynamic quality of growth, then the profession could indeed benefit from a Cashian sense of the development of nonrational perceptions over a long period of time. Jordan attempted approximately this for the slave-owners of colonial Virginia, as did Williamson for the violent Negrophobes of the 1890s and for the genteel Volksgeistian conservatives of the 1920s. Profoundly useful as are these investigations, they underscore yet again the extreme complexity of racial issues, for—despite forays—neither Jordan nor Williamson has been able to take the Cashian and Epimethean insight very far past rather localized places and rather limited periods of time. Although Woodward has expressed admiration for Williamson and for Jordan, while also providing them real help, he has never expressed much appreciation for the debt each man owes to Cash, although he has sometimes implied a sense of the liability which comes with their usages of Cash. As with so much else, this work remains uncompleted, even barely begun: perhaps future historians will start with Cash's ideas, amending them to acknowledge the profound economic transformation wrought by the Civil War, amending them further to acknowledge the widely varying regional and temporal degrees of racism, and finally taking full account of the dissidents in occasionally successful rebellion against racist and class oppression. After making such Promethean amendments, the historians could then employ an analysis essentially inspired by Cash to explain the psychic dimensions of racism; and such an analysis would have far more explanatory power than Woodward has conceded.

During these same "times of trouble," he also failed to perceive the power of other analyses in the fields of Reconstruction and of New South segregation. The latter, having to do with Jim Crow studies, was a more recently developed astigmatism, and one that he would cure after 1974; but the former, having to do with abolitionism, was never and would never be effectively in his field of vision. The abolitionists he had always disdained, and the only weak essays in *The Burden of Southern History* had concerned them; now in "Seeds of Failure in Radical Race Policy" and "The Northern Crusade against Slavery," he perpetuated this misreading, insisting that Reconstruction failed largely because of racism in the North: not only the racism of the man in the street but also the racism of the abolitionist leaders who prepared to direct Reconstruction. While many abolitionists deserved censure on many counts, certainly including a degree of racism, Woodward showed a curiously ahistorical perspective on this matter, tarring every member of a disparate, variegated group with the same brush. Again, his late friend Potter, who had equal dislike for the abolitionists, had once summed up such questions succinctly with the remark that if one thinks some people of recent years have been racist, one should try to conceive the degree of racism it took to *enslave* humans; and this Woodward did not do. As to Jim Crow, "The Strange Career of a Historical Controversy" showed him at his worst, explaining away his own pathbreaking essay by qualifying into nothingness his controversial original insights while talking around the signal contributions of those scholars inspired by him who questioned some of his conclusions. In both essays, there are moments of uncharacteristic and unattractive slipperiness and evasiveness.[38]

By contradistinction, Woodward sounded notes strong and true as he played on the newly emerging themes in Old South historiography. There the peculiar institution, a subject nearly worked to death by traditional narrative history, was being extensively and healthfully reconsidered in comparative perspective, and Woodward seized on the new work, both good and bad, to make some of the most useful generalizations proffered by historians of any ideological or methodological camp. Exciting but often barely comprehensible things were being done for slavery studies by self-styled New Historians attuned to the stories told in demographics by data previously inaccessible because of their bulk but digestible with sophisticated quantification techniques. And thoroughly comprehensible but equally exciting things were being done by scholars comparing the patterns formed by Latin slavery with the patterns formed by southern thralldom.

With "Southern Slaves in the World of Thomas Malthus," Woodward brought to the fore the gleanings of the quantifiers, especially the studies of the slave trade conducted by Philip Curtin. While he still did not know how to do such research, he at least knew how to read it with critical discernment after a trip to Ann Arbor to learn from the practitioners at the computer research center at the University of Michigan; this was a trip which he described to Manning Dauer as being crucial to those hoping to keep up with new trends. Thus informed, he presented a summary of new findings in a speech before the Yale Law School in which he suggested new directions which social historians might take after assimilating the research of Curtin and others; now, refining both interpretation and suggestion, he limned the outlines of a new picture of comparative slavery by considering the data of the trans-Atlantic slave trade and of slave populations in Latin America, the Caribbean, and the United States. From Curtin in particular he learned three facts previously unknown or obscured. For one, the sheer magnitude of the legal slave trade overwhelmed the illicit slave smuggling. For another, the trade remained legitimate for Brazil and Cuba two generations after it was outlawed for the United States. For a third, which did not at all "follow" from the preceding, the slave population of the South was significantly larger than the slave population of any single Latin country despite the smaller number of slaves imported. Putting these three facts together and recalling the Malthusian description of war, pestilence, disease, and drought as the final "check" on population, Woodward was no longer able to give credence to the claim that southern slavery was physically harsher than Latin. Only hinting at the controversial conclusions already being developed and disseminated by the Cliometricians Robert William Fogel and Stanley L. Engerman, he closed with the loaded understatement that one could not link up slave population with slave importation, for the former was separated from the latter by a host of intervening factors such as treatment, diet, weather, working environment, and physical anthropology. [39]

Having crossed the boundaries of disciplines into the land of New History, Woodward next visited and reported on cross-cultural studies, a kind of historiographical United Nations in which was debated the slave systems of Virginia and Cuba, of Carolina and Barbados. Of the spate of cross-cultural monographs available, the life's work of the Brazilian Gilberto de Mello Freyre at that time best exemplified this scholarship. Freyre, born in the rural and isolated Brazilian northeast, was educated at Baylor University and then took a graduate degree from Columbia University before returning to his land to gain positions of power and influence in the government which emerged after the downfall of the dictator Getulio Vargas in 1945. While discharging his many duties of state, Freyre produced a multivolume history of Brazil and thus was in many ways a modern counterpart to George Bancroft in the U.S. republic of the previous century. However, unlike Bancroft and the great narrative tradition, Freyre was less interested in following the line of a developing story than he was in locating and exploring the general organizing laws of his society. Thinking thus like a sociologist, Freyre nevertheless wrote with the compelling verve and energy of the best narrative scholars, and his essays describing the Freudian basis for the super-masculine slave society attracted the attention of southern historians: especially when Freyre drew parallels between what he had studied of the U.S. South and what he had lived back home.

But it was Woodward's contention that the Brazilian, and especially anyone using his translated works, was likely to overdraw the analogy between Freyre's own Pernambucan subtropics and his adoptive Waco plains. With gentle sardonicism, Woodward developed some of his richest imagery in "Protestant Slavery in a Catholic

World," where he reestablished the distinctive characteristics of the antebellum South.

> The culture contrast suggests setting a flock of gray and white mockingbirds down in a tropical jungle filled with gaudy parakeets. To Puritan New England, life along the James, the Sewanee, or the Lower Mississippi may have appeared lushly exotic and outlandishly bizarre. But set side-by-side with life along the Amazon the colors of the antebellum society in the Old South fade to temperate-zone greys and russets and muted saffrons that went well enough with magnolia or Spanish moss, but were not quite the thing for promenades under palm and breadfruit. Beside the garish social scene in the tropics, the Old South was a subdued affair of demure ladies in crinoline and pantolettes, gentlemen in black stock and broadcloth, and sweaty Sunday mornings in Episcopal pews or plain white Methodist chapels. Gaiety there was and spontaneity too, along with some luxury and display, more than a dash of wicked exuberance, and a pervading undertone of more or less repressed sexuality. But it was all under the umbrella of Protestant, Anglo-Saxon restraint and inhibition.

Finally, "perhaps it would have been better, for that matter, never to have broken with Rome, never to have quarreled with monarchy, never to have established those proudly autonomous colonial assemblies, and never to have married such women as they did. But, then, that would have been somebody else's history and not our own."[40]

This question, what is our history? also concerned the passage of time, and Woodward was distressed by an increasing tendency to take the religiosity of the modern hot-gospeler and read that cultural experience back into the story of an antebellum people who simply did not live and think that way. In "The Southern Ethic in a Puritan World" he criticized not only this tendency but also one among historians of religion who blurred the distinctions between Protestantism North and Protestantism South. His Yale colleague Edmund Sears Morgan, once a prized pupil of Perry Miller and now himself the preeminent historian of the New England mind, had become Woodward's friend and coworker on the *National Experience* textbook project, but that did not spare Morgan a full share of ironic wrist slaps for oversimplifying things in this manner. It seemed that Morgan "appointed" James Madison an "honorary" Puritan, and that struck an exposed nerve with Woodward, who hated to see the southern Enlightenment given anything less than its full due as a unique and vital episode of intellectual history: here was Morgan taking a significant thinker and leader and making him into a mere follower of an ancient New England sect. Puritans who traveled south in the seventeenth or eighteenth century, like their descendants who traveled there in the nineteenth, were invariably struck by the cultural differences they encountered, and with good reason, for "the great majority of Southerners—including those concerned about their 'election,' shamelessly and notoriously stole time, and sometimes more than time, for luxury. . . . It is extremely unlikely that a sports event—horse race, fox hunt, cock fight, or gander pulling anywhere from the Tidewater to the Delta was typically preceded by a prayerful debate over whether it 'served a rational purpose' or was 'necessary for physical efficiency.' "[41]

In general these Old South interpretive essays not only delighted with their witty perspicacity but also raised the question what was the identity of the Old South? Here, as he did not do in the Reconstruction and New South essays of the collection, he gave guideposts for answers: agrarianism, patriarchal tradition, caste system, martial spirit, racial etiquette, and familial charisma. Research which filled in the shading of southern meaning within those outlines would be meaningful and valuable indeed; research which filled in the shading of outlines other than these was by and large superfluous. If only his companion essays about the postbellum South had followed the master's own prescription, *American Counterpoint* could be considered the full equal of his volumes of previous eras. Instead, it remained a failure pregnant with the seed of future success; but it seemed likely at the time that others would have to tend the crop for the man who had planted and then had virtually withdrawn from the labor.

This was the more exasperating because he retained the ability to see where academic scholarship and much broader social patterns were going; and he occasionally spoke with a clear, strong voice which again lent a sense of direction to his fellow historians and to other intellectuals. As president of the Organization of American Historians (OAH), 1968–69, and as president of the American Historical Association (AHA), 1969–70, Woodward took full advantage of the opportunities afforded by such an unprecedented level of national recognition to demonstrate his perceptivity; but again, these performances were of uneven quality, for in the OAH speech he boldly showed the way to still another era in scholarship on race relations, but in the AHA speech he was almost fey in his mordant predictions. Before the OAH, he delivered "Clio with Soul," the address subject to Potter's admonitions and also one fully the equal of his best scholarship, in which he scored all historians, not excluding himself, for a poor handling of black history: all too often, he lamented, blacks were either ignored or treated as passive recipients of white actions and attitudes. Correctly predicting the emergence of black historians who could in large part redress the balance, he also offered wise advice on how white historians could proceed to write better history; and he made it quite clear that this task of understanding blacks as an integral part of American history would not and could not be realized by blacks acting alone, but rather was the privilege and the duty of all serious scholars. Much as he had done with *The Strange Career of Jim Crow*, he was simultaneously sensing a trend in the making and speeding its development by seizing the forum at the propitious moment and using it effectively.[42]

Only a few months later, addressing the AHA, he described a gloomy outlook for all in the country who professed to be historians, partly because total college enrollments were about to decline, but largely because of fundamental changes in curriculum borne of a significant revolution in student attitudes toward their instruction and their instructors. Few at a school like Yale were then this keenly aware of the developing problem, and it was courageous as well as necessary for him to point out the impending crisis to the more comfortably established professionals in attendance. But unlike the OAH speech, with its guidelines for effective action, this one offered no prescriptions for redress, and given the security of his own richly endowed Sterling chair, the hint of cleverness in his tone was regrettable, since it implied lack of sympathy for those younger scholars who were already on the edge of the coming disaster. Of course, he did care about the plight of these new Ph.D.s, and they were best served by learning the bad news now, no matter what the style of the delivery; but the address and responses to it underscored once more the magnitude and complexity of the frustrations which were all around him.[43] For these and other reasons, T. S. Eliot's description of the end of life appeared entirely likely to apply to the sexagenarian Woodward of the 1970s, who was hardly threatening to leave the world with a bang.

III

Fittingly for one who had raised irony to new heights as an interpretive device, Woodward's career was reinvigorated—indeed, almost resurrected—after the reappearance on the scene of a genuine scoundrel. Lyndon Johnson's passion for learning scabrous secrets about his friends and foes, along with his pursuit of the Vietnamese folly, had inspired bands of students to chant derisively about him as if he were the singular tyrant of the era. But for all of his faults he did not merit the title of knave: he retained a redeeming capacity for accomplishing good; and he lacked the requisite insensitivity to go on and on in his error. In other words, his decision not to run for reelection in 1968 was two parts shrewd vote counting of a kind he had discarded for a season of military adventurism, but it was also three parts recognition that he ought to stop, acknowledgment that he had done all the good and all the bad that he could and that he should step aside. Vice-President Hubert Horatio Humphrey, once recognized for his courage in the civil rights movement—especially after the mythic dimensions of his speech at the 1948 Democratic convention—but now widely viewed as Johnson's captive, inherited the nomination: unable to disengage himself from the LBJ policies in Indochina and the Caribbean, he too became the target for often vicious attacks from the Left. Meanwhile, Martin Luther King, Jr., and Robert Fitzgerald Kennedy were assassinated in actions which further discouraged and disillusioned a young Left that was likely held together as much by force of personality as by commitment to ideas. While the Democratic party imploded in the heat of Chicago's summer, Richard Milhous Nixon bided his time patiently, assured of election in the fall if he could run against a fractured party.

Editorialists spoke often of a "new Nixon," and this appeared a possibility to the optimistic, what with all the impressive Nixon talk in 1968: talk about making the "better" Johnson social programs work, talk about retaining the commitment to civil rights, talk about reconsidering the Vietnamese commitment, talk about changing the military draft, talk generally about an American Disraeli who could accept and build on the achievements of the Great Society's Gladstone. But within the first months of his administration, Nixon demonstrated that he had not really changed. Casting aside the various Daniel Patrick Moynihan schemes to make welfare programs work, Nixon returned to what he did best, which was to appeal to the basest emotions in the working middle class whose members were feeling neglected by the liberal reform programs and oppressed by taxes and the likelihood of monetary inflation. Moreover, now he had the assistance of Vice-President Spiro Agnew and Attorney General John Mitchell, the two in particular who could successfully enunciate the values of "law and order" for that constituency. In foreign affairs, the creation of a professional mercenary army removed the personal threat to college students and thus relieved the consciences of most, greatly diminishing campus protests as Nixon expanded the Vietnam War into the backward and previously inoffensive land of Cambodia. There were, furthermore, moments of undeniable triumph, for without Nixon to call one a Communist for doing so, the president was free to visit China and to establish relations with that land, whose "loss" so many academics and career foreign servants had been unable to explain satisfactorily to the younger Senator Nixon in the early 1950s. In addition, Alexander Haig was whipping the troops of the North Atlantic Treaty Organization into shape, and Secretary of State Henry Kissinger was speaking the tough language of machtpolitik. Nixon, in short, was not so different after all, but perhaps Americans were; and many delighted in his displays of power in the courts of Europe and Asia, whisked about on two special jets, shielded from bothersome reporters by an odd double helix of plainclothes secret servicemen and a gaudily attired Swiss Guard.

There was in any case little organized opposition to Nixon, since in 1972 the Democratic party became the possession of South Dakota senator George McGovern, a veteran of the Left who had resisted the Vietnam War on the hustings in the many state primaries held in the country. "Politics as usual" the Democrats proudly discarded in favor of greater accessibility to the political leaders for spokesmen representing the public mood, or moods. Woodward supported McGovern with some reluctance, fearing that the Dakotan, while solid on social issues, might be a political naif. Moreover, McGovern's camp included members of the New Left, a collection of widely varying mentalities whose only common trait was a desire to revise Marxist and neo-Marxist ideas to fit the obviously different modern American environment; although Woodward, especially in his youth, was not at all unlike some of the New Left scholars in this regard, he in the early 1970s judged them to be uniformly shallow. There was, finally, the style of McGovern's young supporters, many of whom articulated a politics which the historian found ostentatious, not the stuff of genuine dissidence. But the opposition was Nixon, and so Woodward once again vowed "to vote against" one candidate rather than for another.[44]

Actually, what Woodward or anybody else did mattered quite little in the 1972 election, for it was always Nixon's. Yet in a domestic version of the "arrogance of power," there were persisting reports that Nixon was again orchestrating "dirty tricks," this time in the campaign to defeat McGovern. And shortly after Nixon had swept to a resounding victory over a maladroit Democratic campaign organization, the revelations began: despite the weak opposition, at least one Nixon reelection organization, incredibly enough styling itself CREEP, had attempted to spy on the McGovern headquarters. Woodwardian ironies and complexities were developed with a vengeance when it was revealed that these "second-rate burglars" who were caught peeping in on a third-rate campaign in a first-rate architectural complex were actually part of a much larger story. There were other schemes to pry into the lives of politicians—a so-called hit list of enemies included moderate Republican congressmen who had been meeting to pray with Nixon—and there were schemes to cover up the schemes as well as schemes to cover up the cover-up. The whole thing was quite Hydra-headed, and one did not have to like Nixon to wish that it would just go away, as one did not have to dislike him to wish that he would just go away. In all, during an era of gory body counts, the casualties of the Nixon administration were one president, one vice-president, two attorneys general, eight other cabinet members, and ten White House staffers.

But the toll of the punished easily could have been confined to the handful of Cuban prowlers who probably thought that they were in some way evening the score with Fidel Castro. Initially, Nixon had more than his share of defenders, and it took quite a concerted campaign to oust him. In some ways the thing could have been scripted by Woodward, since at the crucial point in the senatorial prosecution before the House of Representatives the action was dominated by Sen. Sam Erving, Jr., a shrewd "country lawyer" from the Old Democrat school of the Carolina Piedmont who was intensely wary of the smooth rhetoric of such Carolina business representatives from the New Republican school as Harry Dent, Fred Dent, or J. Fred Buzhardt. In fact, there was a distinct southern accent in the whole debate, not only in the often otiose point/ counterpoint between Ervin and self-styled "Sun Belt" Republicans, but also in the quieter, more restrained voices of Georgia's Sam Nunn, South Carolina's Jim Mann, Tennessee's Howard Baker. On the other hand, the mass of southerners remained overwhelmingly loyal to Nixon in the early phases of the investigation and hearings, and the refrain of William Frank Buckley, Jr., "He's only doing what other presidents have done," was echoed in volume down south.

Regardless of Woodward's contemporaneous pessimism about everything in general—a pessimism so profound at that time that he was spending much energy to convince people, especially himself, that he had never been hopeful about social reform—he could not resist plunging into the fray of Nixon's "eighth crisis." Even after the embarrassing failure of the Wierarta memorandum on the Caribbean policy, it felt good to consult again with Manning Dauer and with other friends such as his former student William McFeeley to prepare a report for Rep. Peter Rodino, Democrat of New Jersey, whose committee was investigating the actions of the Nixon White House. What Rodino's committee staff wanted was a historical treatment of the questions of executive misconduct in the United States: what kind of things had previous presidents been accused of doing and how did these earlier presidents respond to such charges? That is, was Nixon doing only what Lincoln and both Roosevelts had done? Organizing a team of fourteen historians, which included William Leuchtenburg, the superb analyst of presidential politics and policies between the world wars, and Jefferson's best biographer, Merrill D. Peterson, Woodward proved a tough taskmaster, for he realized that no one had before attempted such a comprehensive view of presidential misconduct, and that this type of study more than most thus risked the dangers of "abstraction and dispro-portion."[45]

Once the study was completed and submitted to Rodino, Wood-ward as editor summed up its findings for the general citizenry in a subsequently published volume, *Responses of the Presidents to Charges of Misconduct:*

> Heretofore, no president has been proved to be the chief coor-dinator of the crime and misdemeanor charged against his own administration as a deliberate course of conduct or plan. Here-tofore, no president has been held to be the chief personal beneficiary of misconduct in his administration or of measures taken to destroy or cover up evidence of it. Heretofore, the malfeasance and misdemeanor have had no confessed ideologi-cal purpose, no constitutionally subversive ends. Heretofore, no president has been accused of extensively subverting and secretly using established government agencies to defame or discredit political opponents and critics, to obstruct justice, to conceal misconduct and protect criminals, or to deprive cit-izens of their rights and liberties. Heretofore, no president has been accused of creating secret investigative units to engage in covert and unlawful activities against private citizens and their rights. For all the great variations in style and sensitivity in the conscience of the White House from 1789 to 1969, they do little to prepare us for the innovations of the ensuing period of five and a half years. A search of the long history of misconduct charged against the presidents down to 1969—the record that follows—will fail to disclose many of the abuses of that office, many combinations and concentrations of abuses, and many new uses and purposes of such abuses, that have subsequently become increasingly familiar to American citizens.[46]

The report, and the committee's astute use of it, so effectively countered what had earlier seemed the credible assumption that "everybody's done it" that soon no one was really defending Nixon anymore. His defensive strategy deteriorated to the evasiveness of strict legalism—can you absolutely *prove* that he did this when that witness says he did?—and his friendliest political operatives put all their faith in the ability of Alexander Haig to persuade Nixon to resign before he could be convicted formally. By August of 1974

Haig had persuaded him to stand down, with a new and nicer vice-president, Gerald Ford, sure to pardon him.

These were initially exhilarating days for intellectuals, since the defeat of so prominent an antiintellectual as Nixon seemed to reverse the tide of distrust of the experts which had rolled in during the final hours of the Johnson presidency, after the awkward efforts of the "best and the brightest" in support of the failing Indochinese campaign. It seemed in some ways a tragicomic fulfillment of Nixon's oldest nightmare, where the liberal press "gets him"; but reading the nightmare instead as an opportunity, perhaps now liberals could usher in a second era of cross-pollination of ideas between academe and Capitol Hill. Of course, it was conceded that there would be an obligatory period of waiting around while Gerald Ford's caretaker government tidied up the wreckage: but that very period of waiting around could well provide the moment for thinking men and women to enunciate again a direction for the country.

In fact, during that moment, thinking people and others enunciated much, but nothing could reverse the incredible momentum of the culture's intellectual and moral centrifuge. Defeat and doubt pervaded the atmosphere as the long Vietnam War ended desultorily, with the evening news burning into the memory the image of advanced-technology helicopters straining to lift off from the former buildings of state, desperate people clinging to the landing struts as even more desperate people clawed upward at the retreating machines. Inflation and unemployment continued to increase simultaneously, and economic laws as popularly understood by citizens of both left- and right-wing factions failed of application. Municipal New York's financial house of cards tumbled down as the increasing expenses of its swelling social programs combined with the declining revenues from its shrinking tax base to ruin its credit rating; while in the private sector, the automobile industry and its sprawling ancillary businesses faced a crisis first made apparent by the oil embargo but increasingly recognized since as a fundamental structural problem.

By the middle of the 1970s, Woodward was hardly alone in describing irony, although his use of the perspective was markedly different from that employed by most. In fact, every bored sophomore could explain how discrepancies between word and deed, how the distance between intent and consequences, "proved" that politics was utterly hopeless. This was a long, long remove from the ironies of Niebuhr, Voegelin, and Penn Warren, all of whom had emphasized the urgency of political action exactly when the situation was desperate and the available political leaders were less than inspiring. Woodward was further dismayed to see that some former activists now flagellated themselves—or their former allies—with the whip of guilt, thereby actually serving the causes of reactionaries while reinforcing the attitudes of the apathetic.[47] What passed for the day's irony tasted of wormwood, and Woodward was stirred finally to reintroduce the stuff of real irony by returning to a more effective scholarship in the years after 1974.

10

The Gift

Returning from the Achillean tent, Woodward entered the old fray with all the energy of his uniquely ironic enthusiasm. Although his most significant scholarship has been completed and he willingly became emeritus at Yale University in 1978, he has by no means retired from the field. In fact, in some ways he has been more active in the 1980s than he was in the early 1970s. During this decade, he has again staked out positions consistent with his character and his career, and while he may be wrong about certain issues, he has cast aside both ambiguity and reticence. These latest acts in his lengthy scholarly and public career have been tough-minded, dissident, and effective; and he is exiting the stage in the same way he entered it, asking hard questions of the shamans charged with tending the day's icons. What he has done and what he has said, the history he has helped to make, along with the history that he has written, constitute a gift for all of us. What are the nature and the value of that gift?

I

There were two significant controversies in which the elder Woodward took a prominent role, the Herbert Aptheker controversy of 1974–78 and the voting rights extension campaign of 1981–82. In the former his actions stunned many of the New Left—and the Old Left and many mainstream liberals—who had been drawn to his works because of his dissidence and because of his class analysis of politics. In the latter his actions were a fundamental rejection of the newly respectable Right and an even more fundamental rejection of a newly respectable defeatism in matters of race relations. On the Communist Aptheker, William Frank Buckley, Jr., could quote Woodward with approval to "thoughtful conservatives" poring over the *National Review* or reverently witnessing "Firing Line" on public television. Of course, the spiritual descendants of Ab's back in Chapel Hill or of *Bozart* back in Atlanta were appalled by what they regarded as nothing less than apostasy. On the other hand, Woodward's ringing reaffirmation of voting rights disturbed many of the southern Right who were newly restored to prominence and power even as it delighted many of the nation's Left who were otherwise effectively disfranchised in most contemporary political processes. Given these stark contrasts, one could easily suspect eccentricity or caprice, but neither was a characteristic trait. No, the two decisions were both consistent with his political ideals and experiences, that is, consistent at least with those he has expressed since 1932.[1]

In an essay for a special issue of *Daedulus* in 1974 Woodward enunciated some principles of politics which, taken together with his own reading of the Angelo Herndon episode, foretold almost perfectly how he would react both to Aptheker's candidacy for a teaching position at Yale and to the 1981–82 drive to extend the voting rights law. While these instances of controversy were certainly intertwined, they must be examined individually. As marked earlier, the civil rights movement until 1966 was a relatively compact and cohesive thing which provided a sharp focus on reform of particular abuses in the South; but since that year the movement has become increasingly diffuse, and the surviving leaders of the disintegrating coalition have competed with each other as well as with leaders of other causes, so that the sprawling and centrifugal nature of today's reform impulses has worked against the kind of effective focus once attained in Birmingham or in Selma. To large degree, the great reform movement which shaped such a large part of Woodward's identity has died; and there is no question that its disappearance has greatly affected both his politics and his scholarship. Nevertheless, in the case of Aptheker and in the case of voting rights extension, Woodward responded as one committed to a certain kind of liberal dissent and to a certain kind of liberal activism: above all else, he insisted on rational debate as opposed to absolutely free debate. Further, he insisted on historical equity as opposed to theoretical equality.[2]

In *Daedulus* Woodward had sharp words for his colleagues of the Left during the historian's "decade" from 1968 to 1974. This entire number of the journal was given over to reconsiderations of the academy's experiences during a time of intense politicization for the nation's campuses. All of the essayists were taking aim at some of the slowest-moving Kewpie targets ever exhibited at any carnival, and with at least some justification. The old abolitionist cry that problems are *immediate* had been twisted out of context and was now applied with a vengeance by curriculum tinkerers and fiddlers seeking relevance for college students who, as grade schoolers, had been the original subjects of the essays "Why Johnny Can't Read" and "Why Susie's Afraid of Math." Foreign language and classical literature lost, perhaps forever, their status as the very embodiment of the university education; and the history and philosophy and modern literature once required for graduation increasingly became "options" to select—or to reject—from a wide range of elective courses. The result for those disciplines of the humanities was a catastrophic decline in enrollment; and the inertia, the secondary force, of that decline was the very real "irrelevance" of the humanities to the thoughts and actions of students on most campuses. Meanwhile, laboratory science and mathematics, while sufficiently enrolled, became more and more things "done" almost exclusively by a certain kind of specialist until the procedures and the assumptions of the scientific disciplines slipped away from the consciousness of students of the liberal arts. What C. P. Snow had warned about the segregation of the scientist from the humanist appeared to be at hand; and Woodward began to fear that his own quest for the relevant and the usable past had contributed to the contemporary declaration that the whole of the past was unusable because irrelevant.[3]

As for campus political discourse, especially at the more interesting and innovative universities, much of it took a sharp turn down the left alleyway of Herbert Marcuse and Robert Paul Wolff, who largely redefined the nature of the debate. Marcuse's ambitious attempt to fuse the Marxian with the Freudian produced among other things a considerable contempt for "one dimensional man" and the "unfree" nature of liberal debate. For Marcuse, the supposedly untrammeled debate of Western liberalism was actually so hamstrung by the de facto prior censorship of tacit agreements about "proper" discourse and what not to talk about that the whole system was morally bankrupt; for Woodward, Marcuse's critique was deeply flawed by an overemphasis on Freudian analysis, and it also implied a threat to the kind of academic and political debate which informed the historian's career.[4]

Moreover, Wolff's discussion of John Stuart Mill, a discussion which was clearly derivative of Marcuse, was such a scathing attack on the hypocrisy of bourgeois tolerance that Woodward perceived an even more palpable threat to the rational procedures of discussion and debate. With so much fundamental questioning about what really mattered in life, Woodward insisted all the harder on the need for Mill's classic marketplace of ideas; but such processes obviously moved slowly and fitfully, so much so that Wolff doubted the possibility of a radical probing of values under Mill's system. Further, Wolff's unique perspective on the McCarthy hearings—he was fully as critical of the liberal response of Lillian Hellman as he was of the McCarthyites themselves—was for Woodward a nightmare of specious reasoning which could make possible more of the kinds of abuses he had witnessed in the 1950s.[5]

As Woodward read the developments, the New Left was tough without being tough-minded, it was less dissident against old gods than it was fanatically devoted to new gods, and it called back no echoes from the Atlanta days of the triumvirate. Or to put a finer point on it, as he understood things, there *were* echoes from that day, but not from Atlanta: the echoes were instead sounded from Berlin and Rome and Vienna and signaled the wholesale retreat from conviction at quickstep time. The ideals one encounters in college should change one's subsequent behavior, said Woodward; but he thought that this had not happened in the 1960s and 1970s, when instead the "serious betrayal of ideals" of liberal tolerance matched that of post-Weimar Germany. A more accurate description would be that the students of the 1960s and the 1970s certainly did change their subsequent behavior because of campus ideals, but the ideals and the behavior constituted a fundamental rejection of Woodward's own ideals; and he considered that the ideals of more traditional liberalism had not received a real hearing on the radicalized campuses.[6]

Then Woodward went even farther with his criticism of the New Left educators and scholars of that era: he believed, he wrote, that academic privileges and immunities had been eroded because American intellectuals had indulged caprice and cowardliness. A plurality of academics, exercising no meaningful standards of rational discourse for their own house, had themselves to blame for much of the subsequent damage done to the academy by the college and university administrators who were the most obvious heavy players in the act. This did not excuse the actions of the administrators in removing many academic privileges, but it did suggest that administrators got away with their misbehavior primarily because faculties had reneged on their duties of self-governance by presuming privilege without accepting the responsibility concomitant with such privilege. Too many scholars had shrugged their shoulders before the task of ensuring that tenure and promotion were awarded on the basis of academic merit; and too many had thrown up their hands and abandoned any notion of building meaningful curricula or of making individual courses substantial. By the time administrators used the financial exigencies of the next decade as excuses for removing faculty privileges, little really changed at all, for those who do not use their freedom responsibly have already lost it.[7]

Behind this essay was a panoramic nightmare which took personal memories of very real abuses and then combined them in somewhat distorted fashion with contemporary perceptions of a hectic era. As noted, the young Woodward had seen an Arkansas lynch mob, and he had seen an otherwise staid minister of the local Methodist church accepting donations at the worship service from the white-robed klansmen. Later in Berlin he had seen and heard the Fascist thugs who boasted of someday exterminating the "impure" non-Aryans. In the 1970s some self-styled radical group had blown up a research laboratory and faculty office building on the campus of the University of Wisconsin, in the process killing a scientist who was in fact active in opposition to the Vietnam War. And in his own New Haven, members of the Black Panthers had become quite violent after an initial period of very substantive service to the poor of the area; and the revelations of the kidnapping, torture with scalding water, and murder of black man Alex Rackley had dismayed Woodward as the story was unwound in the long trial of Panther leader Bobby G. Seale in 1971.[8]

In addition, the era's radicals were often rowdy, being filled with youthful energies which were alternatively creative and destructive. Particularly upsetting to Woodward was the response of his liberal friends to the radicalism: back in the 1930s his Jewish friends in Berlin had grievously underestimated the Nazis by regarding them as uninfluential; and now he worried that liberals were similarly underestimating the dangers posed by a new violence and a new disorder. For instance, his friend Kingman Brewster, whose presidency at Yale Woodward otherwise admired and supported, seemed to be unaware of the terrible things done by some of the New Haven Black Panthers. Instead, Brewster worried publicly that a revolutionary like Seale could never get a fair trial in America; and then, when a mistrial was declared because of a "hopelessly deadlocked jury" and Seale was acquitted by ruling of Judge Harold M. Mulvey, Brewster praised the jurist for the verdict despite the evidence that an extremely dangerous man was being released. Moreover, while the sporadically occurring excesses of American radicals in the period 1968–74 hardly equaled in kind or in degree the damage perpetuated by the Fascists, the disruptions did have the effect of slowing down the pursuit of "the subject"—or sometimes, the pursuit of any subject.[9]

Woodward's own works and words originally had inspired many of these very radicals, for he was classically antimilitaristic and pro–civil rights; and he was always one to deflate pride or pretension whenever either became puffed up among the members of the established elites. Thus students and professors with Marxian perspectives on things historical worked successfully with him: he trained and sent into the professional world the excellent Marxian historians Bruce Palmer (winner of the Sydnor Award), Steven Hahn (winner of the Nevins Award), Barbara Jeanne Fields, Otto Olsen, and James Green; and he brought to Yale as a visitor the exciting and innovative Marxian analyst Eugene D. Genovese. While Woodward himself might look like the man from Tennessee Life & Casualty Insurance, as the black musician-essayist Albert Murray expressed it, he reveled in Palmer's oversized porkpie hats, blue jeans, and fatigue jackets, and he encouraged his students to press behind the official explanations for black poverty or for the Indochinese war. As he had said of his own work in another context, "In all those books there is a generous amount of class analysis" for any such problems, and so he continued to press for answers to questions pointedly aimed at class structure and the conflicts produced by that structure. Moreover, as he told his student Green, he was flattered that many of the New Left were influenced by him; and he was pleased that this kind of class analysis of conflict had developed as an antidote to the doldrums created by the preexisting cold-war debate among liberals, conservatives, and the older Marxists. [10]

However, as the protest era wore on, the New Left pulled up stakes and roamed places Woodward had never contemplated going. Nor did he now. It is impossible to overstate his passion for the intellectual marketplace of ideas as the modus operandi to effect reform; for him, this was no mere theory: it was part of his very life, and with his circle of personal friends so drastically diminished, it was an even larger part of that life. Furthermore, though publications such as the *New Republic,* the *Reporter,* the *New York Review of Books, Harper's,* and the *New York Times* were valuable forums, none was the equal of the college classroom as the arena for informing debate. This kind of debate was often threatened by the political authorities and by the university administrators beholden in many cases to those authorities; but now the debate was cut off by students and by professors who closed down the seminars, lectures, and library research sessions *from the inside.* At Henderson-Brown College in the 1920s, at the Georgia Institute of Technology in the 1930s, at Scripps College in the 1940s, and at the Johns Hopkins University in the 1950s, the exchange of fact and opinion had been threatened for professors and students by administrators and politicians; but now, in a sad reversal, professors and students shut down their own operations. It infuriated Woodward, and when he learned of armed students occupying offices and classrooms at Cornell University, he exploded at his friend Dauer, "I hope the faculty throws them out on their ears!" [11]

These protest demonstrations and actions were arrayed loosely around both antiwar and black-pride movements, but students and academics on campuses were deeply involved in many other reformist causes. In the shifting sands of avant-garde politics it was obviously difficult to find one's footing on all the different issues; and to some degree Woodward's own prescription of ironic perception failed of application as he responded to these forces. Whether described as richly variegated panoply or as Babel's cacophony, expressions of radicalism during the Nixon administrations were surely less unified, less dangerous, and more reasonable than Woodward considered them to be. Worthy as were the impulses, his own youthful iconoclasm in Arkadelphia and in Atlanta was not uniformly characterized by keen focus and judicious perspective: after all, he and Amy Jean Green and Dick Huie and Glenn Rainey themselves had disrupted life on campus. Despite this caveat, the fact remains that academic processes were in deep crisis, and Woodward was especially angered to see self-appointed spokesmen for the radical chic, in their myriads of contradictory forms, attempting to exercise power over curriculum, over tenure and promotion, even over entire departments in some schools. With so much of substance under profound question, Woodward grasped for form and procedure as a kind of salvation. This was hardly inspiring, and he expressed advocacy of the strategy without much of his characteristic skepticism or humor; but a great deal of what he prescribed was very sound policy, and it was significant that he spoke when he spoke, for it showed that the old energies of the controversialist were stirring and that he was again engaged with the larger issues.

In 1974 Kingman Brewster offered him the chance to report on the recent history of academic freedom at Yale. Anxious to do so, he paused long enough to warn his friend that the report would likely be critical of the administration; but when Brewster reiterated his desire for a frank assessment, Woodward pounced on the subject with a vigor and a force which belied the earlier hints of an end-of-life hibernation. He was unequivocal in his demand for absolute freedom of speech on the campus; and he documented three occasions when students and their campus guests had prevented individuals from speaking: they had shouted down Alabama segregationist George Corley Wallace; then they had so disrupted the address of the racist geneticist William B. Shockley that he left the podium; and a demonstration prior to an address by a Nixon cabinet officer caused it to be canceled. In each instance, Woodward ruled that freedom of speech had been denied; and the ultimate responsibility for each infraction he laid at Brewster's feet, though he also had sharp words for the students and the professors involved. Such an "old-fashioned" insistence that the absolute guarantee of free speech be extended to the extreme Right "was unpopular with the Left on the campus," he recalled; "I heard from them—about [Herbert] Marcuse."[12]

Questioned elsewhere about issues such as recruiting blacks and other minorities for graduate posts and for faculty chairs, Woodward urged Yale to use its seemingly bottomless coffers to compete for the best available minority talent, but he qualified this version of affirmative action significantly: "It [must be] quite clear that I had one standard, no special treatment, some blacks didn't measure up; but they knew the rules." Black students Thomas Holt, John Blassingame, and Barbara Jeanne Fields, just like his white students, earned his warm support only after a rather harrowing rite of passage in his infamous graduate examination sessions. William McFeely saw this spectacle from both sides of the examination board, having endured a stiff interrogation from Woodward to earn his doctorate and then later having served as a professorial questioner on Holt's examination, where McFeely witnessed Woodward going "after him, *after* him—it was awful!" But, McFeely realized, "Holt was ready" with the barrage of statistics and bibliographic references which his mentor wanted to hear. The process was hardly pleasant, but Woodward deemed it justified to prepare scholars, regardless of race, for the rigors of the profession. He detested the very sound of the rumors he heard that other colleges were developing more lenient standards for their own black students, and he permitted no such rumors to develop in the Hall of Graduate Studies on York Street.[13]

By and large, he thought, the Yale practices went against the day's grain in that racial integration there was proceeding the way Woodward had always wanted it to, by merit, slow as that was; and classes were ordinarily uninterrupted by protest strikes. There was, however, one exception, and that was oddly enough a by-product of the Oxbridge system of dormitory colleges, a system intended to guarantee both quality and diversity by letting resident students of certain colleges on campus invite scholars from outside the Yale community to lecture as guests for a term. Many were delighted with the concept, for it blended the traditional college resident scholar with the innovative college guest lecturer; presumably the former produced a higher level of accomplished scholarship, while the latter introduced divergent perspectives concerning the use of knowledge, and the two were said to be fully incorporated in the resident-guest lectureship at Yale. In actual practice, the seminars varied widely in quality, and as completion of one earned only a small number of credit hours—often not counted toward the major course of study—many students, by 1974 more serious and "career-oriented," eschewed them altogether, while many more came to regard them as relatively insignificant, and utterly harmless, diversions. But Woodward regarded the seminars as being quite significant—and *bad:* students had begun to bring in unscholarly celebrities, the quality of guest-resident instruction was slipping as a result, and faculty departments were not exercising real oversight of the process. [14]

By the time Howard Cosell, of television's Monday Night Football fame, had fretted and strutted across the academy's stage, Woodward had had more than enough of the experiment. He moved from not liking it to disdaining it and vowed to watch closely whatever guest the historians were asked to sponsor. "Of course," he ruefully recalled, "Cosell was not [invited] by an historian." But in 1975 the department was asked by the students of Davenport College to sponsor a guest, Herbert Aptheker, and this was a name and a past to conjure with. Moreover, it became Woodward's to conjure with after Henry Turner, the head of the department, appointed him, along with John Morton Blum and John W. Blassingame, to the committee to review the nomination. Blum, a well-respected authority on Theodore Roosevelt, Woodrow Wilson, and other aspects of modern political history, was increasingly the organizing force for the highly successful *National Experience* textbook, which he wrote in collaboration with Woodward and four others; and Blassingame, whose father had worked as a custodian back at the Oxford Junior College where Woodward's own father served as dean, was rapidly becoming a leading historian of slavery. Nevertheless, Woodward's was the big name on the committee and the one which would inevitably be associated with its report. [15]

Woodward treated this question almost as if Aptheker were applying for a chair in the history department, despite the fact that this Davenport seminar instructorship was by invitation, not application, and despite the fact that practically nobody else regarded the appointment as a significant one for whoever filled it. In fact, Woodward had recently quarreled with Aptheker over the issue of a project by the University of Massachusetts Press to produce an edited collection of the papers of the seminal poet-historian-philosopher-activist W. E. B. Du Bois, who was an intimate friend of Aptheker's and who had appointed the Brooklyn-born Communist to be executor of his papers and other literary effects. Woodward was adamant that this unique figure Du Bois deserved a full scholarly treatment in such a project, though it was a massive undertaking in view of the polymath's lengthy life and vigorous activities in a wide array of causes, and thus Woodward and his former student Louis R. Harlan (biographer of Du Bois's nemesis Booker Taliafero Washington) in 1973 had both joined the project advisory board, which already included the eminent scholars Henry Steele Commager, Kenneth B. Clarke, and John Hope Franklin. [16]

By February of 1974, however, Woodward resigned from the board after the publication of the first volume of a planned ten: this first volume was a distillation of Du Bois's correspondence through the year 1937, thus encompassing the first sixty-nine years of his life. Woodward wanted *two* fully annotated volumes for the correspondence of this period, instead of one, and he was disappointed by Aptheker's search for Du Bois's letters—he named six prominent men whose papers had not been consulted although "known to contain Du Bois' letters." Withal, Woodward criticized Aptheker for giving "no clear idea of the principle of selection" of items and for possessing no clear rationale for "the grounds of omission of some correspondence and the enclosure of other correspondence." Woodward's resignation, followed shortly by Harlan's, dealt a blow to the project, which had twice failed to win support from the National Endowment for the Humanities even with its distinguished board of advisers and which now sought funding without the endorsement of these two prominent and previously sympathetic historians and biographers. Subsequently very short on monetary resources in a time of rapidly escalating printing costs, Aptheker's project was necessarily defined anew, with a more limited compass reflecting the sad realities of more limited financial means. Aptheker immediately suspected a degree of ideological prejudging, if not blatant anticommunism, in Woodward's evaluation; and while this seems a strained interpretation, the editor-in-charge, Malcolm Call, and the press director, Leone Stein, were right to feel frustration with the timing of the resignations as well as with the subsequent lukewarm responses to the eventually published five volumes, which, despite their limitations, should have provided an occasion of more note for a profession whose members had been instructed so much by the black radical's penetrating idealism. [17]

The stage was thus set, and not entirely by the muses, for a large-scale confrontation over a kind of appointment which would usually draw a much smaller degree of attention. As Woodward, Blum, and Blassingame studied the Aptheker dossier, thinking about it as a basis for an instructorship endorsed by the Yale History Department, they understandably found little of genuine merit: a significant and provocative 1938 Columbia University dissertation on slave revolts; the dissertation transformed into a scholarly volume which Blassingame had cited in his own work; the completed volume of Du Bois's correspondence to 1937; a massive in-production annotated bibliography of Du Bois's writings; and quite a bit of obviously propagandistic writing. While Aptheker had been teaching history part time for decades on an irregular basis with the city university system of New York, he was in no sense a practicing historian, and the affairs of the American Communist party kept him much too busy for scholarship. Blassingame, despite his previous selective usage of *American Negro Slave Revolts,* considered the overall interpretation to be flawed; and now involved in an ambitious editing project of his own, he concurred with Woodward in the judgment that the first volume of the Du Bois papers was "a partisan job." Further, Blassingame and Blum agreed with Woodward when he stated that the answer was "on the shelves," by which he meant that Aptheker's published works were not equal to the academic standards of the Yale historians. Thus they recommended against sponsoring the seminar, and the majority of the history department agreed with the trio, as Turner informed the students at Davenport residence hall. [18]

Having decided thus, however, Woodward's little group still faced the fact of the political weather: storm clouds were already massed on the left horizon. Even as radicalism began to lose respectability at the polling place, it gained esteem in many alcoves in the academy. Aristotle could bemoan the futility of man's mastering an impeccable dialectic before attempting to rule, and Aeschylus could concede that art is weaker than necessity; but many radical historians of the early 1970s would have none of this Greek evasiveness, seeking instead after ideological purity and correct historicity. By the lights of the ideologue, of course, Aptheker's inaccuracies and oversimplifications were but parts of larger truth, and to deny him his forum was to defy the very progress of history. On the other hand, many historians who had rejected the teleological dimensions of Marxism were still grateful for the new approaches to historical problems which this perspective provided; and these people worried about the pratfalls of excluding an important Marxist from a campus such as Yale's. Besides these aspects of ideological and methodological consideration, there were simply many, many historians who could not agree that the issue deserved such a high level of attention from Woodward, since this was, after all, a visiting instructorship involving perhaps twenty students in a one-semester course and not a "ladder" or "track" appointment leading to a serious consideration for tenure at an Ivy League school. Also, Yale students, who had grown accustomed to the exercise of essentially unchecked power in these resident-seminar appointments, would obviously be embarrassed and angered by the department's rejection of their request; and students across the country, many of whom had grown accustomed to the exercise of much broader powers in the process of hiring and deciding tenure, would likely perceive this denial of the Yale student will as a point at issue in continuing debates about prerogative and privilege. All of these things meant that Woodward by his actions was bound to involve the entire history department in a great deal of controversy. Woodward thought he understood most of this ahead of time, and as he remembered it, "We considered the reaction and we said, 'okay, we're big boys now,' so we just clammed up" after issuing the negative report. [19]

Clamming up, however, was hardly a typical response to this issue. Essayists and columnists of the Left were usually opposed, while the support of conservative and reactionary scribes was not really appreciated, since many of them did in fact oppose Aptheker's appointment on anti-Communist grounds. The leading Marxist historians in the land, Eric Foner and Eugene Genovese, provided no support for Aptheker, Genovese indeed being rather loud and abrasive, since he and Aptheker had had their disagreements before this episode. On the other hand, Woodward "had to face my own faculty," many of whom "were outraged," as were many of his former students. His correspondence was "drenched with" acrimony, and "the freedom-of-speech report I had just gotten up for Yale was held up as inconsistent with [the] Aptheker [decision]." For all that, "I much prefer to be called reactionary and inconsistent than to defend a weak action."[20]

Defining actions as weak or strong is a judgment call at best, and the Yale political scientists, chaired by Joseph LaPalombara, defined the Aptheker appointment as a strong, not a weak, action. In addition, some twenty-two hundred students signed a petition on behalf of Aptheker's candidacy. Thus, in 1976, the political scientists invited Aptheker to serve as resident lecturer sponsored by their department. Again, Woodward and Blassingame issued a negative report, this time at a meeting of the entire faculty, and again Aptheker was denied, but in a close vote in which many supporters of Aptheker were absent because they considered the matter of his appointment to be a foregone, and favorable, decision. Again, there was great anger expressed by students as well as by sympathetic members of the faculty; Aptheker was pointedly invited in February of 1976 to give a public lecture on campus, and attendance at the large lecture hall was pointedly at full capacity. In the spring the department of political science again nominated Aptheker for the residence instructorship, with the important clarification that Aptheker would teach the seminar not as a historian nor as a political scientist but rather on the basis of his warm friendship and long years of cooperation with Du Bois and his directorship of the correspondence and papers. Because of advance notice and because of the memories of the small faculty turnout at the earlier voting, attendance was high, with ninety-four professors in session for three hours while a crowd of students demonstrated conspicuously outside the meeting room. A majority, fifty-three, voted for the appointment, but with thirty-nine negative notes and two abstentions, the issue by rules of normal procedure was referred to the executive committee of the Faculty of Arts and Sciences, because less than two-thirds had approved. This board ruled in favor of the appointment, and Aptheker was invited to hold the seminar in the fall of 1976, which invitation he accepted. The compromise resolution of the conflict was compromising for Woodward's academic standards and sense of responsibility, and it was certainly compromising for those who felt that Aptheker had been unnecessarily embarrassed by the public discussion of his academic credentials and general fitness for the job. Still, within Woodward's own department, and for his fellow historians, he had certainly made his point.[21]

Subsequently, in defense of their actions, Turner and Woodward introduced a new accusation against Aptheker, that he had been guilty of plagiarism of the bibliography concerning Du Bois. This charge, uttered by Turner in a letter to the *Yale Alumni Magazine* in 1978 and cited subsequently with approval by Woodward, was a serious distortion of a legal matter in which the Yale historians declined the opportunity to consult the official records of the case. Back in 1963, while Aptheker and the Kraus-Thomson reprint publishers were developing a complete and annotated bibliography of Du Bois's writings, a young California scholar named Paul G. Partington tried to help by sending his own bibliography and some clippings from articles about Du Bois. The Brooklynite considered the bibliography to be flawed by typographical and factual errors, and he judged the clippings to be a fan's memorabilia; therefore Aptheker thanked Partington for his interest but set all of his material to one side and seldom consulted it, "because I didn't want to confuse myself" with the inaccuracies. Partington expressed some annoyance at being excluded from the project, but otherwise was quiet until 1971. In that year an eager but uninformed young agent of Kraus-Thomson met Partington, saw the bibliography manuscript, and signed him to a provisional contract for the bibliography volume. Herbert W. Gstalder, newly elevated to directorship of the press, was furious with the agent because he knew that Aptheker had the rights as legal executor to the Du Bois papers, and he immediately proposed an alternative agreement, with Partington becoming an assistant to Aptheker in the project. Partington initially accepted this arrangement but was unable to work effectively with Aptheker and thus agreed with Gstalder to have the contract canceled, with the provision that he retain his original advance, share in a portion of the royalties, and receive credit in the book's "acknowledgments" section for his work.[22]

Then in 1976 Partington filed suit against the Kraus-Thomson Organization for breach of contract, and Gstalder, against his own initial reaction that he should fight out the issue for the record in a courtroom, decided to settle out of court by paying a "nuisance fee" of a thousand dollars to Partington and his lawyer on condition that Partington withdraw any claims on the canceled 1971 contract and forfeit any future claims against Kraus-Thomson. "I regret to this day that we settled the suit," wrote Gstalder. "I feared at the time that a settlement would be misconstrued as a de facto admission of guilt." He added, "Ludicrous as the allegations by Mr. Partington were, the suit which he brought against Dr. Aptheker and our publishing firm never mentioned plagiarism." Yet Turner wrote to the *Alumni Magazine:* "The finding of this report by six distinguished historians [representing the joint committee of the AHA and the OAH], along with the outcome of the recent plagiarism suit against Aptheker, will presumably give pause for thought even to those who at the time insinuated that the whole affair amounted only to a denial, on political grounds, by Yale's historians of a 'minor appointment' to 'a good, solid Communist intellectual.' " And Woodward would say, "Eventually the magazine published a letter from Henry Turner which related that Aptheker settled out of court in a suit for plagiarism, that Aptheker paid the plaintiff." In a letter which was kept confidential until 1986, Gstalder wrote to Turner informing him of the full facts of the case, enclosing copies of the documents of the settlement; but Turner never responded.[23]

For his part Aptheker was not particularly embarrassed, as so many worried that he would be; instead he was angry, especially since he tended to see a continuing "social democratic" (that is, left-wing but profoundly anti-Communist) ideological line in Woodward's actions: first, withdrawing from the board of advisors for the collection project; later, twice resisting the political science appointment; and finally repeating Turner's remark about plagiarism. "On my attitude towards Vann Woodward," he said, "this whole affair shocked me. I knew we had our differences, of course, but our relationship had always been at least 'correct' and sometimes friendly. That he or anyone else would challenge my competence to teach a course on Du Bois seemed (and still seems) incredible." Although the two men have retained mutual friends and although the two men speak to each other when they meet at conferences— neither is exactly the type of person who would duck around the corner to avoid an unpleasant encounter—Aptheker has said firmly, "It is not possible for me to forgive Woodward's actions in connection with the Yale appointment." And it seems that many others will never forgive Woodward for these actions.[24]

Considerably less pain for everybody would have ensued if Woodward had simply let Aptheker hold this seminar for a brief season, but he regarded that choice as only one more flight from the responsibility which comes with the privilege of academic governance. "His classes went to pieces, he was reading bibliography to students; as a teacher [Aptheker] was an utter failure," said Woodward, although student evaluations of the course were overwhelmingly enthusiastic, with the one source of complaint coming from the student "planted" by the *Yale Daily News*. Otherwise, Woodward continued to insist on the statement of the original report from his subcommittee: "This was a question of the quality of scholarship: we had certain standards and he didn't meet them. I couldn't have lived with" one more evasion of academic duty. And so, in action which some of his closest friends regarded as disproportionately severe, Woodward helped to lower the boom on this feisty character who in some way had come to stand for much more than he actually was. However one judges Woodward's actions—and the evaluation offered here is that he was severe but within his rights as a representative of the history department, arrogantly but not improperly out of his field in the deliberations of the political science department, and plain wrong to repeat the charge of plagiarism—the effect was hardly what he planned. The liberal historian Arthur Meier Schlesinger, Jr., remarked to Blum that Woodward's behavior had given Aptheker "tenure forever in the pantheon of the Left" by virtually martyring Du Bois's comrade. As Blum commented, "Vann's a controversialist and thrives on such disputes"; but one still suspects that Woodward underestimated both the extent of the response to his actions and the extent of unspoken and perhaps even unacknowledged pleasure which he took in settling an old score with the American Communist party for its behavior in the Angelo Herndon case in 1932.[25]

A result more important, certainly one motivated by fewer and simpler—and better—beliefs, but one far more difficult of achievement was the Voting Rights Extension Act of 1982. On this issue, of course, Woodward was one among a number of academics attempting to work an influence on politicians; but he stood out above the crowd, for after all, Martin Luther King, Jr., had singled his work out on the march to Montgomery. Moreover, the ranks of civil rights workers were thinned by death, by disaffection, and by defeat at the polls. Remembrance of the 1965 Voting Rights Act called up the names King, Lyndon Johnson, Everett Dirksen, Hubert Humphrey, Robert Kennedy, all dead by 1981; but there were also Arthur Schlesinger, Jr., Theodore White, Richard Strout, Gilbert Harrison, Benjamin Bradlee, that is, a host of intellectuals still very much alive but politically beyond the pale in the first two years of Ronald Reagan's White House, when *liberal* was a bad word and *reformism* anathema.

The changes in the script and in the players were both enormous: where once Edward Kennedy protected black voting rights through the Senate Judiciary Committee and Allen Ellender simultaneously protected farmers and the poor consumers of both races with generous food stamp disbursal from the Senate Agricultural Committee, now the original Dixiecrat filibusterer J. Strom Thurmond presided over the Judiciary Committee and the dominant force of the self-proclaimed Moral Majority, Jesse Helms, sat astride the Senate Agricultural Committee. And where once the chief executive might talk edgily with Anthony Lewis or Thomas Wicker of the *New York Times* about the black plight and the deferred commitment to racial justice, the new president dined in elegance with George Will and gloried in the purported arrival of the American Dream. John Kenneth Galbraith and Robert Lekachman discussing jobs and education were out, George Gilder and Milton Friedman discussing the recovery of marketplace realism were in. Thus it was hardly the time for legislation in which the muscle of the federal government was set over against the new money of the South and West or against the older conservatism of the religious fundamentalist, for these were the drive wheels of the Reagan campaign: Reagan the president could hardly be expected to turn against the truly faithful among the supporters of Reagan the candidate.

Moreover, there were special problems in explaining the need for such legislation; wrenched out of its historical context, voting rights protection seemed at best superfluous and at worst unfair to southern states. Many who were by no means racists often asked why the voting systems of southern states were constantly scrutinized when the rest of the country was left alone; and in the same vein, these people added that southern states had successfully enfranchised black citizens since 1965. For this mentality, it followed, then, that the problems were solved and that federal legislation was no longer useful. The error in this approach was caused by the delusion of the ahistorical approach, the kind of approach against which George Washington Cable had protested nearly a century before.[26]

Equity, the legal concept of fairness, was the judicious term the Louisianan finally seized on to explain why the freedman needed more than abstract, ahistorical equality in the postbellum South. Given the history of slavery, the Negro, newly emergent as citizen, could hope for fair treatment only if the national state intervened on his behalf to protect his constitutional rights against an openly hostile home rule by ex-Confederate whites. Of course, Cable's plea was denied; he was all but run out of town on a rail; and subsequently, the southern freedman came to suffer more severely than even the author of *Old Creole Days* had feared. This incident and this personality had been invoked by Woodward in earlier civil rights discussions, and they continued to serve him well in this current phase of the long struggle to enforce the Fourteenth and Fifteenth Amendments successfully enough to make the Thirteenth meaningful. In the working of history, and because many people had worked hard to make that history, Cable's call was at last answered: equity finally was served in the 1965 voting rights legislation.[27]

By 1980, however, the history of racism was declared completed by the triumphant Reaganites; perhaps it would some day merit antiquarian study, as it was an event of the distant past. No one now living in the South had ever abused black rights, it was said by people of the type remembered by the novelist Marcel Proust when he wrote of Frenchmen in the postwar Third Republic incapable of remembering antisemitism among the regnant elders:

> And this ignorance was not merely ignorance of society, but of politics, of everything. For memory was of shorter duration in individuals than life, and besides, the very young, who had never possessed the recollections which had vanished from the minds of the elders, now formed part of society (and with perfect legitimacy, even in the genealogical sense of the word), and the origins of the people whom they saw there being forgotten or unknown, they accepted then at the particular point of their elevation or their fall at which they found them. . . . [Thus those without memory presumed] that Clemenceau . . . had always been [reactionary]. And as certain facts have a greater power of survival than others, the detested

memory of the Dreyfus case persisting vaguely in these young people thanks to what they had heard their fathers say, if one told them Clemenceau had been a Dreyfusard, they replied: "Impossible, you are making a confusion, he is absolutely on the other side of the fence." Ministers with tarnished reputation and women who had started life as prostitutes were now held to be paragons of virtue.[28]

This country also had its paragons of virtue, made chaste by electoral success, and so, if no French leader in 1920 was remembered as a persecutor of the Jewish officer Dreyfus in 1894, no American leader in 1980 was remembered as a persecutor of the black voter in 1964. It was, as Proust also described it, the curious effect worked by mental horizons with differing vanishing points: if Jesse Helms and John East of North Carolina or Newt Gingrich of Georgia or Trent Lott of Mississippi insisted that the black voter was perfectly safe in the exercise of his or her franchise at the local polling place back home, who was to deny them? History, of course, could deny them, but only if its practitioners forced their countrymen to "regain time," to quote Proust for a final time.[29]

The best way to recover that elusive entity was *to be southern,* in Woodward's ironic sense of that identity. Being southern, his way, taking on the burden of knowledge, one understood exactly why the 1965 act specified states of the former Confederacy as discriminators against black voters and therefore forbade those states to change their election laws without advance approval by the federal government. Nearly fifty years earlier, Woodward had been studying and discussing the machinations of the state of Georgia which removed the black vote. A crucial point was that years of "clean" voting procedures were no guarantee of subsequent fair practice: after all, blacks had voted, had held office, had been very active politically from 1865 to 1894 (and later in some areas), but were then gerrymandered, grandfather-claused, poll-taxed, literacy-tested, night-ridden, and otherwise counted out. This pattern held especially in those areas with huge, and active, black electorates. The uses of ironic memory vaccinated one against the otherwise powerful germ of a notion that good behavior by local officials since 1965 in some way guaranteed black rights subsequently.[30]

In fact, the thinness of the guarantee was partially betrayed by

Jesse Helms, who spoke volumes with his short rhetorical question: what *crime* have these places committed? Only, he emphasized shrilly in answer to himself, *only* literacy tests. Or, in other words, not all that much of a much had ever happened anyway. It was this kind of argument by denial of the past that portended the greatest threat to a rule of reason: the aged Proust heard it in fashionable salons, the aged Woodward read it in the papers. Nevertheless, things seemed the same, for the Reagan preference for high living matched that of Proust's fictitious Guermantes. Faced with the question of a voting rights extension, Reagan ordered a six months' study of the issue by his attorney general, William French Smith; but career staffers in the Civil Rights Division of the Justice Department were distrustful of Smith and of William Bradford Reynolds, head of the division. Many feared that Reagan intended to treat the issue by ignoring it, relying on his enormous personal popularity to overwhelm the scattered and disparate voices of dissent.[31]

In fact, however, dissent from such a policy was not really disparate, although those who favored extension were indeed scattered; what was needed was an effective call to face the issue in unison. Congress was a useful forum for such a call, especially since congressmen enjoyed the privilege of investigative travel throughout the country to gather information on such questions and, in the process, to hear very clearly those voices calling for justice. Before now, Woodward had noted often that congressmen, especially Democratic congressmen, needed black voters more than Reagan needed the votes of the Helms forces. As Woodward had suggested, not morality but *practicality* impelled the Democratic congressmen with black constituencies to look after the rights of southern black voters, all of whom seemed to be related to northern populations. Where before southern congressmen had answered to black constituencies, now congressmen from urban areas throughout the nation were held accountable by such groups, and it was thus not surprising that New Jersey's Peter Wallace Rodino immediately set his House Judiciary Committee to work on an extension bill. Nor was it surprising that the subcommittee on civil and constitutional rights established to report to Rodino was headed by Don Edwards, an old-style liberal, and included among its most active members Harold Washington, a black man with like constituency from his native Chicago South Side and a man who would later be elected mayor of that city. Woodward and J. Morgan Kousser, a Tennessean once a student of his and now a professor at the California Institute of Technology, were called in to testify concerning the post-Reconstruction story on voting and black rights and whether that story taught any lessons for the present. Woodward performed effectively, even gleefully: his review of the record quickly gave the lie to any claim that southern states were being "picked on unfairly." He felt dissident again, and as always, political activism made more sense to him within the context of racial problems than within other contexts, especially given the kaleidoscope of causes after 1965.[32]

Cautioning against presentism and conceding the oversimplification of his own term *Second Reconstruction,* Woodward could still say to his hosts, "Exploring the past, I was continually encountering the present—or something like it—and living in the present, I was constantly running head-on into the past." The particular specter that moved across time this way was racism, a racism too powerful for any local southern leader to overcome: it was a force so strong that only the "power and authority of the federal government" could check it. In the two decades after 1877, "once that authority, or the will to enforce it, was withdrawn, a vacuum of permissiveness expanded that the prestige and influence of no leader could fill." The result, as Woodward had said often in his Populist studies, was charged up at the "cost of popular government and democratic principles" for both races: "almost total disfranchisement of blacks, sharp reduction of white voters, reduction of the overall voter turnout by an average of 37 percent (66 percent in Louisiana), the elimination of opposition parties, and the establishment of one-party rule that lasted half a century."[33]

Concerning the 1980s, Woodward said,

> I do not expect so drastic a counter-revolution to end the Second Reconstruction or anything so extreme to result from your decision about the Voting Rights Act of 1965. I do think it reasonable, however, to warn that a weakening of that act . . . will open the door to a rush of measures to abridge, and dilute, if not emasculate the power of the black vote in southern states. Previous testimony before your committee has shown how persistent and effective such efforts have been even with the . . . law in effect. Remove that law and the permissiveness

will likely become irresistible—in spite of promises to the contrary. The coming reallocation of congressional seats in the South as a consequence of the 1980 census will open many temptations for manipulation of laws affecting voting. I hope that retreat from the Second Reconstruction will not make it necessary for some future generation to face a Third.[34]

These poignant words were followed by sharp barbs from Kousser, exactly as Woodward had warned in his prepared statement: where Woodward had some sympathy for the "gentry" who had promised to protect black rights and portrayed them as initially well-meaning men broken by overwhelming pressures brought by a combination of racial attitudes, political exigencies, and economic revolution, Kousser "really came down hard[,] . . . the pretenses of the [Gov. Charles Brantley] Aycock period" of southern Progressivism in the Carolinas and elsewhere. When the two presentations were completed, Harold Washington was moved to ask Woodward if the recent assurances of southern politicians were "designed to lull blacks asleep," as had been the case a hundred years earlier. Woodward replied evenly, "I'm afraid so. . . . [T]he permissiveness[,] . . . the reliance on States, without Federal supervision, would be a temptation that very few, over the long run, would be able to resist."[35]

After other exchanges, Ivy L. Davis, assistant counsel for the House subcommittee, remarked that her investigations, which drew parallels between the end of the first Reconstruction and the present day, "have been poo-pooed." Serving a pitch at very slow speed, Davis wondered if Woodward would comment on assertions that events of the earlier century had no bearing on this one. He could hardly miss such a chance: "It is . . . clear that revolutions and advances in popular rights and democratic rights can be reversed; that history can move backwards; that enormous gains can be lost and jeopardized, eroded, or diluted, and abridged in spite of the enormous costs. . . . The first reconstruction cost us our greatest bloodshed and tragedy. It would seem that if anything has been paid for at a higher price, it was these advances. And yet, they were eroded and lost, and only a century later they were restored. My history teaches me that if it can happen once, it can happen again."[36]

The majority of men on this congressional committee were likely predisposed to extend the law on voting rights no matter what expert witnesses told them. The significance of Woodward's testimony, however, was that he provided ammunition for their siege guns when the battle was joined on the floors of the House and Senate. All such weapons were needed, for the only way to awaken Reagan and win his support was to overwhelm the right flank in Congress. This, in fact, happened, with the House voting 389 to 24 to extend the act, establishing a powerful momentum and drawing attention to the issues and the votes. Soon crafty old Sen. Strom Thurmond, often prone to rigid ideological stances but always keenly aware of the voters back home, saw the need to get right with South Carolina's black voters and came out in favor of the measure, leaving Jesse Helms and John East, like David's lieutenant Uriah, unsupported on the plain.[37] The resultant din awoke Reagan, who came late but facilely to the side of what were now the big battalions; and in August of 1982 a smiling chief executive signed the measure into law.

Besides performing a valuable service to civil rights, Woodward's acts and words completed the circle of a long public career, reminding everyone, perhaps most of all himself, of the basic quality of his life's work. As before, he had recaptured a sense of the past and then forcefully reminded southerners that the past was not dead, nor, as Gavin Stephens said for Faulkner, was it even *past*. As before, he had extended that sense of the past beyond the South and then forcefully reminded lawmakers from New Jersey, Illinois, and California that they, too, shared responsibility for the guarantees of citizenship and equality for blacks. Thus the gift of this particular action, far more than the Aptheker case, was its simple, succinct characterization of the reinvigorated scholarship of his final years after the lull of his "times of trouble" in the early 1970s.

II

Among historians, Woodward also engaged again in conspicuous confrontation with the big issues; as in his politics, in his latest scholarly writing he has been firm and clear. While still ironic, his style has been resonant with conviction rather than satiric with cuteness. An elder statesman of dissidence in the 1980s when many have become defensive about their social institutions, unquestioningly acquiescent before the abuses of their economy, and cynical about their politics, Woodward, characteristically, has been again at the center but pressing to get out. With his ambitious editing projects and his pithy homilies in crucial essays, he has late in life attained a special stature as a revered critic, a moral force sui generis, able to prick our consciences without preaching at us.

Moreover, during the course of this final season, he has taken account of the way in which the larger culture around him has been victim of the giant centrifuge which has flung the former organizing, ordering, sense-making ideas beyond the system's gravity. Perhaps nothing at all can be believed any more, perhaps nothing known, perhaps nothing understood; and if that is so, if no values can have relevance, what else is there to do but tend the body? Or so it seems to many. Without fully solving the dilemma posed by the cultural centrifuge, Woodward has at least demonstrated a stoic's resolution of it. For him, contemporary notions of defeatism and impotence actually constitute a new rationale enabling those with privileges to retain their many material possessions while eschewing societal responsibilities. Essentially, these were fashionable defenses for the "world's most unrestrained capitalism," as he said to an Alabama reformist. Once, in the 1890s, the Populists had stood up to this dangerously uninhibited, unrestrained economic force— "There was some sham and it didn't work, but at least for once someone said no to utterly unrestrained capitalism."[38]

In the lengthening shadows before his moment ends, Woodward has forthrightly announced himself to be "the last living Populist" and thus has dedicated his remaining energies to dispelling the new myths of individual irrelevance which would delude the average citizen into relinquishing his or her power. In fact, he has even discerned still another mask for "unrestrained capitalism," one available after people have tired of using defeatism and impotence as excuses for irresponsibility and have begun to seek instead a revitalized sense of success and omnipotence as the justification for doing what they want to do. He has remained, in short, ready for almost any form of argument, and as much as ever, large numbers of intellectuals have been ready to hear him.

After decades of trying to destroy the twin delusions of invincibility and innocence, Woodward discovered to his chagrin that responses to the experiences of presidential guilt in Watergate and of congressional guilt in Koreagate had done more of a job of deflating the national character than was actually needed: Alice in Wonderland, once swollen too large for her quarters, was now about to disappear altogether. Speaking in 1981 to his fellow members of the American Academy of Arts and Sciences, he recorded a useful warning against the "relatively recent inversion of traditional myths and especially the shift from collective innocence toward collective guilt." Having entered the academic arena by protesting the delusory fairy tales of purity, he now prepared to make his exit by protesting both the old myth of innocence and the more recent obsession with its opposite.[39]

Briefly covering again the already burned-over ground of 1950 consensus history, he remarked, "It was the virtues of the past the historians were praising, but the character of the modern period during which they voiced their pride is worth recalling," that is, the era when the United States was "at once the policeman of the world and the self acclaimed model for revolutions of liberation." Despite the protests of scholars such as Reinhold Niebuhr or statesmen such as James William Fulbright, the celebration went on and on, through the yeasty 1960s and even into the obviously less successful 1970s; but at last, by 1980, the party was over. The guests having departed, the hosts—historians, theologians, sociologists, intellectuals, public figures—were rather suddenly "overwhelmed by spreading convictions of national guilt."[40]

In fact, there was a bona fide "seller's market for guilt," though it was a peculiar market, for the demand came from the present, but "bargains in guilt are to be found mainly in the past." And so it was that some 1980s essayists created the high-technology enterprise of "transposition of symbols and inversions of myths." Yet these exercises grew curiouser and curiouser, for the "new collective guilt" did not seek to identify oppressors but instead "might be called in a sense, unilateral," describing, as it did, "offenses . . . unprovoked, unique, and confined to the dominant group." As flatly foolish as was one generation's ethnocentric worship of the dominant group, this day's ethnocentric fixation on the victims was no wiser by comparison. Moreover, "other nations with bloodier disgraces on their hands . . . all seemed to manage recovery without excesses of self detestation or self revilement."[41]

A serious self-examination to consider wrongdoing would be therapeutic, he granted, but not this odd session of group groping in which Americans laid all the blame either on their parents or, more recently, on everyone. He quoted Hannah Arendt, the analyst nonpareil of revolution and tyranny, to the effect that if all were guilty, then no one, no single one of us, would have to acknowledge personal responsibility. It was, then, yet another way to flee from one's duties, and it developed that "inverting myths may be a way of preserving them." Surely enough, the subsequent fascination with Ronald Reagan and the enthusiastic endorsement of his own brand of innocence and invincibility portended yet another shift in mood; perhaps "the national conscience is preparing to take on new and unpredictable burdens," this time in the form of a new "counterfeit innocence." As Reagan subsequently rode the tide of popular favor following the invasion of Grenada, the economic recovery, and the athletic successes of the Los Angeles Olympiad, there did appear to be not only ebullience but also quite a bit of "counterfeit innocence."[42]

How appropriate, then, that Robert Penn Warren revised his *Brother to Dragons,* a lyric examination of slavery and its responsibilities past and present, to have one of the characters announce that "the burden of innocence is heavier than the burden of guilt."[43] For Woodward, there was no burden of guilt or innocence but rather the burden of knowledge and the responsibility to use that knowledge. Heavy burdens, these, in their way, but burdens to be shouldered by each one of us, not by the "collective all" of nobodies. Partly in response to these new cultural trends, he has involved himself in two major editing assignments, each valuable both for the intelligent laity and for the sincere professional; and in promoting these volumes, he has repeated with force and clarity his criteria for the useful historian. Again he has insisted that the historian use irony to strip away delusion; he has followed class lines to find conflict rather than consensus; he has examined the eccentric with loving attention to detail; and he has presented all of it his way with a wry sense for the hero's clay feet and for the villain's mitigating circumstances (to recall Wesley Frank Craven's apt one-liner, for Woodward only the American Whig party remained as proof of original sin). One of these projects was the *Oxford History of the*

United States, the multivolume edition originally planned in conjunction with Richard Hofstadter; the other was a singular and unified editing of the "diary"—which turned out to be written in several versions long after the fact—of Mary Boykin Chesnut, a shrewd critic from the inner circle of the Confederacy.

The *Oxford History* provided a special opportunity to develop a highly readable but fully competent account of American history, one which embraced the findings of innovative and sophisticated modern social history without sacrificing accessibility of language. Hofstadter and he, despite their differences in interpretation, were an ideal team for this task, since each man was a pastmaster in the art of translating the writings of the specialist into the language of the generalist. Neither man was going to permit obscure language, neither was going to tolerate dullness, neither was going to permit an oversimplification of his own point of view concerning pivotal issues; and the nature of their friendly rivalry would guarantee high editorial standards. Unfortunately, as noted, Hofstadter's death during a time of diminished scholarship for Woodward had slowed the process throughout the 1970s; but by 1980 Woodward was again moving steadily and confidently to recruit good scholars for the project; and in 1982 the volume chronicling the Revolutionary War was ready for distribution.[44] Given the chance by the *New York Times* to describe the development of American historiography on the occasion of the volume's unveiling, Woodward chose as his theme "the historian as pro" and used the space to protest some current trends. Nowadays, he said, "science meant more than a rhetorical commitment to objectivity and austerity. It meant extensive innovation in method, technique, training, subject matter, source, style, and intelligibility. . . . The New Historians were analytical rather than narrative, used statistical rather than 'literary' and 'traditional' sources and concentrated on circumstances and 'behavior' rather than on events, actions, and policy." Moreover, "they adopted social sciences whole heartedly, at a moment when those were in some self doubt," but for their pains, they discovered only that "printouts overwhelmed the quantifiers," for "computers abhor ambiguity." Thus "history was once called a habitation of many mansions, but it has been more recently described as scattered suburbs, trailer camps, and a deteriorating central city." Even worse, the intelligent lay people, who in this land had always consumed history with gusto if not with full understanding, stayed away in droves from these New History servants of Clio.[45]

This much had been said before and essentially reaffirmed the traditional humanist passion for the particularities of narrative, but now Woodward sounded a different note, a single note of thanksgiving for the new questions, new directions, previously unexplored subjects, and general invigoration which the New History had brought to professional historians. No one really serving the muse could ignore the new science and its studies even though the new science so ill served the nonspecialist public. Woodward was here being hard on all concerned, demanding the maximum tithe from everyone: there remained an ancient obligation, one unique to historians, whose echoes Woodward was awakening. An "enduring faith holds that it is the duty and privilege of historians, unlike scholars of other disciplines, to present the results of the guild's researchers, or at least their significance, to the layman in readable, unspecialized prose he can understand and enjoy." This was not, then, another call to return to unanalytical narrative, nor was it a call to the excitement of the simple drama of Progressivism, with its passion for the democratic revelation of justice over time. It was instead a demand that the professional recapture "the art of the craft" and then use that art and that craft to instruct a badly misinformed but still intelligent general public. As he exhorted his colleagues, Woodward suggested names as examples of people "doing" history right; these, including Peter Gay and David Potter, had always succeeded in talking intelligibly with both the specialists and generalist thinkers, and thus in mediating effectively between these two populations. Now it was not only a good idea to follow their lead; it was necessary to do so to ensure the survival of the profession.[46]

Omitted from his list was his own name, but the essay was essentially a statement of the personal principles which have guided the way he has written history. Few things better illustrated his practice of these principles than the edition of the Mary Chesnut writings, a lovely synthesis of the most advanced techniques and interpretations, and all done with his accustomed felicity of expression. It was a natural project for him, since Woodward had been developing an analysis of the antebellum and wartime Souths and since Chesnut was such a thoroughly Woodwardian character, often brilliant, occasionally dyspeptic, always insightful. William Faulkner could not have dreamed up anyone any more interesting, and she had indeed attracted the attentions of the novelist Ben Ames Williams and of others who had separately published her writings in editions entitled *Diary from Dixie*. Unfortunately, neither of the available versions was professionally edited; there had been no sincere effort to bring this woman's opinions before a thinking public. Instead, Williams in every case had sought the novelistic touch to ensure a "good read," while Isabella D. Martin, a kind of matron saint of the Lost Cause, in every case had sought the defense of the Confederacy. So misleading were these two editions that many historians routinely dismissed Chesnut from their reading lists and from their lectures, leaving her available only to the professional search work of graduate students, archivists, and professors who came to the South Caroliniana Library on the campus of the University of South Carolina.[47]

As he explored the Chesnut papers, at first reluctantly at the behest of others, but increasingly with a self-regenerating fervor of discovery, Woodward became what he had been over twenty years before, a "hands-on" researcher, a mole—and happy about it. Not since the intensive research which produced *Tom Watson, Origins of the New South, Reunion and Reaction,* and *The Strange Career of Jim Crow* had he labored so long or so hard in the primary sources. The day of the essayist drawing on general knowledge, the career from 1955 to 1977, was completed, and he occasionally dismissed the whole of that previous era's work as "journalism." He still wrote essays, of course, but now as a man getting his hands dirty in the archives. Still speaking to the laity, still following his own lead concerning the historian's role, he has done his job of instructing the intelligent public with a verve and a force which seem to increase as he has aged. Directing a team of graduate students, other historians, literary experts, and archivists, he became fully engaged with the daily labor of collating the five thousand pages of manuscript with their idiosyncratic punctuation and spelling. And he became fully engaged with Mary Chesnut as a character, so much so that crusty old Bill Carleton would chide him that he thought she was "really something," real aristocracy, "the real thing"—when of course Carleton and many others considered all of the antebellum and wartime elite to be parvenu.[48]

"Real thing" or not, what she actually attempted was nothing less than an artist's intensely evocative portraiture of a social disaster, and what Woodward achieved was nothing less than an equally evocative work of art, for he provided her, at last, with a proper medium for expression of what she saw, heard, and felt. Despite her eye for detail and her ear for subtlety, despite her undeniable powers as a writer, her recollections were not left in a unified, accessible form, but were instead set down in several uncompleted novels and in several memoirs. "What she was doing," he explained to audiences at conferences across the South, "was an artistic recreation of experience. . . . It was a work of creative literature . . . in unique form and with unique commitments. . . . She was representing flesh-and-blood people. She didn't invent anybody and she was evoking a historical experience that she [realized] was the greatest calamity of her time, catastrophic for her own people—and one of which she was very much a part. Yet she was detached as artists should be. . . . Mary had the detachment to see what was happening, the corrupt politicians, the scheming generals. She saw that the world was crazy and that mad men were in charge." To preserve these observations, she had indeed kept a kind of diary during 1861 and during 1865, but her most interesting remarks were written down in the 1880s, and it was in those postbellum reflections and reconsiderations that she explored most usefully the crucial years 1862, 1863, and 1864.[49] Unless scholars sorted out the disjointed fragments of analysis to demonstrate her overriding perspective, her voice would remain essentially unheard; and thus Woodward created a provocative synthesis from her previously undigested papers.

"History is chaos," said the editor, "and the [literary, artistic] writer makes some order out of it. He or she has a creative act to perform that the historian doesn't share. The historian has to report what happened accurately and make sense of it if he can. The artist's duty is to make you feel and comprehend the emotions and the experiences." Just as the historian must stand ready to convey the discoveries of the social scientists to the laity, so must he stand ready to convey the discoveries of the artist, especially those of an artist who left her work in disarray. Moreover, he repeated the ironic call to action, that need to awaken the world to those otherwise forgotten dissidents who stripped away delusions. And "intelligence breeds intelligence and any preservation of a clear, honest perception of a well-informed mind, which not only speaks frankly and forthrightly but has cultivated the capacity for writing in an effective and readable way, will influence those it meets, and I hope, for the good."[50] There it was again, the long-running faith in the power of good ideas given a fair hearing.

Those allowed thus to meet Mary Chesnut, a goodly number thanks to Woodward's popularity and prestige, encountered more than the admittedly delicious gossip from the inner chambers displayed in earlier editions. Funny stories and the macabre were still there, for Chesnut used both to show the paunchy nakedness of the Confederate emperors once they were stripped of the clothes provided posthumously by glorifiers of the Lost Cause. But significantly, there was a perspective to all of this, there was Woodward's kind of activist irony wielded by a mentality which was in the nineteenth-century context both antislavery and feminist. Even more important, Chesnut for him showed the linkage between feminism and antislavery: she showed how the man's world of sexual dominance in which women were a pedestalized property was necessarily also the world of racist dominance and of military adventurism. It was, finally, the latter which destroyed that world, for she could see early on that the generals were quite beneath their monumental task and would fail. In a crowning irony to this "play" which men "wrote," it was a woman who survived it all with her wits intact to record their knavishness and foolishness for people of another day to witness.[51]

Ever the realist in his artistry, Woodward insisted that all of Chesnut's character be introduced to the modern visitors. Thus, for all her feminist inclinations, she was revealed as no friend to the women of her day, understanding their plight more than their personhoods, neither trusting them nor trusted by them. Most women were scared of her, Woodward noted, and that reaction was often fully justified, for "she manipulated people." And her antislavery was not racial justice, since her starting point and her finishing point were basically white; she asked, namely, in what ways does slavery harm white women? In fact, during the 1880s her expressions of racism grew even more strident. Nor did her detestation of slavery, of sexual chauvinism, of militarism, of so much of the South, make her any more receptive to the rest of the country, which she largely disdained. To a remarkable degree, Woodward resisted the temptation to make her fully palatable to this era, instead laboring to fit her accurately within her own Boykin, Camden, Richmond, and Columbia contexts of 1850, 1860, 1865, and 1880.[52]

This edition drew enormous attention, although by no means unanimous appreciation. Carl Degler expressed admiration for the painstaking annotation, which fully identified even minute historical figures or events mentioned in her writings; but the Stanford historian also suggested that Woodward had failed to appreciate how much Chesnut was a whining and spoiled character who was more sensitive to her own desires than she was to the dominant trends of her subculture. Then, in the *New York Times Book Review,* literary and cultural critic Kenneth Schuyler Lynn attempted a sharp rebuttal to Woodward, scolding the liberal for transposing twentieth-century feminism into the identity of a nineteenth-century woman. But Degler had not intended his qualifying remarks to be sharply critical, and there was little substantiation for Lynn's intemperate attack. More to the point was the shrewd analysis of historian Michael P. Johnson, who questioned Woodward's editorial decision to print the 1880s material, supplemented by selections from the 1861 and 1865 diaries. Johnson emphasized that the "instinct" of all historians was to focus on the contemporaneously recorded Civil War notes; and after laboriously working through the printed Yale text and the South Caroliniana manuscripts, he concluded that the historian's instincts were indeed a better guide than Woodward's controversial decision. Johnson further complained that Chesnut's 1880s observations were likelier to be the "wisdom" of hindsight than proof of her percipience in the otherwise confusing rush of wartime events; and he lamented that the insertions for the 1860s notations, "welcome as they are," were inadequate to demonstrate Chesnut's actual contemporaneous opinions and perceptions. He found this especially troubling because only a few readers would have the opportunity, much less the expertise, to examine the original manuscripts in the archives; Woodward's editorial judgment, therefore, would virtually mandate his own interpretation as the only possible one for most readers. Finally, Johnson questioned the assertion that Chesnut was developing some exciting new form of literary art; he insisted instead that the writing—much of which he admired—was "fully within the tradition" of the "prophetic autobiography," which "flourishes in times of crisis."[53]

Most historians disagreed with Lynn, and most generalist readers, if they knew of Johnson's insightful critique at all, were baffled by its complexity; as a result, *Mary Chesnut's Civil War* sold well and earned for its editor the 1982 Pulitzer Prize. It was significant that Brandeis University, a quintessentially liberal institution whose seal proclaimed the pursuit of "truth, even unto its innermost parts," later presented Woodward its Poses Creative Arts Award because of this work and also because his "lifetime practice as scholar, citizen, and teacher serves as a model for those seeking to sustain intellectual debate, human dignity, and democratic and liberal practices." But Woodward was enjoying the controversy with his critics as well as the acclaim of admirers, and he subsequently published *The Private Mary Chesnut,* a unified compilation of the documents and also an opportunity to write an introduction in which he belittled the criticisms of Lynn. Further, he took the unusual, although not unprecedented, step of responding publicly to Johnson's review by announcing in the *Journal of Southern History* that *The Private Mary Chesnut* was forthcoming: "The truth must out, I say! . . . The historians will have more evidence of whatever mischief Mary Chesnut and her conspiratorial editor may have been hiding. Patience! And may curiosity whet the market."[54]

The nature of this controversy about the Mary Chesnut editing projects and especially the nature of Woodward's response to the criticism revealed that despite his frequent demurrers, he was concerned about his place in history; he cares deeply about the present and future status of the scholarship he has produced, and in this last phase of his life and career since 1974, he has been willing and occasionally rather anxious to defend his past works. Once, in an introduction to a reprint edition of Ulrich Phillips's *Life and Labor in the Old South,* he had sketched a vignette for the career of that book: it gained critical acceptance and then popular approval until it was the coin of the realm; then it came under attack and was largely discredited; later still it fell completely from the memory of the general public, which forgot even its identity as a "bad" book; and still later it passed from the scholars' usage, becoming a book whose title and author the specialist could associate with a discredited interpretation—but it was no longer a book that even the specialist would actually read. He did not think this a just fate for Phillips's scholarship, much as he disagreed with his conservative predecessor at Yale, and thus he did more than his part to keep up some interest in *Life and Labor.* To an even greater degree, he disliked the idea of such future neglect of his own work. By 1984, *Life and Labor* was again out of print, and perhaps beyond salvaging, but Woodward seemed intent on defending his own works so successfully and so memorably that his oeuvre might escape this eventuality after his own death—or at the very least, intent on mounting such a defense that he could significantly prolong the day of neglect.[55]

Obviously, all active scholars suffer such anxieties, and most take some kind of action to forestall the inevitable, even knowing the futility of such labors; but with Woodward the defense has been more notable for several related reasons. He has retained such an unusual amount of energy that he can travel to speak effectively across the country; he has continued throughout the 1980s to review books, often as the centerpiece or feature review essay, for the *New York Times Book Review,* the *New York Review of Books,* and the *New Republic;* he has continued to participate in the programs at the conferences of the major historical associations; and he has frequently appeared as lead speaker at special conferences—in 1984–85, for instance, at campuses as widely dispersed as San Diego, Charlottesville, South Hadley, Massachusetts, and Athens, Georgia. He has few other places to direct his considerable energies, as the already-shrunken circle of friends and relatives has diminished further with the death from cancer of his wife, Glenn, in 1982, the death of Bill Carleton the same year, and the debilitating stroke which has taken away his long and informing discussions with former student Willie Lee Rose of Johns Hopkins University. In a 1986 note to a friend he observed that his last blood relatives were gone and that "everywhere I look is cancer of some kind among friends, especially older ones or their closest relatives—Warrens, Brookses, Erskines, on and on." These losses have been partly counterbalanced, as much as such things can be, by new professional associations and sometimes by new friendships among younger scholars with whom he continues to work actively.[56]

But there is still another reason why this recent campaign of defense—unattractive as it sometimes is—has been indulged in. It is because many historians deeply respect him, even though other historians will probably be remembered as achieving more than he and others have been more prominent publicly. In the former category the mind runs to David Potter, Richard Hofstadter, or Peter Gay, while in the latter the mind calls up Arthur Meier Schlesinger, Jr., when he was conspicuously "in" with the Kennedy White House, and Eugene Genovese, when he was conspicuously "out" during the New Jersey campaign to "get the Reds out of Rutgers." But Woodward has won a remarkably widespread recognition as a good person who is a good scholar as well and who is also prominent as a cultural spokesman; and this quality of respect has assured him a hearing for much of what he says about his own historiography and others'. Finally, there is a smaller, but still sizable, group of men and women who now dislike him intensely—some because of the Aptheker controversy, some because of his actions and words in the period 1969–74, when he was often passively ironic and disingenuous and occasionally even meanspirited, others for their own judgments of other issues. And these, without intending to do so, often provide him the opportunity to defend his work by so conspicuously attacking it.

If he had to make such a self-assessment as a summing-up, then he at least found an appropriate forum in 1985 with what could be called Fleming II. Louisiana State University provides an annual series of lectures by a leading historian to honor the scholarship of Walter Lynwood Fleming, one of the great conservatives, who, after the fashion of his teacher William Archibald Dunning, emphasized the study of politics and of political institutions in the service of a genteel and paternal racism. The speeches have varied widely in quality, but often they have been the occasion for the unveiling of significant and controversial interpretations such as Avery Odelle Craven's revisionist version of the path to the Civil War or Carl Degler's reaffirmation of the continuity of social attitudes and practices in the South. One of the dividends paid by the lectureship has been the subsequent publication of the speeches by the Louisiana State University Press; and over the years, the appearance of the slender volume of provocative essays has become a special event for students of "the subject." Woodward had delivered his Fleming addresses in 1955 during the time when his commitments to the uses of history were especially political, especially reformist, and especially atypical for the era's politics and scholarship. Yet despite the fact that he published so much and with such impact that he was called by some historians "our Dixie Express comin' through," Woodward never delivered his essays to the press for publication. Now, after three decades, the press offered him another such opportunity, and he produced a set of witty and sprightly essays as an analysis of some major interpretive trends in the historiography of the modern South; these were titled, appropriately, *Thinking Back: The Perils of Writing History.*[57]

While the motives behind this publication are a complex mixture, the collection is quite useful for those who read the essays with the understanding that a very definite point of view is in force and that despite the wide range of authorities cited, the interpretation is intensive, not extensive. He establishes restricting categories by focusing on the debate about continuity and discontinuity, in the process creating the clever but somewhat misleading term *continuatarian* to describe those who find a *longue durée* of social and economic institutions, attitudes, and practices: "Continuatarians [are] a kind of Presbyterian sect who believe that the faith continues without change," as he put it once in an address. By contrast, he himself much prefers Charles Austin Beard's formulation that the Civil War was a Second American Revolution, "a bourgeois revolution which displaced an agrarian upper class." To those such as Jonathan Wiener who emphasize that the same antebellum planting families, and sometimes even the same planters, emerge as New South industrial leaders, he repeats an earlier observation: these researchers evince a "fascination with names," for they point out that Daniel Thompkins, Wade Hampton, and Joseph Brown were planters important in both eras, Old and New South; "but if Thompkins and Hampton became industrialists, if [they were becoming] interested in banks and railroads and mills, that is *not* a continuation of planter dominance, but instead a transformation in the interests and even occupations of the old elite." In other words, the same people play such an entirely different role in such a new social context that their identity is transformed. Furthermore, he again draws on David Carlton's depiction of upcountry South Carolina textile business to substantiate his claim that essentially new people, men new to the region of the Piedmont or new to this class of leadership, were in charge of New South economic development.[58]

As a statement reaffirming the need to examine class lines and the actual control of the means of production and as a reminder that class conflict can hardly be ignored in New South development, his lectures provide a valuable corrective to some recent trends in which such analysis is downplayed or ignored; and it is worthwhile to state again in such clear form his Beardian theme of discontinuity between antebellum and postbellum leadership, as that issue remains in dispute. On the other hand, he has forced so many different kinds of historians into one camp or school that he has blurred issues of racism, culture, class, and economics in a way that does some disservice to nonspecialists as they try to comprehend the issues. Briefly, he says that men as different as Ulrich Phillips and Joel Williamson are describing a continuing theme of racism, while Carl Degler is interested in the persistence and transcendence of more broadly cast cultural attitudes, which include racism but also much else; Jonathan Wiener and Dwight Billings are using a Marxian, but not an economic determinist, analysis of the ways that a planter class self-consciously manages industrialization in a region; and James Cobb is employing an economic determinist, but not a Marxian, analysis of the patterns of industrial development.[59] Acting individually as they have, these scholars have so thoroughly damaged Woodward's interpretation from so many different angles of approach that one could as well label Woodward the continuatarian, the one clinging to a virtually unchanging faith in Beard. However, if these essays fail as a comprehensive review of what the critics have said, they serve to reiterate Woodward's informing vision in a volume which will remain accessible long after *Origins of the New South* meets the inevitable fate of all works and passes into the status of a ruined monument visited only by the specialists.

To large degree, these debates over interpretation, compelling as they can be, are simply not the issue, since the very nature of the study of history mandates revision, and sometimes outright rejection, of major theses. Far more important is the way in which some historians inspire a process of significant and enlightening questioning about the past; and this Woodward has done both in direct teaching of his Johns Hopkins and his Yale students and in less

direct "teaching" of other scholars attracted to "the subject" by
Woodward's works. By the 1980s, Woodward's students have established themselves as leaders in the field, and it is difficult to name
any contemporary who has trained such a number of high-quality
historians—although in this respect he falls far behind the records
of his predecessors of two previous generations, Herbert Baxter
Adams at Johns Hopkins and Fletcher Melvin Green at the University of North Carolina, each of whom trained over a hundred doctoral students who collectively wrote at least that many books.[60]

In 1982, seventeen of Woodward's students produced a festschrift,
Region, Race, and Reconstruction: Essays in Honor of C. Vann Woodward,
despite the fact that he was so obviously unready to be "shriven."
This was a collection of dissident gems which sparkled in the best of
the Woodward tradition; the essays in it were without exception
well written, and they covered a wide range of attitudes and approaches. For instance, Tilden Edelstein analyzed how racial attitudes have changed over time by following the cultural and racial
meanings of the character and the role of the Moor Othello in American theater productions; but Barbara Jeanne Fields provided a
powerful argument that the whole concept of race is essentially
ideological, and thus class analysis must subsume studies of racism,
just as class conflict subsumes attitudes which most historians label
"racist." There were some very compelling narratives of characters
who demonstrated the eccentricity of the South: William McFeely
told the story of Amos Tappan Akerman, a New Hampshire–born
Georgia slaveowner and veteran of the Confederacy who served as
Grant's attorney general and was quite vigorous in prosecuting the
Ku Klux Klan; Charles B. Dew provided a charming picture of Sam
Williams, a black foreman who exercised a surprising amount of
independent power and exhibited remarkable expertise on the plantation where he served as a slave; and Louis R. Harlan demonstrated
the previously little-known fact that Booker Taliafero Washington
was riotously successful in raising money by tapping the eleemosyn-
ary resources of a small group of wealthy northern Jews. There were
also very sophisticated examinations of social patterns by astute
quantifiers of the New History tradition: Steven Hahn presented a
complex portraiture of the people who became Georgia Populists,
showing in the process that there was such a commingling of cultural traditionalism and economic radicalism in these agrarian pol-

itics that historians may be forced to reconsider the whole question of the character of this movement; and J. Mills Thornton picked at the scab of the old wound of Reconstruction finances in an effort to show that important as racism was, much southern white resistance to Reconstruction programs actually had to do with the characteristic fiscal conservatism of a farming people. As a group, these essays were perfectly in the tone of the mentor, their sardonicism acting as a corrosive agent on the composition of the delusions by which we live. Perhaps not surprisingly, the essays have since sparked controversies in their own right; and also in keeping with an established pattern, Woodward promptly sent each of the authors a thoughtful and usually helpful critique of his or her essay.[61]

Significant as are these obvious and direct influences on the men and women whom he has taught and significant as are his less direct influences on the kinds of questions which historians ask, Woodward's most valuable gift has been of another kind. He has artfully shouldered a burden of knowledge, a knowledge not of guilt or of innocence, but of responsibility; and he has provided a concrete example of the way the rest of us can shoulder the new burdens to come. The essential gift which this man has presented us is, in fact, the whole of his career: in all that he has said and done, in all that he has written and taught, even when he was wrong and even in questions where the very idea of a final verdict of "right" or "wrong" is problematic, he has found a past that he can use, he has used it well, and he leaves us with a clear sense of the privilege conferred by the past he has showed us and an equally clear sense of the duty imposed by that past.

Appendix A

Ph.D. Students from Johns Hopkins University, 1947–1960

Warren W. Hassler, Jr.   Otto H. Olsen
Ludwell H. Johnson   James M. McPherson
Daniel H. Calhoun   Charles F. Kellogg
Louis R. Harlan   Charles B. Dew
Robert P. Sharkey   Bertram Wyatt-Brown
Willie Lee Rose   Tilden H. Edelstein

Note: List supplied by C. Vann Woodward.

Appendix B

Ph.D. Students from Yale University, 1961–1979

Student	Graduation Date	Dissertation
John Blassingame	1971	A Social and Economic Study of the Negro in New Orleans, 1860–1880
Frederick A. Bode	1969	Southern White Protestantism and the Crisis of the New South, North Carolina, 1894–1903
David I. Carlton	1977	Mill and Town: The Cotton Mill Workers and the Middle Class in South Carolina, 1880–1920
Ruth F. Claus	1975	Militancy in the English and American Suffrage Movements
Daniel W. Crofts	1968	The Blair Bill and the Elections Bill: The Congressional Aftermath to Reconstruction
Robert F. Engs	1972	The Development of Black Culture and Community in the Emancipation Era: Hampton Roads, Virginia, 1861–1870
Barbara J. Fields	1978	The Maryland Way from Slavery to Freedom

James R. Green	1972	Socialism in the Southwestern Class Struggle, 1898–1918: A Study of Radical Movements in Oklahoma, Texas, Louisiana, and Arkansas
Francis Sheldon Hackney	1966	From Populism to Progressivism in Alabama, 1890–1910
Frank J. Huffman	1974	Old South, New South: Continuity and Change in a Georgia County, 1850–1880
J. Morgan Kousser	1971	The Shaping of Southern Politics: Suffrage Restriction and the Establishment of the One-Party South, 1880–1910
Marc W. Kruman	1978	Parties and Politics in North Carolina, 1846–1865
John L. McCarthy	1970	Reconstruction Legislation and Voting Assignments in the House of Representatives, 1863–1869
Richard L. McCormick	1976	Shaping Republican Strategy: Political Change in New York State, 1893–1910
Geraldine M. McTigue	1975	Forms of Racial Interaction in Louisiana, 1860–1880
Bruce Palmer	1972	The Rhetoric of Southern Populists: Metaphor and Imagery in the Language of Reform

Robert Dean Pope	1976	Senatorial Baron: The Long Political Career of Kenneth D. McKellar
Lawrence N. Powell	1976	New Masters: Northern Planters during the Civil War and Reconstruction
Daniel T. Rodgers	1973	The Work Ethic in Industrial America, 1865–1917
Richard Skolnick	1964	The Crystallization of Reform in New York City, 1890–1917
J. Mills Thornton III	1974	Politics and Power in a Slave Society: Alabama, 1806–1860
Bert H. Thurber	1973	The Negro at the Nation's Capital, 1913–1921
Michael S. Wayne	1979	Ante-Bellum Planters in the Post-Bellum South: The Natchez District, 1860–1880
John A. Williams	1966	Davis and Elkins of West Virginia: Businessmen in Politics

Note: List supplied by Registrar, Department of History, Yale University.

Notes

INTRODUCTION

1. Cf. Brooks, *The Well-Wrought Urn;* Warren, *The Legacy of the Civil War.*

2. Minter, *William Faulkner, His Life and Work* (Baltimore: Johns Hopkins University Press, 1980), p. ix.

3. Interviews: Cecil Slaton Johnson (28 February 1974), Bell Irvin Wiley (13 September 1974), Mabel Phillips Parker (12–14 July 1974).

4. Comer Vann Woodward to John Herbert Roper, 25 June 1981. Unless otherwise noted, all Roper correspondence is filed in the Roper Papers.

5. Howard Washington Odum to Jackson Davis, 25 March 1936, Odum Papers.

6. Daspit, "Dean Pipkin."

7. Woodward, *Responses of the Presidents;* idem., "Times of Trouble"; Woodward to Roper, 25 June 1981.

CHAPTER 1. *Arkansas Youth, 1908–1928*

1. Interviews: Comer Vann Woodward (18 and 19 July 1978, 12 October 1980, 20 June 1983); Van Dyne, "Vann Woodward"; O'Sheel, "The Uses of Adversity"; Woodward to Glenn Weddington Rainey, 13 September 1957, Rainey Papers.

2. Interviews: Woodward (20 June 1983), James William Fulbright (21 March 1983).

3. Interviews: Woodward (18 and 19 July 1978, 12 October 1980, 20 June 1983).

4. Interviews: William G. Carleton (21 July 1979), Woodward (18 July 1978).

5. Interviews: Woodward (18 and 19 July 1978, 12 October 1980, 20 June 1983).

6. Powdermaker, *After Freedom;* Williamson, *After Slavery;* Kolchin, *First Freedom;* Bleser, *The Promised Land.*

7. Cf. Bleser, *The Promised Land;* Kolchin, *First Freedom;* Williamson, *After Slavery;* Higgs, *Competition and Coercion.*

8. Higgs, *Competition and Coercion.*

9. Ibid.; Foner, *Nothing but Freedom.*

10. Ford, "Rednecks and Merchants."

11. Ransom and Sutch, *One Kind of Freedom,* makes a strong case for the existence of "territorial" or "regional" monopoly of credit. See also "Historian Extols University Life"; Woodward to Roper, 7 June 1984. This attitude pervades Woodward's *Origins of the New South* and was expressed frankly in an interview: Woodward (4–5 November 1982).

12. Lebergott, "Through the Blockade"; Wright, "Cotton Competition"; De-Canio, *Agriculture in the Postbellum South.* Cf. some opposing views in the January 1979 issue of *Explorations in Economic History,* and see a good textbook summary of the literature in Niemi, *U.S. Economic History,* pp. 214–31.

13. Goodspeed Brothers, *Biographical and Historical Memoirs of Eastern Arkansas* (Chicago and St. Louis: Goodspeed Brothers, 1890); interview: Woodward (12 October 1980); Van Dyne, "Vann Woodward"; O'Sheel, "The Uses of Adversity"; interview: Woodward (20 June 1983).

14. Goodspeed Brothers, *Biographical and Historical Memoirs of Eastern Arkansas.*

15. Bond for Marriage License, H. A. Woodward and Emily Branch Hare, 27 June 1907, Cross County Historical Society; Hall, "Woodward."

16. Hall, "Woodward."

17. Interview: Woodward (12 October 1980).

18. Comer McDonald Woodward Papers (hereinafter cited as Comer Woodward Papers): see especially Hugh Allison Woodward to Comer McDonald Woodward, 6 March and 28 February 1926; C. M. Woodward to H. A. Woodward, 27 and 13 February 1926.

19. Interviews: Woodward (18 July 1978, 12 October 1980, 20 June 1983); Woodward, "Times of Trouble."

20. Interview: Woodward (18 July 1978); "Charles Hillman Brough," *National Cyclopedia of American Biography* (1958), 42:141.

21. Interviews: Woodward (18 July 1978, 12 October 1980), Glenn Weddington Rainey (25 and 26 March 1980).

22. Interviews: Rainey (25 and 26 March 1980), Woodward (20 June 1983); C. R. Huie to Roper, 15 September 1983.

23. Huie to Roper, 15 September 1983; interview: Thomas H. English (24 March 1980); Thomas H. English to Roper, 28 January 1980; interview: Woodward (20 June 1983).

24. Interviews: Woodward (20 June 1983), English (24 March 1980); English to Roper, 28 January 1980.

25. Interviews: Woodward (20 June 1983), English (24 March 1980); English

to Roper, 28 January 1980; Daspit, "Dean Pipkin"; Hall, *Henderson State College,* pp. 5, 170.

26. Interview: Woodward (18 July 1978); Tindall, "Rupert Bayless Vance"; interview: Woodward (20 June 1983).

27. Interview: Woodward (20 June 1983).

28. Ibid.

29. Ibid.; interview: Woodward (4–5 November 1982); Woodward Scrapbook, Cross County Historical Society; C. R. Huie to Roper, 1 September 1983.

30. Hall, "Woodward," pp. 1–100; Hall, *Henderson State College,* pp. 159–60; interview: Boulware Martin Ohls (18 March 1984).

31. Hall, "Woodward," pp. 1–100; Hall, *Henderson State College,* pp. 159–60; interview: Boulware Martin Ohls (18 March 1984); *Oracle* (student newspaper) files, 1926–27 (hereinafter cited as *Oracle*).

32. Hall, *Henderson State College,* pp. 128–60; "Fire Razes Men's Dormitory," *Oracle,* 23 February 1928, p. 1.

33. Hall, *Henderson State College,* pp. 128–30; Percy, *The Last Gentleman,* pp. 47–74; Hall, "Woodward."

34. Interview: Julia Hall (19 March 1984); Huie to Roper, 1 September 1983.

35. Interview: Boulware Martin Ohls (18 March 1984).

36. "Garland Society" column on last page of *Oracle,* especially 22 March 1928 and 13 January, 3 February, 21 April, and 26 January 1927.

37. Interview: Ohls (18 March 1984); "Memorial: Mrs. Robert Huie," Huie Library, Henderson State University; Hall, *Henderson State College,* pp. 128–60.

38. Interview: Ohls (18 March 1984); Huie to Roper, 1 September 1983.

39. Interview: James William Fulbright (21 March 1983); Huie to Roper, 1 September 1983; correspondence between Woodward and Rainey, 1938–67, Rainey Papers. In the 1930s and the early years of World War II, Woodward evinced considerable sympathy for the Russian Communists.

40. Hall, "Woodward"; "Garland," *Oracle,* 27 October 1927, p. 3; Woodward to Rainey, 20 October 1938, Rainey Papers; interview: Woodward (15 November 1979).

41. "Garland," *Oracle,* 27 October 1927, p. 3; Hall, *Henderson State College,* pp. 128–60.

42. Hall, *Henderson State College,* pp. 128–60; interview: Julia Hall (19 March 1984); "Scholarship First," *Oracle,* 10 February 1927, p. 2; "On Growing Ears," ibid., 1 April 1927, p. 2; "Garland," ibid., 19 January 1928, p. 3; "Miss Martin Proves Valuable Class Sponsor," ibid., 7 April 1927, p. 1.

43. Hall, *Henderson State College.*

44. Comer M. Woodward to Hugh Allison Woodward, 6 March 1926, Comer Woodward Papers.

45. Ibid.; Howard Washington Odum to Jackson Davis, 25 March 1936, Odum Papers.

46. Hall, "Woodward"; [Gunn,] "Arkansan Wins Fame"; "Ten Victories as Debating Season Closes; Best Record in State," *Oracle,* 17 May 1928, p. 1; interviews: Jack R. Pole (11 November 1983), Boulware Martin Ohls (18 March 1984).

CHAPTER 2. *The City, 1928–1934*

1. Gerschenkron, *Economic Backwardness in Historical Perspective,* pp. 1–10 and passim. Woodward the mature scholar, in *Origins of the New South,* denounces these forces of industrial development in language which is drenched with a disdainful satire; he recalls that as a youth, he "took an instant distaste" to the city of Atlanta (Green, "Interview with Vann Woodward"; Green was kind enough to show the author an early version of the typescript interview and to share some observations about the process: Green to Roper, with enclosure, 26 March 1984).

2. Comer M. Woodward to Walter C. Woodward, 20 October 1930, and Comer M. Woodward to H. A. Woodward, 19 June 1931, Comer Woodward Papers; Thomas H. English to Roper, 28 February 1980.

3. Cf. Bullock, *A History of Emory University.* Bullock takes a more charitable view of the school's history. Candler, *Asa Griggs Candler,* while almost ancestor worship, provides useful information.

4. Interview: Carl D. Stewart (26 June 1979).

5. Ibid.

6. Sledd, "The Negro."

7. Carl D. Stewart to Roper, 9 August 1979; "Message of 14 November 1901," *Georgia House of Representatives Journal,* 1901, pp. 429–430.

8. Woodward, *Origins of the New South,* p. 445; Smith, "Professor Sledd and Emory College." The details of Sledd's banishment are in Sledd Papers. Williamson, *The Crucible of Race,* has pointed out details of this story which were only partially explored by Woodward.

9. Woodward, *Origins of the New South,* p. 445; Smith, "Professor Sledd and Emory College"; Sledd Papers; Williamson, *The Crucible of Race;* interview: Stewart (26 June 1979); Stewart to Roper, 9 August and 22 November 1979.

10. See Stewart to Roper, 22 November 1979, for the particularities of the Emory events. For more generalized patterns of racism in the South, Woodward's *Origins of the New South* and *The Strange Career of Jim Crow* have been supplemented usefully by Williamson, *The Crucible of Race.*

11. Interview: LeRoy E. Loemker (11 August 1979).

12. Interviews: Thomas H. English (26 March 1980), Carl D. Stewart (26 June 1979), Glenn Weddington Rainey (25 and 26 March 1980), Martin D. Young (20 June 1979).

13. Ernest Hartsock, "Strange Splendor," 1930 typescript in Ernest Hartsock Collection.

14. Interview: Woodward (13 April 1979); O'Sheel, "The Uses of Adversity." Scruggs, *The Sage in Harlem,* demonstrates that Mencken was actually very helpful to many individuals, such as particular black writers and particular southern white writers, whom he criticized severely in a generic sense in his *American Mercury.*

15. Interview: Woodward (13 April 1979); Woodward to Rainey, 14 December 1931, Rainey Papers.

16. Interviews: Rainey (25 and 26 March 1980); correspondence between Rainey and Woodward in the Rainey Papers, 1930–33; Woodward, "Emory Landlubber"; Rainey to Roper, 11 February 1980.

17. Rainey, in fact, took an A.M. degree in 1927 in history under Theodore Jack at Emory University, writing a thesis on the Atlanta race riot of 1906. He then entered doctoral studies in political science at Northwestern University, examining for decades the Independent Movement and race relations in Georgia, 1877–92, and eventually producing a manuscript of some five hundred pages which he never submitted for dissertation approval. Although he also studied and translated Geoffrey Chaucer, Rainey evinced an unending fascination with racial history in the South. See interviews: Rainey (25 and 26 March 1980), and Woodward-Rainey correspondence, 1930–66, Rainey Papers.

18. Loemker to Roper, 2 June 1979; Potter, "Woodward and the Uses of History"; Johann von Goethe, *Faustus,* part 1, lines 2038–39.

19. Interviews: Loemker (11 August 1979), Rainey (25 and 26 March 1980); Dittmer, *Black Georgia in the Progressive Era.*

20. Interview: Loemker (11 August 1979); I have extrapolated from the typescripts of Loemker's remarks.

21. Ibid.

22. Murphy, *Present Problems of the South,* best exemplifies such conservatism. Williamson, *The Crucible of Race,* painstakingly diagnoses the Hegelian influence on the "racial mentalities" of the era.

23. Woodward to Rainey, 11 May 1931, 12 July 1936, and spring 1932, Rainey Papers.

24. Interview: Loemker (11 August 1979); Loemker shared his student notebook covering the Vierkundt lectures.

25. Interview: Rainey (26 March 1980); Loemker to Roper, 2 June 1979; interview: Loemker (11 August 1979).

26. Interview: Rainey (26 March 1980); Loemker to Roper, 2 June 1979; interview: Loemker (11 August 1979).

27. Ibid.

28. Interview: Woodward (18 July 1978); Dittmer, *Black Georgia in the Progressive Era,* pp. 141–62; Woodward, *Thinking Back,* p. 85.

29. Interview: Woodward (18 July 1978); Redding, *The Lonesome Road;* idem, *On Being Negro.*

30. Woodward remained fascinated with this technique of the "inner dialogue" long after it had ceased to be avant-garde and had become in fact a fully accepted literary device, as is shown especially in his reading of Mary Boykin Chesnut's Civil War remembrances: see his Introduction to his edition of *Mary Chesnut's Civil War* and his "What Happened to the Diary of Mary Boykin Chesnut?" For Brutus Jones and Saunders Redding, see O'Neill, *The Emperor Jones;* Redding, *On Being Negro.*

31. "Two Emory Men Get Fellowships in Social Science," clipping, 1932, Rainey Papers.

32. Interview: Woodward (18 July 1978); Woodward to Rainey, [spring?] 1932, Rainey Papers.

33. Interviews: Woodward (18 July 1978), Rainey (26 March 1980), Woodward (20 June 1983); Woodward to Rainey, 20 October and 1 December 1931, Rainey Papers.

34. Interview: Woodward (13 April 1979).

35. Ibid. (18 July 1978).

36. Ibid.; Woodward to Rainey, 11 August 1932, Rainey Papers; Carter, *Scottsboro.*

37. Carter, *Scottsboro;* Green, "Interview with Vann Woodward." Cf. idem, "Rewriting Southern History."

38. Interview: Rainey (26 March 1980).

39. Martin, *The Angelo Herndon Case,* reads the CP and its actions quite differently from the way that Woodward and Rainey do; although I find Woodward's interpretation severe, it still makes more sense than do those of Martin and others relatively sympathetic to the CP. See also Herndon, *Let Me Live.*

40. Martin, The Angelo Herndon Case; Herndon, *Let Me Live.*

41. Ibid.; interview: Loemker (11 August 1979).

42. Interviews: Woodward (18 and 19 July 1978, 11 August 1979, 26 March 1980).

43. Interviews: Woodward (18 and 19 July 1978), Loemker (11 August 1979), Bennett Harrison Wall (12 April 1979), Rainey (26 March 1980), Robert McMath (24 May 1979).

44. Interviews: Woodward (18 and 19 July 1978), Loemker (11 August 1979), Wall (12 April 1979), Rainey (26 March 1980), McMath (24 May 1979).

45. Interviews: Woodward (18 and 19 July 1978); Dykeman and Stokely, *Seeds of Southern Change.*

46. *Daily Worker,* 8 May 1933; interviews: Woodward (18 and 19 July 1978); *Atlanta Constitution,* 8 May 1933; *Atlanta Georgian,* 8 May 1933.

47. Interviews: Rainey (25 March 1980), McMath (24 May 1979).

48. Interviews: Woodward (13 April 1979), McMath (24 May 1979). McMath

has recalled a session of a conference when Woodward, functioning as moderator, casually remarked to the audience that he had been fired at Georgia Tech because of Herndon. This offhand remark has become an accepted version for many who know of the series of incidents. However, in the 13 April interview, Woodward is at pains to straighten out the details for the record, and in *Thinking Back,* pp. 86–87, he corroborates the interview.

49. Interview: Rainey (25 March 1980). Cf. Martin, *The Angelo Herndon Case.*

CHAPTER 3. *Discovery of Agrarian Radicalism, 1934*

1. Woodward to Rainey, 17 June 1934, Rainey Papers; interviews: Rainey (25 and 27 March 1980).

2. Woodward to Rainey, 17 June 1934, Rainey Papers.

3. Interviews: Rainey (25 and 27 March 1980).

4. Ibid. (25 March 1980).

5. The conclusion is my own, distilled from my reading of Woodward's works, my examination of his contemporaneous correspondence, especially with Rainey (Rainey Papers), and my interviews with Woodward and others. The activist and politically purposeful intent, at least of the young Woodward, has been pointed out in critical context by Potter in "Woodward and the Uses of History" and by O'Brien in "Woodward and the Burden of Southern Liberalism." While agreeing with their description of the tension which this historian has experienced because of the opposing pulls of committed reformism and disinterested, detached scholarship, I judge this development a good thing, whereas they clearly regret it. Woodward himself, especially after living through the period 1968–74 (see chapter 9), after hearing the critique from his friend Potter, and after reading O'Brien's piece, has often expressed some embarrassment at youthful "excess" and has occasionally reinterpreted his scholarship and activities of the period 1932–55 (interviews: Woodward [18 and 19 July 1978]; Woodward to Roper, 6 September 1977). But the contemporaneous records belie such reinterpretation of past attitudes or actions, for this young man was unmistakably involved in scholarship which was both leftist and activist; and the embarrassment is inappropriate, even misguided, the product of a man who, between 1968 and 1974 (his personal "time of troubles"), lost the edge of former commitments and who, in that process of loss, produced scholarship which failed to match the exceptionally high standards of his earlier efforts.

6. Potter, "Woodward and the Uses of History"; O'Brien, "Woodward and the Burden of Southern Liberalism"; interview: Bennett Harrison Wall (12 April 1979). Cf. Schorske, *Fin-de-Siècle Vienna,* pp. xvii–xxx.

7. Macaulay, *History of England from the Ascension of James II;* idem, *Critical and Historical Essays.*

8. Gay, *Style in History;* Weber, *The Protestant Ethic and the Spirit of Capitalism.*

9. Motley, *The Rise of the Dutch Republic;* Bancroft, *History of the United States.*

10. Woodward, "A Short History of American History." Woodward's own choice for a headline was "The Historian as 'Pro,'" a preference which tells much about the critical focus of the piece (interview: Woodward [4–5 November 1982]). Cf. Adams, *Historical Scholarship in the United States;* Carr, *What Is History?* Dunning, *A History of Political Theories;* Higham, *History;* Wise, *American Historical Explanations.* My interpretation differs significantly from all of these perspectives, but it is derived from them.

11. Woodward, "A Short History of American History."

12. Adams, *Historical Scholarship.*

13. Ibid.; Woodward describes this "compromise of 1877" in *Reunion and Reaction* and then expands the racial and cultural implications in several essays: "Equality: America's Deferred Commitment"; "The Political Legacy of Reconstruction"; "Seeds of Failure in Radical Race Policy"; and "Point Counterpoint: A Preface," in *American Counterpoint,* pp. 3–11.

14. Billington, *Frederick Jackson Turner;* Turner, *Frontier and Section;* Hofstadter, *The Progressive Historians;* Ray Allen Billington to Roper, 14 November 1975, 27 January 1976.

15. Quoted in Billington, *Frederick Jackson Turner,* pp. 98–99.

16. Curti and Carstensen, *The University of Wisconsin,* vol. 2; Programme of American Historical Association, 1907, Frederick Jackson Turner Papers, University Archives, University of Wisconsin, Madison; Roper, *U. B. Phillips,* pp. 67–81.

17. May, *The End of American Innocence;* interview: Woodward (4–5 November 1982).

18. Interview: Woodward (4–5 November 1982); Hofstadter, *The Progressive Historians,* pp. 349–466, 486–94; Muzzey, *American History.* Cf. Fitzgerald, "Onward and Upward with the Arts: Rewriting American History," part 1, pp. 41–60; Beard and Beard, *The Rise of American Civilization.*

19. Beard and Beard, *The Rise of American Civilization;* Nore, *Charles A. Beard.*

20. Nye, *Midwestern Progressive Politics;* Graham, *Encore for Reform.* Johnson, "Nine Milestones," codifies this interpretation for the political laity. See also Stein, *The Fiscal Revolution in America,* pp. 1–38 and passim.

21. Beard, *Economic Interpretation of the Constitution of the United States.*

22. Beard and Beard, *The Rise of American Civilization.*

23. Hofstadter, *The Age of Reform,* pp. 316–17.

24. Interviews: Woodward (18 July 1978, 13 April 1979).

25. Correspondence between Woodward and Rainey, 1934–36, including newspaper clippings of Woodward book reviews from the *Atlanta Journal,* Rainey Papers.

26. Interviews: Woodward (18 and 19 July 1978); Potter, "Woodward and the

Uses of History"; interviews: Rainey (25 and 27 March 1980). Woodward does not recall the names of all seven demagogues, but Rainey remembers that Huey Pierce Long was among them.

27. Interviews: Rainey (25 and 27 March 1980).

28. Ulrich Bonnell Phillips, "The Situation of the South in 1903," manuscript in Phillips Papers; interview: Rainey (27 March 1980); Woodward to Roper, 6 September 1977 and 28 January 1980.

29. See especially correspondence between Avery Odelle Craven and Ulrich Bonnell Phillips, Phillips Papers; interview: Avery Odelle Craven (12 November 1975); Smith, "Keep 'em in a Fire-proof Vault."

30. Interviews: Rainey (25 and 27 March 1980); Woodward to Georgia Watson Craven, 3 October 1933, and Georgia Watson Craven to Roper, 18 June 1979, with enclosures, both in possession of author.

31. Interview: Woodward (18 July 1978).

32. Howard Washington Odum to Will W. Alexander, 11 October 1933, and Alexander to Odum, 12 and 18 October 1933, Odum Papers.

33. Interview: Woodward (18 July 1978).

34. Ibid.; Woodward to Georgia Watson, 3 October 1933 and 26 June and 1 April 1938, in possession of author.

35. Woodward to Roper, 6 September 1977.

CHAPTER 4. *The Hill*

1. *Yale Alumni Review,* 1975.

2. Weldon A. Brown, "Upward" (1936), p. 291, typescript in the Weldon A. Brown Papers (hereinafter cited as "Upward").

3. Interview: Woodward (18 July 1978).

4. "Upward," pp. 298–99.

5. Ibid., passim.

6. Woodward to Rainey, 20 August 1939, Rainey Papers; interviews: Woodward (18 and 19 July 1978, 12 October 1980).

7. Woodward to Rainey, 20 August 1939, Rainey Papers; interviews: Woodward (18 and 19 July 1978, 12 October 1980).

8. Cf. Woodward, *Thinking Back;* see chapter 3 above for description of the state of contemporaneous southern historical research. The History Department Papers of the University of North Carolina (hereinafter cited as History Papers) show Chairman Albert Ray Newsome—a fine scholar trained under Ulrich Bonnell Phillips at the University of Michigan—awash in the overwhelming details of administering a program running on an expense account of less than six hundred dollars. Cecil Slaton Johnson and Carl Pegg were good research scholars, but in the 1930s their energies were largely given over to teaching huge numbers of

students. All of this was about to change dramatically because of Fletcher Melvin Green, who joined the faculty in 1936; but Green's emphasis on high-quality professional research and writing bore little fruit before 1940, three years after Woodward was graduated. See especially Howard Kennedy Beale to William Heath, 9 June 1936, History Papers. For examples of racial moderation and even liberalism in Newsome, see "Minutes of the Division of Cooperation in Education and Race Relations, 1935," and correspondence between W. A. Cooper, a black minister, and Newsome, History Papers. For Woodward's contemporaneous response to the graduate instruction, see Woodward to Rainey, 24 September and 4 February 1934, Rainey Papers. On Hamilton, see interviews: Woodward (18 July 1978), J. Carlyle Sitterson (10 November 1978), J. Isaac Copeland (19 November 1979), William Terry Couch (10–11 January 1980).

9. Interviews: Bennett Harrison Wall (12 April 1979), Manning J. Dauer (21 July 1979; Dauer was close friends with Woodward during the latter's first job after graduate school, and he recalls that Woodward complained of one seminar instructor who fell asleep during the sessions), Woodward (18 July 1978).

10. Woodward to Rainey, 17 May 1936, Rainey Papers. See also History Papers for 1935–36.

11. Interviews: Frank Winkler Ryan (15 March 1981; Ryan recalled these observations from Carl Pegg, who also described Woodward as "the worst instructor who walked the earth"), James R. Caldwell (8 October 1982); Caldwell to Roper, 2 February 1980. Caldwell has preserved a generally more positive image of those days, but he has also noted that Woodward did slight his studies.

12. Ashby, *Frank Porter Graham;* Herzenberg, "Frank Porter Graham"; interviews: Guy Johnson and Guion Johnson (11 January 1980); Kousser, *The Shaping of Southern Politics;* interview: Georgia Watson Craven (11 November 1975); Craven to Roper, 10 August 1978; interviews: Woodward (18 July 1978), Rainey (25 and 27 March 1980).

13. Interviews: Guy Johnson and Guion Johnson (11 January 1980), William Terry Couch (10–11 January 1980). Cf. Brazil, "Howard W. Odum"; Brazil reads Odum psychologically and finds changes in behavior resulting from historical shocks redolent of childhood trauma. In combination with later traumas in adult life involving controversies, memories of these childhood events then caused Odum to retreat from confrontation—and eventually Odum became much less activist, according to Brazil. The argument fails to explain fully Odum's continuing scholarly and political activism after his series of adult "shocks," which occurred between 1924 and 1928; nevertheless, the reading of the relationship between character and environment is compelling.

14. Gatewood, " 'Embattled' Scholar," pp. 375–82; idem, *Preachers, Pedagogues, and Politicians;* Brazil, "Howard W. Odum," pp. 427–41; idem, "Social Forces and Sectional Self-Scrutiny."

15. Turner, *The Significance of Sections in American History;* Odum, *An American*

Epoch; idem, *Southern Regions of the United States;* interviews: Rainey (25 and 27 March 1980), William Terry Couch (10–11 January 1980).

16. Interviews: J. Isaac Copeland (10–11 November 1979), William Terry Couch (10–11 January 1980); Howell, *Kenan Professorships.*

17. Howell, *Kenan Professorships;* interviews: J. Isaac Copeland (10–11 November 1979), Woodward (18 July 1978).

18. Interview: J. Isaac Copeland, (10–11 November 1979); Williams, *Capitalism and Slavery;* Poteat, "Religion in the South"; interview: Couch, (10–11 January 1980).

19. The phrase is Albert Murray's in *South to a Very Old Place,* pp. 84, 200.

20. Couch, "Reflections on the Southern Tradition"; idem, "The Agrarian Romance" (this is the text of the speech which inspired Tate's exit from the session); interview: Woodward (18 July 1978). Cf. Woodward, *Thinking Back,* pp. 17–20.

21. Interview: John Hope Franklin (10 November 1978); Tindall, "Rupert Bayless Vance"; Reed, Introduction to *Regionalism and the South;* Vance, *Human Geography of the South.*

22. Interview: Paul Green with Joseph A. Herzenberg (1975); Parker, "Paul Green."

23. Parker, "Paul Green"; interview: Woodward (18 July 1978).

24. Interviews: Bennett Harrison Wall (12 April 1979), Guy Johnson and Guion Johnson (11 January 1980), Couch (10–11 January 1980).

25. Interviews: Couch (10–11 January 1980); Woodward (18 July 1978). Cf. Buttitta, *After the Good Gay Times.*

26. Pope, *Millhands and Preachers.*

27. Woodward, letter to the editor and editorial clipping [from *Chapel Hill Tar Heel,* n.d.], enclosures, in Woodward to Rainey, 3 March 1935, Rainey Papers.

28. Ibid.

29. Ibid. See also correspondence with Rainey, 1933–38, Rainey Papers.

30. Interviews: J. Carlyle Sitterson (10 November 1978), Woodward (18 July 1978), Joseph R. Caldwell (8 October 1982); Woodward to Rainey, 3 March 1935, Rainey Papers.

31. Interviews: Sitterson (10 November 1978), Caldwell (8 October 1982), Frank Winkler Ryan (15 March 1981), Bennett Harrison Wall (12 April 1979); Woodward to Rainey, 17 May 1936, Rainey Papers.

32. Hugh Talmadge Lefler, To Whom It May Concern, 1935, History Papers; Caldwell to Roper, 2 February 1980; interview: Caldwell (8 October 1982).

33. Beale to Charles Austin Beard, 10 October 1936, and Beale, To Whom It May Concern, 31 March 1937, History Papers.

34. Interviews: Frank Weir Klingberg (10 November 1978), Sitterson (10 November 1978), Copeland (10 November 1979), Woodward (18 July 1978), Guion Johnson (11 January 1980); Joseph Steelman to Roper, 3 December 1979;

Beale to Martin A. Roberts, 13 November 1936, and Beale to Conyers Read, 17 December 1935, History Papers; interview: August Meier (20 April 1985, with corrections and amendments, 17 June 1985).

35. Beale to Robert Felsenthal, 15 March 1937, History Papers.

36. Beale to James R. Angel, 13 November 1936, History Papers. See also other correspondence, 1936–37, History Papers.

37. Interview: Woodward (18 July 1978).

38. Woodward, "The Political and Literary Career of Thomas E. Watson."

39. Interviews: Woodward (18 July 1978), Rainey (24, 25, and 27 March 1980), Guy Johnson and Guion Johnson (11 January 1980). The 24 March 1980 interview with Rainey is in possession of the author.

CHAPTER 5. *Two Kinds of Travel, 1937–1946*

1. Howard Kennedy Beale to John Musser, 20 February 1937, and Beale to Louis C. Hunter, 9 March 1937, History Papers; interviews: Manning J. Dauer (21 July 1979), Woodward (18 July 1978).

2. Interviews: Woodward (18 July 1978, 13 April 1979), Dauer (21 July 1979), William G. Carleton (21 July 1979).

3. Interviews: Woodward (18 July 1978), Dauer (21 July 1979). Dauer was speaking not only from memory but also from a recent search in the University Archives, the Library of the University of Florida, Gainesville.

4. Interviews: Dauer (21 July 1979), Carleton (21 July 1979); Woodward to Rainey, [fall?] 1937, Rainey Papers.

5. Interview: Dauer (21 July 1979).

6. Interviews: Dauer (21 July 1979), Ralph Henry Gabriel (13 March 1975); University of Florida Catalogue, 1937; Hutchins, *The Higher Learning in America*.

7. Interview: Dauer (21 July 1979). Again, Dauer was speaking after a search of the records in University Archives.

8. Ibid.; interview: Woodward (18 July 1978).

9. Woodward to Georgia Watson, 26 June 1938, in possession of author; interviews: Rainey, 25 and 27 March 1980; Woodward to Rainey, [fall?] 1937, Rainey Papers.

10. Interviews: Dauer (21 July 1979), Bennett Harrison Wall (12 April 1979), Jack R. Pole (11 November 1983). Even his dear friend Pole labels Woodward a "throwaway lecturer."

11. Interviews: Dauer (21 July 1979), Carleton (21 July 1979), Woodward (18 July 1978).

12. Interview: Woodward (18 July 1978); Odum to Woodward, [?] 1938, Odum Papers.

13. Woodward to Rainey, 11 September 1937, Rainey Papers.

14. Interviews: Woodward (18 July 1978, 13 April 1979). See Woodward and Rainey correspondence, 1937–38, Rainey Papers.

15. Interview: Woodward (13 April 1979).

16. Ibid.

17. Woodward and Rainey correspondence, 1937–39, Rainey Papers, especially Woodward to Rainey, 26 March 1939; interviews: Dauer (21 July 1979), Carleton (21 July 1979). Cf. Woodward, *Thinking Back,* p. 86: actually, Woodward had unsuccessfully approached Du Bois as early as 1932, but was given short shrift and dismissed "after he heard that Deep South accent of mine."

18. Nevins, "Tom Watson and the New South"; Hackney, *"Origins of the New South* in Retrospect."

19. Hofstadter, *Age of Reform;* Bell, *The New American Right;* Viereck, *The Unadjusted Man.* Cf. Woodward, "The Populist Heritage and the Intellectual"; Pollack, *The Populist Mind;* idem, *The Populist Response to Industrial America.*

20. Hackney, *Populism to Progressivism in Alabama;* Goodwyn, *Democratic Promise.*

21. Hunt, "The Making of a Populist"; Hahn, *The Roots of Southern Populism* (Hahn is a Woodward—and Howard Lamar—student using a complex Marxist perspective on these issues, but he emphasizes the cultural values of a traditionalist peasantry more than he does the concept of a rational and a forward-looking economic planning and pragmatism described by his mentor in *Tom Watson*); Shaw, *The Wool-Hat Boys* (Shaw's book impressed historians sufficiently to win the 1985 Frederick Jackson Turner Award, and this quotation is from a favorable review by Charles L. Flynn, Jr., in the *Journal of American History*).

22. Crowe, "Tom Watson, Populists, and Blacks Reconsidered"; Shaw, *The Wool-Hat Boys;* Williamson, *The Crucible of Race;* Genovese, *The World the Slaveowners Made,* p. 111; Nugent, *The Tolerant Populists;* Dittmer, "Woodward with Soul" (this paper, used and cited here with Dittmer's permission, shows that Woodward himself in these Populist studies was often guilty of describing the black electorate as a kind of "passive" group who "ought to" have followed the Populists but who were often drawn into allegiance with southern Democrats in the 1892–98 period—an insight of Dittmer's which prepares the way for Shaw's insistence that it was rational for blacks to respond to the opportunities, where they existed and when they existed, in the dominant Democratic party in Georgia); Goodwyn, *Democratic Promise.*

23. Durden, "The Cowbird Grounded"; Palmer, *"Man over Money."*

24. Palmer, *"Man over Money"*; Goodwyn, *Democratic Promise.*

25. Woodward, "The South in Search of a Philosophy"; interview: Dauer (21 July 1979).

26. Woodward, "The South in Search"; interview: Woodward (18 July 1978).

27. Woodward, "The South in Search," pp. 4–6. In its class analysis, this speech is naive compared with his later writings, where he would discuss in great

depth and with great sensitivity the antebellum planters as an upper-class, specifically an agrarian, elite; later writings would also display a much more complex sense of the transition to industrialism and of the class and family allegiances of those leading the transition.

28. Ibid., pp. 7–9; interviews: Rainey (25 and 27 March 1980).

29. Woodward, "The South in Search," pp. 10–11.

30. Ibid., p. 11.

31. Ibid., pp. 13–14.

32. Ibid., pp. 14–16.

33. Ibid., p. 16.

34. Ibid., p. 20; Will W. Alexander, correspondence with Odum, 1935–37, Odum Papers.

35. Woodward, "The South in Search."

36. Rupert Bayless Vance to Woodward, 10 and 31 October 1938 and 21 and 31 January 1939, Institute for Research in the Social Sciences Papers (hereinafter cited as Institute Papers).

37. Vance to Woodward, 20 March 1939, Institute Papers; Michael V. Woodward, "Ellis Merton Coulter." Cf. Woodward's unique recollections, including the discovery that at least one editor for the series disdained the young man's ability to write: *Thinking Back,* pp. 60–65.

38. Woodward to Rainey, 26 March 1939, Rainey Papers; Chandler et al., *The South in the Building of the Nation;* interviews: Dauer (21 July 1979), Carleton (21 July 1979).

39. Interviews: Rainey (25 and 27 March 1980). Woodward to Rainey, 25 May 1939, Rainey Papers, indicates that he gave up $400 in salary to make the change to Virginia, a sizable drop in pay in 1939 wages, but the letter also indicates that his duties were "half the work" asked at Gainesville.

40. Woodward to Rainey, 27 October 1939, Rainey Papers; interview: Woodward (18 July 1978); Woodward to Roper, 15 November 1981; Woodward to Rainey, 11 February 1940.

41. Woodward to Roper, 15 November 1981; Woodward to Rainey, 4 April 1943, Rainey Papers.

42. Woodward to Rainey, 5 May 1940, Rainey Papers; Woodward to Roper, 25 June 1981; Morris, *North toward Home.*

43. Woodward to Rainey, 28 October 1941, Rainey Papers; Woodward, *Origins of the New South,* pp. 23–24; Woodward, *Reunion and Reaction.* For an even more succinct version, see Blum et al., *The National Experience,* 2:416–22.

44. Woodward to Rainey, 28 October 1941, 19 October 1942, Rainey Papers; Woodward to Roper, 15 November 1981.

45. Woodward to Roper, 15 November 1981; interview: John Morton Blum (13 December 1984).

46. Woodward to Rainey, 4 December, 19 October 1942, Rainey Papers. On Warren's role as wartime governor and Japanese detention, see Schwartz, *The Unpublished Opinions of the Warren Court*, introduction, also pp. 485–90.

47. Woodward to Rainey, 4 April 1943, Rainey Papers; Woodward to Roper, 15 November 1981; Woodward to Rainey, 13 July 1943, Rainey Papers; interview: Bennett Harrison Wall (12 April 1979).

48. Woodward to Rainey, 13 July 1943, Rainey Papers; quotations from Woodward, *Thinking Back*, pp. 46–47.

49. Woodward, *Thinking Back*, pp. 46–47; idem, *The Battle for Leyte Gulf*, p. 162.

50. Woodward, *The Battle for Leyte Gulf*, p. 233; interviews: Woodward (18 and 19 July 1978); Warren, *Selected Poems;* Robert Penn Warren to Roper, 22 August 1984; Eleanor Warren to Roper, 7 December 1984.

CHAPTER 6. *Questions of Provenance, 1946–1954*

1. Hofstadter, *The Progressive Historians*, pp. 437–66, 489–94.

2. Hofstadter, *The American Political Tradition and the Men Who Made It*, p. ix.

3. The phrase is from Hellman, *Scoundrel Time*.

4. Hofstadter, *The Paranoid Style in American Politics;* idem, *Anti-intellectualism in American Life*.

5. Baker, *Radical Beginnings;* Parrington, *Main Currents in American Thought*, pp. 39–75; Miller, *The New England Mind;* idem, *Errand into the Wilderness*.

6. Hofstadter, *The Age of Reform*.

7. Boorstin, *The Genius of American Politics;* idem, "The Place of Thought in American Life"; idem, *The Americans*, vol. 1, *The Colonial Experience*, pp. 188, 33–84, 307, 19, 72–98.

8. Hartz, *The Liberal Tradition in America*. The source for Woodward's rather atypically ungenerous evaluation of Hartz is an interview: William G. Carleton (21 July 1979).

9. Hofstadter, in *The Progressive Historians*, pp. 444–66, indicates that as an elder statesman among scholars he came to harbor grave doubts about the consensus "school" and began to prefer much of the older Progressivism, which he himself had championed in his youthful writing. See also Higham, *History;* Wise, *American Historical Explanations*.

10. Interviews: William Samuel McFeely (4 December 1984), Woodward (11 November 1982).

11. Interview: Woodward (11 November 1982); Woodward (Hall interviewed a number of JHU students who recalled both the demanding sessions and Woodward's high expectations of their work in general); interview: John Morton Blum

(13 December 1984). Among the very fine historians who studied with Woodward at JHU were Otto Olsen, Willie Lee Rose, James McPherson, and Bertram Wyatt-Brown (see appendix A for full list).

12. Woodward, *Reunion and Reaction,* preface.

13. Roper, *U. B. Phillips;* Singal, *The War Within.*

14. Mitchell, *Alexander Hamilton;* idem, *The Rise of Cotton Mills in the South,* Mitchell and Mitchell, *The Industrial Revolution in the South;* Cash, *The Mind of the South.* Morrison, *Wilbur J. Cash,* rejects both suppositions about Cash, preferring a medical explanation that Cash was depressed by a combination of illness and medicine at the time of his suicide.

15. James Tice Moore and Jonathan M. Wiener, addresses (Southern Historical Association, November 1979); Moore, "Redeemers Reconsidered"; Wiener, *Social Origins of the New South;* Degler, *Place over Time;* Roper, "Progress and History"; Billings, *Planters and the Making of a "New South";* Mandle, *The Roots of Black Poverty.*

16. Wiener, *Social Origins of the New South;* Moore, *Social Origins of Dictatorship and Democracy.*

17. Wiener, *Social Origins of the New South.* Schorske, *German Social Democracy,* is especially useful for a discussion of class conflict in early modern Germany.

18. Carlton, *Mill and Town in South Carolina;* Steven Hahn and Barbara Jeanne Fields, addresses (Southern Historical Association, November 1982).

19. Degler, *Place over Time;* Bloch, *French Rural History;* Cobb, *Industrialization and Southern Society;* Mandle, *The Roots of Black Poverty.*

20. Gaston, *The New South Creed;* Hackney, "*Origins of the New South* in Retrospect."

21. Green, "Interview with Vann Woodward" (Green, a Marxist student of radicalism in the Southwest, studied under Woodward and interviewed him in July 1983, at which time Green was kind enough to share the typescript with the author); Buck, *Road to Reunion.*

22. Woodward, *Origins of the New South;* idem, *Reunion and Reaction.*

23. Woodward, *Reunion and Reaction.*

24. Blum et al., *The National Experience,* 2:416–22.

25. Peskin, "Was There a Compromise of 1877?"; Woodward, "Communication: Yes, There Was a Compromise of 1877."

26. Benedict, "Southern Democrats in the Crisis of 1876–1877"; Polakoff, *The Politics of Inertia,* quotations from pp. 313, 319.

27. Gillette, *Retreat from Reconstruction;* Meier, "An Epitaph for the Writing of Reconstruction History?"

28. Woodward, *Origins of the New South;* Milton Friedman and Anna Jacobsen Schwartz, *A Monetary History of the United States, 1867–1960* (Princeton: Princeton University Press, 1963).

29. Woodward, *Origins of the New South.*

30. Ibid.

31. Cf. Cobb, *Industrialization and Southern Society;* Shaw, *The Wool-Hat Boys;* Hunt, "The Making of a Populist." See discussions in chapter 5 of their revisionist contributions to these debates concerning continuity and change in the postbellum New South.

32. Woodward, *Origins of the New South.* See also Williamson, *The Crucible of Race,* for convincing demonstrations that the southern elite was deeply involved in the most extreme Neogrophobic acts, specifically lynchings and paramilitary violence in the race riots of Wilmington, N.C., 1898, and Atlanta, 1906.

33. Hackney, *"Origins of the New South* in Retrospect."

34. Interviews: Woodward (18 and 19 July 1978).

35. Woodward to Rainey, 26 September 1951, Rainey Papers; Edwards, "Link Lattimore to Red Doctrine."

36. Woodward to Rainey, 26 September 1951, Rainey Papers; White, "McCarran Critical of Jessup Record"; idem, "Wallace Disowns 'Soft' China Policy"; "Three at Harvard Deny role as Pro-Reds"; "Jessup Is Accused as Red Party Liner." The IPR, although essentially a "think tank" of independent scholars, was employed to produce pamphlets of government propaganda during World War II; the pamphlets, distributed to soldiers and to schoolchildren, frequently dealt with the issue of the Russian allies and often took a rather naive approach to the Stalinists. By contrast, after the war members of the IPR were among the first to perceive that Communist China was very different from Communist Russia for reasons of cultural distinctiveness and that because of those differences and its own needs for national security, it might be unlikely to make common cause with the USSR in every issue; but this message, that the Red Chinese were not solidly in league with Moscow, was regarded as a pro-Communist subterfuge by the hard-line cold warriors.

37. "Full Text of Wallace Note to Truman"; Woodward to Rainey, 26 September 1951, Rainey Papers.

38. Interviews: Manning J. Dauer (21 July 1979), Bennett Harrison Wall (12 April 1979), LeRoy P. Graf (12 April 1979), John Hope Franklin (10 November 1978).

39. Interview: Dauer (21 July 1979); Woodward to Roper, 25 June 1981; Schwartz, ed., *The Unpublished Opinions of the Warren Court,* pp. 485–90 and passim.

40. Interview: William Samuel McFeely (4 December 1984).

41. Interviews: Woodward (18 and 19 July 1978), John Hope Franklin and Aurelia Franklin (10 November 1978), August Meier (20 April 1985), Meier to Roper, 17 June 1985 (amended typescript of interview, with eighteen pages of additional information) and 24 June 1985.

42. Bell Irvin Wiley to Roper, 27 November 1978; Meier to Roper, 24 June 1985.

43. Wiley to Roper, 27 November 1978; Meier to Roper, 24 June 1985; interview: John Hope Franklin and Aurelia Franklin (10 November 1978); Meier to Roper, 17 June 1985.

44. Wiley to Roper, 27 November 1978; Meier to Roper, 17 June 1985; interviews: Wall (12 April 1979), Graf (12 April 1979).

45. Cf. interview: John Hope Franklin (10 November 1978). Meier and Graf specifically recall dining with Franklin, in the company of other white historians, at the Williamsburg Inn; and after checking his own records of correspondence—noting, "If LeRoy Graf said it, it's right"—Franklin has found that he was permitted to dine at that restaurant with the white historians (Meier to Roper, 17 June 1985).

46. Interview: John Hope Franklin and Aurelia Franklin (10 November 1978).

47. Ibid.

48. Interviews: Wall (12 April 1979), Graf (12 April 1979). This address, "The Irony of Southern History," is discussed in detail in chapter 8.

49. Interviews: John Hope Franklin and Aurelia Franklin (10 November 1978), Woodward (18 July 1978).

50. Interview: Graf (12 April 1979).

51. Interview: Woodward (18 July 1978).

52. Ibid. Meier has pointed out that much work remained to be done before the SHA offered real service to the Negro historians, that Franklin at one point became so frustrated with lack of progress after his 1949 Williamsburg speech and after Woodward's Whittle Springs address that he declined to attend one conference (this recollection was independently corroborated by Bell Wiley in a note to Roper, 27 November 1978), and that the leadership of the SHA campaign passed to Meier, Zinn, and others partly because Woodward and Franklin became engaged with other issues. After 1952 these integrationists, none of whom was then prominent, often came from black colleges, and evidently several of them considered that they had litle to lose professionally by publicity about such activities (interview: Meier [20 April 1985]).

CHAPTER 7. *The Strange Career of Jim Crow, 1954–1955*

1. Kammen, *People of Paradox.*

2. Ransom and Sutch, *One Kind of Freedom.*

3. Pettigrew, *A Profile of the Negro American,* p. 10 and passim.

4. Ibid.; McNeil, *Groundwork;* Kellogg, *NAACP.*

5. Goldsmith, "The Traveller." The actual wording may be Samuel Johnson's.

6. Sumner, *Folkways and Mores;* Phillips, "The Central Theme of Southern History."

7. Woodward, *The Strange Career of Jim Crow.* Except where noted, the original edition is the source for this reading.

8. Ibid., pp. 111–12; for the striking imagery of the man on the cliff Woodward credits Maurice S. Evans, but much of the sense of "engulfment" and many of these themes are from Paton, *Cry, the Beloved Country;* and idem, "The Grave Problem of South Africa." Scholarly treatments following the same line, but with more subtlety, are Fredrickson, *White Supremacy;* and Cell, *The Highest Stage of White Supremacy.*

9. The anecdote was repeated at the PEN Conference, Moscow, 1985.

10. Wharton, *The Negro in Mississippi;* Tindall, *South Carolina Negroes.*

11. Interviews: Woodward (18 and 19 July 1978), J. Carlyle Sitterson (10 November 1978). It should be marked that Fletcher Green significantly modified his views toward segregation and integration, but not while Wharton was a student at Chapel Hill.

12. Simkins and Woody, *South Carolina during Reconstruction.*

13. Wharton, *The Negro in Mississippi,* pp. 274–75.

14. Interviews: Woodward (15 November 1979, 11 November 1982); Allport, *The Nature of Prejudice;* Lorenz, *On Aggression.*

15. Lorenz, *On Aggression.*

16. Allport, *ABC's of Scapegoating,* p. 5.

17. Ibid., pp. 9, 13.

18. Woodward to Roper, 6 September 1979.

19. Woodward, "The South in Search of a Philosophy," p. 14.

20. Woodward, *The Strange Career of Jim Crow,* p. 45.

21. Ibid., p. 45.

22. Ibid., pp. 47–59.

23. Ibid., pp. 60–65.

24. Interview: William G. Carleton (21 July 1979).

25. Woodward, *The Strange Career of Jim Crow,* pp. 44–47.

26. Interview: John Hope Franklin (10 November 1978).

27. Interview: Woodward (19 July 1978).

28. Interview: Joel Randolph Williamson (12 April 1977).

29. Carleton to Woodward, [1955?], carbon in possession of Manning J. Dauer and used here with his permission; interview: Woodward (19 July 1978).

30. Cf. Woodward, *The Strange Career of Jim Crow,* 3d rev. ed. (1974); while the 1957 and the 1968 revised editions are essentially unchanged from the 1955 edition, this 1974 revision includes as a new concluding chapter a brilliant and very useful summary of the modern civil rights movement since the Voting Rights Act of 1965 (pp. 189–220).

31. Williamson, *After Slavery;* idem, *Origins of Segregation;* idem, "The Strange Career of *The Strange Career of Jim Crow*," (Graduate History Student Association,

University of South Carolina, 1970); idem, *The Crucible of Race,* especially preface; interview: Williamson (12 April 1977); Woodward, "The Strange Career of a Historical Controversy"; interview: Woodward (19 July 1978).

32. Interview: John Hope Franklin (10 November 1978: Franklin tells an especially charming story of taking the then-graduate student Rabinowitz to the manuscript collections at Duke University and at the University of North Carolina, in the process instructing him at several levels about the meaning and the methods of Woodward's thesis); Rabinowitz, *Race Relations in the Urban South,* pp. 133–97, 125. See Woodward, Review of *Race Relations in the Urban South.*

33. Fredrickson, *White Supremacy;* Cell, *The Highest Stage of White Supremacy;* Rabinowitz, "The Not-So-Strange Career of Jim Crow."

34. On Woodward's attitudes since 1968 and for the King quotation, see interviews: Woodward. Cf. interviews: William Samuel McFeely (4 December 1984; McFeely was glad to see the "Tory Period" end), Jack R. Pole (10 November 1983; Pole was concerned about the quality of Woodward's works "of political enthusiasm," such as the Tom Watson biography or *The Strange Career of Jim Crow*).

35. On pertinence and impertinence in intellectual development, see Adler, *The Paideia Proposal.*

36. Ellison, *Going to the Territory;* Genovese, *Roll, Jordan, Roll;* Litwack, *Been in the Storm So Long;* Wood, *Black Majority;* Joyner, *Down by the Riverside;* Faulkner, *Absalom, Absalom!* p. 139.

37. Murray, *South to a Very Old Place,* pp. 16–26.

CHAPTER 8. *The Burden of Southern History, 1955–1965*

1. Lewis, "The Civil Rights Movement"; idem, *King;* Brooks, "Irony as a Principle of Structure"; idem, *The Well-Wrought Urn;* Alvarez, "The Noble Poet."

2. The periodization given here simply states the obvious; each of the phases of Woodward's march toward disbelief likely began earlier than the date given. Hall, "Woodward"; *Oracle* (student newspaper), 1926–27, on file in Alumni House, Henderson State College, Arkadelphia (this newspaper indicates that Woodward was still active in attending Sunday School classes taught by his favorite Henderson-Brown teachers); interviews: Boulware Martin Ohls (18 March 1984), Julia Hall (19 March 1984), Glenn Weddington Rainey (25 and 27 March 1980), Woodward (18 July 1978); Auden, "Homage to Clio"; Jefferson, *Writings,* 10:157–58.

3. Niebuhr, *The Children of Light,* pp. 18–19.

4. On the intellectual, as opposed to the personal, influence, see Woodward, *Thinking Back,* pp. 105–10, 137.

5. Ibid.; Niebuhr, *The Children of Light;* idem, *The Irony of American History.*

6. Brooks, "Irony as a Principle of Structure," p. 738.

7. Brooks, *The Well-Wrought Urn,* p. 102; idem, "Irony as a Principle of Structure," p. 738. Alvarez, in "The Noble Poet," says that the "nobility" of the ironist lies in his status as the "enemy of delusion."

8. Hughes, *The Sea Change* (for the concept "sea change," from Shakespeare's phrase); Voegelin, *Order and History.*

9. Voegelin, *Order and History,* vol. 1, *Israel and Revelation,* pp. xiv, 144, 345, vol. 2, *The World of the Polis,* pp. 1, 3, 7. The literary critic Thomas McHaney was kind enough to point out the influence which Voegelin exercised over Brooks and Warren, (interview: McHaney [16 September 1985]).

10. Warren, "William Faulkner," p. 467; note that Warren's article originally appeared in two successive installments in *The New Republic* during 1946. The lines of Warren's argument and even his language are strikingly parallel to Voegelin's: see *The World of the Polis,* pp. 1, 3, 7. On Warren's ironic style and interest in history, see Graziano, *Homage to Robert Penn Warren,* passim, but especially, on his "fires of irony," Smith, "Notes on a Form to Be Lived," and Brooks, "Being Here."

11. Brooks, "Irony as a Principle of Structure," p. 741; interview: Ralph Henry Gabriel (13 March 1975). Gabriel was instrumental in bringing Phillips to Yale and was also involved in bringing Woodward to Yale; cf. interview: Woodward (11 November 1982, concerning the decision to go to Yale).

12. Woodward, "The Irony of Southern History," pp. 3–6.

13. Ibid.

14. Ibid., pp. 3–8 and passim.

15. Ibid., passim. Cf. Buckley, *McCarthy and His Enemies.*

16. Woodward, "The Irony of Southen History," p. 7.

17. Ibid.; Niebuhr, *The Irony of American History.* Cf. Woodward, *Thinking Back,* pp. 106–10.

18. Woodward to Rainey, 25 March 1952, Rainey Papers; interviews: Woodward (18 July 1978), Rainey (16 November 1979, 25 March 1980); Woodward, "A Southern Critique for the Gilded Age" (this essay, like others from *The Burden of Southern History,* is cited from the 1968 ed.).

19. Woodward, "Southern Critique," pp. 111–13, 116.

20. Ibid., pp. 123, 125, 128; Adams, *The Education of Henry Adams;* idem, *Mont-Saint-Michel and Chartres.* Cf. Woodward, "History with Compassion and Contempt," review of Library of America reprint edition of Henry Adams, *History of the United States of America during the Administrations of Thomas Jefferson, New York Times Book Review,* 6 July 1986, pp. 3, 19.

21. Woodward, "Southern Critique," pp. 132–33.

22. Ibid., p. 140.

23. Woodward, "John Brown's Private War," in *The Burden of Southern History,* pp. 41–68.

24. Ibid., pp. 48, 49, 66, 68.

25. Woodward, "Equality: The Deferred Commitment," in *The Burden of Southern History,* pp. 69–88; idem, "The Political Legacy of Reconstruction," in ibid., pp. 89–108.

26. Woodward, "The Political Legacy of Reconstruction," p. 97. Cf. Parrington, *Main Currents in American Thought,* vol. 3, *The Beginnings of Critical Realism,* pp. 23–47.

27. Woodward, "The Political Legacy of Reconstruction," p. 100.

28. Ibid., p. 79.

29. Ibid., pp. 84–86.

30. Woodward, "The Populist Heritage," in *The Burden of Southern History,* pp. 141–66; Parrington, *Main Currents in American Thought,* 3:259–88; Hicks, *The Populist Revolt;* Hostadter, *The Age of Reform;* Bell, *The New American Right,* with essays by Hofstadter, Peter Viereck, Talcott Parsons, and Seymour Martin Lipset.

31. The words are Peter Viereck's in *The Unadjusted Man.*

32. Woodward, "The Populist Heritage," pp. 141–66.

33. Ibid., p. 166.

34. Tindall, "Populism"; Durden, "The Cowbird Grounded."

35. Woodward, "A Southerner's Answer"; idem, "From the First Reconstruction," in *The Burden of Southern History,* pp. 127–33.

36. Cf. Hofstadter, *The Age of Reform,* pp. 23–59, 148–73.

37. Woodward, "A Southerner's Answer," p. 41.

38. Ibid., p. 44.

39. Ibid., passim.

40. Ibid., p. 41.

41. Woodward, *A Southern Prophecy;* interviews: William G. Carleton (21 July 1979), William Samuel McFeely (4 December 1984). Carleton and McFeely emphasize Woodward's optimism and enthusiasm about Johnson's programs during the first year of the Great Society.

42. Woodward, "From the First Reconstruction." Note the influence of this perspective in Brauer, *John F. Kennedy.*

43. Woodward, "From the First Reconstruction," pp. 129–31.

44. Phillips, "The Central Theme of Southern History"; Zinn, *The Southern Mystique;* August Meier to Roper, 17 June 1985; Warren, *The Legacy of the Civil War.*

45. Woodward, "From the First Reconstruction," p. 133.

46. Interview: Woodward (18 July 1978); Woodward to Roper, 6 September 1977; interview: Jack R. Pole (11 November 1983).

47. Richard L. Wentworth to Roper, 22 June 1984, with enclosure from William S. McFeely; interview: McFeely (4–6 December 1984).

CHAPTER 9. *Irony in a Centrifuge, 1965–1974*

1. Interviews: William G. Carleton (21 July 1979), Woodward (18 July 1978); Woodward to Roper, 6 September 1977. Cf. Butterfield, *The Whig Interpretation of History,* which makes the telling point that the Whig historians' presentist fascination with the "winners," that is, with the liberal philosophy of emergent Protestantism and capitalism, has caused such historiography to neglect the achievements of the "losers," those who stood against the forces which ultimately prevailed. Woodward likely avoided this particular fault of liberal presentism, although he still fell prey to other dangers inherent in this perspective.

2. Alvarez, "The Noble Poet." This is a question of the subtleties of tone, and few people, either in writing or in conversation, are as subtle of tone as Woodward, who is, in any case, seldom harsh in criticism. Note, however, the evasiveness and overly clever character of his responses to basic questions raised by Joel Randolph Williamson, by David Herbert Donald, and by neo-abolitionist critics: "The Strange Career of a Historical Controversy"; "W. J. Cash Reconsidered"; remarks at the University of South Carolina Conference on *Time on the Cross,* 2 November 1974; and "The Future of Southern History."

3. Interview: William Samuel McFeely (4 December 1984).

4. Interviews: Woodward (11 November 1982), John Morton Blum (13 December 1984); Woodward to Rainey, 4 December 1963, Rainey Papers.

5. Interviews: Woodward (11 November 1982), McFeely (4 December 1984).

6. Interview: Woodward (18 July 1978); Hall, "Woodward." Hall was able to interview a number of Woodward's former Yale students, most of whom remember him as a poor lecturer and poor leader of seminar discussions but as a stimulating and painstaking director of their dissertations; above all else, the students with whom Hall talked recall struggling to meet the highest possible standards of scholarly rigor.

7. Interviews: Woodward (18 and 19 July 1978, 20 June 1983, 14 December 1984).

8. Interview: Blum (13 December 1984).

9. Interview: Manning J. Dauer (21 July 1979); Richard Wentworth to Roper, [?] June 1984, with enclosure (William Samuel McFeely to Wentworth [1984], in possession of author); interview: McFeely (4–5 December 1984).

10. Interview: McFeely (4–5 December 1984); Santayana, *The Last Puritan,* p. 177.

11. Interview: Woodward (19 July 1978).

12. The New Haven novel was written by Helen Lane, wife of a political scientist at Yale University; now out of print, it was widely read by Yale students and faculty members, who could recognize their colleagues thinly disguised among the story's characters (interviews: Joseph A. Herzenberg [15 June 1983], McFeely [4–5 December 1984]). Potter's desire to go to Stanford University was

both professional—because of the marvelous opportunity there—and also personal, as he revealed to long-time friend Mabel Phillips Parker, daughter of his teacher Ulrich Bonnell Phillips (interview: Parker [14 July 1974, 9–10 December 1984]); in possession of author]); Potter shared similar expressions of sadness and dissatisfaction with his colleague Blum (interview: Blum [13 December 1984]). See also Potter, *People of Plenty;* idem, *The South and the Sectional Conflict.*

13. Potter, "Historical Development of Eastern-Southern Freight Rates Relationships"; idem, *The South and the Sectional Conflict,* p. 11; interview: Woodward (19 July 1978); Plutarch, *Plutarch's Lives,* vol. 3.

14. Hofstadter, *The Age of Reform;* idem, *The Progressive Historians;* interviews: Woodward (19 July 1978), Jack R. Pole (10 November 1983).

15. Woodward, "A Short History of American History"; interview: Woodward (11 November 1982).

16. Bickel, *Politics and the Warren Court;* interview: Woodward (19 July 1978); Joanne Bickel to Roper, 15 August 1984.

17. Interviews: Woodward (18 and 19 July 1978, 11 November 1982, 9–10 November 1983), McFeely (4–5 December 1984); Hall, "Woodward."

18. Interview: Woodward (19 July 1978).

19. Ibid.; interviews: Dauer (21 July 1979), Carleton (21 July 1979); Woodward, review of *Lyndon,* by Merle Miller.

20. Interviews: Dauer (21 July 1979), Carleton (21 July 1979).

21. Halberstam, *The Best and the Brightest,* interviews: Dauer (21 July 1979), Carleton (21 July 1979).

22. Interviews: Dauer (21 July 1979), Carleton (21 July 1979); Fulbright, *The Arrogance of Power,* pp. 3–5.

23. Fulbright to Roper, 25 May 1982, in possession of author; interviews: Woodward (18 and 19 July 1978), Fulbright (21 March 1983).

24. Woodward to Rainey, 4 October 1966, Rainey Papers; interviews: Dauer (21 July 1979), Carleton (21 July 1979); Woodward, *The Strange Career of Jim Crow,* pp. 189–220 (3d rev. ed.): despite these flaws in his reading of separatism and pan-Africanism, this added chapter was essentially wise and judicious and has remained very useful as an overview for students of the movement.

25. Carson, *In Struggle;* on pan-Africanism, see also Clarke, *Marcus Garvey.*

26. Thornton, "The Civil Rights Movement." Cf. remarks by Carson, William Chafe, David Levering Lewis, Nancy Weiss, and David Garrow in Eagles, ed., *The Civil Rights Movement;* Kammen, *People of Paradox;* Thurow, *The Zero-Sum Society.*

27. Woodward to Rainey, 4 October 1966, Rainey Papers.

28. Virgil, *The Aeneid,* p. 360.

29. Schorske, *Fin-de-Siècle Vienna,* pp. xxiv, xxiii.

30. Woodward explained Curtin's *The Atlantic Slave Trade,* with a full histo-

riographical and cultural interpretation which Curtin himself had not then attempted, before law and history students at the Yale University School of Law (interview: Woodward [4–5 December 1984]); subsequent to this lecture, Woodward's *American Counterpoint* included a chapter, "Southern Slaves in the World of Thomas Malthus," which developed Curtin's, and other demographers', insights much more fully. Cf. Jordan, *White over Black;* Woodward, review of *White over Black.*

31. Interview: Woodward (19 July 1978).

32. Woodward, Introduction to *American Counterpoint,* pp. 3–11.

33. Ibid., pp. 3–11. See also idem, "The North and South of It."

34. Woodward, Introduction to *American Counterpoint,* pp. 3–11.

35. Woodward, "The Elusive Mind of the South."

36. Ibid.

37. Cf. Jordan, *White over Black;* Williamson, *The Crucible of Race.*

38. Woodward, "The Northern Crusade against Slavery," in *American Counterpoint,* pp. 140–62; idem, "Seeds of Failure in Radical Race Policy," in ibid., pp. 163–83; idem, "The Strange Career of a Historical Controversy."

39. Woodward, "Southern Slaves in the World of Thomas Malthus"; interview: Dauer (21 July 1979); Fogel and Engerman, *Time on the Cross.* Fogel and Engerman were appearing at college campuses and research centers to share their controversial conclusions at least as early as 1973, and they had shared early drafts of the manuscript with many scholars before 1973.

40. Woodward, "Protestant Slavery in a Catholic World," pp. 69, 76–77.

41. Woodward, "The Southern Ethic in a Puritan World," in *American Counterpoint,* pp. 13–46, quotation from p. 30.

42. Woodward, "Clio with Soul."

43. Woodward, "The Future of the Past."

44. Woodward to Carleton and Dauer, 16 July 1972, in possession of Dauer and cited here with his permission; interview: Woodward (12 October 1980).

45. Woodward, "That Other Impeachment"; Woodward to Dauer, 24 October 1972 and 5 December 1973, both in possession of Dauer and cited here with his permission.

46. Woodward, *Responses of the Presidents,* p. xxvi.

47. On the development of such activist irony, see Woodward, "The Fall of the American Adam."

CHAPTER 10. *The Gift*

1. See chapter 2 for discussion of Woodward's turn away from radicalism in the year 1932; see also Buckley, interview with Morris Abram.

2. Woodward, "The Erosion of Academic Privileges."

3. Ibid. This entire issue of *Daedalus,* entitled "American Higher Education: Toward an Uncertain Future," is noteworthy: see especially Grabard, Preface; Frankel, "Reflections on a Worn-Out Model"; Gerschenkron, "The Legacies of Evil"; Ulam, "Where Do We Go From Here?" David E. Apter, "An Epitaph for the Revolutions That Failed." See Snow, *Appendix to Science and Government,* for a statement of the theme of the divorce between science and the humanities, a theme developed in many of Snow's novels.

4. Marcuse, *One Dimensional Man;* Woodward, "The Erosion of Academic Privileges"; interview: Woodward (14 December 1984).

5. Wolff, *The Poverty of Liberalism;* Woodward, "The Erosion of Academic Privileges"; interview: Woodward (14 December 1984).

6. Woodward, "The Erosion of Academic Privileges."

7. Ibid.; interview: Woodward (19 July 1978).

8. Woodward, "The Erosion of Academic Privileges"; interview: Woodward (19 July 1978); see Green, "Interview with Vann Woodward."

9. Epstein, in "A Reporter at Large (Black Panthers)," makes the point that with the awful exception of the police assassination of Freddie Hampton, there was no "police persecution" of the Panthers resulting in twenty-eight deaths, as claimed by Seale's lawyer Charles R. Garry—a claim accepted by the Urban League, the NAACP, the American Civil Liberties Union, the *New York Times,* and the *Washington Post.* Epstein, a legal investigative reporter, painstakingly reviewed each case of a Panther's death, finding most to have resulted from shootouts with police initiated by the Panthers. "Melee Puzzles Music-Arts School" describes the beating of a Jewish teacher by Panther youth. "Seale Asks Court to Authorize Goatee," despite its rather frivolous headline, is a substantive discussion of the efforts of Judge Harold M. Mulvey to ensure a fair trial and decent treatment for the accused Panther leader. For summaries of courtroom proceedings and rulings, see Oelsner, "Charges Dropped in the Seale Case"; idem, "Deadlock by Jury Results in Seale-Huggins Mistrial." On Brewster's statement, made at the 1971 baccalaureate address at Yale, see "Brewster Praises Trial Judge."

10. Murray, *South to a Very Old Place,* pp. 16–26; Green, "Interview with Vann Woodward"; Palmer, *Man over Money;* interviews: Woodward (4–5 November 1982, 19 July 1978).

11. Woodward to Rainey, 26 September 1951, Rainey Papers; interviews: Woodward (18 and 19 July 1978, 4–5 November 1982, 14 December 1984), Manning J. Dauer (21 July 1979).

12. Interviews: Woodward (14 December 1984 [citing Woodward's "Report on Freedom of Expression at Yale University," 1975], 4–5 November 1982). Woodward's "Report" is distilled and published for all undergraduates in *Undergraduate Regulations* (New Haven: Yale University, 1986–87), pp. 9–11. In fall 1986, Woodward was again embroiled in controversy, defending the right of a

student, Wayne Dick, to display on the Yale campus crude posters which belittled homosexuals during a gay rights and lesbian rights awareness week. Woodward deplored Dick's attitudes and expressions, but was even more upset by the action of the faculty and student tribunal which in academic year 1985–86 censured Dick by issuing a suspended sentence for violating the civil rights of minorities on the campus. When newly selected university president Benno Schmidt agreed to schedule an appeal in the fall term of academic year 1986–87, Woodward accepted the position of faculty counsel on the student's behalf. After winning this appeal, Woodward also published an opinion piece in the *New York Times* in which he again pounded home the themes of an absolute freedom of expression on university campuses. An interesting aspect of this dispute is that Schmidt is a legal scholar and jurist who was close to Woodward's friend Alexander Bickel; Woodward has noted that Schmidt delivered an address to the faculty in which he resoundingly upheld the concept of an unqualified and unambiguous freedom of expression on the campus. He has noted further that Schmidt rather conspicuously took Woodward to luncheon soon after the dispute was resolved. See also Woodward to Roper, 9 October 1986, with enclosures (Woodward, "Freedom of Speech, Not Selectivity"; Romanoff, "Woodward Defends Freedom of Speech"; idem, "Interview with Vann Woodward"; Schmidt, Address, Yale University Faculty.

13. Interviews: Woodward (4–5 November 1982), William Samuel McFeely (4–5 December 1984).

14. Interview: Woodward (4–5 November 1982).

15. Ibid.; interviews: Woodward (13 April 1979), John Morton Blum (13 December 1984), McFeely (4–5 December 1984).

16. Interviews: Woodward (4–5 November 1982, 13 April 1979), Blum (13 December 1984); Malcolm L. Call to Roper, 24 September 1984, with enclosures of letters in possession of Call and cited here with his permission (Call to Louis R. Harlan, 13 February 1974; Leone Stein to Herbert Aptheker, 12 February 1974; Woodward to Stein, 24 April 1974; Stein to Woodward, 19 April 1974; Memorandum Regarding National Advisory Board for the Press Du Bois Series to Randolph Bromery from Call, 2 April 1974; Memorandum Regarding Du Bois Series to "File" from Stein, 13 March 1974); "Yale University and Dr. Herbert Aptheker"; Aptheker, "Comment on the Report of the Joint AHA-OAH Committee." Cf. Brookhiser, "Aptheker and Samarin at Yale."

17. Call to Roper, with enclosures cited in preceding note. On the nature of Du Bois's idealism, especially concerning his "Hegelian Phase" and its influence on all of us, cf. Williamson, *The Crucible of Race,* pp. 397–413.

18. Interviews: Woodward (4–5 November 1982, 13 April 1979), Blum (13 December 1984); "Yale University and Dr. Herbert Aptheker."

19. "Interviews: Woodward (4–5 November 1982, 13 April 1979).

20. Ibid. See Green, "Interview with Vann Woodward": this interview demon-

strates the complexities both of Woodward's later views of Marxism and of his long relationships with Genovese and with Aptheker. Woodward attended the 1966 Socialist Scholars' Conference and saw Genovese "waving [figuratively] the flag of black nationalism"; but such a focus on one group and on the phenomenon of nationalism was inherently antagonistic to the internalism and holism of most Marxist thought, even as its separatist tendencies offended Woodward's integrationist values. Woodward himself, after conferring with Aptheker, then "read the platform of the Communist Party denouncing black nationalism"! As usual, he plainly enjoyed the confrontation and the discussions; and he especially enjoyed "scoring one on Gene." However, Woodward's long-running relationship with Genovese has been both personally warm and professionally supportive.

21. "Yale University and Dr. Herbert Aptheker."

22. Henry A. Turner to Roper, 2 March 1983, with enclosure from *Yale Alumni Magazine,* February 1984, pp. 10, 52–53; interviews: Woodward (4–5 November 1982, 13 April 1979, 13 December 1984), Aptheker (23 March 1985); Herbert W. Gstalder to Roper, 28 June 1985, with enclosures (Gstalder to Henry Turner, 2 March 1978 [machine copy], and Settlement Agreement, Paul G. Partington and Kraus-Thomson Organization, Ltd. [machine copy], 22 September 1977). Gstalder also made available to the author the complete files on the Partington case, the offer earlier made to Turner: Partington Files, 1963–78, Kraus-Thomson Organization, Ltd., White Plains, N.Y. A summary of notes from the extensive correspondence and documents is provided in Roper Papers.

23. Turner to Roper, 2 March 1983, with enclosure from *Yale Alumni Magazine;* interview: Gstalder (26 June 1986); notes on Partington agreements, 3 May and 21 September 1971, Roper Papers.

24. Interview: Aptheker (23 March 1985); Aptheker to Roper, 1 and 16 July 1985.

25. Aptheker to Roper, 16 July 1985; interviews: Woodward (4–5 November 1982, 13 December 1984), Blum (13 December 1984). See discussion of the Herndon case in chapter 3.

26. Turner, *George W. Cable;* Cable, *The Negro Question,* citing speeches and essays from 1877–90. See also Rubin, *George W. Cable.*

27. Turner, *George W. Cable,* pp. 208–26; Woodward, *The Strange Career of Jim Crow;* interview: Don Edwards (22 March 1983).

28. Proust, *Remembrance of Things Past,* 3:1000–1001.

29. Ibid., pp. 957, 999.

30. House Committee on the Judiciary, *Extension of the Voting Rights Act: Hearing,* pp. 1999–2028 (hereinafter cited as *Hearing,* 1981); Woodward to Roper, 25 June 1981.

31. "Late and Limp on Voting Rights"; interview: staffers of House Committee on the Judiciary (22 March 1983); Roper, "Essay on the Voting Rights Extension Act."

32. Interviews: Don Edwards (22 March 1983), staffers of House Committee on the Judiciary (22 March 1983); *Hearing,* 1981, pp. 1999–2001; Woodward to Roper, 25 June 1981; Paul Zingg to Roper, 21 June 1984, with enclosure (Woodward, "Times of Trouble").

33. *Hearing,* 1981, pp. 1999–2001.

34. Ibid., p. 2001.

35. Ibid., pp. 2001–3; interview: Woodward (12 October 1980).

36. *Hearing,* 1981, p. 2027.

37. Interview: Don Edwards (22 March 1983); Roper, "Essay on the Voting Rights Extension," p. 196. Woodward by no means left the public stage of such controversies after this incident: see his protest of Reagan policies in the Caribbean, "Correspondence from Contributors," *New Republic.*

38. Interview: Woodward (4–5 November 1982).

39. Woodward, "The Fall of the American Adam," p. 24.

40. Ibid., pp. 27, 28.

41. Ibid., pp. 31–32.

42. Ibid., p. 33.

43. Quoted in ibid., p. 34.

44. Woodward, *Oxford History,* vol. 2, *The Revolutionary War,* by Robert Middlekauff.

45. Woodward, "A Short History of American History," pp. 3, 14.

46. Ibid. See also Starr, "Historian Says History Is an Extension of One's Memory," a record of an interview with Woodward on these subjects.

47. Woodward, *Mary Chesnut's Civil War;* Munger, Review of *Mary Chesnut's Civil War;* Williams, *Diary from Dixie;* Martin and Avary, *Diary from Dixie.*

48. Interview: William G. Carleton (21 July 1979).

49. Munger, Review of *Mary Chesnut's Civil War.* See also notes from conference of Organization of American Historians, filed with interview: Woodward (13 April 1979).

50. Munger, Review of *Mary Chesnut's Civil War.*

51. Ibid.

52. Ibid.; Woodward, *Mary Chesnut's Civil War.*

53. Degler, Review of *Mary Chesnut's Civil War;* Lynn, Review of *Mary Chesnut's Civil War;* Johnson, "Mary Boykin Chesnut's Autobiography and Biography."

54. "Sessions, Sylvia Plath, and Updike"; M. J. Dubis to Roper, 26 January 1983, with enclosure ("Poses Commemoration," in possession of author); Woodward, "Communication," *Journal of Southern History.*

55. See all interviews: Woodward (1977–84): a subtheme running through these sessions is that Woodward expresses the opinion that his life and career are not important enough to warrant a historiographical study; yet the same sessions usually involve discussions of recent criticism of his work, and in his responses to the criticism, he is usually both well informed and careful to defend his own

works. See also Woodward, Introduction to *Life and Labor in the Old South,* by Ulrich Bonnell Phillips.

56. See interview: Woodward (4–5 November 1982), for description of the rather strenuous schedule which Woodward keeps at a conference. See also Woodward to Roper, 4 April and 22 July 1986.

57. Ann Firor Scott quoted Flannery O'Connor's remark about William Faulkner being "the Dixie Express comin' through" in comments on Woodward, "What Happened to the Diary of Mary Boykin Chesnut?"

58. Woodward, *Thinking Back,* pp. 73–75. See also notes filed with interview: Woodward (4–5 November 1982), to see how consistently he has worked with the same themes in defense of his work.

59. Interview: Woodward (4–5 November 1982). Cf. Williamson, *The Crucible of Race;* Degler, *Place over Time;* Wiener, *Social Origins of the New South;* Billings, *Planters and the Making of a "New South";* Cobb, *Industrialization and Southern Society.*

60. See lists of Woodward graduate students in appendixes A and B. On Green's and Adams's graduate students, see Stephenson, *Southern History in the Making,* pp. 24–25.

61. Kousser and McPherson, *Region, Race, and Reconstruction;* interview: William Samuel McFeely (4–5 December 1984).

Bibliography

The Writings of Comer Vann Woodward

BOOKS

Ed. *After the War: A Tour of the Southern States, 1865–1866,* by Whitelaw Reid.
  1866. Reprint. New York: Peter Smith, 1965.
American Attitudes toward History. Oxford: Clarendon Press, 1955.
American Counterpoint: Slavery and Racism in the North-South Dialogue. Boston:
  Little, Brown, 1971. 2d ed., 1983.
The Battle for Leyte Gulf. New York: Macmillan, 1947. Reprint. New York:
  Norton, 1965.
*The Bougainville Landing and the Battle of Empress Augusta Bay, 27 October–2
  November 1943.* Restricted distribution. Washington, D.C.: U.S.
  Government Printing Office, n.d. [ca. 1947].
The Burden of Southern History. Baton Rouge: Louisiana State University Press,
  1960. Rev. ed., 1968.
Ed. *Cannibals All! or, Slaves without Masters,* by George Fitzhugh. 1857.
  Reprint. Cambridge: Harvard University Press, 1960.
The Civil Rights Movement Re-examined: Three Essays, with Paul Feldman and
  Bayard Rustin. New York: A. Phillip Randolph Education Fund, n.d. [ca.
  1956].
Ed. *The Comparative Approach to American History.* New York: Basic Books,
  1968.
Kolombangara and Vella Lavella, 6 August–7 October, 1943. Restricted
  distribution. Washington, D.C.: U.S. Government Printing Office, n.d. [ca.
  1947].
Ed. *Mary Chesnut's Civil War.* New Haven: Yale University Press, 1981.
The National Experience: A History of the United States, with John Morton Blum,
  Edmund Sears Morgan, Willie Lee Rose, Arthur Meier Schlesinger, Jr., and
  Kenneth Milton Stampp. New York: Harcourt Brace Jovanovich, 1963. Rev.
  ed., 1968. 2d rev. ed., 1977. 3d rev. ed., 4th rev. ed., 1981. 5th rev. ed.,
  1984. 6th rev. ed., 1985.

Origins of the New South, 1877–1913. Volume 9 of *The History of the South,* edited by Ellis Merton Coulter and Wendell Holmes Stephenson. Baton Rouge: Louisiana State University Press, 1951. 2d ed. with revised bibliographic essay by Charles B. Dew, 1971.

Ed. *Oxford History of the United States.* Vol. 1 and 2. New York: Oxford University Press, 1982, 1983.

Ed. *The Private Mary Chesnut: The Unpublished Civil War Diaries.* New Haven: Yale University Press, 1984.

Ed. *Responses of the Presidents to Charges of Misconduct.* New York: Delacorte, 1974.

Reunion and Reaction: The Compromise of 1877 and the End of Reconstruction. Boston: Little, Brown, 1951. Rev. ed., Garden City, N.Y.: Doubleday, 1956.

Ed. *A Southern Prophecy: The Prosperity of the South Dependent upon the Elevation of the Negro,* by Lewis Harvie Blair. Boston: Little, Brown, 1964.

The Strange Career of Jim Crow. New York: Oxford University Press, 1955. Rev. ed., 1957. 2d rev. ed., 1966. 3d rev. ed., 1974.

Thinking Back: The Perils of Writing History. Baton Rouge: Louisiana State University Press, 1985.

Tom Watson: Agrarian Rebel. New York: Macmillan, 1938.

ARTICLES AND ADDRESSES

"After Watts—Where Is the Negro Revolution Headed?" *New York Times Magazine,* 29 August 1965, pp. 24–25, 81–89.

"The Age of Reinterpretation." *American Historical Review* 66 (1960): 1–19.

"American Attitudes toward History: An Inaugural Lecture Delivered before the University of Oxford." 22 February 1955.

"American History (White Man's Version) Needs an Infusion of Soul." *New York Times Magazine,* 20 April 1969, pp. 32–33, 108–14.

"The Antislavery Myth." *American Scholar* 31 (1962): 312–28.

"Bourbonism in Georgia." Address, Southern Historical Association, Durham, N.C., 1937. *North Carolina Historical Review* 16 (1939): 23–35.

"Can We Believe Our Own History?" *Johns Hopkins Magazine* 5 (1954): 1–6, 16.

"The Case of the Louisiana Traveler (Plessy v. Ferguson, 163 U.S. 537)." In *Quarrels That Have Shaped the Constitution,* edited by John Arthur Garraty, pp. 135–58. New York: Harper and Row, 1964.

"Clio with Soul." *Journal of American History* 56 (1969): 5–20.

"Collapse of Activism: What Became of the 1960's?" *New Republic,* 9 November 1974, pp. 18–25.

"Comment: What Is a Liberal—Who Is a Conservative? A Symposium." *Commentary* 62 (1976): 110–11.

"Comment on Eugene D. Genovese, 'The Legacy of Slavery and the Roots of Black Nationalism.'" *Studies on the Left* 6 (1966): 35–43.

"Comments by Writers and Scholars on Books of the Past Ten Years." *American Scholar* 24 (1965): 492.

"Communication." *Journal of Southern History* 48 (1982): 160.

"Communication: Yes, There Was a Compromise of 1877." *Journal of American History* 60 (1973): 215–23. Reply to Allan Peskin, "Was There a Compromise of 1877?" *Journal of American History* 60 (1973): 63–75.

"The Comparability of American History." In *The Comparative Approach to American History,* edited by Woodward, pp. 3–17. New York: Basic Books, 1968.

"Confessions of a Rebel: 1831." *New Republic,* 7 October 1967, pp. 25–28. Reprinted in *The Nat Turner Rebellion: The Historical Event and the Modern Controversy,* edited by John B. Duff and Peter M. Mitchell, pp. 168–73. New York: Harper and Row, 1971.

"Correspondence." *Commentary* 25 (1958): 76.

"Correspondence from Contributors." *New Republic,* 14 April 1986, pp. 4, 41.

"Defending Liberalism." *Daily Tar Heel* (Chapel Hill), February 193[6?]. Clipping in Glenn Weddington Rainey Papers. Manuscript Division. Emory University Library, Atlanta.

"The Disturbed Southerners." *Current History* 32 (1957): 278–82.

"The Elusive Mind of the South." *New York Review of Books,* 4 December 1969. Reprinted with revisions in *American Counterpoint,* pp. 261–83, q.v.

"Emancipations and Reconstructions: A Comparative Study." In *XIII International Congress of Historical studies, Moscow.* 1970. Reprint. Moscow: Navka Publishing, 1970.

"Emory Landlubber Goes to Sea." *Atlanta Journal,* 8 September 1929, p. 7.

"Equality: America's Deferred Commitment." *American Scholar* 27 (1958): 459–72. Reprinted in *The Burden of Southern History,* pp. 69–88 (rev. ed.), q.v.

"The Erosion of Academic Privileges and Immunities." *Daedalus,* 103 (1974): 33–37.

"An Expert Pick of the Pack." *New York Times Book Review,* 5 December 1965, pp. 5, 52–54.

"The Fall of the American Adam." *American Academy of Arts and Sciences Bulletin* 35 (1981): 24–33.

"Flight from History: The Heritage of the Negro." *Nation,* 20 September 1965, pp. 142–46. Reprinted in *The State of the Nation,* edited by David Boroff, pp. 174–82. Englewood Cliffs, N.J.: Prentice-Hall, 1965.

Foreword to *France and England in North America,* vol. 1, by Francis Parkman. Edited by David Levin. New York: Library of America, 1984.

Foreword to *Mary Boykin Chesnut: A Biography,* by Elizabeth Muhlenfeld. Baton Rouge: Louisiana State University Press, 1981.

Foreword to *Southern Negroes,* by Bell Irvin Wiley. 1938. Reprint. New Haven: Yale University Press, 1965.

"Fortenbraugh Lecture on the American Character." Robert Fortenbraugh Memorial Lecture, Gettysburg, Pa., 1981.

"Freedom of Speech, Not Selectivity." *New York Times,* 15 October 1986, sec. A, p. 27.

"From the First Reconstruction to the Second." *Harper's,* April 1965, pp. 126–33. Reprinted in *The Burden of Southern History,* pp. 127–33 (rev. ed.), q.v.

"The Future of Southern History." In *The Future of History: Essays in the Vanderbilt University Centennial Symposium,* edited by Charles F. Delzell, pp. 135–50. Nashville: Vanderbilt University Press, 1977.

"The Future of the Past." *American Historical Review* 75 (1970): 711–26.

"The Ghost of Populism Walks Again." *New York Times Magazine,* 4 June 1972, pp. 16–17, 60–69.

"The Graying of America: Reflections upon Our Most Enduring National Myth as We Put the Bicentennial Behind Us, and Move On." *New York Times,* 29 December 1976, p. 25.

"The Great Civil Rights Debate: The Ghost of Thaddeus Stevens in the Senate Chamber." *Commentary* 24 (1957): 283–91.

"The Hidden Sources of Negro History." *Saturday Review,* 18 January 1969, pp. 18–22.

"Hillbilly Realism." *Southern Review* 4 (1939): 676–81.

"The Historian's Verdict on the Johnson Years." *Newsweek,* 20 January 1969, p. 19.

"The Historical Dimension." *Virginia Quarterly Review* 32 (1956): 258–67.

"History and the Third Culture." *Journal of Contemporary History* 3 (1968): 23–35.

"History from Slave Sources." *American Historical Review* 79 (1974): 470–81.

Introduction to *Life and Labor in the Old South,* by Ulrich Bonnell Phillips. Boston: Little, Brown, 1963.

Introduction to *Rehearsal for Reconstruction: The Port Royal Experiment,* by Willie Lee Rose. Indianapolis: Bobbs-Merrill, 1964.

"The Irony of Southern History." *Journal of Southern History* 19 (1953): 3–19.

"Jefferson Memorial Address on the National Character." National Endowment for the Humanities Lecture, Washington, D.C., 1978.

"John Brown's Private War." In *America in Crisis,* edited by Daniel Aaron, pp. 109–32. New York: Knopf, 1952. Reprinted in *The Burden of Southern History,* pp. 41–68 (rev. ed.), q.v.

"The Jolly Institution." *New York Review of Books,* 2 May 1974, pp. 3–6.

"Letter." *New York Review of Books*, 7 February 1980, p. 53.

"Letter: Academic Freedom: Whose Story," with Edmund Sears Morgan. *Columbia University Forum* 11 (1968): 42–43.

"Letter: Adam Clayton Powell as Symbol." *New York Times*, 18 January 1967, p. 42.

"Letter: Concern for Cambodia and Campus," with Felix Gilbert, Richard Hofstadter, H. Stuart Hughes, Leonard Krieger, Fritz Stern, and Gordon Wright. *New York Times*, 10 May 1970, sec. 4, p. 17.

"Letter: Indignity at Princeton's Institute for Advanced Study." *New York Times*, 13 March 1973, p. 38.

"Letter: On David Donald's 'Radical Historians on the Move.'" *New York Times Book Review*, 30 August 1970, p. 22.

"Letter: On Forestalling Watergates." *New York Times*, 26 June 1975, p. 38.

"Letter: Scottsboro: A Reply." *New York Times Book Review*, 22 June 1969, p. 34.

"Letter: Time on the Cross, A Reply." *New York Review of Books*, 13 June 1974, p. 41.

"The Lowest Ebb." *American Heritage* 8 (1957): 106–9.

"Mary Chesnut in Search of Her Genre." *Yale Review* 73 (1984): 199–209.

"Monograph on the History of Reconstruction in the South to Brief for Oliver Brown et al., v. Board of Education of Topeka, et al." Filed in U.S. Supreme Court, 16 November 1953.

"National Decision against Equality." *American Heritage* 15 (1964): 52–55.

"The 'New Reconstruction' in the South: Desegregation in Historical Perspective." *Commentary* 21 (1956): 501–8.

"The North and South of It." *American Scholar* 35 (1966): 647–58.

"The Northern Crusade against Slavery." *New York Review of Books*, 27 February 1969. Reprinted in *American Counterpoint*, pp. 140–62, q.v.

"Our Past Isn't What It Used to Be." *New York Times Book Review*, 28 July 1963, pp. 1, 24–25.

"Plessy v. Ferguson: The Birth of Jim Crow." *American Heritage* 15 (1964): 52–55, 100–103.

"The Political Legacy of Reconstruction." *Journal of Negro Education* 26 (1957): 231–40. Reprinted in *The Burden of Southern History*, pp. 89–108 (rev. ed.), q.v.

"The Populist Heritage and the Intellectual." *American Scholar* 28 (1959): 55–72. Reprinted in *The Burden of Southern History*, pp. 141–66 (rev. ed.), q.v.

"The Price of Freedom." In *What Was Freedom's Price?* edited by David G. Sansing, pp. 93–113. Jackson: University Press of Mississippi, 1978.

"Protestant Slavery in a Catholic World." In *American Counterpoint*, pp. 46–77, q.v.

"The Question of Loyalty." *American Scholar* 33 (1964): 561–67.
"Race Prejudice Is Itself a Form of Violence." Comment for "Is America by Nature a Violent Society?" *New York Times Magazine,* 28 April 1968, p. 114.
"Reading, Writing, and Revolution: Comments by Historians on Books in American History." *Washington Post,* 22 February 1976, sec. E, pp. 1, 4.
"Recommended Summer Reading." *American Scholar* 37 (1968): 553–54.
"Reflections on a Centennial: The American Civil War." *Yale Review* 50 (1961): 481–90.
"Reflections on the Fate of the Union: Kennedy and After." *New York Review of Books,* 26 December 1963, pp. 8–9.
Remarks, University of South Carolina Conference on *Time on the Cross,* 2 November 1974, Columbia.
"Report on Current Research." *Saturday Review,* 4 April 1953, pp. 16–17, 48.
"Richard Hofstadter, 1916–1970." *New York Review of Books,* 3 December 1970, p. 10.
"The Search for Southern Identity." *Virginia Quarterly Review* 34 (1958): 321–28.
"Seeds of Failure in Radical Race Policy." *Proceedings of the American Philosophical Society* 105 (1966): 1–9. Reprinted with substantial revisions in *American Counterpoint,* pp. 163–83, q.v.
"Segregation." In *Encyclopedia Americana,* 24:523–24. 1978.
"Share-the-Wealth Movements." In *Dictionary of American History,* vol. 5, edited by James Truslow Adams, p. 64. New York: Scribner, 1940 and following editions.
"Shop from Which Tech Grew." *Atlanta Journal,* [1933?]. Clipping in Glenn Weddington Rainey Papers. Manuscript Division. Emory University Library, Atlanta.
"A Short History of American History." *New York Times Book Review,* 8 August 1982, pp. 3, 14.
"The Sources of Southern History." Fiftieth Anniversary Celebration of the Southern Historical Collection, Chapel Hill, N.C., 24 October 1980.
"The South and the Law of the Land: The Present Resistance and Its Prospects." *Commentary* 26 (1958): 369–74.
"The South in Search of a Philosophy." *Phi Beta Kappa Addresses at the University of Florida* 1 (1938): 1–20.
"A Southern Critique for the Gilded Age." In *The Burden of Southern History,* pp. 109–40 (rev. ed.), q.v.
"A Southerner's Answer to the Race Question." *Reporter* 30 (1964): 39–44.
"The Southern Ethic in a Puritan World." *William and Mary Quarterly,* 3d ser., 25 (1968): 343–70. Reprinted in *American Counterpoint,* pp. 13–46, q.v.
"Southern Mythology." *Commentary* 39 (1965): 60–63.

"Southern Slaves in the World of Thomas Malthus." In *American Counterpoint,* pp. 78–106. q.v.

"Statement in Favor of Abolishing Poll Taxes." *Congressional Digest* 20 (1941): 309–10.

"Statement in Favor of Extending the 1965 Voting Rights Act." In *Extension of the Voting Rights Act: Hearing,* 97th Cong., 1st sess., 24 June 1981, pt. 3: 1999–2028.

"The Strange Career of a Historical Controversy." In *American Counterpoint,* pp. 234–66, q.v.

"The Test of Comparison." In *The Comparative Approach to American History,* edited by Woodward, pp. 346–58. New York: Basic Books, 1968.

"That Other Impeachment." *New York Times Magazine,* 11 August 1974, pp. 9, 26–32.

"Thomas Edward Watson." In *Dictionary of American Biography,* 19:549–51. 1936.

"Times of Trouble." *Pennsylvania Gazette,* December 1981, pp. 16–19.

"Tom Watson and the Negro in Agrarian Politics." *Journal of Southern History* 4 (1938): 14–33.

"Townsend Plan." In *Dictionary of American History,* vol. 5, edited by James Truslow Adams, p. 288. New York: Scribner, 1940 and following editions.

"Toynbee and Metahistory." *American Scholar* 27 (1958): 384–92.

"The Unreported Crisis in Southern Colleges." *Harper's,* October 1962, pp. 82–89.

"The Uses of History in Fiction: A Discussion with Ralph Ellison, William Styron, and Robert Penn Warren." *Southern Literary Journal* 1 (1969): 57–90.

"W. J. Cash Reconsidered." *New York Review of Books,* 4 December 1969, pp. 28–34.

"Weill Lecture on European Images of America." Weill Memorial Lecture, Chapel Hill, N.C., 1983.

"What Happened to the Civil Rights Movement?" *Harper's,* January 1967, pp. 29–37.

"What Happened to the Diary of Mary Boykin Chesnut?" Address, Organization of American Historians, New Orleans, 13 April 1979.

"What Is the Chesnut Diary?" In *South Carolina Women Writers: Proceedings of the Reynolds Conference, 24–25 October 1975,* edited by James B. Meriwether, pp. 193–206, 263–85. Spartanburg, S.C.: Reprint Company, 1979.

"White Racism and Black 'Emancipation.' " *New York Review of Books,* 27 February 1969, pp. 5–11.

"Why the Southern Renaissance?" *Virginia Quarterly Review* 51 (1975): 222–39.

"Young Jim Crow." *Nation,* 7 July 1956, pp. 9–10.

BOOK REVIEWS

Aaron, Daniel, *The Unwritten War: American Writers and the Civil War*. New York *Review of Books,* 21 February 1974, pp. 26–29.

Adams, Henry, Library of America reprint ed. of *History of the United States of America during the Administrations of Thomas Jefferson. New York Times Book Review,* 6 July 1986.

Ashmore, Harry, *An Epitaph for Dixie. Virginia Quarterly Review* 34 (1958): 292–94.

Barnard, Harry, *Rutherford B. Hayes and His America. Nation,* 28 May 1955, p. 467.

Baruch, Bernard, *My Own Story. Saturday Review,* 31 August 1957, pp. 13–14.

Barzun, Jacques, *The House of Intellect. Key Reporter* 25 (1959): 6.

Bazelon, David T., *Power in America: The Politics of the New Class. Commentary* 44 (1967): 92–95.

Beale, Howard Kennedy, ed., *Charles A. Beard: An Appraisal. New York Times Book Review,* 5 September 1954, p. 9.

————, *The Diary of Gideon Welles. Key Reporter* 26 (1960): 6.

Beard, Chares Austin, *The Republic;* Henry Steele Commager, *Majority Rule and Minority Rights;* Wilfred Binkley, *American Political Parties: Their National History. Virginia Quarterly Review* 20 (1944): 150–54.

Beard, Charles Austin, and Mary Ritter Beard, *America in Midpassage;* Howard Washington Odum, *American Social Problems;* William Terry Couch, ed., *These Are Our Lives. Virginia Quarterly Review* 15 (1939): 632–36.

Belden, Thomas, and Marva Belden, *So Fell the Angels. New York Herald Tribune Book Review,* 29 July 1956, p. 3.

Beringer, Richard E., Herman Hattaway, Archer Jones, and William N. Still, Jr., *Why the South Lost the Civil War. New York Review of Books,* 17 July 1986, pp. 3–6.

Bernstein, Barton J., ed., *Towards a New Past: Dissenting Essays in American History. New York Review of Books,* 1 August 1968, pp. 8–12.

Berwanger, Eugene, *The Frontier against Slavery. New York Review of Books,* 27 February 1969, pp. 5–11.

Billington, Ray Allen, *Land of Savagery, Land of Promise: The European Image of the American Frontier in the Nineteenth Century. New York Review of Books,* 11 June 1981, pp. 33–35.

Binkley, Wilfred, *American Political Parties: Their National History. Virginia Quarterly Review* 20 (1944): 150–54.

Bleser, Carol, ed., *The Hammonds of Redcliffe. New York Review of Books,* 22 October 1981, pp. 47–48.

Brodie, Fawn, *Thaddeus Stevens: Scourge of the South. New York Times Book Review,* 22 November 1959, pp. 66–67.

Bruckberger, R. L., *Image of America. Key Reporter* 25 (1959): 6.

Burger, Nash K., and John K. Bettersworth, *South of Appomattox. New York Times Book Review,* 29 September 1959, p. 46.

Burton, Orville Vernon, *In My Father's House Are Many Mansions. New York Review of Books,* 10 October 1985, pp. 30–31.

Cahnman, Werner, and Alvin Boskoff, eds., *Sociology and History: Theory and Research. New York Times Book Review,* 24 January 1965, pp. 1, 44–45.

Cappon, Lester J., ed., *The Adams-Jefferson Letters,* vols. 1–2; R. R. Palmer, *The Age of the Democratic Revolution,* vol. 1; Stefan Lorant, *The Life and Times of Theodore Roosevelt. Key Reporter* 25 (1960): 7.

Carter, Dan T., *Scottsboro: A Tragedy of the American South. New York Times Book Review,* 9 March 1969, p. 5.

Carter, Hodding, *The Angry Scar: The Story of Reconstruction. New York Times Book Review,* 1 February 1959, pp. 5, 33.

Cash, Wilbur J., *The Mind of the South. Journal of Southern History* 7 (1941): 400–401.

Commager, Henry Steele, *Majority Rule and Minority Rights. Virginia Quarterly Review* 20 (1944): 150–54.

———— and Richard B. Morris, eds., *The Spirit of Seventy-Six. New York Herald Tribune Book Review,* 2 November 1958, p. 4.

Connelly, Thomas L., *The Marble Man: Robert E. Lee and His Image in American Society. New York Times Book Review,* 3 April 1977, p. 12.

Conway, Alan, *The Reconstruction of Georgia. American Historical Review* 72 (1967): 1502–3.

Couch, William Terry, ed., *These Are Our Lives. Virginia Quarterly Review* 15 (1939): 632–36.

Cunningham, Noble E., *The Jeffersonian Republicans: The Formation of Party Organization, 1789–1801. Key Reporter* 24 (1958): 7.

Current, Richard N., *The Lincoln Nobody Knows. Key Reporter* 24 (1959): 6.

Dabbs, James McBride, *The Southern Heritage. Nation,* 15 November 1958, p. 365.

Dabney, Virginius, *The Jefferson Scandals: A Rebuttal. New York Times Book Review,* 5 July 1981, pp. 1, 14.

Dalleck, Robert, *Ronald Reagan. New Republic,* 2 April 1984, pp. 31–35.

Daniel, Pete, *The Shadow of Slavery: Peonage in the South, 1901–1969. Journal of American History* 59 (1973): 1030–31.

Daniels, Josephus, *Editor in Politics. Mississippi Valley Historical Review* 28 (1941): 285–86.

————, *Tar Heel Editor. New Republic,* 1 January 1940, pp. 27–28.

Davidson, Chandler, *Biracial Politics: Conflict and Coalition in the Metropolitan South. New York Review of Books,* 14 December 1972, pp. 37–40.

Davidson, Elizabeth H., *Child Labor Legislation in the Southern Textile States. Journal of Southern History* 5 (1939): 407–8.

Degler, Carl N., *The Other South: Southern Dissenters in the Nineteenth Century.* New York Times Book Review, 10 March 1974, p. 4.

DeLeon, David, *The American as Anarchist: Reflections on Indigenous Radicalism;* James R. Green, *Grass-Roots Socialism: Radical Movements in the Southwest, 1895–1943.* New York Review of Books, 5 April 1979, pp. 3–5.

Donald, David Herbert, ed., *Inside Lincoln's Cabinet: The Civil War Diaries of Salmon P. Chase.* Pennsylvania Magazine of History and Biography 79 (1955): 131–32.

———, *Liberty and Union.* New York Times Book Review, 19 November 1978, p. 13.

Donald, Henderson H., *The Negro Freedmen: Life Conditions of the American Negro in the Early Years after Emancipation.* Saturday Review, 13 June 1953, p. 45.

Dovring, Folke, *History as a Social Science: An Essay on the Nature and Purpose of Historical Studies.* American Historical Review 66 (1961): 1079.

Draper, Theodore, *The Roots of American Communism.* Key Reporter 22 (1957): 5.

Dugan, James, *The Great Iron Ship.* Saturday Review, 6 February 1954, p. 19.

Durden, Robert F., *Reconstruction Bonds and Twentieth-Century Politics: South Dakota v. North Carolina.* American Historical Review 68 (1963): 840.

Dykeman, Wilma, and James Stokely, *Neither Black nor White;* Harry Ashmore, *An Epitaph for Dixie.* Virginia Quarterly Review 34 (1958): 292–94.

Eaton, Clement, *Henry Clay and the Art of American Politics.* New York Herald Tribune Book Review, 14 July 1957, p. 9.

Faulkner, Harold Underwood, *Politics, Reform, and Expansion, 1890–1900.* Key Reporter 25 (1959): 6.

Fehrenbacher, Don E., *The Dred Scott Case: Its Significance in American Law and Politics.* New York Review of Books, 7 December 1978, pp. 30–31.

———, and Carl N. Degler, eds., *The South and the Concurrent Majority,* by David Morris Potter. Journal of American History 60 (1973): 123–24.

Field, James A., Jr., *The Japanese at Leyte Gulf: The Sho Operation.* American Historical Review 53 (1947): 82–84.

Fitzgerald, Frances, *America Revised: History Schoolbooks in the Twentieth Century.* New York Review of Books, 20 December 1979, pp. 16–19.

Floan, Howard, *The South in Northern Eyes, 1831–1861.* Key Reporter 23 (1958): 4.

Fogel, Robert William, and Stanley L. Engerman, *Time on the Cross: The Economics of American Negro Slavery;* idem, *Time on the Cross: Evidence and Methods, a Supplement.* New York Review of Books, 2 May 1974, pp. 3–6.

Foner, Eric, *Politics and Ideology in the Age of the Civil War.* New Republic, 22 November 1980, pp. 34–35.

Foote, Shelby, *The Civil War: A Narrative,* vol. 3. New York Review of Books, 6 March 1972, p. 12.

Franklin, John Hope, *The Militant South, 1800–1861. New York Times Book Review,* 23 September 1956, p. 3.

———, *Racial Equality in America. Journal of American History* 64 (1977): 776–77.

Fraser, Hugh Russell, *Democracy in the Making. New Republic,* 4 January 1939, p. 265.

Fredrickson, George M., *The Black Image in the White Mind: The Debate on Afro-American Character and Destiny, 1817–1914;* Eugene D. Genovese, *In Red and Black: Marxian Explorations in Southern and Afro-American History. New York Review of Books,* 12 August 1971, pp. 11–14.

———, *White Supremacy: A Comparative Study in American and South African History. New York Review of Books,* 5 March 1981, pp. 26–28.

Friedel, Frank, *Franklin D. Roosevelt: The Ordeal. New York Herald Tribune Book Review,* 31 January 1954, p. 7.

———, *Franklin D. Roosevelt: The Triumph. New York Herald Tribune Book Review,* 9 September 1956, p. 4.

Genovese, Eugene D., *In Red and Black: Marxian Explorations in Southern and Afro-American History. New York Review of Books,* 12 August 1971, pp. 11–14.

———, *Roll, Jordan, Roll: The World the Slaves Made. New York Review of Books,* 3 October 1974, pp. 19–21.

Gillette, William, *Retreat from Reconstruction, 1869–1879;* Otto H. Olsen, ed., *Reconstruction and Redemption in the South. New York Review of Books,* 20 November 1980, pp. 49–51.

Ginzberg, Eli, *The Negro Potential. Commentary* 20 (1956): 288–92.

Going, Allen Johnston, *Bourbon Democracy in Alabama, 1874–1890. Mississippi Valley Historical Review* 38 (1952): 719–20.

Goodwyn, Lawrence, *Democratic Promise: The Populist Movement in America. New York Review of Books,* 28 October 1976, pp. 28–29.

Gore, Albert, *Let the Glory Out: My South and Its Politics. New York Review of Books,* 14 December 1972, pp. 37–40.

Green, James R., *Grass-Roots Socialism: Radical Movements in the Southwest, 1895–1943. New York Review of Books,* 5 April 1979, pp. 3–5.

Guerin, Daniel, *Negroes on the March;* Eli Ginzberg, *The Negro Potential Commentary* 20 (1956): 288–92.

Halsey, William F., *Admiral Halsey's Story. American Historical Review* 63 (1948): 898.

Hammond, Bray, *Banks and Politics in America from the Revolution to the Civil War. Key Reporter* 23 (1958): 4.

Harlan, Louis R., ed., *Booker T. Washington,* vol. 2. *New York Times Book Review,* 22 May 1983, pp. 13, 36.

———, *The Booker T. Washington Papers,* vols. 1–2; idem, *Booker T. Washington:*

The Making of a Black Leader, 1865–1901. New Republic, 11 November 1972, pp. 20–22.

Harvard, William C., ed., *The Changing Politics of the South;* Chandler Davidson, *Biracial Politics: Conflict and Coalition in the Metropolitan South;* Albert Gore, *Let the Glory Out: My South and Its Politics. New York Review of Books*, 14 December 1972, pp. 37–40.

Hesseltine, William B., *Confederate Leaders in the New South. Journal of Southern History* 17 (1951): 270–71.

Higgs, Robert, *Competition and Coercion: Blacks in the American Economy, 1865–1914. Agricultural History* 52 (1978): 194–95.

Hofstadter, Richard, *The American Political Tradition and the Men Who Made It. Mississippi Valley Historical Review* 35 (1949): 681–82.

————, *The Paranoid Style in American Politics and Other Essays. New York Times Book Review*, 14 November 1965, pp. 3, 84.

Horn, Stanley F., *Invisible Empire: The Story of the Ku Klux Klan, 1866–1871. New Republic*, 26 July 1939, pp. 341–42.

Hough, Frank O., *The Island War: The United States Marine Corps in the Pacific. Pacific Historical Review* 16 (1947): 459–60.

Howe, Irving, *Socialism and America. New York Review of Books*, 30 January 1986, pp. 26–29.

James, Marquis, *Mr. Garner of Texas. Virginia Quarterly Review* 16 (1940): 129–34.

Jocher, Katharine, Guy B. Johnson, George L. Simpson, and Rupert B. Vance, eds., *Folk, Region, and Society: Selected Papers of Howard W. Odum. New York Times Book Review*, 27 September 1964, p. 48.

Johnson, Gerald W., *America's Silver Age: The Statecraft of Clay, Webster, Calhoun. New Republic*, 29 November 1939, pp. 176–77.

Jordan, Winthrop D., *White over Black: American Attitudes toward the Negro, 1550–1812. New York Times Book Review*, 31 March 1968, pp. 6, 43.

Kahler, Erich, *The Meaning of History. New York Times Book Review*, 26 July 1964, p. 5.

Key, V. O., Jr., *Southern Politics in State and Nation. Yale Review* 39 (1949): 374–76.

Kilpatrick, James Jackson, *The Sovereign States: Notes of a Citizen of Virginia. Commentary* 24 (1957): 465–66.

King, Ernest J., and Walter Muir Whitehall, *Fleet Admiral King: A Naval Record. Saturday Review*, 22 November 1952, p. 26.

Kirwan, Albert Dennis, *Revolt of the Rednecks: Mississippi Politics, 1876–1925. American Historical Review* 56 (1951); 918–19.

Kohn, Hans, *American Nationalism: An Interpretive Essay. Key Reporter* 22 (1957): 5.

Kraditor, Aileen, *Means and Ends in American Abolitionism;* Eugene Berwanger,

The Frontier against Slavery; Lorman Ratner, *Powder Keg: Northern Opposition to the Antislavery Movement, 1831–1840;* V. Jacques Voegeli, *Free but Not Equal: The Midwest and the Negro during the Civil War;* Forrest G. Wood, *Black Scare: The Racist Response to Emancipation and Reconstruction;* William Samuel McFeely, *Yankee Stepfather: General O. O. Howard and the Freedmen. New York Review of Books,* 27 February 1969, pp. 5–11.

Lambert, John R., *Arthur Pue Gorman. American Historical Review* 59 (1954): 1027–28.

Levenson, J. C., *The Mind and the Art of Henry Adams;* Theodore Draper, *The Roots of American Communism;* Charles Grier Sellers, Jr., *James K. Polk: Jacksonian, 1795–1843;* Broadus Mitchell, *Alexander Hamilton: Youth to Maturity, 1755–1788;* Hans Kohn, *American Nationalism: An Interpretive Essay;* Henry Pelling, *America and the British Left. Key Reporter* 22 (1957): 5.

Lief, Alfred, *Democracy's Norris. Virginia Quarterly Review* 16 (1940): 129–34.

Link, Arthur Stanley, *Wilson: The Road to the White House. Pennsylvania Magazine of History and Biography* 72 (1948): 97–98.

Litwack, Leon F., *Been in the Storm So Long: The Aftermath of Slavery. New York Review of Books,* 16 August 1979, pp. 8–9.

Logan, Frenise A., *The Negro in North Carolina, 1876–1894. American Historical Review* 70 (1965): 584.

Logan, Rayford A., *The Negro in American Life and Thought: The Nadir, 1877–1901;* Louis Ruchames, *Race, Jobs, and Politics: The Story of FEPC;* Lee Nichols, *Breakthrough on the Color Front. Yale Review* 43 (1954): 604–7.

Lorant, Stefan, *The Life and Times of Theodore Roosevelt. Key Reporter* 25 (1960): 7.

Lord, Russell, *The Wallaces of Iowa. Mississippi Valley Historical Review* 34 (1948): 703.

Lumpkin, Katharine DuPre, *The Making of a Southerner. Mississippi Valley Historical Review* 34 (1947): 141–42.

Mabry, William A., *The Negro in North Carolina Politics since Reconstruction. North Carolina Historical Review* 18 (1941): 82–83.

McDonald, Forrest, *We the People: The Economic Origins of the Constitution. Key Reporter* 24 (1959): 6.

McFeely, William Samuel, *Grant: A Biography. New York Review of Books,* 19 March 1981, pp. 3–6.

———, *Yankee Stepfather: General O. O. Howard and the Freedmen. New York Review of Books,* 27 February 1969, pp. 5–11.

McKitrick, Eric, *Andrew Johnson and Reconstruction. New York Times Book Review,* 25 September 1960, pp. 3, 24.

McPherson, James M., *The Struggle for Equality: Abolitionists and the Negro in the Civil War and Reconstruction. New York Times Book Review,* 3 January 1965, p. 6.

Malone, Dumas, *The Sage of Monticello,* vol. 6; Virginius Dabney, *The Jefferson Scandals: A Rebuttal. New York Times Book Review,* 5 July 1981, pp. 1, 14.

Marcosson, Isaac F., *"Marse Henry": A Biography of Henry Watterson. Journal of Southern History* 18 (1952): 97.

May, Henry F., *The End of American Innocence: A Study of the First Years of Our Own Time, 1912–1917. American Historical Review* 65 (1960): 637–38.

Mazlich, Bruce, and Edwin Diamond, *Jimmy Carter: A Character Portrait. New York Review of Books,* 3 April 1980, pp. 9–11.

Meade, Robert D., *Patrick Henry: Patriot in the Making. Key Reporter* 23 (1957): 5.

Meyers, Marvin, *The Jacksonian Persuasion;* Bray Hammond, *Banks and Politics in America from the Revolution to the Civil War;* Howard Floan, *The South in Northern Eyes, 1831–1861;* Rexford Guy Tugwell, *The Democratic Roosevelt;* Frank E. Vandiver, *Mighty Stonewall. Key Reporter* 23 (1958): 4.

Michie, Allan, and Frank Ryhlick, *Dixie Demagogues;* Marquis James, *Mr. Garner of Texas;* Alfred Lief, *Democracy's Norris. Virginia Quarterly Review* 16 (1940): 129–34.

Miers, Earl Schenck, *Robert E. Lee: A Great Life in Brief. New York Herald Tribune Book Review,* 10 June 1956, p. 3.

Miller, Merle, *Lyndon. New Republic,* 1 November 1980, pp. 29–31.

Miller, William D., *Memphis during the Progressive Era, 1900–1917. American Historical Review* 64 (1958): 200–201.

Mitchell, Broadus, *Alexander Hamilton: Youth to Maturity, 1755–1788. Key Reporter* 22 (1957): 5.

Mollenhoff, Clark R., *The President Who Failed: Carter out of Control;* Bruce Mazlich and Edwin Diamond, *Jimmy Carter: A Character Portrait. New York Review of Books,* 3 April 1980, pp. 9–11.

Moore, Barrington, Jr., *Social Origins of Dictatorship and Democracy: Lord and Peasant in the Making of the Modern World. Yale Review* 56 (1967): 450–53.

Moore, John Hammond, ed., *Before and After; or, The Relations of the Races at the South,* by Isaac DuBose Seabrook. *American Historical Review* 73 (1968): 1255–56.

Morgan, Edmund Sears, *The Puritan Dilemma: The Story of John Winthrop. Key Reporter* 24 (1958): 7.

Morgenstern, George, *Pearl Harbor: The Story of the Secret War. American Historical Review* 53 (1947): 188.

Morison, Samuel Eliot, *History of United States Naval Operations in World War II: Aleutians, Gilberts, and Marshalls, June 1942–April 1944. Saturday Review of Literature,* 24 November 1951, pp. 14–15, 45.

———, *History of United States Naval Operations in World War II: Breaking the Bismarck's Barrier, 22 July 1942–May 1944. Saturday Review of Literature,* 24 February 1951, pp. 15, 16.

———, *History of United States Naval Operations in World War II: Coral Sea,*

Midway, and Submarine Actions, May 1942–August 1942. Saturday Review of Literature, 29 October 1949, pp. 20–21.

———, *History of United States Naval Operations in World War II: Leyte, June 1944–January 1945. Key Reporter* 24 (1959): 6.

———, *John Paul Jones: A Sailor's Biography. New York Times Book Review*, 13 September 1959, p. 3.

Morris, Richard B., ed., *Encyclopedia of American History. Saturday Review*, 13 June 1953, p. 45.

Morrison, Joseph L., *W. J. Cash: Southern Prophet. New Republic*, 9 December 1967, *pp. 28–30.*

Mowry, George E., *The Era of Theodore Roosevelt, 1900–1912. Key Reporter* 24 (1958): 7.

Mudge, Eugene Tenbroek, *The Social Philosophy of John Taylor of Caroline. North Carolina Historical Review* 17 (1940): 273–75.

Nevins, Allan, *Allan Nevins on History. Reviews in American History* 4 (1976): 25–26.

———, *The War for the Union: The Improvised War, 1861–1862;* Jacques Barzun, *The House of Intellect;* Harold Underwood Faulkner, *Politics, Reform, and Expansion, 1890–1900;* R. L. Bruckberger, *Image of America. Key Reporter* 25 (1959): 6.

———. *The War for the Union*, vols. 2 and 4. *New York Times Book Review*, 26 December 1971, pp. 5, 17.

Nichols, Alice, *Bleeding Kansas. New York Herald Tribune Book Review*, 25 July 1954, p. 3.

Nichols, Lee, *Breakthrough on the Color Front. Yale Review* 43 (1954): 604–7.

Nixon, Raymond B., *Henry W. Grady: Spokesman of the New South. Journal of Southern History* 10 (1944): 114–15.

Noblin, Stuart, *Leonidas Lafayette Polk: Agrarian Crusader. American Historical Review* 55 (1950): 1002–3.

Nugent, Walter T. K., *The Tolerant Populists: Kansas Populism and Nativism. Mississippi Valley Historical Review* 50 (1963): 516–17.

Odum, Howard Washington, *American Social Problems. Virginia Quarterly Review* 15 (1939): 632–36.

Oliphant, Mary C. Simms, Alfred Taylor Odell, and T. C. Duncan Eaves, eds., *The Letters of William Gilmore Simms*, vols. 1–2. *American Historical Review* 59 (1954): 466–67.

———, *The Letters of William Gilmore Simms*, vols. 3–5. *American Historical Review* 63 (1958): 529–30.

Olsen, Otto H., ed., *Reconstruction and Redemption in the South, New York Review of Books*, 20 November 1980 pp. 49–51.

Palmer, R. R., *The Age of the Democratic Revolution*, vol. 1. *Key Reporter* 25 (1960): 7.

Parkman, Francis, *France and England in North America,* edited by David Levin. *New York Times Book Review,* 3 July 1983, pp. 3, 18.

Peirce, Neal R., *The People's President: The Electoral College in American History and the Direct-Vote Alternative. New Republic,* 1 June 1968, pp. 33–34.

Pelling, Henry, *America and the British Left. Key Reporter* 22 (1957): 8.

Perkins, Dexter, *The New Age of Franklin Roosevelt, 1932–1945. Saturday Review,* 6 July 1957, p. 16.

Peterson, H. C., and Gilbert C. Fite, *Opponents of War, 1917–1918. American Historical Review* 63 (1957): 155–56.

Pole, J. R., *Paths to the American Past. Times Literary Supplement,* 30 May 1980, p. 609.

Rabinowitz, Howard N., *Race Relations in the Urban South, 1865–1890. Journal of Southern History* 44 (1978): 476–78.

Ramsdell, Charles W., *Behind the Lines of the Southern Confederacy,* edited by Wendell Holmes Stephenson. *American Historical Review* 49 (1944): 754–55.

Ratner, Lorman, *Powder Keg: Northern Opposition to the Antislavery Movement, 1831–1840. New York Review of Books,* 27 February 1969, pp. 5–11.

Riencourt, Amaury de, *The Coming Caesars. Key Reporter* 23 (1957): 5.

Roseboom, Eugene H., *A History of Presidential Elections. Key Reporter* 23 (1957): 5.

Rowan, Carl T., *Go South to Sorrow. Commentary* 24 (1957): 271–72.

Ruchames, Louis, *Race, Jobs, and Politics: The Story of FEPC. Yale Review* 43 (1954): 604–7.

Samuels, Ernest, *Henry Adams: The Middle Years, 1877–1891;* Richard N. Current, *The Lincoln Nobody Knows;* Forrest McDonald, *We the People: The Economic Origins of the Constitution;* Cushing Strout, *The Pragmatic Revolt in American History;* Samuel Eliot Morison, *History of United States Naval Operations in World War II: Leyte, June 1944–January 1945. Key Reporter* 24 (1959): 6.

Saveth, Edward N., ed., *American History and the Social Sciences;* Werner Cahnman and Alvin Boskoff, eds., *Sociology and History: Theory and Research. New York Times Book Review,* 24 January 1965, pp. 1, 44–45.

Schlesinger, Arthur Meier, Jr., *The Age of Roosevelt: The Crisis of the Old Order. Saturday Review,* 2 March 1957, pp. 11–12.

Sellers, Charles Grier, Jr., *James K. Polk: Jacksonian, 1795–1843. Key Reporter* 22 (1957): 5.

———, ed., *The Southerner as American. Journal of Southern History* 27 (1961): 92–94.

Silver, James W., *Mississippi: The Closed Society. New York Review of Books,* 20 August 1964, pp. 13–14.

Simkins, Francis Butler, *Pitchfork Ben Tillman: South Carolinian. North Carolina Historical Review* 23 (1945): 378–79.

Singletary, Otis A., *Negro Militia and Reconstruction.* Key Reporter 23 (1957): 5.

Smith, Page, *The Historian and History;* Erich Kahler, *The Meaning of History.* New York Times Book Review, 26 July 1964, p. 5.

Stampp, Kenneth Milton, *The Peculiar Institution: Slavery in the Antebellum South.* New York Herald Tribune Book Review, 21 October 1956, p. 6.

Sternsher, Bernard, *Consensus, Conflict, and American Historians.* American Historical Review 81 (1976): 438–39.

Strout, Cushing, *The Pragmatic Revolt in American History.* Key Reporter 24 (1959): 6.

Styron, William, *Confessions of Nat Turner.* New Republic, 7 October 1967, pp. 25–28.

Taft, Philip, *The A.F.L. in the Time of Gompers.* Key Reporter 23 (1957): 5.

Takaki, Ronald, *Iron Cages: Race and Culture in Nineteenth Century America.* New York Review of Books, 22 November 1979, pp. 14–16.

Taylor, Joe Gray, *Louisiana Reconstructed, 1863–1877.* Louisiana History 17 (1976): 97–98.

Taylor, William R., *Cavalier and Yankee: The Old South and American National Character.* New York Times Book Review, 24 December 1961, p. 6.

Thomas, Emory M., *The Confederate Nation, 1861–1865.* New Republic, 17 March 1979, pp. 25–28.

Thomas, John, *The Liberator, William Lloyd Garrison: A Biography.* New York Times Book Review, 30 June 1963, p. 6.

Thorp, Willard, *A Southern Reader.* American Quarterly 8 (1956): 284–85.

Trelease, Allen W., *White Terror: The Ku Klux Klan Conspiracy and Southern Reconstruction.* New York Times Book Review, 23 May 1971, pp. 5, 28.

Trowbridge, John T., *The Desolate South, 1865–1866.* New York Herald Tribune Book Review, 13 May 1956, p. 4.

Tugwell, Rexford Guy, *The Democratic Roosevelt.* Key Reporter 23 (1958): 4.

Turner, Arlin, *George W. Cable: A Biography.* Journal of Southern History 23 (1957): 133–34.

———, ed., *The Negro Question: A Selection of Writings on Civil Rights in the South,* by George Washington Cable. New York Times Book Review, 27 July 1958, p. 6.

Van Deusen, Glyndon G., *The Jackson Era, 1828–1848.* New York Herald Tribune Book Review, 22 March 1959, p. 4.

Vandiver, Frank E., *Mighty Stonewall.* Key Reporter 23 (1958): 4.

Voegeli, V. Jacques, *Free but Not Equal: The Midwest and the Negro during the Civil War.* New York Review of Books, 27 February 1969, pp. 5–11.

Wall, Joseph Frazier, *Henry Watterson: Reconstructed Rebel.* Mississippi Valley Historical Review 43 (1956): 137–38.

Walters, Raymond, Jr., *Albert Gallatin: Jeffersonian Financier;* Eugene H. Roseboom, *A History of Presidential Elections;* Philip Taft, *The A.F.L. in the*

Time of Gompers; Robert D. Meade, *Patrick Henry: Patriot in the Making;* Otis A. Singletary, *Negro Militia and Reconstruction;* Amaury de Riencourt, *The Coming Caesars. Key Reporter* 23 (1957): 5.

Warren, Robert Penn, *Who Speaks for the Negro? New Republic,* 22 May 1965, pp. 21–23.

White, Leonard D., *The Republican Era, 1869–1901: A Study in Administrative History. New York Times Book Review,* 30 March 1958, pp. 3, 26.

Wilkins, Thomas, *Clarence King: A Biography;* George E. Mowry, *The Era of Theodore Roosevelt, 1900–1912.* Noble E. Cunningham, *The Jeffersonian Republicans: The Formation of Party Organization, 1789–1801;* Edmund Sears Morgan, *The Puritan Dilemma: The Story of John Winthrop. Key Reporter* 24 (1958): 7.

Wilkinson III, J. Harvie, *From "Brown" to "Bakke": The Supreme Court and School Integration, 1954–1978. New Republic,* 23 June 1979, pp. 27–29.

Williamson, Joel Randolph, *The Crucible of Race: Black-White Relations in the American South since Reconstruction. New Republic,* 15 October 1985, pp. 29–32.

Wilson, Edmund, *Patriotic Gore: Studies in the Literature of the American Civil War. American Scholar* 31 (1962): 638–42.

Wood, Forrest G., *Black Scare: The Racist Response to Emancipation and Reconstruction. New York Review of Books,* 27 February 1969, pp. 5–11.

Primary Sources

MANUSCRIPT AND ARCHIVAL COLLECTIONS

Atlanta University, Trever Arnett Library, Atlanta, Ga.
 Association of Southern Women for the Prevention of Lynching, Papers
Cross County Historical Society, Wynne, Ark.
 Comer Vann Woodward Scrapbook
Emory University, Robert M. Woodruff Library, Atlanta, Ga.
 Ernest Hartsock Collection
 Glenn Weddington Rainey Papers
 Comer McDonald Woodward Papers
 Andrew Sledd Papers
 University Alumni Office
 University Alumni Records, Class of 1930
Henderson State University, Arkadelphia, Ark.
 Henderson-Brown College Archives
 Oracle Newspaper Files

University of North Carolina, Louis Round Wilson Library, Chapel Hill, N.C.
    Southern Historical Collection
        Weldon A. Brown Papers
        Howard Washington Odum Papers
        J. Fred Rippy Papers
        John Herbert Roper Papers
        Southern Historical Association Papers
    Southern Oral History Project
        Paul Green interview by Joseph Herzenberg
    University Archives
        History Department Papers
        Institute for Research in the Social Sciences Papers
University of Wisconsin, Madison, Wis. University Archives
    Frederick Jackson Turner Papers
Yale University, New Haven, Conn. Manuscript Division
    Ulrich Bonnell Phillips Papers

PERSONAL COLLECTIONS OF CORRESPONDENCE

Georgia Watson Craven
Manning J. Dauer
J. Merton England
Kraus-Thomson Organization, Ltd.

INTERVIEWS

(Unless otherwise noted with *, typescripts are deposited in the Roper Papers, Southern Historical Collection, University of North Carolina, Louis Round Wilson Library, Chapel Hill, N.C. Asterisked interviews are in possession of the author.)

Herbert Aptheker	Manning J. Dauer
John Morton Blum	Don Edwards
James R. Caldwell	Thomas H. English*
William G. Carleton	John Hope and Aurelia Franklin
J. Isaac Copeland	James William Fulbright
William Terry Couch	Ralph Henry Gabriel
Avery Odelle Craven*	LeRoy P. Graf
Georgia Watson Craven*	Herbert W. Gstalder

John and Julia Hall*
Joseph A. Herzenberg*
Cecil Slaton Johnson
Guy Johnson
Guion Johnson
Frank Weir Klingberg*
LeRoy E. Loemker
William Samuel McFeely
Thomas McHaney*
Robert McMath*
August Meier
Boulware Martin Ohls
Mabel Phillips Parker (*1984 only)

Jack R. Pole
Glenn Weddington Rainey
Frank Winkler Ryan*
J. Carlyle Sitterson
Staffers, House of Representatives
    Committee on the Judiciary
Carl D. Stewart
Bennett Harrison Wall
Bell Irvin Wiley
Joel Randolph Williamson*
Comer Vann Woodward
Edwin Milton Yoder
Martin D. Young*

Secondary Sources

Adams, Henry. *The Education of Henry Adams.* 1907. Reprint. Boston: Houghton Mifflin, 1974.
──────. *Mont-Saint-Michel and Chartres.* 1904. Reprint. New York: Doubleday, 1959.
Adams, Herbert Baxter. *Historical Scholarship in the United States, 1876–1901: As Revealed in the Correspondence of Herbert B. Adams.* Ed. William Stull Holt. Baltimore: Johns Hopkins Press, 1938.
Adler, Mortimer J. *The Paideia Proposal: An Educational Manifesto.* New York: Macmillan, 1982.
Allport, Gordon W. *ABC's of Scapegoating.* 6th rev. ed. New York: Freedom Pamphlets of Anti-Defamation League of B'nai B'rith, 1969.
──────. *The Nature of Prejudice.* Reading, Mass.: Addison-Wesley, 1954.
Alvarez, A. "The Noble Poet." *New York Review of Books,* 18 July 1985, pp. 7–10.
Apter, David E. "An Epitaph for the Revolutions That Failed." *Daedalus* 103 (1974): 85–103.
Aptheker, Herbert. *American Negro Slave Revolts.* New York: International Publishers, 1961.
──────. "Comment on the Report of the Joint AHA-OAH Committee for the Defense of Historians under the First Amendment in the Yale-Aptheker Controversy." *American Historical Association Newsletter* 16 (1978): 3–4.
──────, ed. *The Papers of W. E. B. Du Bois.* Vols. 1–2. Amherst: University of Massachusetts Press, 1974, 1976.
Ashby, Warren. *Frank Porter Graham: A Southern Liberal.* Winston-Salem, N.C.: John Blair, 1980.

Auden, Wystan Hugh. Foreword to *The Sorrows of Young Werther and Novella,* by Johann Wolfgang von Goethe, translated by Elizabeth Mayer and Louise Bogan. New York: Random House, 1971.

―――. "Homage to Clio." In *Collected Poems,* edited by Edward Mendelson, p. 464. New York: Random House, 1976.

Baker, Susan Stout. *Radical Beginnings: Richard Hofstadter and the 1930s.* Westport, Conn.: Greenwood Press, 1985.

Bancroft, George. *The History of the United States from the Discovery of the Continent.* 6 vols. 1886. Reprint. Port Washington, N.Y.: Kennikat Press, 1967.

Bartley, Numan V. "Beyond Southern Politics: Some Suggestions for Research." In *Perspectives on the American South: An Annual Review of Society, Politics, and Culture,* vol. 2, edited by Merle Black and John Shelton Reed, pp. 35–47. London: Gordon and Breech for the University of North Carolina, 1985.

Beale, Howard Kennedy. "On Rewriting Reconstruction History." *American Historical Review* 45 (1940): 807–27.

―――, ed. *Charles A. Beard: An Appraisal.* Lexington: University of Kentucky Press, 1954.

Beard, Charles Austin. *An Economic Interpretation of the Constitution of the United States.* 1913. Reprint. New York: Free Press, 1965.

―――, and Mary Ritter Beard. *The Rise of American Civilization.* 2 vols. Rev. ed. New York: Macmillan, 1939.

Bell, Daniel, ed. *The New American Right.* New York: Criterion Books, 1955.

Benedict, Michael Les. "Southern Democrats in the Crisis of 1876–1877: A Reconsideration of Reunion and Reaction." *Journal of Southern History* 46 (1980): 489–524.

Bickel, Alexander Mordecai. *Politics and the Warren Court.* New York: Harper and Row, 1965.

Billings, Dwight B. *Planters and the Making of a "New South": Class, Politics, and Development in North Carolina, 1865-1900.* Chapel Hill: University of North Carolina Press, 1979.

Billington, Ray Allen. *Frederick Jackson Turner: Historian, Scholar, Teacher.* New York: Oxford University Press, 1973.

Bleser, Carol. *The Promised Land: The History of the South Carolina Land Commission.* Columbia: University of South Carolina Press, 1969.

Bloch, Marc Leopold Benjamin. *French Rural History: An Essay on Its Basic Characteristics.* Translated by Janet Sondheimer. Berkeley and Los Angeles: University of California Press, 1966.

Blum, John Morton, et al. *The National Experience: A History of the United States.* Vol. 2. 6th ed. New York: Harcourt Brace Jovanovich, 1985.

Boorstin, Daniel Joseph. *The Americans: The Colonial Experience.* New York: Random House, 1958.

_____. *The Genius of American Politics.* 1953. Reprint. Chicago: University of Chicago Press, Phoenix Books, 1958.

_____. "The Place of Thought in American Life." *American Scholar* 25 (1957): 137–50.

Bragdon, Henry Wilkinson, and Samuel Proctor McCutchen. *History of a Free People.* New York: Macmillan, 1954.

"Brandeis Awards to Go to Nine Today." *New York Times,* 29 April 1982, sec. C, p. 21.

Brauer, Carl M. *John F. Kennedy and the Second Reconstruction.* New York: Columbia University Press, 1977.

Brazil, Wayne Douglas. "Howard W. Odum: The Building Years, 1884–1930." Ph.D. diss., Harvard University, 1975.

_____. "*Social Forces* and Sectional Self-Scrutiny." In *Perspectives on the American South: An Annual Review of Society, Politics, and Culture,* vol. 2, edited by Merle Black and John Shelton Reed, pp. 73–104. London: Gordon and Breach for the University of North Carolina, 1985.

"Brewster Praises Trial Judge on Handling of Seale Case." *New York Times,* 14 June 1971, p. 74.

Brogan, Denis. "David M. Potter." In *Pastmasters: Some Essays on American Historians,* edited by Marcus Cunliffe and Robin W. Winks, pp. 316–44. New York: Harper and Row, 1968.

Brookhiser, Richard. "Aptheker and Samarin at Yale." *National Review,* 26 November 1976, p. 1289.

Brooks, Cleanth. "The Impending Crisis of the Deep South." *Harper's Magazine,* Centennial Supplement, 9 April 1965, pp. 147–51.

_____. "Irony as a Principle of Structure." In *Literary Opinion in America,* edited by Morton D. Zabel, 2:729–41. 1951. 3d rev. ed. New York: Harper and Row, 1962.

_____. *The Well-Wrought Urn: Studies in the Structure of Poetry.* New York: Harcourt, Brace, 1947.

Brooks, David. "Being Here." In *Homage to Robert Penn Warren: A Collection of Critical Essays,* edited by Frank Graziano, pp. 57–92. Durango, Colo.: Logbridge and Rhodes, 1985.

Buck, Paul. *Road to Reunion.* Boston: Little, Brown, 1937.

Buckley, William Frank, Jr. Interview with Morris Abram. "Firing Line." 10 November 1982. South Carolina Educational Television transcription.

_____. *McCarthy and His Enemies.* Chicago: Henry Regnery, 1954.

Bullock, Henry Morton. *A History of Emory University.* Nashville: Vanderbilt University Press, 1936.

Butterfield, Herbert. *The Whig Interpretation of History.* 1931. Reprint. New York: Scribner, 1951.

Buttitta, Tony. *After the Good Gay Times.* New York, Viking Press, 1974.

Cable, George Washington. "Does the Negro Pay for His Education?" *Forum* 13 (1892): 640–49.

———. *The Negro Question.* New York: Scribner, 1890.

Candler, Charles Howard. *Asa Griggs Candler.* Atlanta: Emory University Press, 1950.

Carlton, David. *Mill and Town in South Carolina, 1880–1920.* Baton Rouge: Louisiana State University Press, 1982.

Carr, Edward Halleck. *What Is History?* New York: Random House, 1967.

Carson, Clayborne. *In Struggle: SNCC and the Black Awakening of the 1960s.* Cambridge: Harvard University Press, 1981.

Carter, Dan T. "From the Old South to the New: Another Look at the Theme of Change and Continuity." In *From the Old South to the New: Essays on the Transitional South,* edited by Walter J. Fraser and Winfred B. Moore, Jr., pp. 23–32. Westport, Conn.: Greenwood Press, 1981.

———. *Scottsboro: A Tragedy of the American South.* Baton Rouge: Louisiana State University Press, 1969.

Cash, Wilbur J. *The Mind of the South.* New York: Knopf, 1939.

Cell, John W. *The Highest Stage of White Supremacy: The Origins of Segregation in South Africa and the American South.* Cambridge: Cambridge University Press, 1982.

Chandler, Julian Alvin Carroll et al. *The South in the Building of the Nation.* 13 vols. Richmond, Va.: Southern Publication Society, 1909.

Clarke, John H., ed. *Marcus Garvey and the Vision of Africa.* New York: Random House, 1982.

Clayton, Bruce. *The Savage Ideal: Intolerance and Intellectual Leadership in the South, 1890–1914.* Baltimore: Johns Hopkins University Press, 1972.

Clinton, Catherine. Review of *Mary Chesnut's Civil War. Journal of American History* 68 (1982): 939–41.

Cobb, James Charles. *Industrialization and Southern Society, 1877–1984.* Lexington: University of Kentucky Press, 1984.

Coles, Robert. "Jimmy Carter: Agrarian Rebel?" *New Republic,* 26 June 1976, pp. 14–19.

Cooper, William James, Jr. *The Conservative Regime: South Carolina, 1877–1890.* Baltimore: Johns Hopkins Press, 1968.

Cott, N. F. Review of *Mary Chesnut's Civil War. Yale Review* 71 (1981): 121–28.

Cotterill, Robert S. "The Old South to the New." *Journal of Southern History* 15 (1949): 3–8.

Couch, William Terry. "The Agrarian Romance." *South Atlantic Quarterly* 36 (1937): 414–30.

———. "Reflections on the Southern Tradition." *South Atlantic Quarterly* 35 (1936): 284–97.

Cox, La Wanda. *Lincoln and Black Freedom: A Study in Presidential Leadership.* Columbia: University of South Carolina Press, 1981.

Crawford, Martin. Review of *Mary Chesnut's Civil War. History* 67 (1982): 427.

Crowe, Charles R. "Tom Watson, Populists, and Blacks Reconsidered." *Journal of Negro History* 55 (1970): 99–116.

Curti, Merle, and Vernon L. Carstensen. *The University of Wisconsin: A History.* Vol. 2. Madison: University of Wisconsin Press, 1949.

Curtin, Philip D. *The Atlantic Slave Trade: A Census.* Madison: University of Wisconsin Press, 1969.

Daniel, Frank. Review of *Tom Watson: Agrarian Rebel. Atlanta Journal,* 27 March 1938.

Daspit, Alex. "Dean Pipkin." *Louisiana State University Graduate Report* 21 (1976): 5.

Davenport, F. Garvin, Jr. *The Myth of Southern History: Historical Consciousness in Twentieth-Century Southern Literature.* Nashville: Vanderbilt University Press, 1970.

Davidson, Donald. "The Class Approach to Southern Problems." *Southern Review* 2 (1939): 261–72.

DeCanio, Stephen J. *Agriculture in the Postbellum South.* Cambridge: MIT Press, 1974.

Degler, Carl N. Review of *Mary Chesnut's Civil War. American Historical Review* 87 (1982): 261.

———. *The Other South: Southern Dissenters in the Nineteenth Century.* New York: Harper and Row, 1974.

———. *Place over Time: The Continuity of Southern Distinctiveness.* Baton Rouge: Louisiana State University Press, 1977.

Dittmer, John. *Black Georgia in the Progressive Era, 1900–1920.* Urbana: University of Illinois Press, 1977.

———. "C. Vann Woodward with Soul: The Treatment of Blacks in History; A Reconsideration." Unpublished research seminar paper, National Endowment for the Humanities Scholars Seminar, Vanderbilt University, 1976.

Dunning, William Archibald. *A History of Political Theories.* 3 vols. New York: Macmillan, 1920.

Durden, Robert F. "The Cowbird Grounded: The Populist Nomination of Bryan and Tom Watson in 1896." *Journal of American History* 50 (1964): 397–423.

Dykeman, Wilma, and James Stokely. *Seeds of Southern Change: The Life of Will W. Alexander.* Chicago: University of Chicago Press, 1962.

Eagles, Charles, ed. *The Civil Rights Movement.* Jackson: University Presses of Mississippi, 1986.

Edwards, Willard. "Link Lattimore to Red Doctrines Fed to Schools." *Chicago Tribune,* 27 September 1951, p. 3.

Ellison, Ralph Waldo. *Going to the Territory.* New York: Random House, 1986.

Ellsworth, Scott. *Death in a Promised Land: The Tulsa Race Riot of 1921.* Baton Rouge: Louisiana State University Press, 1982.

Epstein, Edwin Jay. "A Reporter at Large (Black Panthers)." *New Yorker,* 13 February 1971, pp. 45–77.

Explorations in Economic History 16 (January 1979): whole issue.

Faulkner, William. *Absalom, Absalom!* New York: Random House, 1936.

Felton, Rebecca Latimer. "Message of 14 November 1901." Georgia. House of Representatives. *Journal,* 1901. pp. 429–30.

Fields, Barbara Jeanne. *Slavery and Freedom in the Middle Ground.* New Haven: Yale University Press, 1985.

Fitzgerald, Frances. "Onward and Upward with the Arts: Rewriting American History." Part 1. *New Yorker,* 26 February 1979, pp. 41–77.

_____. "Onward and Upward with the Arts: Rewriting American History." Part 2. *New Yorker,* 5 March 1979, pp. 40–91.

_____. "Onward and Upward with the Arts: Rewriting American History." Part 3. *New Yorker,* 12 March 1979, pp. 48–106.

Flynn, Charles L., Jr. Review of *The Wool-Hat Boys. Journal of American History* 72 (1985): 165.

Fogel, Robert William, and Stanley L. Engerman. *Time on the Cross: The Economics of American Negro Slavery.* Boston: Little, Brown, 1974.

Foner, Eric. *Nothing but Freedom.* Baton Rouge: Louisiana State University Press, 1985.

Ford, Lacy K. "Rednecks and Merchants: Economic Development and Social Tensions in the South Carolina Upcountry, 1865–1900." *Journal of American History* 71 (1984): 294–318.

Foster, Gaines M. "Woodward and Southern Identity." *Southern Review* 21 (1985): 351–60.

Frankel, Charles. "Reflections on a Worn-Out Model." *Daedalus* 103 (1974): 25–32.

Franklin, John Hope. "Desegregation: The South's Newest Dilemma." *Journal of Negro Education* 25 (1956): 95–100.

_____. *From Slavery to Freedom: A History of Negro Americans.* 3d ed. New York: Random House, 1969.

_____. *The Historian and Public Policy: Nora and Edward Ryerson Lecture, 23 April 1974.* Chicago: University of Chicago Press, 1974.

_____. "Legal Disfranchisement of the Negro." *Journal of Negro Education* 26 (1957): 241–48.

_____. "Whither Reconstruction Historiography?" *Journal of Negro Education* 17 (1948): 446–61.

Fredrickson, George M. *White Supremacy: A Comparative Study in American and South African History.* New York: Oxford University Press, 1980.

Friedman, Lawrence J. *The White Savage: Racial Fantasies in the Postbellum South.*
Englewood Cliffs, N.J.: Prentice-Hall, 1970.

Friedman, Milton, and Anna Jacobsen Schwartz. *A Monetary History of the United States, 1867–1960.* Princeton: Princeton University Press, 1963.

Fulbright, James William. *The Arrogance of Power.* New York: Random House, 1966.

"Full Text of Wallace Note to Truman." *New York Times,* 24 September 1951, p. 20.

Gabriel, Ralph Henry, and Mabel B. Casner. *The Story of American Democracy.* New York: Harcourt, Brace and World, 1955.

Garner, James W. et al. *Studies in Southern History and Politics Inscribed to William Archibald Dunning.* New York: Columbia University Press, 1914.

Gaston, Paul M. *The New South Creed.* 1970. Reprint. Baton Rouge: Louisiana State University Press, 1976.

Gatewood, Willard B., Jr. "Embattled Scholar: Howard W. Odum and the Fundamentalists, 1925–1927." *Journal of Southern History* 31 (1965): 375–92.

———. *Preachers, Pedagogues, and Politicians: The Evolution Controversy in North Carolina, 1920–1927.* Chapel Hill: University of North Carolina Press, 1966.

Gay, Peter. *Style in History.* New York: Basic Books, 1974.

Genovese, Eugene D. "Potter and Woodward on the South." In Genovese, *In Red and Black: Marxian Explorations in Southern and Afro-American History,* pp. 299–314. New York: Random House, 1971.

———. *Roll, Jordan, Roll: The World the Slaves Made.* New York: Knopf, 1974.

———. *The World the Slaveowners Made: Two Essays in Interpretation.* New York: Random House, 1969.

Georgia House of Representatives. *Journal,* 1901, pp. 429–430.

Gerschenkron, Aleksandr. *Economic Backwardness in Historical Perspective: A Book of Essays.* Cambridge: Harvard University Press, 1966.

———. "The Legacies of Evil." *Daedalus* 103 (1974): 44–49.

Gillette, William. *Retreat from Reconstruction, 1869–1879.* Baton Rouge: Louisiana State University Press, 1979.

Goethe, Johann Wolfgang von. *The Sorrows of Young Werther and Novella.* Translated by Elizabeth Mayer, Louise Bogan, and W. H. Auden. New York: Random House, 1971.

Goldsmith, Oliver. "The Traveller." In *Collected Works of Oliver Goldsmith,* edited by Arthur Friedman, 4: 269. Oxford: Clarendon Press, 1966.

Goodspeed Brothers. *Biographical and Historical Memoirs of Eastern Arkansas.* Chicago and St. Louis: Goodspeed Bros., 1890.

Goodwyn, Lawrence. *Democratic Promise: The Populist Movement in America.* New York: Oxford University Press, 1976.

Grabard, Stephen R. Preface to "American Higher Education: Toward an Uncertain Future." *Daedulus* 103 (1974): v–x.

Graham, Otis L., Jr. *Encore for Reform: The Old Progressives and the New Deal.* New York: Oxford University Press, 1967.

Graziano, Frank, ed. *Homage to Robert Penn Warren: A Collection of Critical Essays.* Durango, Colo.: Logbridge and Rhodes, 1985.

Green, James R. "Past and Present in Southern History: An Interview with C. Vann Woodward." *Radical History Review* 36 (1986): 80–100.

———. "Rewriting Southern History: An Interview with C. Vann Woodward." *Southern Exposure* 12 (1984): 87–92.

Greenberg, Paul. "The Making of Reason." *Arkansas Times,* December 1982, p. 14–15.

Grew, Raymond. "The Case for Comparing Histories." *American Historical Review* 85 (1980): 763–78.

[Gunn, Bill.] "Arkansan Wins Fame as Author of Biography of South's Famous 'Agrarian Rebel.'" 1938. Clipping in Woodward Scrapbook. Cross County Historical Society, Wynne, Ark.

Hackney, Sheldon. "*Origins of the New South* in Retrospect." *Journal of Southern History* 38 (1972): 191–216.

———. *Populism to Progressivism in Alabama.* Princeton: Princeton University Press, 1969.

Hahn, Steven. *The Roots of Southern Populism: Yeomen Farmers and the Transformation of the Georgia Upcountry, 1850–1890.* New York: Oxford University Press, 1983.

Halberstam, David. *The Best and the Brightest.* New York: Random House, 1972.

Hall, John Gladden. *Henderson State College: The Methodist Years, 1890–1929.* Arkadelphia, Ark.: Henderson State College Alumni Association, 1974.

Hall, Julia. "C. Vann Woodward, Historian and Educator." Ph.D. diss., University of Mississippi, 1977.

Harris, Carl V. "Right Fork or Left Fork? The Section-Party Alignments of Southern Democrats in Congress, 1873–1897." *Journal of Southern History* 42 (1976): 471–506.

Hartz, Louis. *The Liberal Tradition in America: An Interpretation of American Political Thought since the Revolution.* Cambridge: Harvard University Press, 1955.

Hellmann, Lillian. *Scoundrel Time.* Boston: Little, Brown, 1977.

Herndon, Angelo. *Let Me Live.* Preface by Howard N. Meyer. New York: Arno/New York Times, 1969.

Herzenberg, Joseph A. "Frank Porter Graham." In *Encyclopedia of Southern History,* edited by David C. Roller and Robert W. Twyman. Baton Rouge: Louisiana State University Press, 1983.

Hicks, John D. *The Populist Revolt: A History of the Farmers' Alliance and the People's Party.* Minneapolis: University of Minnesota Press, 1931.

Higgins, Nancy. "Woodward Grew Close to 'Mary.'" Reprinted from *Camden (S.C.) Chronicle,* 16 April 1981, in the (Hartsville, S.C.) *Pee Dee Recorder,* September 1981, p. 3.

Higgs, Robert. *Competition and Coercion: Blacks in the American Economy, 1865–1914.* Cambridge: Cambridge University Press, 1977.

Higham, John. *History: Professional Scholarship in America.* New York: Harper and Row, 1965.

"Historian Extols University Life." *Richmond* (Va.) *Times-Dispatch,* 21 May 1984, sec. B., p. 3.

Hofstadter, Richard. *The Age of Reform: From Bryan to F.D.R.* New York: Random House, Vintage Books, 1955.

———. *The American Political Tradition and the Men Who Made It.* New York: Knopf, 1948.

———. *Anti-intellectualism in American Life.* New York: Knopf, 1963.

———. *The Paranoid Style in American Politics and Other Essays.* 1965. Reprint. Chicago: University of Chicago Press, Phoenix Books, 1979.

———. *The Progressive Historians: Turner, Beard, Parrington.* New York: Knopf, 1968.

Houghton, Walter E. *Victorian Frame of Mind.* New Haven: Yale University Press, 1957.

Howell, Almonte Charles. *Kenan Professorships.* Chapel Hill: University of North Carolina Press, 1956.

Hughes, Henry Stuart. *The Sea Change: The Migration of Social Thought, 1930–1965.* Rev. ed. New York: McGraw-Hill, 1977.

Hunt, James L. "The Making of a Populist: Marion Butler, 1863–1895." Part 1. *North Carolina Historical Review* 62 (1985): 53–77.

Hutchins, Robert Maynard. *The Higher Learning in America.* New Haven: Yale University Press, 1936.

"[Interview with] C. Vann Woodward." In *Conversations with Historians,* edited by John Arthur Garraty, 2 vols., 1: 45–68. New York: Macmillan, 1970.

Intress, Ruth. "Historian Extols University Life." *Richmond* (Va.) *Times-Dispatch,* 21 May 1984, sec. B, p. 3.

Jefferson, Thomas. *The Writings of Thomas Jefferson.* Edited by Paul Leicester Ford. Vol. 10. New York: Putnam, 1899.

"Jessup Is Accused as Red Party Liner." *New York Times,* 26 September 1951, p. 16.

Johannsen, Robert W. "Historical News and Notices." *Journal of Southern History* 49 (1983): 73–98.

Johnson, Gerald W. "Faith, Fear, and the Future of America." *New Republic,* 4 and 11 January 1975, pp. 14–16.

_____. "Nine Milestones." *New Republic,* 13 December 1975, pp. 8–9.

Johnson, Michael P. "Mary Boykin Chesnut's Autobiography and Biography: A Review Essay." *Journal of Southern History* 47 (1980): 583–88.

Jordan, Winthrop D. *White over Black: American Attitudes toward the Negro, 1550–1812.* Chapel Hill: University of North Carolina Press, 1968.

Josephson, Matthew. *Zola and His Time.* New York: Macmillan, 1928.

Joyner, Charles W. *Down by the Riverside.* Urbana: University of Illinois Press, 1984.

Kammen, Michael. *People of Paradox: An Inquiry concerning the Origins of American Civilization.* New York: Knopf, 1972.

Kant, Immanuel. *The Philosophy of Kant: Immanuel Kant's Moral and Political Writings.* Edited with an introduction by Carl J. Friedrich. New York: Random House, Modern Library, 1940.

Kellogg, Charles Flint. *NAACP: A History of the National Association for the Advancement of Colored People.* Baltimore: Johns Hopkins Press, 1967.

King, Richard H. *A Southern Renaissance: The Cultural Awakening of the American South, 1930–1955.* New York: Oxford University Press, 1980.

Kolchin, Peter. *First Freedom: The Responses of Alabama's Blacks to Emancipation and Reconstruction.* Westport, Conn.: Greenwood Press, 1972.

_____. "In Defense of Servitude: American Proslavery and Russian Pro-Serfdom Arguments, 1760–1860." *American Historical Review* 85 (1980): 809–27.

Kousser, J. Morgan. *The Shaping of Southern Politics: Suffrage Restrictions and the Establishment of the One-Party South, 1880–1910.* New Haven: Yale University Press, 1974.

_____, and James McPherson, eds. *Region, Race, and Reconstruction: Essays in Honor of C. Vann Woodward.* New York: Oxford University Press, 1982.

"Late and Limp on Voting Rights." *New York Times,* 13 April 1982, sec. A, p. 26.

Lebergott, Stanley. "Through the Blockade: The Profitability and Extent of Cotton Smuggling, 1861–1865." *Journal of Economic History* 41 (1981): 867–88.

Leibniz, Gottfried Wilhelm. *Discourse on Metaphysics; Correspondence with Arnaud; Monadology.* Translated by George R. Montgomery. LaSalle, Ill.: Open Court, 1957.

Lewis, David Levering. "The Civil Rights Movement: Background and Causes." Address. Porter L. Fortune Symposium on Southern History, 2 October 1985, University of Mississippi, Oxford.

_____. *King: A Biography.* 2d ed. Urbana: University of Illinois Press, 1978.

Litwack, Leon. *Been in the Storm So Long: The Aftermath of Slavery.* New York: Random House, 1980.

Lorenz, Konrad. *On Aggression.* Translated by Marjorie Kerr Wilson. 1966. Reprint. New York: Harcourt Brace Jovanovich, 1974.

Lynn, Kenneth Schuyler. *The Airline to Seattle: Studies in Literary and Historical Writing about America.* Chicago: University of Chicago Press, 1983.

————. Review of *Mary Chesnut's Civil War. New York Times Book Review,* 26 April 1981, p. 9.

Macaulay, Thomas Babington. *Critical and Historical Essays.* London: Dent, 1907.

————. *The History of England from the Ascension of James II.* 5 vols. Boston: Crosby, Nichols, 1861.

McFeely, William Samuel. *Grant: A Biography.* New York: Norton, 1982.

McNeil, Genna Rae. *Groundwork: Charles Hamilton Houston and the Struggle for Civil Rights.* Philadelphia: University of Pennsylvania Press, 1983.

McPherson, James M. "Antebellum Southern Exceptionalism: A New Look at an Old Question." *Civil War History* 29 (1983): 230–44.

McWhiney, Grady. "Continuity in Celtic Welfare." *Continuity: A Journal of History* 1 (1981): 1–17.

Mandle, Jay R. *The Roots of Black Poverty: The Southern Plantation Economy after the Civil War.* Durham, N.C.: Duke University Press, 1978.

Marcuse, Herbert. *One Dimensional Man: Studies in the Ideology of Advanced Industrial Society.* Boston: Beacon Press, 1964.

Martin, Charles H. *The Angelo Herndon Case and Southern Justice.* Baton Rouge: Louisiana State University Press, 1976.

Martin, Isabella D., and Myrta Lockett Avary, eds. *A Diary from Dixie.* New York: Peter Smith, 1929.

Matthews, Fred. "'Hobbesian Populism': Interpretive Paradigms and Moral Vision in American Historiography." *Journal of American History* 72 (1985): 92–115.

May, Henry F. *The End of American Innocence: A Study of the First Years of Our Own Time, 1912–1917.* New York: Knopf, 1959.

Meier, August. "An Epitaph for the Writing of Reconstruction History?" *Reviews in American History* 9 (1981): 82–87.

————, and Elliott Rudwick. "A Strange Chapter in the Career of Jim Crow." In *The Making of Black America: Essays in Negro Life and History,* edited by August Meier and Elliott Rudwick, 2:14–19. New York: Atheneum, 1969.

"Melee Puzzles Music-Art School; Beaten Teacher Lauds Its Spirit." *New York Times,* 7 March 1971, p. 44.

Mering, John Vollmer. "Persistent Whiggery in the Confederate South: A Reconsideration." *South Atlantic Quarterly* 69 (1970): 126–42.

Miller, Perry G. E. *Errand into the Wilderness.* Cambridge: Harvard University Press, 1956.

————. *The New England Mind.* 3 vols. Cambridge: Harvard University Press, 1954, 1971.

Minter, David. *William Faulkner: His Life and Work.* Baltimore: Johns Hopkins University Press, 1980.

Mitchell, Broadus. *Alexander Hamilton.* 2 vols. New York: Macmillan, 1957, 1962.

———. *The Rise of Cotton Mills in the South.* 1921. Reprint. New York: Peter Smith, 1966.

———, and George Sinclair Mitchell. *The Industrial Revolution in the South.* 1930. Reprint. Westport, Conn.: Greenwood Press, 1968.

Montaigne, Michel de. *Essays of Michel de Montaigne.* 1580. Reprint. New York: Doubleday, 1947.

Moore, Barrington, Jr. *Social Origins of Dictatorship and Democracy: Lord and Peasant in the Making of the Modern World.* Boston: Beacon Press, 1966.

Moore, James Tice. "Redeemers Reconsidered: Change and Continuity in the Democratic South, 1870–1900." *Journal of Southern History* 44 (1978): 357–78.

Morris, Willie. *North toward Home.* 1967. Reprint. Marietta, Ga.: Larlin, 1977.

Morrison, Joseph L. *Wilbur J. Cash: Southern Prophet.* New York: Knopf, 1967.

Motley, John Lothrop. *The Rise of the Dutch Republic.* 3 vols. New York: Harper and Bros., 1883.

Muhlenfeld, Elizabeth. "C. Vann Woodward." *Dictionary of Literary Biography* 17 (1983): 465–82.

Munger, Guy. Review of *Mary Chesnut's Civil War.* Raleigh (N.C.) *News and Observer,* 19 April 1981, pp. 1, 7.

Murphy, Edgar Gardner. *Present Problems of the South.* New York: Macmillan, 1904.

Murray, Albert. *South to a Very Old Place.* New York: McGraw-Hill, 1971.

Muzzey, David Saville. *American History.* New York: Ginn, 1911.

National Cyclopedia of American Biography. Vol 42. New York: James T. White, 1958.

Nettels, Curtis Putnam. *The Roots of American Civilization.* New York: Appleton-Century-Crofts, 1938.

Nevins, Allan. "Tom Watson and the New South." Review of *Tom Watson: Agrarian Rebel.* *New York Times Book Review,* 3 April 1938, pp. 1, 26.

Niebuhr, Reinhold. *The Children of Light and the Children of Darkness: A Vindication of Democracy and a Critique of Its Traditional Defense.* New York: Scribner, 1944.

———. *The Irony of American History.* New York: Scribner, 1952.

Niemi, Albert W. *U.S. Economic History.* 2d rev. ed. Chicago: Rand McNally, 1890.

Nore, Ellen. *Charles A. Beard: An Intellectual Biography.* Carbondale: Southern Illinois University Press, 1983.

Nugent, Walter T. K. *The Tolerant Populists: Kansas Populism and Nativism.* Chicago: University of Chicago Press, 1963.

Nye, Russell Blaine. *Midwestern Progressive Politics: A Historical Study of Its*

Origins and Development, 1870–1958. East Lansing: Michigan State University Press, 1959.

O'Brien, Michael. "C. Vann Woodward and the Burden of Southern Liberalism." *American Historical Review* 78 (1973): 589–604.

Odum, Howard Washington. *An American Epoch: Southern Portraiture in the National Picture.* New York: Holt, 1930.

————. *The Regional Approach to National Social Planning.* Chapel Hill: University of North Carolina Press, 1935.

————. *Southern Regions of the United States.* Chapel Hill: University of North Carolina Press, 1936.

Oelsner, Lesley. "Charges Dropped in the Seale Case; 'Publicity' Cited." *New York Times,* 26 May 1971, pp. 1, 88.

————. "Deadlock by Jury Results in Seale-Huggins Mistrial." *New York Times,* 25 May 1971, pp. 1, 27.

O'Neill, Eugene. *The Emperor Jones.* New York: Liveright, 1921.

O'Sheel, Patrick. "The Uses of Adversity." *National Endowment for the Humanities* 8 (1978): 1–6.

Palmer, Bruce. *"Man over money": The Southern Populist Critique of American Capitalism.* Chapel Hill: University of North Carolina Press, 1982.

Parker, Roy, Jr. "Paul Green, 'Apostle of Light,' 1894–1981." *Fayetteville* (N.C.) *Times,* 6 May 1981, sec. A, p. 4.

Parker, William Nelson. "The South in the National Economy, 1865–1970." *Southern Economics Journal* 46 (1980): 1019–48.

————, ed. "The Structure of the Cotton Economy of the Ante-bellum South." *Agricultural History* 44 (1970): 1–165.

Parrington, Vernon Louis. *Main Currents in American Thought.* Vol. 3, *The Beginnings of Critical Realism in America, 1866–1920.* New York: Harcourt, Brace and World, 1930.

Paton, Alan. *Cry, the Beloved Country.* New York: Scribner, 1948.

————. "The Grave Problem of South Africa." *New York Herald Tribune,* 26 October 1949. Reprinted as "Why I Write" in *Knocking on the Door,* edited by Colin Gardner, pp. 75–80. New York: Scribner, 1975.

————. "This Is My Own, My Native Land." *Common Sense,* 1946. Reprinted in *Knocking on the Door,* edited by Colin Gardner, pp. 24–28. New York: Scribner, 1975.

Patterson, Daniel W. "A Woman of the Hills: The Works of Maude Minish Sutton." *Southern Exposure* 5 (1977): 105–10.

Patterson, Orlando. *Slavery and Social Death: A Comparative Study.* Cambridge: Harvard University Press, 1982.

Percy, Walker. *The Last Gentleman.* New York: Farrar, Straus and Giroux, 1966.

————. "Random Thoughts on Southern Literature, Southern Politics, and the American Future." *Georgia Review* 32 (1979): 499–511.

Perman, Michael. *The Road to Redemption: Southern Politics, 1869–1879.* Chapel Hill: University of North Carolina Press, 1984.

Peskin, Allan. "Was There a Compromise of 1877?" *Journal of American History* 60 (1973): 63–75.

Pettigrew, Thomas F. *A Profile of the Negro American.* Princeton: Princeton University Press, 1964.

Phillips, Ulrich Bonnell. "The Central Theme of Southern History." *American Historical Review* 34 (1928): 30–43.

Plutarch. *Plutarch's Lives.* Translated by Bernadotte Perrin. New York: Macmillan, 1914–28. Vol. 3.

Polakoff, Keith Ian. *The Politics of Inertia: The Election of 1876 and the End of Reconstruction.* Baton Rouge: Louisiana State University Press, 1973.

Pollack, Norman. *The Populist Mind.* Indianapolis: Bobbs-Merrill, 1967.

———. *The Populist Response to Industrial America: Midwestern Populist Thought.* 1962. Reprint. New York: Norton, 1966.

Pope, Liston. *Millhands and Preachers: A Study of Gastonia.* New Haven: Yale University Press, 1942.

Poteat, Edwin McNeill, Jr. "Religion in the South." In *Culture in the South,* edited by William Terry Couch, pp. 248–69. Chapel Hill: University of North Carolina Press, 1939.

Potter, David Morris. "C. Vann Woodward and the Uses of History." In *History and American Society: Essays of David Potter,* edited by Donald E. Fehrenbacher. New York: Oxford University Press, 1972.

———. "The Historical Development of Eastern-Southern Freight Rates Relationships." *Law and Contemporary Politics* 12 (1947): 446–48.

———. *People of Plenty: Economic Abundance and the American Character.* Chicago: University of Chicago Press, 1959.

———. *The South and the Sectional Conflict.* Baton Rouge: Louisiana State University Press, 1968.

Powdermaker, Hortense. *After Freedom: A Cultural Study in the Deep South.* New York: Viking Press, 1939.

"Professor Sledd and Emory College," *Nation.* 21 August 1902, p. 142.

Proust, Marcel. *Remembrance of Things Past.* Translated by Terence Kilmartin and Andreas Mayor. Vol. 3. New York: Random House, 1979.

Rabinowitz, Howard N. "The Not-So-Strange Career of Jim Crow." *Reviews in American History* 12 (1984): 58–64.

———. *Race Relations in the Urban South, 1865–1890.* Champaign-Urbana: University of Illinois Press, 1978.

Rable, George C. "Southern Interests and the Election of 1876: A Reappraisal." *Civil War History* 26 (1980): 347–61.

Rainey, Glenn Weddington. "Ernest Hartsock's Strange Splendor." In Southern Ballet of Atlanta Program, 1964. No pagination.

———. "Strange Splendor in the Sahara of the Bozart." *Emory University Quarterly* 14 (1958): 82–92.

Ranson, Roger L., and Richard Sutch. *One Kind of Freedom: The Economic Consequences of Emancipation.* Cambridge: Cambridge University Press, 1977.

Redding, J. Saunders. *The Lonesome Road.* New York: Doubleday, 1958.

———. *On Being Negro in America.* Indianapolis: Bobbs-Merrill, 1951. 2d ed., 1962.

Reed, John Shelton. Introduction to *Regionalism and the South: Selected Papers of Rupert Vance.* Chapel Hill: University of North Carolina Press, 1978.

Reich, Michael. *Racial Inequality: A Political-Economic Analysis.* Princeton: Princeton University Press, 1981.

Reid, Joseph D., Jr. "Sharecropping as an Understandable Market Response: The Post-Bellum South." *Journal of Economic History* 33 (1973): 106–30.

Review of *Mary Chesnut's Civil War. Economist,* 28 November 1981, p. 99.

Romanoff, Andrew. "Interview with Vann Woodward." *Yale Daily News,* 23 September 1986, p. 2.

———. "Woodward Defends Freedom of Speech." *Yale Daily News,* 19 September 1986, p. 3.

Roper, John Herbert. "Essay on the Voting Rights Extension Act." *Phylon* 45 (1984): 188–96.

———. "Progress and History." *Southern Humanities Review* 17 (1983): 101–19.

———. *U. B. Phillips: A Southern Mind.* Macon, Ga.: Mercer University Press, 1984.

Rostow, Walt Whitman. *Economics of Take-Off into Sustained Growth.* New York: St. Martin, 1963.

———. *Process of Economic Growth.* Rev. ed. New York: Norton, 1962.

Rubin, Louis Decimus. "A Classic Rediscovered." *New Republic,* 21 March 1981, pp. 34–36.

———. *George W. Cable: The Life and Times of a Southern Heretic.* New York: Pegasus, 1969.

Santayana, George. *The Last Puritan: A Memoir in the Form of a Novel.* New York: Scribner, 1936.

Saunders, Robert. "Southern Populists and the Negro, 1893–1895." *Journal of Negro History* 54 (1969): 240–61.

———. "The Transformation of Tom Watson, 1894–1895." *Georgia Historical Quarterly* 54 (1970): 339–56.

Schmidt, Benno. Address. Yale University Faculty, 20 September 1986. Reprinted in *Yale Weekly Bulletin and Calendar,* 29 September–6 October 1986.

Schorske, Carl E. *Fin-de-Siècle Vienna: Politics and Culture.* New York: Random House, Vintage Books, 1981.

———. *German Social Democracy, 1905–1917: The Development of the Great Schism.* 1955. Reprint. New York: Russell and Russell, 1970.

Schumacher, Richard. "Wayne Dick Acquitted." *Yale Daily News,* 2 October 1986, pp. 1, 4.

Schwartz, Bernard, ed. *The Unpublished Opinions of the Warren Court.* New York: Oxford University Press, 1985.

Scruggs, Charles. *The Sage in Harlem: H. L. Mencken and the Black Writers of the 1920s.* Baltimore: Johns Hopkins University Press, 1983.

"Seale Asks Court to Authorize Goatee Forbidden by Jail Rules." *New York Times,* 14 February 1971, p. 50.

Seip, Terry L. *The South Returns to Congress: Men, Economic Measures, and Intersectional Relationships, 1868–1879.* Baton Rouge: Louisiana State University Press, 1983.

"Sessions, Sylvia Plath, and Updike Are American Pulitzer Prize Winners." *New York Times,* 13 April 1982, sec. A, p. 1, sec. B, p. 4.

Sharkey, Robert P. *Money, Class & Party: An Economic Study of Civil War and Reconstruction.* Baltimore: Johns Hopkins Press, 1959.

Shaw, Barton C. *The Wool-Hat Boys: Georgia's Populist Party.* Baton Rouge: Louisiana State University Press, 1984.

Simkins, Francis Butler, and Robert Hilliard Woody. *South Carolina during Reconstruction.* Chapel Hill: University of North Carolina Press, 1932.

Simpson, Lewis P. *"The Southern Review* and Post-Bellum American Letters." *Tri-Quarterly* 43 (1978): 87–88.

Singal, Daniel Joseph. *The War Within: From Victorian to Modernist Thought in the South, 1919–1945.* Chapel Hill: University of North Carolina Press, 1982.

Sledd, Andrew. "The Negro: Another View." *Atlantic Monthly* 90 (1902): 65–73.

Smith, Charles Forster. "Professor Sledd and Emory College." *Nation,* 25 November 1902, p. 245.

Smith, Dave. "Notes on a Form to Be Lived." In *Homage to Robert Penn Warren: A Collection of Critical Essays,* edited by Frank Graziano, pp. 35–53. Durango, Colo.: Logbridge and Rhodes, 1985.

Smith, John David. "Keep 'em in a Fire-proof Vault: Pioneer Southern Historians Discover Plantation Records." *South Atlantic Quarterly* 78 (1979): 379–91.

Smith, Lillian. *Killers of the Dream.* New York: Norton, 1949.

――――. *Strange Fruit.* New York: Reynal and Hitchcock, 1944.

Snow, C. P. *Appendix to Science and Government.* Cambridge: Harvard University Press, 1962.

Starr, William W. "First Volume of History Continues Proud Tradition." *Columbia* (S.C.) *State,* 27 June 1982, sec. E, p. 9.

――――. "Historian Says History Is an Extension of One's Memory." *Columbia* (S.C.) *State,* 27 June 1982, sec. E, pp. 9, 13.

Stein, Herbert. *The Fiscal Revolution in America.* Chicago: University of Chicago Press, 1969.

Stephenson, Wendell Holmes. *Southern History in the Making: Pioneer Historians of the South.* Baton Rouge: Louisiana State University Press, 1964.

Stokely, James, and Wilma Dykeman. *Seeds of Social Change: The Life of Will Alexander.* Chicago: University of Chicago Press, 1962.

Styron, William. Review of *Mary Chesnut's Civil War. New York Review of Books,* 13 August 1981, pp. 24–25.

Sumner, William Graham. *Folkways and Mores.* Edited by Edward Sagarin. 1924. Reprint. New York: Schocken, 1979.

Taylor, William R. *Cavalier and Yankee: The Old South and American National Character.* New York: Harper and Row, 1957.

Tentarelli, Ronda C. *"The Southern Review:* An Episode in Southern Intellectual History, 1935–1942." Ph.D. diss., Louisiana State University, 1980.

Thomas, Emory M. "The Paradoxes of Confederate Historiography." In *The Southern Enigma: Essays on Race, Class, and Folk Culture,* edited by Walter L. Fraser, Jr., and Winfred B. Moore, Jr., pp. 217–24. Westport, Conn.: Greenwood Press, 1983.

Thornton, J. Mills. "The Civil Rights Movement: Results." Address. Porter L. Fortune Symposium on Southern History, 4 October 1985, University of Mississippi, Oxford.

———. "Politics and Power in a Slave Society: Alabama, 1806–1860s." Ph.D. diss., Yale University, 1974.

"Three at Harvard Deny Role as Pro-Reds." *New York Times,* 27 September 1951, p. 18.

Thurow, Lester C. *The Zero-Sum Society: Distribution and the Possibilities for Economic Change.* New York: Basic Books, 1980.

Tindall, George Brown. *The Persistent Tradition in New South Politics.* Baton Rouge: Louisiana State University Press, 1975.

———. "Populism: A Semantic Identity Crisis." *Virginia Quarterly Review* 48 (1972): 501–18.

———. "Rupert Bayless Vance, 1899–1975: A Memorial." Faculty Council of the University of North Carolina, Chapel Hill, 17 October 1975.

———. *South Carolina Negroes, 1877–1900.* Columbia: University of South Carolina Press, 1952.

Turner, Arlin. *George W. Cable: A Biography.* Baton Rouge: Louisiana State University Press, 1966.

Turner, Frederick Jackson. *Frontier and Section: Selected Essays.* Edited by Ray Allen Billington. Englewood Cliffs, N.J.: Prentice-Hall, 1961.

———. *The Significance of Sections in American History.* 1932. Reprint. New York: Peter Smith, 1981.

Ulam, Adam B. "Where Do We Go from Here?" *Daedalus* 103 (1974): 80–89.

U.S. Congress. House of Representatives. *Extension of the Voting Rights Act: Hearing.* 97th Cong., 1st sess., 24 June 1981, pt. 3.

Vance, Rupert Bayless. *Human Geography of the South: A Study of Regional Resources and Human Adequacy.* Chapel Hill: University of North Carolina Press, 1935.

Van Dyne, Larry. "Vann Woodward: Penetrating the Romantic Haze." *Chronicle of Higher Education,* 8 May 1978, pp. 13–14.

Viereck, Peter. *The Unadjusted Man.* Boston: Beacon Press, 1956.

Virgil. *The Aeneid.* Translated by Rolfe Humphries. New York: Scribner, 1951.

Voegelin, Eric. *Order and History.* Vol. 1, *Israel and Revelation.* Vol. 2, *The World of the Polis.* Baton Rouge: Louisiana State University Press, 1956, 1957.

Warren, Robert Penn. *Brother to Dragons.* New York: Random House, 1953.

_____. *The Legacy of the Civil War.* 1965. Reprint, Cambridge: Harvard University Press, 1983.

_____. *Selected Poems, 1924–1975.* New York: Random House, 1975.

_____. *Who Speaks for the Negro?* New York: Random House, 1965.

_____. "William Faulkner." *New Republic,* 1946. Republished in *Literary Opinion in America,* edited by Morton Dauwen Zabel, 3d rev. ed., 1: 467–70. New York: Harper and Row, 1962.

Wayne, Michael. *The Reshaping of Plantation Society: The Natchez District, 1860–1880.* Baton Rouge: Louisiana State University Press, 1983.

Weber, Max. *The Protestant Ethic and the Spirit of Capitalism.* Translated by Talcott Parsons. New York: Scribner, 1930.

Weisberger, Bernard A. "Making History: An Interview with C. Vann Woodward." *American Heritage* 32 (1981): 105–7.

Westbrook, Robert B. "C. Vann Woodward: The Southerner as Liberal Realist." *South Atlantic Quarterly* 77 (1978): 54–71.

Wharton, Vernon Lane. *The Negro in Mississippi, 1865–1890.* Chapel Hill: University of North Carolina Press, 1947.

White, Walter Francis. *Rope and Faggot: A Biography of Judge Lynch.* New York: Knopf, 1929.

White, William S. "McCarran Critical of Jessup Record." *New York Times,* 21 September 1951, pp. 1, 10.

_____. "Wallace Disowns 'Soft' China Policy." *New York Times,* 24 September 1951, pp. 1, 20.

Wiener, Jonathan M. "Class Structure and Economic Development in the American South, 1865–1955." *American Historical Review* 84 (1979): 970–92.

_____. *Social Origins of the New South: Alabama, 1860–1885.* Baton Rouge: Louisiana State University Press, 1980.

Williams, Ben Ames, ed. *A Diary from Dixie.* Boston: Houghton Mifflin, 1949.

Williams, Eric. *Capitalism and Slavery.* Chapel Hill: University of North Carolina Press, 1939.

Williamson, Joel Randolph. *After Slavery: The Negro in South Carolina during*

Reconstruction, 1861–1877. Chapel Hill: University of North Carolina Press, 1965.

———. *The Crucible of Race: Black-White Relations in the American South since Reconstruction.* New York: Oxford University Press, 1984.

———. *New People.* New York: Macmillan, 1980.

———, ed. *Origins of Segregation.* Lexington, Mass.: Heath, n.d.

———. "The Strange Career of *The Strange Career of Jim Crow.*" Address. Graduate History Student Association, University of South Carolina, Columbia, 1970.

Wise, Gene. *American Historical Explanations: A Strategy for Grounded Inquiry.* Homewood, Ill.: Dorsey, 1973.

Wolff, Robert Paul. *The Poverty of Liberalism.* Boston: Beacon Press, 1968.

———, Barrington Moore, Jr., and Herbert Marcuse. *A Critique of Pure Tolerance.* Boston: Beacon Press, 1968.

Wood, Peter H. *Black Majority: Negroes in Colonial South Carolina from 1670 through the Stono Rebellion.* New York: Knopf, 1974.

Woodman, Harold D. "Economic Reconstruction: Change and Continuity in the Postbellum Era." Address, Organization of American Historians, Cincinnati, 1983.

———. "Post-Civil War Southern Agriculture and the Law." *Agricultural History* 53 (1979): 319–37.

Woodward, Michael Vaughn. "Ellis Merton Coulter." Ph.D. diss., University of Georgia, 1982.

Wright, Gavin. "Cotton Competition and the Post-Bellum Recovery of the American South." *Journal of Economic History* 56 (1974): 610–35.

———. *The Political Economy of the Cotton South: Households, Markets, and Wealth in the Nineteenth Century.* New York: Norton, 1978.

Wyatt-Brown, Bertram. "The Sound and the Fury." Review of *Thinking Back. New York Review of Books,* 13 February 1986, pp. 12–15.

———. *Southern Honor: Ethics and Behavior in the Old South.* New York: Oxford University Press, 1982.

Yale Alumni Magazine 10 (1978): 52–53.

Yale Alumni Review, 1975.

"Yale University and Dr. Herbert Aptheker." Report of American Historical Association-Organization of American Historians Committee on the Defense of the Rights of Historians under the First Amendment." December 1977.

Yoder, Edward Milton. "Historian Woodward Shows How Past Shapes Present." *Charlotte* (N.C.) *Observer,* 21 February 1986, sec. A, p. 23.

Zinn, Howard. *The Southern Mystique.* New York: Knopf, 1964.

Index